The Methuen Drama Book
of Naturalist Plays

The Methuen Drama Book of Naturalist Plays

A Doll's House
Henrik Ibsen
translated by Michael Meyer

Miss Julie
August Strindberg
translated by Michael Meyer

The Weavers
Gerhart Hauptmann
translated by Frank Marcus

Mrs Warren's Profession
Bernard Shaw

Three Sisters
Anton Chekhov
translated by Michael Frayn

Strife
John Galsworthy

Edited and with an introduction by
Chris Megson

Methuen Drama

Published by Methuen Drama 2010

1 3 5 7 9 10 8 6 4 2

This collection first published in Great Britain in 2010 by Methuen Drama

Methuen Drama
A & C Black Publishers Limited
36 Soho Square
London W1D 3QY
www.methuendrama.com

ISBN 978 1 408 12843 5

A CIP catalogue record for this book is available from the British Library

Typeset by MPS Limited, A Macmillan Company
Printed and bound in Great Britain by CPI Cox & Wyman, Reading, Berkshire

Caution

Contents

Introduction

by Chris Megson

Naturalism in context

In the popular imagination, Naturalist playwriting is often associated with fusty drawing-rooms, corseted emotion and the provincial life of a bygone era. The impact of Naturalism has been so pervasive over the past century, its conventions so widely adopted and the canon of plays so frequently performed, that it is easy to overlook its revolutionary qualities. The six landmark plays in this anthology demonstrate that 'Naturalism' is not a monolithic term but accommodates a range of styles and preoccupations. And although Naturalist playwriting carries the imprint of the social and cultural tensions specific to its historical context, its concerns still resonate today.

Naturalism emerged in European culture in the second half of the nineteenth century influenced by the seismic political, sociological and scientific ferment that followed on the heels of the Industrial Revolution. Naturalist art, whether in painting, literature or theatre, is characterised by the pursuit of documentary veracity in the portrayal of subject matter. The Naturalist quest for verisimilitude via the forensic reproduction of the observable world reflects the gravitation of art towards the new visual perspectives opened up by the invention of the camera at this historical juncture. '[T]he age of Photography,' argues the philosopher Roland Barthes in *Camera Lucida* (1980), 'corresponds precisely to the explosion of the private into the public, or rather into the creation of a new social value, which is the publicity of the private: the private is consumed as such, publicly'.[1] Naturalist drama, which modelled its aesthetic on the photograph, helped engender this 'social value' by placing domestic life at the centre of theatrical performance. In so doing, it revolutionised theatre's engagement with social reality, sexual politics and the public sphere.

The philosophical roots of Naturalism lie deep in the intellectual maelstrom of the *fin-de-siècle*. By the mid-nineteenth century, the production of empirical knowledge resulting from advances in science and technology had led to the reification of scientific methods across an ever-increasing number of disciplines. A key object of philosophical scrutiny was the interdependency of life, including human social organisation, and its environment. The seminal work of Auguste Comte, Karl Marx and Charles Darwin, in the respective fields of sociology, political economy and natural science, emerged more or less contemporaneously and had a particularly strong impact on the wider culture. The conceptual insights at the core of their writings were absorbed directly into the bloodstream of Naturalist theory.

Comte, a French philosopher, published his *Course of Positive Philosophy* between 1830 and 1842. It sets out the philosophy of positivism and explores some of its social ramifications. Positivism takes up the baton of the Enlightenment project, perceiving in the movement of history the onward march of scientific progress. Comte argues that human society passes inexorably through three stages of development: in the 'theological' stage, human beings explain the world by appealing to the will of a god or gods; in the 'metaphysical' stage, events are explained by appealing to abstract forces or concepts; in the final or 'positive' stage, which for Comte represents the apex of human achievement, science alone is mobilised to explain the nexus of causality in the phenomenal world. Comte envisages the ultimate ideal of the positive system as reducing all phenomena to a series of general laws and facts. Following this logic, the adoption of a scientific approach is crucial to effective social reorganisation.

The positivist investment in human development through science is also discernible in the work of Marx and Darwin, the two intellectual titans of the era. In 1848, Karl Marx and Frederick Engels published *The Communist Manifesto*, an extraordinary document that conceives of history in terms of class struggle and anticipates the eventual victory of the proletariat over the bourgeoisie. Marx's later *A Contribution to the Critique of Political Economy*, published in 1859, refined this analysis, describing how the economic conditions of society – particularly the means of production – determine the life of the community and its social and structural formations. In the same year, Charles Darwin's *On*

the Origin of Species by Means of Natural Selection laid the foundations
for modern evolutionary theory. Natural Selection describes a
process of evolution directed by adaptive fitness and challenges
the idea that all species are individually created and immutable.
Darwin's main point is that the young born to any species must
compete for survival: those that manage to survive tend to
embody favourable natural variations that make them better
adapted to their environment, and which are passed on to future
generations via heredity. In this way, each generation is better
adapted for survival than the one that precedes it and, if species
do not adapt, they become extinct.

Naturalism represents the high-water mark of attempts to
create a scientific art form. The plays in this anthology inflect,
in various ways, the positivist and determinist impulses of the
new philosophy. To a lesser or greater degree, the principal aim
of Naturalist drama is to expose the determining impact of
environment on human behaviour. Its theatrical procedure is to
integrate the various elements of performance – from setting and
costume to lighting and gesture – to conjure a seamless illusion of
observable reality. The social critique of the plays emerges from
the spectator's recognition of the chains of causality – that is, the
material, psychological, even physiological, determinants of the
action – which the play makes explicit. The extent to which free
will is circumscribed by determinist causality in Naturalist theatre
became a heated point of contention in the public domain when
these plays were first performed, and critics protested vigorously
at their perceived indulgence of depraved morality. 'He loves
to make his heroes stand in the strong sun of public favour and
estimation,' thundered an 1891 editorial in the *Daily Telegraph*
after a London staging of Henrik Ibsen's *Ghosts*, 'only in order
to throw beside them a dark shadow of baseness and hypocrisy
which he makes out to be their real personalities.'[2] Many of the
plays were either revised (Ibsen himself amended the ending of
A Doll's House to make it more acceptable for theatre manage-
ments and audiences), or censored or banned on the basis of
their controversial content. The New York production of Bernard
Shaw's *Mrs Warren's Profession* in 1905 provides just one example:
the city's police commissioner lambasted its 'revolting, indecent,
and nauseating' subject matter, and the show was pulled.[3]

Émile Zola, the French novelist and critic, published a famous clarion call for theatrical Naturalism in 1881, in which he argued that 'the physiological man [sic] in our modern works is asking more and more compellingly to be determined by his setting, by the environment that produced him'.[4] Zola himself applied the precepts of positivism to literary fiction and recast the novel as a scientific crucible for the examination of human behaviour. The central characters in his first important work, *Thérèse Raquin* (1867), act under the influence of blood and nerves, physical needs and animalistic drives, which direct their relationships in the external world to calamitous effect. Between 1870 and 1893, he wrote a series of twenty novels under the collective title of *Les Rougon-Macquart*, a sprawling family chronicle that sets out the congenital and environmental influences on the protagonists' behaviour. The hardcore physiological determinism at the centre of Zola's Naturalism drew fire from the religious and conservative establishment (he was condemned as a pornographer) but, as one of the earliest advocates of Naturalism in theatre, his influence is inestimable.

It was Zola's colleague, the actor and director André Antoine, who was the first to establish both a theatre and a theatrical method for the performance of Naturalist plays. The Théâtre Libre (Free Theatre), founded in 1887, jettisoned the declamatory recitation and posturing of the traditional acting schools in favour of a system of rehearsal that focused on characters as individuals, not types. Given the relatively small environs of the stage spaces in which he worked, and the proximity of the audience, this quest for psychological veracity in performance marked a turning point in theatre history. The company achieved notoriety for its authentic costumes (which the actors wore in rehearsal), the use of real furniture on stage (dragged from the homes of the actors to the theatre) and authentic stage design. Antoine was the first modern director to understand the organic relationship between stage design and the movement of the actor, and he often waited until a stage setting was complete before beginning rehearsals. His staging involved the meticulous evocation of scenic reality and a renewed focus on the physical expressivity of the actor which was attuned precisely to the given circumstances of the play. The playwright Jean Jullien coined the famous phrase 'fourth wall' to describe the actor–audience configuration in Antoine's theatre. It is this 'fourth wall' – 'transparent for the public, opaque for the actor', as Jullien put it – that separates the visual field of Naturalist performance from its audience of spectator-voyeurs.[5]

The Théâtre Libre inspired a groundswell of independent, experimental theatres across Europe, including Otto Brahm's Freie Bühne in Berlin (1889), Jacob Grein's Independent Theatre in London (1891) and, most famously, Konstantin Stanislavsky's and Vladimir Nemirovich-Danchenko's Moscow Art Theatre (1897). The Naturalist revolution depended on this burgeoning theatrical infrastructure to both nurture and accelerate its propagation.

The plays

Ibsen's Naturalist plays represent only a small portion of his total dramatic output but they exerted a colossal influence during and after his lifetime. *A Doll's House* (1879) is arguably the best known play in the Naturalist pantheon, renowned for its resonant slamming door and co-option by the nascent movement for female equality at the end of the century. The play shows that private and public experience, marriage and money, are indivisibly linked. If environmental determinism is the signature philosophy of theatrical Naturalism, then the home is its primary site of embodiment: as its title makes clear, the sanctuary of bourgeois domesticity has become infantilised in this play.

Ibsen's playwriting adapts the 'well-made' formula popularised in the boulevard theatres of Europe by writers such as Eugène Scribe and Victorien Sardou. The well-made schema relied on 'setpiece' incidents, love intrigue and mistaken identities, with fast-paced action and logical plotting that moved rapidly from exposition to climax and resolution. Ibsen inherits the sturdy dramaturgical carpentry of the well-made play but places an intensive focus on causality to add social depth to his drama.

A Doll's House confronts the so-called 'Woman Question' that vexed the patrician intellectual establishments of Europe at this time. It traces the encroaching feminist awareness of Nora Helmer and her eventual exodus from the private sphere but the sexual politics are folded into a dramatic situation that illuminates how capitalism exerts pressure on the ascendant bourgeois class. The focus of dramatic interest is Nora's debt repayment, and the manner in which she secured this debt from the lawyer, Krogstad. It is the latter's job insecurity that triggers his attempted blackmail of Nora while the financial hardships of Mrs Linde prompt her to seek Nora's help in her hunt for employment. All the characters, it turns out, are ensnared in a network of financial obligation and interdependency. The family itself is portrayed as a unit of consumption, the site of an endless series of transactions, and even the Christmas setting of the play is conceived as a commercialised affair, with gifts and decorations festooning the set of Act One.

It is women, of course, who are the major commodity in this play and all of them live under the shadow of financial ruin. It transpires that lack of money caused Mrs Linde to jilt Krogstad and the servant, Anne-Marie, to relinquish motherhood for domestic service. Torvald refers to Nora as his possession; at different points in the play he exercises direct control over her income, dress, language, diet and time. Nora's realisation is that her marriage represents a crude economic transaction from her father to her husband.

Helmer constructs an image of Nora as mistress and virginal wife ('I pretend to myself that you're my secret mistress, my clandestine little sweetheart', p. 72) as a means of reasserting his control over her, and he is at once both titillated and shamed when she dances in public. The tarantella dance, a stunning *coup-de-théâtre* with its choreography of sex and death, embodies Nora's intractable situation and sexual objectification. In its aftermath, the lengthy exchange between Nora and Torvald is a kind of requiem for a failed marriage that was premised on false consciousness. Helmer attempts to mystify the workings of patriarchy as he tries to persuade Nora to stay ('You don't understand how society works', p. 86); when this fails, he diagnoses Nora as hysterical ('You're feverish. I almost believe you're out of your mind', p. 86). Nora manages to breach the hermetic carapace of the home but her future as a single woman is left deliberately uncertain.

In Ibsen's Naturalism, the causes planted in the past wreak havoc in the present: the process of cause and effect is remorseless, pursued to the end, and it tends to overwhelm his characters. The plays of August Strindberg, in contrast, search for causality all the time, and in all sorts of places. In his preface to *Miss Julie* (1888), Strindberg sketches out a 'modern' mode of characterisation suited to what he calls 'an age of transition'.[6] He denigrates bourgeois drama for its immutable and two-dimensional characters, and proceeds to bombard the reader with a battery of possible motivations for Miss Julie's actions in the play. For Strindberg, 'character' in the new drama should be fractured and fragmentary, comprised of a patchwork of motivations. This conception of split subjectivity marks a new departure for Naturalism and a rupture with the mechanics of Ibsenite causality.

Strindberg's creed of Naturalism is further adumbrated in the preface when he itemises a range of unconventional dramaturgical and staging practices. The passing of time in the world of the play matches the playing time in performance, the interval is abolished, and there are concentrated sequences of nonverbal action. Stage directions furnish an immense level of quotidian detail that locates the 'setting' itself as an extension of the social position of Jean and Christine. The intention is to create an immersive theatrical spectacle enabling the undisrupted scrutiny of social reality.

Miss Julie explores the impact of class on the dynamics of sexual desire and the viability of class mobility in a feudal society on the cusp of change. The play's evocation of 'the problem of social ascent and decline', as Strindberg puts it in the preface, is depicted controversially as a Darwinist struggle for existence.[7] The language of evolutionary determinism is applied to legitimate Julie's defeat as an aristocrat and as a 'half-woman [. . .] synonymous with corruption' while Jean intuits himself as the aspirational man of the future.[8] Miss Julie's authority as an aristocratic woman hinges on her impeccable moral conduct and subordination to patriarchal mores. In Strindberg's analysis, her transgression of these is emblematic of the gradual extinction of an exhausted creed of nobility (incarnated in the absent figure of her father, the Count) that sanctifies family honour above everything else. Julie's suicide, as a result, carries a sense of inevitability that accounts for the play's subtitle, 'A Naturalistic Tragedy'. *Miss Julie* is a troubling and challenging play with a preface held together by misogynist

rhetoric and an embrace of social Darwinism. Yet, in performance, the play is more sympathetic to Miss Julie than the preface
allows, and it remains unrivalled in Naturalism for its concentrated
distillation of determinist causality.

Gerhart Hauptmann's *The Weavers* (1892) is the quintessential
Marxist drama of the nineteenth century. Based on an actual
historical event – a weavers' revolt in Silesia (present-day Poland)
in 1844 – this monumental five-act play exemplifies the reach for
documentary exactitude in the Naturalist staging of history (the
play as written uses the original Silesian dialect). Hauptmann
dramatises the movement of an entire social class into revolutionary consciousness, setting out multiple perspectives on the
weavers' pitiful economic plight. The techniques of Naturalism are
deployed to lay bare the desultory conditions of the weavers that
are symptomatic of the inequities of capital. Each act takes place
in a different location and this allows a spectrum of class positions
to be counterpointed across the play. For example, the cramped
and dimly lit weaver's room in Act Two contrasts starkly with the
plush and airy manufacturer's house in Act Four. The economic
disparity is inscribed in the stage environments but the play's
political critique is carefully nuanced. The weavers are exploited
by factory-owners and nobility, capitalists and landowners, but
Dreissiger, the manufacturer, is a victim of economic circumstances
too: as he points out in Act Four, domestic industry has been
jeopardised by import tariffs and unregulated domestic competition. The play, therefore, locates the cause of social injustice, not
in the wayward actions of individual men, but in the structural
make-up of the capitalist economy.

The motif of living death in the play is inscribed somatically
on the bodies of the weavers. In the opening stage directions,
Hauptmann describes the throng of figures as 'creatures of
the loom, whose knees have become bent as a result of excessive sitting' (p. 140). Unrelenting labour has triggered a kind
of physiological regression that renders the weavers scarcely
recognisable as human beings. A starving boy collapses in Act
One and, at the opening of Act Two, a ghoulish effect is created
when a 'warm glow falls fully upon the face, neck and chest of
[Mother Baumert]: a face emaciated to a skeleton, with folds
and wrinkles in its bloodless skin' (p. 154). In this scene, the

floor, rafters and light are freighted with a sense of decay and the noise of the looms creates a soundscape of relentless clatter. Later, Old Baumert vomits the meat he has tried to keep down. The impact of injurious capitalism is embodied by the weavers and the play is punctuated with shocking tableaux of corporeal decrepitude.

The weavers' 'Song of Blood and Justice' charges the play with an electrifying energy. It carries the momentum of the rebellion but, because the song is the collective 'property' of the entire peasant class, it also signifies the role of culture in catalysing transformations in consciousness. Dreissiger is the first to mention the song disapprovingly in Act One. By the end of the following act, it has irrupted onto the stage, given collective expression by the despairing weavers in Ansorge's house. Old Baumert quotes from the song rhapsodically to ground the truth of his suffering: 'Look at me! What have they done to me? "Your torture will be long and slow." (*He stretches out his arms.*) Here, feel them, skin and bone.' (p. 168) From this point on, 'Blood and Justice' heralds the weavers' increasing solidarity and unity. In the public setting of Act Three, the song becomes the actual trigger for revolution: in the closing sequence, Baecker begins singing and the rest of the weavers gradually join in. At the end of the play, the rebellion is in full force and '*several hundred voices*' (p. 211) are heard singing the weavers' song. The act of singing is the means through which Hauptmann shows the whole community passing into revolutionary consciousness. As with Nora's dance of the tarantella, the affective power of music orchestrates the moment of profound transformation in theatrical terms.

The ending of the play is ambiguous – Old Hilse is shot while tending to his loom – and the outcome of the revolt is left uncertain. The play is more interested in charting the actualities of lived experience and the fathomless despair that makes revolution possible than in propagandising doctrinaire political messages. As such, its impact resounds like an aria of emotional devastation.

Mrs Warren's Profession (1898) typifies Bernard Shaw's highly influential creed of 'thesis play' or 'play of ideas'. Shaw, a fierce champion of Ibsen, wrote a lengthy preface to the play in which he targets the established shibboleths of British playwriting. His comments are worth quoting at length:

> In trying to produce the sensuous effects of opera, the fashionable drama has become so flaccid in its sentimentality, and the intellect of its frequenters so atrophied by disuse, that the reintroduction of problem, with its remorseless logic and iron framework of fact, inevitably produces at first an overwhelming impression of coldness and inhuman rationalism [. . .] only in the problem play is there any real drama, because drama is no mere setting up of the camera to nature: it is the presentation in parable of the conflict between Man's will and environment: in a word, of problem.[9]

What is notable in this defence is Shaw's rejection of photographic Naturalism in favour of the dramatisation of a 'problem' that has its source in the limits that social environment places on human potential. In *Mrs Warren's Profession*, the 'problem' addressed is capitalism's exploitation of women in the sex economy: 'as long as poverty makes virtue hideous,' argues Shaw in his preface, 'and the spare pocket-money of rich bachelordom makes vice dazzling, their daily hand-to-hand fight against prostitution with prayer and persuasion, shelters and scanty alms, will be a losing one'.[10] Shaw's approach to Naturalism infuses storytelling with the imperatives of investigative journalism in such a way as to illuminate Victorian social hypocrisy and particularly its impact on disadvantaged women.

Shaw places a 'New Woman' at the centre of the play in the form of Vivie Warren. The 'New Woman' emerged in the Victorian literature of the 1890s as a prototypical icon of female self-determination. She rejected conventional distinctions between masculine and feminine behaviour, pursued education and often dispensed with traditional 'feminine' appearance. At the end of *Mrs Warren's Profession*, after her mother's history has been revealed, Vivie occupies an office on the top floor of a legal firm in Chancery Lane. This marks the tentative beginning of her working life in 'respectable' employment. However, as in *A Doll's House*, the play concludes with a slamming door – in this case,

Mrs Warren's exit denotes her estrangement from Vivie, and there is no reconciliation between mother and daughter in the closing scene. Once again, the emergence of women into the public sphere is bought at significant personal cost.

The gradual revelation of secrets that casts, retrospectively, the underlying social relations of the characters in a new light is imported by Shaw from Ibsen's drama. Shaw's propensity, however, is to carry the debate forward in dialogue and much of the play unfolds in crackling and sometimes comical exchanges between two or more characters. Dialogic interaction in Shavian Naturalism exposes the plight of those who wrestle with the contradictions of capitalism; as a result, *Mrs Warren's Profession* provoked controversy for its refusal to indict its ebullient central character. The Lord Chamberlain refused the play a licence for performance in 1898, a private staging in 1902 by the Stage Society was roundly condemned, and it was not given a professional public production in England until 1925.

Anton Chekhov's playwriting launches a wholesale assault upon the well-made model. *Three Sisters* (1901) balances the representation of surface reality in the Naturalistic mode with an expressivity and self-conscious theatricality that pushes towards the metaphorical and, at times, overtly symbolic. The distinctiveness of Chekhov's approach is rooted in his treatment of causality: in his plays, causality is unpredictable and liable to comic disruption (it is often accidental or serendipitous events that lead the action forward). Expectations are established, but soon recede or evaporate as the focus of attention moves elsewhere. For example, the first act of *Three Sisters* concludes with Andrey and Natasha's embrace: this implies that their partnership, and its romantic development, will be of paramount importance in what follows. Yet, by the beginning of Act Two, their marriage has already taken place (offstage) and they are settling into parental responsibilities and a decidedly humdrum domestic routine. This is a familiar trope in the architecture of Chekhov's playwriting: the spectator is routinely distanced from overt dramatic incident and experiences a sense of dislocation and anti-climax that is a key part of the dramatic structure. The effect is to open up Naturalism to new vistas of existential anxiety.

In *Three Sisters*, the audience's identification with character is dispersed across a large ensemble and the terms of this identification are liable to sudden transformation. In Act One, Chekhov presents a community of family and friends gathering for Sunday lunch on Irina's naming-day. The dramatic impact of this scene is derived, in part, from the fact that Chekhov captures the cadences of dinner table chitchat and uses this as a framework to explore the emotional states of his characters. It is within the context of everyday experience that strong emotions are generated, perhaps unexpectedly. Masha's anger at Chebutykin's drinking, and Irina's tearful reaction to Solyony's description of black-beetle wine, serve to illustrate this. These outbursts hint at turbulent emotional states that cut beneath the particular context in which they are aroused (the reactions may seem unwarranted) and point to a deeper unhappiness. Throughout the play, profound passions are constituted in apparently inconsequential activity. Many of the characters partake in rampant philosophising focused on the past or speculation about the future. These endless ruminations, Masha's singing, Chebutykin's drinking and Andrey's gambling all seem to be exit strategies from life lived in the present. The general flow of inaction is occasionally disrupted by memorable incidents – such as the taking of the photograph and the observation of the spinning top in Act One, or Chebutykin's accidental dropping of the clock in Act Three – when the present moment is fully inhabited and time seems to stand still.

Act Three follows a typical structure: it opens with the promise of agency, there is a whirl of activity in response to the fire, but the impulse to action falls away. The scene of frenzy and bustle gives way to darkness, silence and an image of stasis in which Irina affirms her resolute determination to go to Moscow. The fact that, at this point, she is preparing to get into bed strikes a deeply ironic note. In such moments, the illusionist credentials of Naturalism break down and Chekhov anticipates the preoccupations of modernist playwrights such as Samuel Beckett.

John Galsworthy's *Strife* (1909) attempts an objective appraisal of class conflict and its structure is premised carefully on the balancing of opposed points of view. The play examines the contortion of personal and industrial relations in the furnace of economic dispute. Galsworthy does not dwell on the actual

causes of this strike, thus implying that the workers' hardships
and the Board's exasperation stem from the perpetuation of
the strike itself rather than the material conditions that give
rise to it. The characters in the play represent the full spectrum
of capital-labour relations; it quickly becomes clear, however,
that the intransigence of the strike is due to the two men whose
class interests are placed in direct opposition: the Chairman of
the Board, John Anthony, and the leader of the strike, David
Roberts.

The first act builds up to the confrontation between Anthony
and Roberts. The massive physical presence of the former
resembles a dormant volcano, and his eyes control people even
though his words are sometimes inaudible. Roberts, meanwhile,
is the showman of the strike, charismatic and witty. As in *The
Weavers*, *Strife* arbitrates the effects of the conflict on the domestic
condition of the workers and it draws attention to the fissuring of
sexual politics as a result of the strike action. Galsworthy's play,
however, exploits theatre's relationship with language as a form
of public rhetoric. In the course of the play, both Anthony and
Roberts exercise a level of rhetorical prowess that reduces their
audiences to cowed silence. In the pivotal scene of the public
meeting, in Act Two: Scene Two, Roberts' oratory works like
sorcery on the hearts of his fellow workers. Such is the impact of
his speaking voice that his wife, in the previous scene, attempts
to copy his style, like a bad actor. Roberts's hold on his men lasts
as long as he speaks and only the death of his wife can inhibit his
voice. Anthony's oratorical abilities reflect those of Roberts: like
his class enemy, he also uses speech to discipline his listeners and
its effect is measured by the indomitable eye contact he makes
with them, especially in the final act.

The intentions underlying the act of public speaking become
the centre of dramatic focus. In the end, Anthony and Roberts,
both incapable of compromise, are defeated by the conciliatory
forces on either side of the dispute. They stand together in the
final scene, with heads respectfully bowed, like siblings in an
elemental struggle for dominance. Galsworthy's play exposes the
mutual distrust at the polarities of the Edwardian social structure
but, in performance, it is difficult not to be seduced by the force
of its protagonists' charisma.

The fragmentation of Naturalism is foreshadowed in the work of all its major practitioners. Ibsen's later plays, for example, push into subjective territory that can only be apprehended by symbolic theatre discourse. Strindberg increasingly embraced Expressionism and archetypes to excavate interior states of life, dreams and the unconscious. In the twentieth century, practitioners such as Bertolt Brecht dismantled the aesthetic of Naturalism, perceiving it to be cobwebbed in Victoriana and too intoxicated with psychological angst. For Brecht, two World Wars and the atom bomb had dealt a final blow to the positivist faith in scientific progress. In ensuing decades, postmodern thinking has questioned the viability of an external and inviolable 'reality' that can be recuperated in theatrical representation. In the light of such scepticism, the claims of Naturalism seem to rest on a theoretical absurdity: '[Naturalism] not only asserts a reality that is natural or unconstructed,' observes the scholar W. B. Worthen, 'it argues that such a reality can only be shown on the stage by effacing the medium [. . .] that discloses it.'[11] These contradictions help explain why contemporary productions of Ibsen and Chekhov often deconstruct or dispense entirely with the illusionist apparatus of Naturalist stagecraft. Thomas Ostermeier's production of *Nora (A Doll's House)* for the Berlin Schaubühne in 2002 was studded with knowing references to ersatz media culture. It reconceived Ibsen's masterpiece by setting it in a chic Bauhaus-style apartment replete with the techno-trinkets of today's consumer society. What's more, to restore the shock of the play's ending, Ostermeier's Nora ends up gunning down her husband. In 2006, for her production of Chekhov's *The Seagull* at the National Theatre, the British director Katie Mitchell drew on anachronistic stage objects, expansive interiors and a pared-down version of the text by Martin Crimp. Her intention was to, as she describes it, 'cut away all the creaky nineteenth-century theatrical conventions' thus releasing the play's intrinsic 'violence and cruelty'.[12]

Naturalism in the theatre remains a lodestar for practitioners and audiences alike, and has exerted a huge influence on the younger media of film and television. The ubiquity of the form might be explained by the particular kinds of pleasure it makes available to the viewer. Naturalist playwriting shows what is at stake when individuals and classes move from one state of consciousness to another. It trawls the subterranean emotion that impels language and action in the social world. It exposes the conditioning that percolates gender identities. And, at its best, Naturalism gives us an idea of what it might feel like to step into the world of a photograph.

Notes

1 Barthes, Roland, *Camera Lucida: Reflections on Photography*, trans. Richard Howard (London: Vintage, 2000 (1980)), p. 98.

2 Quoted in Ledger, Sally, and Roger Luckhurst (eds), *The Fin de Siècle: A Reader in Cultural History c.1880–1900* (Oxford: Oxford University Press, 2000), p. 128.

3 Quoted in Innes, Christopher (ed.), *A Sourcebook on Naturalist Theatre* (London: Routledge, 2000), p. 227.

4 Quoted in Bentley, Eric (ed.), *The Theory of the Modern Stage: An Introduction to Modern Theatre and Drama* (Harmondsworth: Penguin, 1968), p. 370.

5 Quoted in Chothia, Jean, *André Antoine* (Cambridge: Cambridge University Press, 1991), p. 25.

6 Strindberg, August, 'Preface', *Miss Julie,* trans. Michael Meyer (London: Methuen Drama Student Edition, 2006), p. xci.

7 *Ibid.*, p. lxxxviii.

8 *Ibid.*, p. xci.

9 Shaw, Bernard, 'Preface [to *Mrs Warren's Profession*]', *Plays Unpleasant* (London: Penguin Classics, 2000), p. 197.

10 *Ibid.*, p. 184.

11 Worthen, W. B., *Modern Drama and the Rhetoric of Theater* (Berkeley: University of California Press, 1992), p. 14.

12 Mitchell, Katie, 'The Scavengers', *Guardian* (17 June 2006).

HENRIK IBSEN

A Doll's House

translated by Michael Meyer

Characters

Torvald Helmer, *a lawyer*
Nora, *his wife*
Dr Rank
Mrs Linde
Nils Krogstad, *also a lawyer*
Nurse, Anne-Marie
Maid, Helen
The **Helmers'** three small children
A **Porter**

The action takes place in the **Helmers'** *apartment.*

Act One

A comfortably and tastefully, but not expensively furnished room. Backstage right a door leads to the hall; backstage left, another door to **Helmer***'s study. Between these two doors stands a piano. In the middle of the left-hand wall is a door, with a window downstage of it. Near the window, a round table with armchairs and a small sofa. In the right-hand wall, slightly upstage, is a door; downstage of this, against the same wall, a stove lined with porcelain tiles, with a couple of armchairs and a rocking-chair in front of it. Between the stove and the side door is a small table. Engravings on the wall. A what-not with china and other bric-à-brac; a small bookcase with leather-bound books. A carpet on the floor; a fire in the stove. A winter day.*

A bell rings in the hall outside. After a moment we hear the front door being opened. **Nora** *enters the room, humming contentedly to herself. She is wearing outdoor clothes and carrying a lot of parcels, which she puts down on the table right. She leaves the door to the hall open; through it, we can see a* **Porter** *carrying a Christmas tree and a basket. He gives these to the* **Maid***, who has opened the door for them.*

Nora Hide that Christmas tree away, Helen. The children mustn't see it before I've decorated it this evening. (*To the* **Porter***, taking out her purse*) How much – ?

Porter A shilling.

Nora Here's a pound. No, keep it.

The **Porter** *touches his cap and goes.* **Nora** *closes the door. She continues to laugh happily to herself as she removes her coat, etc. She takes from her pocket a bag containing macaroons and eats a couple. Then she tiptoes across and listens at her husband's door.*

Nora Yes, he's here. (*Starts humming again as she goes over to the table, right.*)

Helmer (*from his room*) Is that my skylark twittering out there?

Nora (*opening some of the parcels*) It is!

Helmer Is that my squirrel rustling?

Nora Yes!

Helmer   When did my squirrel come home?

Nora   Just now. (*Pops the bag of macaroons in her pocket and wipes her mouth.*) Come out here, Torvald, and see what I've bought.

Helmer   You mustn't disturb me!

Short pause; then he opens the door and looks in, his pen in his hand.

Helmer   Bought, did you say? All that? Has my little squander-bird been overspending again?

Nora   Oh, Torvald, surely we can let ourselves go a little this year! It's the first Christmas we don't have to scrape.

Helmer   Well, you know, we can't afford to be extravagant.

Nora   Oh yes, Torvald, we can be a little extravagant now. Can't we? Just a tiny bit? You've got a big salary now, and you're going to make lots and lots of money.

Helmer   Next year, yes. But my new salary doesn't start till April.

Nora   Pooh; we can borrow till then.

Helmer   Nora! (*Goes over to her and takes her playfully by the ear.*) What a little spendthrift you are! Suppose I were to borrow fifty pounds today, and you spent it all over Christmas, and then on New Year's Eve a tile fell off a roof on to my head –

Nora (*puts her hand over his mouth*)   Oh, Torvald! Don't say such dreadful things!

Helmer   Yes, but suppose something like that did happen? What then?

Nora   If anything as frightful as that happened, it wouldn't make much difference whether I was in debt or not.

Helmer   But what about the people I'd borrowed from?

Nora   Them? Who cares about them? They're strangers.

Helmer   Oh, Nora, Nora, how like a woman! No, but seriously, Nora, you know how I feel about this. No debts! Never borrow! A home that is founded on debts and borrowing can never be a place of freedom and beauty. We two have stuck it out bravely up to now; and we shall continue to do so for the few weeks that remain.

Nora (*goes over towards the stove*)   Very well, Torvald. As you say.

Helmer (*follows her*)   Now, now! My little songbird mustn't droop her wings. What's this? Is little squirrel sulking? (*Takes out his purse.*) Nora; guess what I've got here!

Nora (*turns quickly*)   Money!

Helmer   Look. (*Hands her some banknotes.*) I know how these small expenses crop up at Christmas.

Nora (*counts them*)   One – two – three – four. Oh, thank you, Torvald, thank you! I should be able to manage with this.

Helmer   You'll have to.

Nora   Yes, yes, of course I will. But come over here, I want to show you everything I've bought. And so cheap! Look, here are new clothes for Ivar – and a sword. And a horse and a trumpet for Bob. And a doll and a cradle for Emmy – they're nothing much, but she'll pull them apart in a few days. And some bits of material and handkerchiefs for the maids. Old Anne-Marie ought to have had something better, really.

Helmer   And what's in that parcel?

Nora (*cries*)   No, Torvald, you mustn't see that before this evening!

Helmer   Very well. But now, tell me, my little spendthrift, what do you want for Christmas?

Nora   Me? Oh, pooh, I don't want anything.

Helmer   Oh yes, you do. Now tell me, what within reason would you most like?

Nora   No, I really don't know. Oh, yes – Torvald – !

Helmer   Well?

Nora (*plays with his coat-buttons; not looking at him*)   If you really want to give me something, you could – you could –

Helmer   Come on, out with it.

Nora (*quickly*)   You could give me money, Torvald. Only as much as you feel you can afford; then later I'll buy something with it.

Helmer   But, Nora –

Nora   Oh yes, Torvald dear, please! Please! Then I'll wrap up the notes in pretty gold paper and hang them on the Christmas tree. Wouldn't that be fun?

Helmer   What's the name of that little bird that can never keep any money?

Nora   Yes, yes, squanderbird; I know. But let's do as I say, Torvald; then I'll have time to think about what I need most. Isn't that the best way? Mm?

Helmer (*smiles*)   To be sure it would be, if you could keep what I give you and really buy yourself something with it. But you'll spend it on all sorts of useless things for the house, and then I'll have to put my hand in my pocket again.

Nora   Oh, but Torvald –

Helmer   You can't deny it, Nora dear. (*Puts his arm around her waist.*) The squanderbird's a pretty little creature, but she gets through an awful lot of money. It's incredible what an expensive pet she is for a man to keep.

Nora   For shame! How can you say such a thing? I save every penny I can.

Helmer (*laughs*)   That's quite true. Every penny you can. But you can't.

Nora (*hums and smiles, quietly gleeful*)   Hm. If you only knew how many expenses we larks and squirrels have, Torvald.

Helmer   You're a funny little creature. Just like your father used to be. Always on the look-out for some way to get money, but as soon as you have any it just runs through your fingers and you never know where it's gone. Well, I suppose I must take you as you are. It's in your blood. Yes, yes, yes, these things are hereditary, Nora.

Nora   Oh, I wish I'd inherited more of papa's qualities.

Helmer   And I wouldn't wish my darling little songbird to be any different from what she is. By the way, that reminds me. You look awfully – how shall I put it? – awfully guilty today.

Nora Do I?

Helmer Yes, you do. Look me in the eyes.

Nora (*looks at him*) Well?

Helmer (*wags his finger*) Has my little sweet-tooth been indulging herself in town today, by any chance?

Nora No, how can you think such a thing?

Helmer Not a tiny little digression into a pastry shop?

Nora No, Torvald, I promise –

Helmer Not just a wee jam tart?

Nora Certainly not.

Helmer Not a little nibble at a macaroon?

Nora No, Torvald – I promise you, honestly – !

Helmer There, there. I was only joking.

Nora (*goes over to the table, right*) You know I could never act against your wishes.

Helmer Of course not. And you've given me your word – (*Goes over to her.*) Well, my beloved Nora, you keep your little Christmas secrets to yourself. They'll be revealed this evening, I've no doubt, once the Christmas tree has been lit.

Nora Have you remembered to invite Dr Rank?

Helmer No. But there's no need; he knows he'll be dining with us. Anyway, I'll ask him when he comes this morning. I've ordered some good wine. Oh, Nora, you can't imagine how I'm looking forward to this evening.

Nora So am I. And, Torvald, how the children will love it!

Helmer Yes, it's a wonderful thing to know that one's position is assured and that one has an ample income. Don't you agree? It's good to know that, isn't it?

Nora Yes, it's almost like a miracle.

Helmer   Do you remember last Christmas? For three whole weeks you shut yourself away every evening to make flowers for the Christmas tree, and all those other things you were going to surprise us with. Ugh, it was the most boring time I've ever had in my life.

Nora   I didn't find it boring.

Helmer (*smiles*)   But it all came to nothing in the end, didn't it?

Nora   Oh, are you going to bring that up again? How could I help the cat getting in and tearing everything to bits?

Helmer   No, my poor little Nora, of course you couldn't. You simply wanted to make us happy, and that's all that matters. But it's good that those hard times are past.

Nora   Yes, it's wonderful.

Helmer   I don't have to sit by myself and be bored. And you don't have to tire your pretty eyes and your delicate little hands –

Nora (*claps her hands*)   No, Torvald, that's true, isn't it? I don't have to any longer! Oh, it's really all just like a miracle. (*Takes his arm.*) Now I'm going to tell you what I thought we might do, Torvald. As soon as Christmas is over –

A bell rings in the hall.

Oh, there's the doorbell. (*Tidies up one or two things in the room.*) Someone's coming. What a bore.

Helmer   I'm not at home to any visitors. Remember!

Maid (*in the doorway*)   A lady's called, madam. A stranger.

Nora   Well, ask her to come in.

Maid   And the doctor's here too, sir.

Helmer   Has he gone to my room?

Maid   Yes, sir.

Helmer *goes into his room. The* **Maid** *shows in* **Mrs Linde**, *who is dressed in travelling clothes; then closes the door.*

Mrs Linde (*shyly and a little hesitantly*)   Good morning, Nora.

Nora (*uncertainly*)   Good morning –

Mrs Linde   I don't suppose you recognize me.

Nora   No, I'm afraid I – Yes, wait a minute – surely – ! (*Exclaims.*) Why, Christine! Is it really you?

Mrs Linde   Yes, it's me.

Nora   Christine! And I didn't recognize you! But how could I – ? (*More quietly.*) How you've changed, Christine!

Mrs Linde   Yes, I know. It's been nine years – nearly ten –

Nora   Is it so long? Yes, it must be. Oh, these last eight years have been such a happy time for me! So you've come to town? All that way in winter! How brave of you!

Mrs Linde   I arrived by the steamer this morning.

Nora   Yes, of course, to enjoy yourself over Christmas. Oh, how splendid! We'll have to celebrate! But take off your coat. You're not cold, are you? (*Helps her off with it.*) There! Now let's sit down here by the stove and be comfortable. No, you take the armchair. I'll sit here in the rocking-chair. (*Clasps* **Mrs Linde**'s *hands.*) Yes, now you look like your old self. Just at first I – you've got a little paler, though, Christine. And perhaps a bit thinner.

Mrs Linde   And older, Nora. Much, much older.

Nora   Yes, perhaps a little older. Just a tiny bit. Not much. (*Checks herself suddenly and says earnestly.*) Oh, but how thoughtless of me to sit here and chatter away like this! Dear, sweet Christine, can you forgive me?

Mrs Linde   What do you mean, Nora?

Nora (*quietly*)   Poor Christine, you've become a widow.

Mrs Linde   Yes. Three years ago.

Nora   I know, I know — I read it in the papers. Oh, Christine, I meant to write to you so often, honestly. But I always put it off, and something else always cropped up.

Mrs Linde   I understand, Nora dear.

Nora   No, Christine, it was beastly of me. Oh, my poor darling, what you've gone through! And he didn't leave you anything?

Mrs Linde   No.

Nora   No children, either?

Mrs Linde   No.

Nora   Nothing at all, then?

Mrs Linde   Not even a feeling of loss or sorrow.

Nora (*looks incredulously at her*)   But, Christine, how is that possible?

Mrs Linde (*smiles sadly and strokes* **Nora***'s hair*)   Oh, these things happen, Nora.

Nora   All alone. How dreadful that must be for you. I've three lovely children. I'm afraid you can't see them now, because they're out with Nanny. But you must tell me everything –

Mrs Linde   No, no, no. I want to hear about you.

Nora   No, you start. I'm not going to be selfish today, I'm just going to think about you. Oh, but there's one thing I *must* tell you. Have you heard of the wonderful luck we've just had?

Mrs Linde   No. What?

Nora   Would you believe it – my husband's just been made vice-president of the bank!

Mrs Linde   Your husband? Oh, how lucky – !

Nora   Yes, isn't it? Being a lawyer is so uncertain, you know, especially if one isn't prepared to touch any case that isn't – well – quite nice. And of course Torvald's been very firm about that – and I'm absolutely with him. Oh, you can imagine how happy we are! He's joining the bank in the New Year, and he'll be getting a big salary, and lots of percentages too. From now on we'll be able to live quite differently – we'll be able to do whatever we want. Oh, Christine, it's such a relief! I feel so happy! Well, I mean, it's lovely to have heaps of money and not to have to worry about anything. Don't you think?

Mrs Linde   It must be lovely to have enough to cover one's needs, anyway.

Nora   Not just our needs! We're going to have heaps and heaps of money!

Mrs Linde (*smiles*)   Nora, Nora, haven't you grown up yet? When we were at school you were a terrible little spendthrift.

Nora (*laughs quietly*)   Yes, Torvald still says that. (*Wags her finger.*) But 'Nora, Nora' isn't as silly as you think. Oh, we've been in no position for me to waste money. We've both had to work.

Mrs Linde   You too?

Nora   Yes, little things – fancy work, crocheting, embroidery and so forth. (*Casually.*) And other things too. I suppose you know Torvald left the Ministry when we got married? There were no prospects of promotion in his department, and of course he needed more money. But the first year he overworked himself dreadfully. He had to take on all sorts of extra jobs, and worked day and night. But it was too much for him, and he became frightfully ill. The doctors said he'd have to go to a warmer climate.

Mrs Linde   Yes, you spent a whole year in Italy, didn't you?

Nora   Yes. It wasn't easy for me to get away, you know. I'd just had Ivar. But, of course, we had to do it. Oh, it was a marvellous trip! And it saved Torvald's life. But it cost an awful lot of money, Christine.

Mrs Linde   I can imagine.

Nora   Two hundred and fifty pounds. That's a lot of money, you know.

Mrs Linde   How lucky you had it.

Nora   Well actually, we got it from my father.

Mrs Linde   Oh, I see. Didn't he die just about that time?

Nora   Yes, Christine, just about then. Wasn't it dreadful, I couldn't go and look after him. I was expecting little Ivar any day. And then I had my poor Torvald to care for – we really didn't think he'd live. Dear, kind papa! I never saw him again, Christine. Oh, it's the saddest thing that's happened to me since I got married.

Mrs Linde   I know you were very fond of him. But you went to Italy – ?

Nora   Yes. Well, we had the money, you see, and the doctors said we mustn't delay. So we went the month after papa died.

Mrs Linde   And your husband came back completely cured?

Nora   Fit as a fiddle!

Mrs Linde   But – the doctor?

Nora   How do you mean?

Mrs Linde   I thought the maid said that the gentleman who arrived with me was the doctor.

Nora   Oh yes, that's Dr Rank, but he doesn't come because anyone's ill. He's our best friend, and he looks us up at least once every day. No, Torvald hasn't had a moment's illness since we went away. And the children are fit and healthy and so am I. (*Jumps up and claps her hands*.) Oh, God, oh God, Christine, isn't it a wonderful thing to be alive and happy! Oh, but how beastly of me! I'm only talking about myself. (*Sits on a footstool and rests her arms on* **Mrs Linde***'s knee*.) Oh, please don't be angry with me! Tell me, is it really true you didn't love your husband? Why did you marry him, then?

Mrs Linde   Well, my mother was still alive; and she was helpless and bedridden. And I had my two little brothers to take care of. I didn't feel I could say no.

Nora   Yes, well, perhaps you're right. He was rich then, was he?

Mrs Linde   Quite comfortably off, I believe. But his business was unsound, you see, Nora. When he died it went bankrupt and there was nothing left.

Nora   What did you do?

Mrs Linde   Well, I had to try to make ends meet somehow, so I started a little shop, and a little school, and anything else I could turn my hand to. These last three years have been just one endless slog for me, without a moment's rest. But now it's over, Nora. My poor dead mother doesn't need me any more; she's passed away. And the boys don't need me either; they've got jobs now and can look after themselves.

Nora   How relieved you must feel –

Mrs Linde   No, Nora. Just unspeakably empty. No one to live for any more. (*Gets up restlessly.*) That's why I couldn't bear to stay out there any longer, cut off from the world. I thought it'd be easier to find some work here that will exercise and occupy my mind. If only I could get a regular job – office work of some kind –

Nora   Oh but, Christine, that's dreadfully exhausting; and you look practically finished already. It'd be much better for you if you could go away somewhere.

Mrs Linde (*goes over to the window*)   I have no pappa to pay for my holidays, Nora.

Nora (*gets up*)   Oh, please don't be angry with me.

Mrs Linde   My dear Nora, it's I who should ask you not to be angry. That's the worst thing about this kind of situation – it makes one so bitter. One has no one to work for; and yet one has to be continually sponging for jobs. One has to live; and so one becomes completely egocentric. When you told me about this luck you've just had with Torvald's new job – can you imagine? – I was happy not so much on your account, as on my own.

Nora   How do you mean? Oh, I understand. You mean Torvald might be able to do something for you?

Mrs Linde   Yes, I was thinking that.

Nora   He will too, Christine. Just you leave it to me. I'll lead up to it so delicately, so delicately; I'll get him in the right mood. Oh, Christine, I do so want to help you.

Mrs Linde   It's sweet of you to bother so much about me, Nora. Especially since you know so little of the worries and hardships of life.

Nora   I? You say *I* know little of – ?

14   A Doll's House

Mrs Linde (*smiles*)   Well, good heavens – those bits of fancy-work of yours – well, really! You're a child, Nora.

Nora (*tosses her head and walks across the room*)   You shouldn't say that so patronizingly.

Mrs Linde   Oh?

Nora   You're like the rest. You all think I'm incapable of getting down to anything serious –

Mrs Linde   My dear –

Nora   You think I've never had any worries like the rest of you.

Mrs Linde   Nora dear, you've just told me about all your difficulties –

Nora   Pooh – that! (*Quietly.*) I haven't told you about the big thing.

Mrs Linde   What big thing? What do you mean?

Nora   You patronize me, Christine; but you shouldn't. You're proud that you've worked so long and so hard for your mother.

Mrs Linde   I don't patronize anyone, Nora. But you're right – I am both proud and happy that I was able to make my mother's last months on earth comparatively easy.

Nora   And you're also proud at what you've done for your brothers.

Mrs Linde   I think I have a right to be.

Nora   I think so too. But let me tell you something, Christine. I too have done something to be proud and happy about.

Mrs Linde   I don't doubt it. But – how do you mean?

Nora   Speak quietly! Suppose Torvald should hear! He mustn't, at any price – no one must know, Christine – no one but you.

Mrs Linde   But what is this?

Nora   Come over here. (*Pulls her down on to the sofa beside her.*) Yes, Christine – I too have done something to be happy and proud about. It was I who saved Torvald's life.

Mrs Linde   Saved his – ? How did you save it?

Nora   I told you about our trip to Italy. Torvald couldn't have lived if he hadn't managed to get down there –

Mrs Linde   Yes, well – your father provided the money –

Nora (*smiles*)   So Torvald and everyone else thinks. But –

Mrs Linde   Yes?

Nora   Papa didn't give us a penny. It was I who found the money.

Mrs Linde   You? All of it?

Nora   Two hundred and fifty pounds. What do you say to that?

Mrs Linde   But, Nora, how could you? Did you win a lottery or something?

Nora (*scornfully*)   Lottery? (*Sniffs.*) What would there be to be proud of in that?

Mrs Linde   But where did you get it from, then?

Nora (*hums and smiles secretively*)   Hm; tra-la-la-la!

Mrs Linde   You couldn't have borrowed it.

Nora   Oh? Why not?

Mrs Linde   Well, a wife can't borrow money without her husband's consent.

Nora (*tosses her head*)   Ah, but when a wife has a little business sense, and knows how to be clever –

Mrs Linde   But Nora, I simply don't understand –

Nora   You don't have to. No one has said I borrowed the money. I could have got it in some other way. (*Throws herself back on the sofa.*) I could have got it from an admirer. When a girl's as pretty as I am –

Mrs Linde   Nora, you're crazy!

Nora   You're dying of curiosity now, aren't you, Christine?

Mrs Linde   Nora dear, you haven't done anything foolish?

Nora (*sits up again*)   Is it foolish to save one's husband's life?

Mrs Linde   I think it's foolish if without his knowledge you –

Nora   But the whole point was that he mustn't know! Great heavens, don't you see? He hadn't to know how dangerously ill he was. It was me they told that his life was in danger and that only going to a warm climate could save him. Do you suppose I didn't try to think of other ways of getting him down there? I told him how wonderful it would be for me to go abroad like other young wives; I cried and prayed; I asked him to remember my condition, and said he ought to be nice and tender to me; and then I suggested he might quite easily borrow the money. But then he got almost angry with me, Christine. He said I was frivolous, and that it was his duty as a husband not to pander to my moods and caprices – I think that's what he called them. Well, well, I thought, you've got to be saved somehow. And then I thought of a way –

Mrs Linde   But didn't your husband find out from your father that the money hadn't come from him?

Nora   No, never. Papa died just then. I'd thought of letting him into the plot and asking him not to tell. But since he was so ill – ! And as things turned out, it didn't become necessary.

Mrs Linde   And you've never told your husband about this?

Nora   For heaven's sake, no! What an idea! He's frightfully strict about such matters. And besides – he's so proud of being a man – it'd be so painful and humiliating for him to know that he owed anything to me. It'd completely wreck our relationship. This life we have built together would no longer exist.

Mrs Linde   Will you never tell him?

Nora (*thoughtfully, half-smiling*)   Yes – some time, perhaps. Years from now, when I'm no longer pretty. You mustn't laugh! I mean, of course, when Torvald no longer loves me as he does now; when it no longer amuses him to see me dance and dress up and play the fool for him. Then it might be useful to have something up my sleeve. (*Breaks off.*) Stupid, stupid, stupid! That time will never come. Well, what do you think of my big secret, Christine?

I'm not completely useless, am I? Mind you, all this has caused me a frightful lot of worry. It hasn't been easy for me to meet my obligations punctually. In case you don't know, in the world of business there are things called quarterly instalments and interest, and they're a terrible problem to cope with. So I've had to scrape a little here and save a little there, as best I can. I haven't been able to save much on the housekeeping money, because Torvald likes to live well; and I couldn't let the children go short of clothes – I couldn't take anything out of what he gives me for them. The poor little angels!

Mrs Linde   So you've had to stint yourself, my poor Nora?

Nora   Of course. Well, after all, it was my problem. Whenever Torvald gave me money to buy myself new clothes, I never used more than half of it; and I always bought what was cheapest and plainest. Thank heaven anything suits me, so that Torvald's never noticed. But it made me a bit sad sometimes, because it's lovely to wear pretty clothes. Don't you think?

Mrs Linde   Indeed it is.

Nora   And then I've found one or two other sources of income. Last winter I managed to get a lot of copying to do. So I shut myself away and wrote every evening, late into the night. Oh, I often got so tired, so tired. But it was great fun, though, sitting there working and earning money. It was almost like being a man.

Mrs Linde   But how much have you managed to pay off like this?

Nora   Well, I can't say exactly. It's awfully difficult to keep an exact check on these kind of transactions. I only know I've paid everything I've managed to scrape together. Sometimes I really didn't know where to turn. (*Smiles.*) Then I'd sit here and imagine some rich old gentleman had fallen in love with me –

Mrs Linde   What! What gentleman?

Nora   Silly! And that now he'd died and when they opened his will it said in big letters: 'Everything I possess is to be paid forthwith to my beloved Mrs Nora Helmer in cash.'

Mrs Linde   But, Nora dear, who was this gentleman?

Nora   Great heavens, don't you understand? There wasn't any old gentleman; he was just something I used to dream up as I sat here evening after evening wondering how on earth I could raise some money. But what does it matter? The old bore can stay imaginary as far as I'm concerned, because now I don't have to worry any longer! (*Jumps up.*) Oh, Christine, isn't it wonderful? I don't have to worry any more! No more troubles! I can play all day with the children, I can fill the house with pretty things, just the way Torvald likes. And, Christine, it'll soon be spring, and the air'll be fresh and the skies blue – and then perhaps we'll be able to take a little trip somewhere. I shall be able to see the sea again. Oh, yes, yes, it's a wonderful thing to be alive and happy!

The bell rings in the hall.

Mrs Linde (*gets up*)   You've a visitor. Perhaps I'd better go.

Nora   No, stay. It won't be for me. It's someone for Torvald –

Maid (*in the doorway*)   Excuse me, madam, a gentleman's called who says he wants to speak to the master. But I didn't know – seeing as the doctor's with him –

Nora   Who is this gentleman?

Krogstad (*in the doorway*)   It's me, Mrs Helmer.

Mrs Linde *starts, composes herself and turns away to the window.*

Nora (*takes a step towards him and whispers tensely*)   You? What is it? What do you want to talk to my husband about?

Krogstad   Business – you might call it. I hold a minor post in the bank, and I hear your husband is to become our new chief –

Nora   Oh – then it isn't – ?

Krogstad   Pure business, Mrs Helmer. Nothing more.

Nora   Well, you'll find him in his study.

Nods indifferently as she closes the hall door behind him. Then she walks across the room and sees to the stove.

Mrs Linde   Nora, who was that man?

Nora   A lawyer called Krogstad.

Mrs Linde   It was him, then.

Nora   Do you know that man?

Mrs Linde   I used to know him – some years ago. He was a solicitor's clerk in our town, for a while.

Nora   Yes, of course, so he was.

Mrs Linde   How he's changed!

Nora   He was very unhappily married, I believe.

Mrs Linde   Is he a widower now?

Nora   Yes, with a lot of children. Ah, now it's alight.

She closes the door of the stove and moves the rocking-chair a little to one side.

Mrs Linde   He does – various things now, I hear?

Nora   Does he? It's quite possible – I really don't know. But don't let's talk about business. It's so boring.

Dr Rank *enters from* **Helmer**'s *study.*

Dr Rank (*still in the doorway*)   No, no, my dear chap, don't see me out. I'll go and have a word with your wife. (*Closes the door and notices* **Mrs Linde**.) Oh, I beg your pardon. I seem to be *de trop* here too.

Nora   Not in the least. (*Introduces them.*) Dr Rank. Mrs Linde.

Rank   Ah! A name I have often heard in this house. I believe I passed you on the stairs as I came up.

Mrs Linde   Yes. Stairs tire me. I have to take them slowly.

Rank   Oh, have you hurt yourself?

Mrs Linde   No, I'm just a little run down.

Rank   Ah, is that all? Then I take it you've come to town to cure yourself by a round of parties?

Mrs Linde   I have come here to find work.

Rank   Is that an approved remedy for being run down?

Mrs Linde   One has to live, Doctor.

Rank   Yes, people do seem to regard it as a necessity.

Nora   Oh, really, Dr Rank. I bet you want to stay alive.

Rank   You bet I do. However wretched I sometimes feel, I still want to go on being tortured for as long as possible. It's the same with all my patients; and with people who are morally sick, too. There's a moral cripple in with Helmer at this very moment –

Mrs Linde (*softly*)   Oh!

Nora   Whom do you mean?

Rank   Oh, a lawyer fellow called Krogstad – you wouldn't know him. He's crippled all right; morally twisted. But even he started off by announcing, as though it were a matter of enormous importance, that he had to live.

Nora   Oh? What did he want to talk to Torvald about?

Rank   I haven't the faintest idea. All I heard was something about the bank.

Nora   I didn't know that Krog – that this man Krogstad had any connection with the bank.

Rank   Yes, he's got some kind of job down there. (*To* **Mrs Linde**.) I wonder if in your part of the world you too have a species of creature that spends its time fussing around trying to smell out moral corruption? And when they find a case they give him some nice, comfortable position so that they can keep a good watch on him. The healthy ones just have to lump it.

Mrs Linde   But surely it's the sick who need care most?

Rank (*shrugs his shoulders*)   Well, there we have it. It's that attitude that's turning human society into a hospital.

Nora, *lost in her own thoughts, laughs half to herself and claps her hands.*

Rank   Why are you laughing? Do you really know what society is?

Nora   What do I care about society? I think it's a bore. I was laughing at something else – something frightfully funny. Tell me, Dr Rank – will everyone who works at the bank come under Torvald now?

Rank   Do you find that particularly funny?

Nora (*smiles and hums*)   Never you mind! Never you mind! (*Walks around the room.*) Yes, I find it very amusing to think that we — I mean, Torvald — has obtained so much influence over so many people. (*Takes the paper bag from her pocket.*) Dr Rank, would you like a small macaroon?

Rank   Macaroons! I say! I thought they were forbidden here.

Nora   Yes, well, these are some Christine gave me.

Mrs Linde   What? I — ?

Nora   All right, all right, don't get frightened. You weren't to know Torvald had forbidden them. He's afraid they'll ruin my teeth. But, dash it — for once — ! Don't you agree, Dr Rank? Here! (*Pops a macaroon into his mouth.*) You too, Christine. And I'll have one too. Just a little one. Two at the most (*Begins to walk round again.*) Yes, now I feel really, really happy. Now there's just one thing in the world I'd really love to do.

Rank   Oh? And what is that?

Nora   Just something I'd love to say to Torvald.

Rank   Well, why don't you say it?

Nora   No, I daren't. It's too dreadful.

Mrs Linde   Dreadful?

Rank   Well then, you'd better not. But you can say it to us. What is it you'd so love to say to Torvald?

Nora   I've the most extraordinary longing to say: 'Bloody hell!'

Rank   Are you mad?

Mrs Linde   My dear Nora — !

Rank   Say it. Here he is.

Nora (*hiding the bag of macaroons*)   Ssh! Ssh!

Helmer, *with his overcoat on his arm and his hat in his hand, enters from his study.*

Nora (*goes to meet him*)   Well, Torvald dear, did you get rid of him?

Helmer   Yes, he's just gone.

Nora   May I introduce you – ? This is Christine. She's just arrived in town.

Helmer   Christine – ? Forgive me, but I don't think –

Nora   Mrs Linde, Torvald dear. Christine Linde.

Helmer   Ah. A childhood friend of my wife's, I presume?

Mrs Linde   Yes, we knew each other in earlier days.

Nora   And imagine, now she's travelled all this way to talk to you.

Helmer   Oh?

Mrs Linde   Well, I didn't really –

Nora   You see, Christine's frightfully good at office work, and she's mad to come under some really clever man who can teach her even more than she knows already –

Helmer   Very sensible, madam.

Nora   So when she heard you'd become head of the bank – it was in her local paper – she came here as quickly as she could and – Torvald, you will, won't you? Do a little something to help Christine? For my sake?

Helmer   Well, that shouldn't be impossible. You are a widow, I take it, Mrs Linde?

Mrs Linde   Yes.

Helmer   And you have experience of office work?

Mrs Linde   Yes, quite a bit.

Helmer   Well then, it's quite likely I may be able to find some job for you –

Nora (*claps her hands*)   You see, you see!

Helmer   You've come at a lucky moment, Mrs Linde.

Mrs Linde   Oh, how can I ever thank you – ?

Helmer   There's absolutely no need. (*Puts on his overcoat.*) But now I'm afraid I must ask you to excuse me –

Rank   Wait. I'll come with you.

He gets his fur coat from the hall and warms it at the stove.

Nora   Don't be long, Torvald dear.

Helmer   I'll only be an hour.

Nora   Are you going too, Christine?

Mrs Linde (*puts on her outdoor clothes*)   Yes, I must start to look round for a room.

Helmer   Then perhaps we can walk part of the way together.

Nora (*helps her*)   It's such a nuisance we're so cramped here – I'm afraid we can't offer to –

Mrs Linde   Oh, I wouldn't dream of it. Goodbye, Nora dear, and thanks for everything.

Nora   *Au revoir.* You'll be coming back this evening, of course. And you too, Dr Rank. What? If you're well enough? Of course you'll be well enough. Wrap up warmly, though.

They go out, talking, into the hall. Children's voices are heard from the stairs.

Nora   Here they are! Here they are!

She runs out and opens the door. The **Nurse**, **Anne-Marie**, *enters with the children.*

Nora   Come in, come in! (*Stoops down and kisses them.*) Oh, my sweet darlings – ? Look at them, Christine! Aren't they beautiful?

Rank   Don't stand here chattering in this draught!

Helmer   Come, Mrs Linde. This is for mothers only.

Dr Rank, **Helmer** *and* **Mrs Linde** *go down the stairs. The* **Nurse** *brings the children into the room.* **Nora** *follows, and closes the door to the hall.*

Nora   How well you look! What red cheeks you've got! Like apples and roses!

The **Children** *answer her inaudibly as she talks to them.*

Nora   Have you had fun? That's splendid. You gave Emmy and Bob a ride on the sledge? What, both together? I say! What a clever boy you are, Ivar! Oh, let me hold her for a moment Anne-Marie! My sweet little baby doll! (*Takes the smallest child from the* **Nurse** *and dances with her.*) Yes, yes, mummy will dance with Bob too. What? Have you been throwing snowballs? Oh, I wish I'd been there! No, don't – I'll undress them myself, Anne-Marie. No, please let me; it's such fun. Go inside and warm yourself; you look frozen. There's some hot coffee on the stove.

The **Nurse** *goes into the room on the left.* **Nora** *takes off the children's outdoor clothes and throws them anywhere while they all chatter simultaneously.*

Nora   What? A big dog ran after you? But he didn't bite you? No, dogs don't bite lovely little baby dolls. Leave those parcels alone, Ivar. What's in them? Ah, wouldn't you like to know! No, no; it's nothing nice. Come on, let's play a game. What shall we play? Hide and seek? Yes, let's play hide and seek. Bob shall hide first. You want me to? All right, let me hide first.

Nora *and the* **Children** *play around the room, and in the adjacent room to the right, laughing and shouting. At length* **Nora** *hides under the table. The* **Children** *rush in, look, but cannot find her. Then they hear her half-stifled laughter, run to the table, lift up the cloth and see her. Great excitement. She crawls out as though to frighten them. Further excitement. Meanwhile, there has been a knock on the door leading from the hall, but no one has noticed it. Now the door is half opened and* **Krogstad** *enters. He waits for a moment; the game continues.*

Krogstad   Excuse me, Mrs Helmer –

Nora (*turns with a stifled cry and half jumps up*)   Oh! What do you want?

Krogstad   I beg your pardon – the front door was ajar. Someone must have forgotten to close it.

Nora (*gets up*)   My husband is not at home, Mr Krogstad.

Krogstad   I know.

Nora   Well, what do you want here, then?

Krogstad A word with you.

Nora With – ? (*To the* **Children**, *quietly*.) Go inside to Anne-Marie. What? No, the strange gentleman won't do anything to hurt mummy. When he's gone we'll start playing again.

She takes the children into the room on the left and closes the door behind them.

Nora (*uneasy, tense*)   You want to speak to me?

Krogstad Yes.

Nora Today? But it's not the first of the month yet.

Krogstad No, it is Christmas Eve. Whether or not you have a merry Christmas depends on you.

Nora What do you want? I can't give you anything today –

Krogstad We won't talk about that for the present. There's something else. You have a moment to spare?

Nora Oh, yes. Yes, I suppose so – though –

Krogstad Good, I was sitting in the café down below and I saw your husband cross the street –

Nora Yes.

Krogstad With a lady.

Nora Well?

Krogstad Might I be so bold as to ask; was not that lady a Mrs Linde?

Nora Yes.

Krogstad Recently arrived in town?

Nora Yes, today.

Krogstad She is a good friend of yours, is she not?

Nora Yes, she is. But I don't see –

Krogstad I used to know her, too, once.

Nora I know.

Krogstad   Oh? You've discovered that. Yes, I thought you would. Well then, may I ask you a straight question: is Mrs Linde to be employed at the bank?

Nora   How dare you presume to cross-examine me, Mr Krogstad? You, one of my husband's employees? But since you ask, you shall have an answer. Yes, Mrs Linde is to be employed by the bank. And I arranged it, Mr Krogstad. Now you know.

Krogstad   I guessed right, then.

Nora (*walks up and down the room*)   Oh, one has a little influence, you know. Just because one's a woman it doesn't necessarily mean that – When one is in a humble position, Mr Krogstad, one should think twice before offending someone who – hm – !

Krogstad   – who has influence?

Nora   Precisely.

Krogstad (*changes his tone*)   Mrs Helmer, will you have the kindness to use your influence on my behalf?

Nora   What? What do you mean?

Krogstad   Will you be so good as to see that I keep my humble position at the bank?

Nora   What do you mean? Who is thinking of removing you from your position?

Krogstad   Oh, you don't need to play the innocent with me. I realize it can't be very pleasant for your friend to risk bumping into me. And now I also realize whom I have to thank for being hounded out like this.

Nora   But I assure you –

Krogstad   Look, let's not beat about the bush. There's still time, and I'd advise you to use your influence to stop it.

Nora   But, Mr Krogstad, I have no influence!

Krogstad   Oh? I thought you just said –

Nora   But I didn't mean it like that! I? How on earth could you imagine that I would have any influence over my husband?

Krogstad   Oh, I've known your husband since we were students together. I imagine he has his weaknesses like other married men.

Nora   If you speak impertinently of my husband, I shall show you the door.

Krogstad   You're a bold woman, Mrs Helmer.

Nora   I'm not afraid of you any longer. Once the New Year is in, I'll soon be rid of you.

Krogstad (*more controlled*)   Now listen to me, Mrs Helmer. If I'm forced to, I shall fight for my little job at the bank as I would fight for my life.

Nora   So it sounds.

Krogstad   It isn't just the money – that's the last thing I care about. There's something else. Well, you might as well know. It's like this, you see. You know of course, as everyone else does, that some years ago I committed an indiscretion.

Nora   I think I did hear something –

Krogstad   It never came into court; but from that day, every opening was barred to me. So I turned my hand to the kind of business you know about. I had to do something; and I don't think I was one of the worst. But now I want to give up all that. My sons are growing up: for their sake, I must try to regain what respectability I can. This job in the bank was the first step on the ladder. And now your husband wants to kick me off that ladder back into the dirt.

Nora   But, my dear Mr Krogstad, it simply isn't in my power to help you.

Krogstad   You say that because you don't want to help me. But I have the means to make you.

Nora   You don't mean you'd tell my husband that I owe you money?

Krogstad   And if I did?

Nora   That'd be a filthy trick! (*Almost in tears.*) This secret that is my pride and my joy – that he should hear about it in such a filthy, beastly way – hear about it from you! It'd involve me in the most dreadful unpleasantness –

Krogstad   Only – unpleasantness?

Nora (*vehemently*)   All right, do it! You'll be the one who'll suffer. It'll show my husband the kind of man you are, and then you'll never keep your job.

Krogstad   I asked you whether it was merely domestic unpleasantness you were afraid of.

Nora   If my husband hears about it, he will of course immediately pay you whatever is owing. And then we shall have nothing more to do with you.

Krogstad (*takes a step closer*)   Listen, Mrs Helmer. Either you've a bad memory or else you know very little about financial transactions. I had better enlighten you.

Nora   What do you mean?

Krogstad   When your husband was ill, you came to me to borrow two hundred and fifty pounds.

Nora   I didn't know anyone else.

Krogstad   I promised to find that sum for you –

Nora   And you did find it.

Krogstad   I promised to find that sum for you on certain conditions. You were so worried about your husband's illness and so keen to get the money to take him abroad that I don't think you bothered much about the details. So it won't be out of place if I refresh your memory. Well – I promised to get you the money in exchange for an I.O.U., which I drew up.

Nora   Yes, and which I signed.

Krogstad   Exactly. But then I added a few lines naming your father as security for the debt. This paragraph was to be signed by your father.

Nora Was to be? He did sign it.

Krogstad I left the date blank for your father to fill in when he signed this paper. You remember, Mrs Helmer?

Nora Yes, I think so –

Krogstad Then I gave you back this I.O.U. for you to post to your father. Is that not correct?

Nora Yes.

Krogstad And of course you posted it at once; for within five or six days you brought it along to me with your father's signature on it. Whereupon I handed you the money.

Nora Yes, well. Haven't I repaid the instalments as agreed?

Krogstad Mm – yes, more or less. But to return to what we were speaking about – that was a difficult time for you just then, wasn't it, Mrs Helmer?

Nora Yes, it was.

Krogstad Your father was very ill, if I am not mistaken.

Nora He was dying.

Krogstad He did in fact die shortly afterwards?

Nora Yes.

Krogstad Tell me, Mrs Helmer, do you by any chance remember the date of your father's death? The day of the month, I mean.

Nora Pappa died on the twenty-ninth of September.

Krogstad Quite correct; I took the trouble to confirm it. And that leaves me with a curious little problem – (*Takes out a paper.*) – which I simply cannot solve.

Nora Problem? I don't see –

Krogstad The problem, Mrs Helmer, is that your father signed this paper three days after his death.

Nora What? I don't understand –

Krogstad Your father died on the twenty-ninth of September. But look at this. Here your father has dated his signature the second of October. Isn't that a curious little problem, Mrs Helmer?

Nora *is silent.*

Krogstad Can you suggest any explanation?

She remains silent.

Krogstad And there's another curious thing. The words 'second of October' and the year are written in a hand which is not your father's, but which I seem to know. Well, there's a simple explanation to that. Your father could have forgotten to write in the date when he signed, and someone else could have added it before the news came of his death. There's nothing criminal about that. It's the signature itself I'm wondering about. It *is* genuine, I suppose, Mrs Helmer? It was your father who wrote his name here?

Nora (*after a short silence, throws back her head and looks defiantly at hint*) No, it was not. It was I who wrote pappa's name there.

Krogstad Look, Mrs Helmer, do you realize this is a dangerous admission?

Nora Why? You'll get your money.

Krogstad May I ask you a question? Why didn't you send this paper to your father?

Nora I couldn't. Pappa was very ill. If I'd asked him to sign this, I'd have had to tell him what the money was for. But I couldn't have told him in his condition that my husband's life was in danger. I couldn't have done that!

Krogstad Then you would have been wiser to have given up your idea of a holiday.

Nora But I couldn't! It was to save my husband's life. I couldn't put it off.

Krogstad But didn't it occur to you that you were being dishonest towards me?

Nora I couldn't bother about that. I didn't care about you. I hated you because of all the beastly difficulties you'd put in my way when you knew how dangerously ill my husband was.

Krogstad Mrs Helmer, you evidently don't appreciate exactly what you have done. But I can assure you that it is no bigger nor worse a crime than the one I once committed and thereby ruined my whole social position.

Nora You? Do you expect me to believe that you would have taken a risk like that to save your wife's life?

Krogstad The law does not concern itself with motives.

Nora Then the law must be very stupid.

Krogstad Stupid or not, if I show this paper to the police, you will be judged according to it.

Nora I don't believe that. Hasn't a daughter the right to shield her father from worry and anxiety when he's old and dying? Hasn't a wife the right to save her husband's life? I don't know much about the law, but there must be something somewhere that says that such things are allowed. You ought to know that, you're meant to be a lawyer, aren't you? You can't be a very good lawyer, Mr Krogstad.

Krogstad Possibly not. But business, the kind of business we two have been transacting – I think you'll admit I understand something about that? Good. Do as you please. But I tell you this. If I get thrown into the gutter for a second time, I shall take you with me.

He bows and goes out through the hall.

Nora (*stands for a moment in thought, then tosses her head*) What nonsense! He's trying to frighten me! I'm not that stupid. (*Busies herself gathering together the children's clothes; then she suddenly stops.*) But – ? No, it's impossible. I did it for love, didn't I?

Children (*in the doorway, left*) Mummy, the strange gentleman has gone out into the street.

Nora Yes, yes, I know. But don't talk to anyone about the strange gentleman. You hear? Not even to Daddy.

Children   No, Mummy. Will you play with us again now?

Nora   No, no. Not now.

Children   Oh but, Mummy, you promised!

Nora   I know, but I can't just now. Go back to the nursery. I've a lot to do. Go away, my darlings, go away.

She pushes them gently into the other room, and closes the door behind them. She sits on the sofa, takes up her embroidery, stitches for a few moments, but soon stops.

Nora   No! (*Throws the embroidery aside, gets up, goes to the door leading to the hall and calls.*) Helen! Bring in the Christmas tree! (*She goes to the table on the left and opens the drawer in it; then pauses again.*) No, but it's utterly impossible!

Maid (*enters with the tree*)   Where shall I put it, madam?

Nora   There, in the middle of the room.

Maid   Will you be wanting anything else?

Nora   No, thank you. I have everything I need.

*The **Maid** puts down the tree and goes out.*

Nora (*busy decorating the tree*)   Now – candles here – and flowers here. That loathsome man! Nonsense, nonsense, there's nothing to be frightened about. The Christmas tree must be beautiful. I'll do everything that you like, Torvald. I'll sing for you, dance for you –

Helmer, *with a bundle of papers under his arm, enters.*

Nora   Oh – are you back already?

Helmer   Yes. Has anyone been here?

Nora   Here? No.

Helmer   That's strange. I saw Krogstad come out of the front door.

Nora   Did you? Oh yes, that's quite right – Krogstad was here for a few minutes.

Helmer   Nora, I can tell from your face, he has been here and asked you to put in a good word for him.

Nora   Yes.

Helmer   And you were to pretend you were doing it of your own accord? You weren't going to tell me he'd been here? He asked you to do that too, didn't he?

Nora   Yes, Torvald. But –

Helmer   Nora, Nora! And you were ready to enter into such a conspiracy? Talking to a man like that, and making him promises – and then, on top of it all, to tell me an untruth!

Nora   An untruth?

Helmer   Didn't you say no one had been here? (*Wags his finger.*) My little songbird must never do that again. A songbird must have a clean beak to sing with. Otherwise she'll start twittering out of tune. (*Puts his arm round her waist.*) Isn't that the way we want things? Yes, of course it is. (*Lets go of her.*) So let's hear no more about that. (*Sits down in front of the stove.*) Ah, how cosy and peaceful it is here! (*Glances for a few moments at his papers.*)

Nora (*busy with the tree; after a short silence*)   Torvald.

Helmer   Yes.

Nora   I'm terribly looking forward to that fancy-dress ball at the Stenborgs on Boxing Day.

Helmer   And I'm terribly curious to see what you're going to surprise me with.

Nora   Oh, it's so maddening.

Helmer   What is?

Nora   I can't think of anything to wear. It all seems so stupid and meaningless.

Helmer   So my little Nora has come to that conclusion, has she?

Nora (*behind his chair, resting her arms on its back*)   Are you very busy, Torvald?

Helmer Oh –

Nora What are those papers?

Helmer Just something to do with the bank.

Nora Already?

Helmer I persuaded the trustees to give me authority to make certain immediate changes in the staff and organization. I want to have everything straight by the New Year.

Nora Then that's why this poor man Krogstad –

Helmer Hm.

Nora (*still leaning over his chair, slowly strokes the back of his head*) If you hadn't been so busy, I was going to ask you an enormous favour, Torvald.

Helmer Well, tell me. What was it to be?

Nora You know I trust your taste more than anyone's. I'm so anxious to look really beautiful at the fancy-dress ball. Torvald, couldn't you help me to decide what I shall go as, and what kind of costume I ought to wear?

Helmer Aha! So little Miss Independent's in trouble and needs a man to rescue her, does she?

Nora Yes, Torvald. I can't get anywhere without your help.

Helmer Well, well, I'll give the matter thought. We'll find something.

Nora Oh, how kind of you! (*Goes back to the tree. Pause.*) How pretty these red flowers look! But, tell me, is it so dreadful, this thing that Krogstad's done?

Helmer He forged someone else's name. Have you any idea what that means?

Nora Mightn't he have been forced to do it by some emergency?

Helmer He probably just didn't think – that's what usually happens. I'm not so heartless as to condemn a man for an isolated action.

Nora No, Torvald, of course not!

Helmer Men often succeed in re-establishing themselves if they admit their crime and take their punishment.

Nora Punishment?

Helmer But Krogstad didn't do that. He chose to try and trick his way out of it. And that's what has morally destroyed him.

Nora You think that would – ?

Helmer Just think how a man with that load on his conscience must always be lying and cheating and dissembling – how he must wear a mask even in the presence of those who are dearest to him, even his own wife and children! Yes, the children. That's the worst danger, Nora.

Nora Why?

Helmer Because an atmosphere of lies contaminates and poisons every corner of the home. Every breath that the children draw in such a house contains the germs of evil.

Nora (*comes closer behind him*)   Do you really believe that?

Helmer Oh, my dear, I've come across it so often in my work at the bar. Nearly all young criminals are the children of mothers who are constitutional liars.

Nora Why do you say mothers?

Helmer It's usually the mother – though of course the father can have the same influence. Every lawyer knows that only too well. And yet this fellow Krogstad has been sitting at home all these years poisoning his children with his lies and pretences. That's why I say that, morally speaking, he is dead. (*Stretches out his hand towards her.*) So my pretty little Nora must promise me not to plead his case. Your hand on it. Come, come, what's this? Give me your hand. There. That's settled, now. I assure you it'd be quite impossible for me to work in the same building as him. I literally feel physically ill in the presence of a man like that.

Nora (*draws her hand from his and goes over to the other side of the Christmas tree*)   How hot it is in here! And I've so much to do.

Helmer (*gets up and gathers his papers*)   Yes, and I must try to get some of this read before dinner. I'll think about your costume too. And I may even have something up my sleeve to hang in gold paper on the Christmas tree. (*Lays his hand on her head.*) My precious little songbird!

He goes into his study and closes the door.

Nora (*softly, after a pause*)   It's nonsense. It must be. It's impossible. It *must* be impossible!

Nurse (*in the doorway, left*)   The children are asking if they can come in to Mummy.

Nora   No, no, no – don't let them in. You stay with them, Anne-Marie.

Nurse   Very good, madam. (*Closes the door.*)

Nora (*pale with fear*)   Corrupt my little children – ! Poison my home! (*Short pause. She throws back her head.*) It isn't true! It *couldn't* be true!

Act Two

The same room. In the corner by the piano the Christmas tree stands, stripped and dishevelled, its candles burned to their sockets, **Nora**'s *outdoor clothes lie on the sofa. She is alone in the room, walking restlessly to and fro. At length she stops by the sofa and picks up her coat.*

Nora (*drops the coat again*)   There's someone coming! (*Goes to the door and listens.*) No, it's no one. Of course – no one'll come today, it's Christmas Day. Nor tomorrow. But perhaps – ! (*Opens the door and looks out.*) No. Nothing in the letter-box. Quite empty. (*Walks across the room.*) Silly, silly. Of course he won't do anything. It couldn't happen. It isn't possible. Why, I've three small children.

The **Nurse,** *carrying a large cardboard box, enters from the room on the left.*

Nurse   I found those fancy dress clothes at last, madam.

Nora   Thank you. Put them on the table.

Nurse (*does so*)   They're all rumpled up.

Nora   Oh, I wish I could tear them into a million pieces!

Nurse   Why, madam! They'll be all right. Just a little patience.

Nora   Yes, of course. I'll go and get Mrs Linde to help me.

Nurse   What, out again? In this dreadful weather? You'll catch a chill, madam.

Nora   Well, that wouldn't be the worst. How are the children?

Nurse   Playing with their Christmas presents, poor little dears. But –

Nora   Are they still asking to see me?

Nurse   They're so used to having their mummy with them.

Nora   Yes, but, Anne-Marie, from now on I shan't be able to spend so much time with them.

Nurse   Well, children get used to anything in time.

Nora   Do you think so? Do you think they'd forget their mother if she went away from them – for ever?

Nurse   Mercy's sake, madam! For ever!

Nora   Tell me, Anne-Marie – I've so often wondered. How could you bear to give your child away – to strangers?

Nurse   But I had to when I came to nurse my little Miss Nora.

Nora   Do you mean you wanted to?

Nurse   When I had the chance of such a good job? A poor girl what's got into trouble can't afford to pick and choose. That good-for-nothing didn't lift a finger.

Nora   But your daughter must have completely forgotten you.

Nurse   Oh no, indeed she hasn't. She's written to me twice, once when she got confirmed and then again when she got married.

Nora (*hugs her*)   Dear old Anne-Marie, you were a good mother to me.

Nurse   Poor little Miss Nora, you never had any mother but me.

Nora   And if my little ones had no one else, I know you would – no, silly, silly, silly! (*Opens the cardboard box.*) Go back to them, Anne-Marie. Now I must – ! Tomorrow you'll see how pretty I shall look.

Nurse   Why, there'll be no one at the ball as beautiful as my Miss Nora.

She goes into the room, left.

Nora (*begins to unpack the clothes from the box, but soon throws them down again*)   Oh, if only I dared go out! If I could be sure no one would come and nothing would happen while I was away! Stupid, stupid! No one will come. I just mustn't think about it. Brush this muff. Pretty gloves, pretty gloves! Don't think about it, don't think about it! One, two, three, four, five, six – (*Cries.*) Ah – they're coming – !

She begins to run towards the door, but stops uncertainly. **Mrs Linde** *enters from the hall, where she has been taking off her outdoor clothes.*

Nora Oh, it's you, Christine. There's no one else outside, is there? Oh, I'm so glad you've come.

Mrs Linde I hear you were at my room asking for me.

Nora Yes, I just happened to be passing. I want to ask you to help me with something. Let's sit down here on the sofa. Look at this. There's going to be a fancy-dress ball tomorrow night upstairs at Consul Stenborg's, and Torvald wants me to go as a Neapolitan fisher-girl and dance the tarantella. I learned it in Capri.

Mrs Linde I say, are you going to give a performance?

Nora Yes, Torvald says I should. Look, here's the dress. Torvald had it made for me in Italy − but now it's all so torn, I don't know −

Mrs Linde Oh, we'll soon put that right − the stitching's just come away. Needle and thread? Ah, here we are.

Nora You're being awfully sweet.

Mrs Linde (*sews*) So you're going to dress up tomorrow, Nora? I must pop over for a moment to see how you look. Oh, but I've completely forgotten to thank you for that nice evening yesterday.

Nora (*gets up and walks across the room*) Oh, I didn't think it was as nice as usual. You ought to have come to town a little earlier, Christine. . . . Yes, Torvald understands how to make a home look attractive.

Mrs Linde I'm sure you do, too. You're not your father's daughter for nothing. But, tell me − is Dr Rank always in such low spirits as he was yesterday?

Nora No, last night it was very noticeable. But he's got a terrible disease − he's got spinal tuberculosis, poor man. His father was a frightful creature who kept mistresses and so on. As a result Dr Rank has been sickly ever since he was a child − you understand −

Mrs Linde (*puts down her sewing*) But, my dear Nora, how on earth did you get to know about such things?

Nora (*walks about the room*) Oh, don't be silly, Christine − when one has three children, one comes into contact with women who – well, who know about medical matters, and they tell one a thing or two.

Mrs Linde (*sews again; a short silence*)   Does Dr Rank visit you every day?

Nora   Yes, every day. He's Torvald's oldest friend, and a good friend to me too. Dr Rank's almost one of the family.

Mrs Linde   But, tell me – is he quite sincere? I mean, doesn't he rather say the sort of thing he thinks people want to hear?

Nora   No, quite the contrary. What gave you that idea?

Mrs Linde   When you introduced me to him yesterday, he said he'd often heard my name mentioned here. But later I noticed your husband had no idea who I was. So how could Dr Rank –

Nora   Yes, that's quite right, Christine. You see, Torvald's so hopelessly in love with me that he wants to have me all to himself – those were his very words. When we were first married, he got quite jealous if I as much as mentioned any of my old friends back home. So naturally, I stopped talking about them. But I often chat with Dr Rank about that kind of thing. He enjoys it, you see.

Mrs Linde   Now listen, Nora. In many ways you're still a child; I'm a bit older than you and have a little more experience of the world. There's something I want to say to you. You ought to give up this business with Dr Rank.

Nora   What business?

Mrs Linde   Well, everything. Last night you were speaking about this rich admirer of yours who was going to give you money –

Nora   Yes, and who doesn't exist – unfortunately. But what's that got to do with – ?

Mrs Linde   Is Dr Rank rich?

Nora   Yes.

Mrs Linde   And he has no dependants?

Nora   No, no one. But –

Mrs Linde   And he comes here to see you every day?

Nora   Yes, I've told you.

Mrs Linde   But how dare a man of his education be so forward?

Nora   What on earth are you talking about?

Mrs Linde   Oh, stop pretending, Nora. Do you think I haven't guessed who it was who lent you that two hundred pounds?

Nora   Are you out of your mind? How could you imagine such a thing? A friend, someone who comes here every day! Why, that'd be an impossible situation!

Mrs Linde   Then it really wasn't him?

Nora   No, of course not. I've never for a moment dreamed of – anyway, he hadn't any money to lend then. He didn't come into that till later.

Mrs Linde   Well, I think that was a lucky thing for you, Nora dear.

Nora   No, I could never have dreamed of asking Dr Rank – Though I'm sure that if ever I did ask him –

Mrs Linde   But of course you won't.

Nora   Of course not. I can't imagine that it should ever become necessary. But I'm perfectly sure that if I did speak to Dr Rank –

Mrs Linde   Behind your husband's back?

Nora   I've got to get out of this other business – and *that's* been going on behind his back. I've *got* to get out of it.

Mrs Linde   Yes, well, that's what I told you yesterday. But –

Nora (*walking up and down*)   It's much easier for a man to arrange these things than a woman –

Mrs Linde   One's own husband, yes.

Nora   Oh, bosh. (*Stops walking.*) When you've completely repaid a debt, you get your I.O.U. back, don't you?

Mrs Linde   Yes, of course.

Nora   And you can tear it into a thousand pieces and burn the filthy, beastly thing!

Mrs Linde (*looks hard at her, puts down her sewing and gets up slowly*)   Nora, you're hiding something from me.

Nora   Can you see that?

Mrs Linde   Something has happened since yesterday morning. Nora, what is it?

Nora (*goes towards her*)   Christine! (*Listens.*) Ssh! There's Torvald. Would you mind going into the nursery for a few minutes? Torvald can't bear to see sewing around. Anne-Marie'll help you.

Mrs Linde (*gathers some of her things together*)   Very well. But 1 shan't leave this house until we've talked this matter out.

She goes into the nursery, left. As she does so, **Helmer** *enters from the hall.*

Nora (*runs to meet him*)   Oh, Torvald dear, I've been so longing for you to come back!

Helmer   Was that the dressmaker?

Nora   No, it was Christine. She's helping me mend my costume. I'm going to look rather splendid in that.

Helmer   Yes, that was quite a bright idea of mine, wasn't it?

Nora   Wonderful! But wasn't it nice of me to give in to you?

Helmer (*takes her chin in his hand*)   Nice – to give in to your husband? All right, little silly, I know you didn't mean it like that. But I won't disturb you. I expect you'll be wanting to try it on.

Nora   Are you going to work now?

Helmer   Yes. (*Shows her a bundle of papers.*) Look at these. I've been down to the bank – (*Turns to go into his study.*)

Nora   Torvald.

Helmer (*stops*)   Yes.

Nora   If little squirrel asked you really prettily to grant her a wish –

Helmer   Well?

Nora   Would you grant it to her?

Helmer   First I should naturally have to know what it was.

Nora   Squirrel would do lots of pretty tricks for you if you granted her wish.

Helmer   Out with it, then.

Nora   Your little skylark would sing in every room –

Helmer   My little skylark does that already.

Nora   I'd turn myself into a little fairy and dance for you in the moonlight, Torvald.

Helmer   Nora, it isn't that business you were talking about this morning?

Nora (*comes closer*)   Yes, Torvald – oh, please! I beg of you!

Helmer   Have you really the nerve to bring that up again?

Nora   Yes, Torvald, yes, you must do as I ask! You must let Krogstad keep his place at the bank!

Helmer   My dear Nora, his is the job I'm giving to Mrs Linde.

Nora   Yes, that's terribly sweet of you. But you can get rid of one of the other clerks instead of Krogstad.

Helmer   Really, you're being incredibly obstinate. Just because you thoughtlessly promised to put in a word for him, you expect me to –

Nora   No, it isn't that, Helmer. It's for your own sake. That man writes for the most beastly newspapers – you said so yourself. He could do you tremendous harm. I'm so dreadfully frightened of him –

Helmer   Oh, I understand. Memories of the past. That's what's frightening you.

Nora   What do you mean?

Helmer   You're thinking of your father, aren't you?

Nora   Yes, yes. Of course. Just think what those dreadful men wrote in the papers about papa! The most frightful slanders.

I really believe it would have lost him his job if the Ministry hadn't sent you down to investigate, and you hadn't been so kind and helpful to him.

Helmer   But, my dear little Nora, there's a considerable difference between your father and me. Your father was not a man of unassailable reputation. But I am. And I hope to remain so all my life.

Nora   But no one knows what spiteful people may not dig up. We could be so peaceful and happy now, Torvald – we could be free from every worry – you and I and the children. Oh, please, Torvald, please – !

Helmer   The very fact of your pleading his cause makes it impossible for me to keep him. Everyone at the bank already knows that I intend to dismiss Krogstad. If the rumour got about that the new vice-president had allowed his wife to persuade him to change his mind –

Nora   Well, what then?

Helmer   Oh, nothing, nothing. As long as my little Miss Obstinate gets her way – ! Do you expect me to make a laughingstock of myself before my entire staff – give people the idea that I am open to outside influence? Believe me, I'd soon feel the consequences! Besides – there's something else that makes it impossible for Krogstad to remain in the bank while I am its manager.

Nora   What is that?

Helmer   I might conceivably have allowed myself to ignore his moral obloquies –

Nora   Yes, Torvald, surely?

Helmer   And I hear he's quite efficient at his job. But we – well, we were school friends. It was one of those friendships that one enters into over-hastily and so often comes to regret later in life. I might as well confess the truth. We – well, we're on Christian name terms. And the tactless idiot makes no attempt to conceal it when other people are present. On the contrary, he thinks it gives him the right to be familiar with me. He shows off the whole time, with 'Torvald this', and 'Torvald that'. I can tell you,

I find it damned annoying. If he stayed, he'd make my position intolerable.

Nora   Torvald, you can't mean this seriously.

Helmer   Oh? And why not?

Nora   But it's so petty.

Helmer   What did you say? Petty? You think *I* am petty?

Nora   No, Torvald dear, of course you're not. That's just why –

Helmer   Don't quibble! You call my motives petty. Then I must be petty too. Petty! I see. Well, I've had enough of this. (*Goes to the door and calls into the hall.*) Helen!

Nora   What are you going to do?

Helmer (*searching among his papers*)   I'm going to settle this matter once and for all.

The **Maid** *enters.*

Helmer   Take this letter downstairs at once. Find a messenger and see that he delivers it. Immediately! The address is on the envelope. Here's the money.

Maid   Very good, sir. (*Goes out with the letter.*)

Helmer (*putting his papers in order*)   There now, little Miss Obstinate.

Nora (*tensely*)   Torvald – what was in that letter?

Helmer   Krogstad's dismissal.

Nora   Call her back, Torvald! There's still time. Oh, Torvald, call her back! Do it for my sake – for your own sake – for the children! Do you hear me, Torvald? Please do it! You don't realize what this may do to us all!

Helmer   Too late.

Nora   Yes. Too late.

Helmer   My dear Nora, I forgive you this anxiety. Though it is a bit of an insult to me. Oh, but it is! Isn't it an insult to imply that

I should be frightened by the vindictiveness of a depraved hack journalist? But I forgive you, because it so charmingly testifies to the love you bear me. (*Takes her in his arms.*) Which is as it should be, my own dearest Nora. Let what will happen, happen. When the real crisis comes, you will not find me lacking in strength or courage. I am man enough to bear the burden for us both.

Nora (*fearfully*)   What do you mean?

Helmer   The whole burden, I say —

Nora (*calmly*)   I shall never let you do that.

Helmer   Very well. We shall share it, Nora — as man and wife. And that's as it should be. (*Caresses her.*) Are you happy now? There, there, there; don't look at me with those frightened little eyes. You're simply imagining things. You go ahead now and do your tarantella, and get some practice on that tambourine. I'll sit in my study and close the door. Then I won't hear anything, and you can make all the noise you want. (*Turns in the doorway.*) When Dr Rank comes, tell him where to find me. (*He nods to her, goes into his room with his papers and closes the door.*)

Nora (*desperate with anxiety, stands as though transfixed, and whispers*)   He said he'd do it. He will do it. He will do it, and nothing'll stop him. No, never that. I'd rather anything. There must be some escape — Some way out — !

The bell rings in the hall.

Nora   Dr Rank — ! Anything but that! Anything, I don't care — !

She passes her hand across her face, composes herself, walks across and opens the door to the hall. **Dr Rank** *is standing there, hanging up his fur coat. During the following scene it begins to grow dark.*

Nora   Good evening, Dr Rank. I recognized your ring. But you mustn't go in to Torvald yet. I think he's busy.

Rank   And — you?

Nora (*as he enters the room and she closes the door behind him*)   Oh, you know very well I've always time to talk to you.

Rank   Thank you. I shall avail myself of that privilege as long as I can.

Nora   What do you mean by that? As long as you *can*?

Rank   Yes. Does that frighten you?

Nora   Well, it's rather a curious expression. Is something going to happen?

Rank   Something I've been expecting to happen for a long time. But I didn't think it would happen quite so soon.

Nora (*seizes his arm*)   What is it? Dr Rank, you must tell me!

Rank (*sits down by the stove*)   I'm on the way out. And there's nothing to be done about it.

Nora (*sighs with relief*)   Oh, it's you – ?

Rank   Who else? No, it's no good lying to oneself. I am the most wretched of all my patients, Mrs Helmer. These last few days I've been going through the books of this poor body of mine, and I find I am bankrupt. Within a month I may be rotting up there in the churchyard.

Nora   Ugh, what a nasty way to talk!

Rank   The facts aren't exactly nice. But the worst is that there's so much else that's nasty that's got to come first. I've only one more test to make. When that's done I'll have a pretty accurate idea of when the final disintegration is likely to begin. I want to ask you a favour. Helmer's a sensitive chap, and I know how he hates anything ugly. I don't want him to visit me when I'm in hospital –

Nora   Oh but, Dr Rank –

Rank   I don't want him there. On any pretext. I shan't have him allowed in. As soon as I know the worst, I'll send you my visiting card with a black cross on it, and then you'll know that the final filthy process has begun.

Nora   Really, you're being quite impossible this evening. And I did hope you'd be in a good mood.

Rank   With death on my hands? And all this to atone for someone else's sin? Is there justice in that? And in every single family, in one way or another, the same merciless law of retribution is at work –

Nora (*holds her hands to her ears*)   Nonsense! Cheer up! Laugh!

Rank   Yes, you're right. Laughter's all the damned thing's fit for. My poor innocent spine must pay for the fun my father had as a gay young lieutenant.

Nora (*at the table, left*)   You mean he was too fond of asparagus and *foie gras*?

Rank   Yes; and truffles too.

Nora   Yes, of course, truffles, yes. And oysters too, I suppose?

Rank   Yes, oysters, oysters. Of course.

Nora   And all that port and champagne to wash them down. It's too sad that all those lovely things should affect one's spine.

Rank   Especially a poor spine that never got any pleasure out of them.

Nora   Oh yes, that's the saddest thing of all.

Rank (*looks searchingly at her*)   Hm –

Nora (*after a moment*)   Why did you smile?

Rank   No, it was you who laughed.

Nora   No, it was you who smiled, Dr Rank!

Rank (*gets up*)   You're a worse little rogue than I thought.

Nora   Oh, I'm full of stupid tricks today.

Rank   So it seems.

Nora (*puts both her hands on his shoulders*)   Dear, dear Dr Rank, you mustn't die and leave Torvald and me.

Rank   Oh, you'll soon get over it. Once one is gone, one is soon forgotten.

Nora (*looks at him anxiously*)   Do you believe that?

Rank   One finds replacements, and then –

Nora Who will find a replacement?

Rank You and Helmer both will, when I am gone. You seem to have made a start already, haven't you? What was this Mrs Linde doing here yesterday evening?

Nora Aha! But surely you can't be jealous of poor Christine?

Rank Indeed I am. She will be my successor in this house. When I have moved on, this lady will –

Nora Ssh – don't speak so loud! She's in there!

Rank Today again? You see!

Nora She's only come to mend my dress. Good heavens, how unreasonable you are! (*Sits on the sofa.*) Be nice now, Dr Rank. Tomorrow you'll see how beautifully I shall dance; and you must imagine I'm doing it just for you. And for Torvald, of course – obviously. (*Takes some things out of the box.*) Dr Rank, sit down here and I'll show you something.

Rank (*sits*) What's this?

Nora Look here! Look!

Rank Silk stockings!

Nora Flesh-coloured. Aren't they beautiful? It's very dark in here now, of course, but tomorrow – ! No, no, no – only the soles. Oh well, I suppose you can look a bit higher if you want to.

Rank Hm –

Nora Why are you looking so critical? Don't you think they'll fit me?

Rank I can't really give you a qualified opinion on that.

Nora (*looks at him for a moment*) Shame on you! (*Flicks him on the ear with the stockings.*) Take that. (*Puts them back in the box.*)

Rank What other wonders are to be revealed to me?

Nora I shan't show you anything else. You're being naughty.

She hums a little and looks among the things in the box.

Rank (*after a short silence*)   When I sit here like this being so intimate with you, I can't think – I cannot imagine what would have become of me if I had never entered this house.

Nora (*smiles*)   Yes, I think you enjoy being with us, don't you?

Rank (*more quietly, looking into the middle distance*)   And now to have to leave it all –

Nora   Nonsense. You're not leaving us.

Rank (*as before*)   And not to be able to leave even the most wretched token of gratitude behind; hardly even a passing sense of loss; only an empty space, to be filled by the next comer.

Nora   Suppose I were to ask you to – ? No –

Rank   To do what?

Nora   To give me proof of your friendship –

Rank   Yes, yes?

Nora   No, I mean – to do me a very great service –

Rank   Would you really for once grant me that happiness?

Nora   But you've no idea what it is.

Rank   Very well, tell me, then.

Nora   No, but, Dr Rank, I can't. It's far too much – I want your help and advice, and I want you to do something for me.

Rank   The more the better. I've no idea what it can be. But tell me. You do trust me, don't you?

Nora   Oh, yes, more than anyone. You're my best and truest friend. Otherwise I couldn't tell you. Well then, Dr Rank, there's something you must help me to prevent. You know how much Torvald loves me – he'd never hesitate for an instant to lay down his life for me –

Rank (*leans over towards her*)   Nora – do you think he is the only one – ?

Nora (*with a slight start*)   What do you mean?

Rank Who would gladly lay down his life for you?

Nora (*sadly*) Oh, I see.

Rank I swore to myself I would let you know that before I go. I shall never have a better opportunity. . . . Well, Nora, now you know that. And now you also know that you can trust me as you can trust nobody else.

Nora (*rises; calmly and quietly*) Let me pass, please

Rank (*makes room for her but remains seated*) Nora –

Nora (*in the doorway to the hall*) Helen, bring the lamp. (*Goes over to the stove.*) Oh, dear, Dr Rank, this was really horrid of you.

Rank (*gets up*) That I have loved you as deeply as anyone else has? Was that horrid of me?

Nora No – but that you should go and tell me. That was quite unnecessary –

Rank What do you mean? Did you know, then – ?

*The **Maid** enters with the lamp, puts it on the table and goes out.*

Rank Nora – Mrs Helmer! I am asking you, did you know this?

Nora Oh, what do I know, what did I know, what didn't I know – ? I really can't say. How could you be so stupid, Dr Rank? Everything was so nice.

Rank Well, at any rate, now you know that I am ready to serve you, body and soul. So – please continue.

Nora (*looks at him*) After this?

Rank Please tell me what it is.

Nora I can't possibly tell you now.

Rank Yes, yes! You mustn't punish me like this. Let me be allowed to do what I can for you.

Nora You can't do anything for me now. Anyway, I don't need any help. It was only my imagination – you'll see. Yes, really. Honestly. (*Sits in the rocking-chair, looks at him and smiles.*) Well, upon my word you *are* a fine gentleman, Dr Rank. Aren't you ashamed of yourself, now that the lamp's been lit?

Rank   Frankly, no. But perhaps I ought to say – *adieu?*

Nora   Of course not. You will naturally continue to visit us as before. You know quite well how Torvald depends on your company.

Rank   Yes, but you?

Nora   Oh, I always think it's enormous fun having you here.

Rank   That was what misled me. You're a riddle to me, you know. I'd often felt you'd just as soon be with me as with Helmer.

Nora   Well, you see, there are some people whom one loves, and others whom it's almost more fun to be with.

Rank   Oh, yes, there's some truth in that.

Nora   When I was at home, of course, I loved papa best. But I always used to think it was terribly amusing to go down and talk to the servants; because they never told me what I ought to do; and they were such fun to listen to.

Rank   I see. So I've taken their place?

Nora (*jumps up and runs over to him*)   Oh, dear, sweet Dr Rank, I didn't mean that at all. But I'm sure you understand – I feel the same about Torvald as I did about papa.

Maid (*enters from the hall*)   Excuse me, madam. (*Whispers to her and hands her a visiting card.*)

Nora (*glances at the card*)   Oh! (*Puts it quickly in her pocket.*)

Rank   Anything wrong?

Nora   No, no, nothing at all. It's just something that – it's my new dress.

Rank   What? But your costume is lying over there.

Nora   Oh – that, yes – but there's another – I ordered it specially – Torvald mustn't know –

Rank   Ah, so that's your big secret?

Nora   Yes, yes. Go in and talk to him – he's in his study – keep him talking for a bit –

Rank   Don't worry. He won't get away from me. (*Goes into* **Helmer***'s study.*)

Nora (*to the* **Maid**)   Is he waiting in the kitchen?

Maid   Yes, madam, he came up the back way –

Nora   But didn't you tell him I had a visitor?

Maid   Yes, but he wouldn't go.

Nora   Wouldn't go?

Maid   No, madam, not until he's spoken with you.

Nora   Very well, show him in. But quietly. Helen, you mustn't tell anyone about this. It's a surprise for my husband.

Maid   Very good, madam. I understand. (*Goes.*)

Nora   It's happening. It's happening after all. No, no, no, it can't happen, it mustn't happen.

She walks across and bolts the door of **Helmer***'s study. The* **Maid** *opens the door from the hall to admit* **Krogstad***, and closes it behind him. He is wearing an overcoat, heavy boots and a fur cap.*

Nora (*goes towards him*)   Speak quietly. My husband's at home.

Krogstad   Let him hear.

Nora   What do you want from me?

Krogstad   Information.

Nora   Hurry up, then. What is it?

Krogstad   I suppose you know I've been given the sack.

Nora   I couldn't stop it, Mr Krogstad. I did my best for you, but it didn't help.

Krogstad   Does your husband love you so little? He knows what I can do to you, and yet he dares to –

Nora   Surely you don't imagine I told him?

Krogstad No, I didn't really think you had. It wouldn't have been like my old friend Torvald Helmer to show that much courage –

Nora Mr Krogstad, I'll trouble you to speak respectfully of my husband.

Krogstad Don't worry, I'll show him all the respect he deserves. But since you're so anxious to keep this matter hushed up, I presume you're better informed than you were yesterday of the gravity of what you've done?

Nora I've learned more than you could ever teach me.

Krogstad Yes, a bad lawyer like me –

Nora What do you want from me?

Krogstad I just wanted to see how things were with you, Mrs Helmer. I've been thinking about you all day. Even duns and hack journalists have hearts, you know.

Nora Show some heart, then. Think of my little children.

Krogstad Have you and your husband thought of mine? Well, let's forget that. I just wanted to tell you, you don't need to take this business too seriously. I'm not going to take any action, for the present.

Nora Oh, no – you won't will you? I knew it.

Krogstad It can all be settled quite amicably. There's no need for it to become public. We'll keep it among the three of us.

Nora My husband must never know about this.

Krogstad How can you stop him? Can you pay the balance of what you owe me?

Nora Not immediately.

Krogstad Have you any means of raising the money during the next few days?

Nora None that I would care to use.

Krogstad Well, it wouldn't have helped anyway. However much money you offered me now I wouldn't give you back that paper.

Nora   What are you going to do with it?

Krogstad   Just keep it. No one else need ever hear about it. So in case you were thinking of doing anything desperate –

Nora   I am.

Krogstad   Such as running away –

Nora   I am.

Krogstad   Or anything more desperate –

Nora   How did you know?

Krogstad   – just give up the idea.

Nora   How did you know?

Krogstad   Most of us think of that at first. I did. But I hadn't the courage –

Nora (*dully*)   Neither have I.

Krogstad (*relieved*)   It's true, isn't it? You haven't the courage, either?

Nora   No. I haven't. I haven't.

Krogstad   It'd be a stupid thing to do anyway. Once the first little domestic explosion is over . . . I've got a letter in my pocket here addressed to your husband –

Nora   Telling him everything?

Krogstad   As delicately as possible.

Nora (*quickly*)   He must never see that letter. Tear it up. I'll find the money somehow –

Krogstad   I'm sorry, Mrs Helmer, I thought I'd explained –

Nora   Oh, I don't mean the money I owe you. Let me know how much you want from my husband, and I'll find it for you.

Krogstad   I'm not asking your husband for money.

Nora   What do you want, then?

Krogstad   I'll tell you. I want to get on my feet again, Mrs Helmer. I want to get to the top. And your husband's going to help me. For eighteen months now my record's been clean. I've been in hard straits all that time: I was content to fight my way back inch by inch. Now I've been chucked back into the mud, and I'm not going to be satisfied with just getting back my job. I'm going to get to the top, I tell you. I'm going to get back into the bank, and it's going to be higher up. Your husband's going to create a new job for me –

Nora   He'll never do that!

Krogstad   Oh yes, he will. I know him. He won't dare to risk a scandal. And once I'm in there with him, you'll see! Within a year I'll be his right-hand man. It'll be Nils Krogstad who'll be running that bank, not Torvald Helmer!

Nora   That will never happen.

Krogstad   Are you thinking of – ?

Nora   Now I *have* the courage.

Krogstad   Oh, you can't frighten me. A pampered little pretty like you –

Nora   You'll see! You'll see!

Krogstad   Under the ice? Down in the cold, black water? And then, in the spring, to float up again, ugly, unrecognizable, hairless – ?

Nora   You can't frighten me.

Krogstad   And you can't frighten me. People don't do such things, Mrs Helmer. And anyway, what'd be the use? I've got him in my pocket.

Nora   But afterwards? When I'm no longer – ?

Krogstad   Have you forgotten that then your reputation will be in my hands?

She looks at him speechlessly.

Krogstad   Well, I've warned you. Don't do anything silly. When Helmer's read my letter, he'll get in touch with me. And remember, it's your husband who has forced me to act like this. And for that

I'll never forgive him. Goodbye, Mrs Helmer. (*He goes out through the hall.*)

Nora (*runs to the hall door, opens it a few inches and listens*)   He's going. He's not going to give him the letter. Oh, no, no, it couldn't possibly happen. (*Opens the door, a little wider.*) What's he doing? Standing outside the front door. He's not going downstairs. Is he changing his mind? Yes, he – !

A letter falls into the letter-box. **Krogstad**'s *footsteps die away down the stairs.*

Nora (*with a stifled cry, runs across the room towards the table by the sofa. A pause*)   In the letter-box. (*Steals timidly over towards the hall door.*) There it is! Oh, Torvald, Torvald! Now we're lost!

Mrs Linde (*enters from the nursery with* **Nora**'s *costume*)   Well, I've done the best I can. Shall we see how it looks – ?

Nora (*whispers hoarsely*)   Christine, come here.

Mrs Linde (*throws the dress on the sofa*)   What's wrong with you? You look as though you'd seen a ghost!

Nora   Come here. Do you see that letter? There – look – through the glass of the letter-box.

Mrs Linde   Yes, yes, I see it.

Nora   That letter's from Krogstad –

Mrs Linde   Nora! It was Krogstad who lent you the money!

Nora   Yes. And now Torvald's going to discover everything.

Mrs Linde   Oh, believe me, Nora, it'll be best for you both.

Nora   You don't know what's happened. I've committed a forgery –

Mrs Linde   But, for heaven's sake – !

Nora   Christine, all I want is for you to be my witness.

Mrs Linde   What do you mean? Witness what?

Nora   If I should go out of my mind – and it might easily happen –

Mrs Linde   Nora!

Nora   Or if anything else should happen to me – so that I wasn't here any longer –

Mrs Linde   Nora, Nora, you don't know what you're saying!

Nora   If anyone should try to take the blame, and say it was all his fault – you understand – ?

Mrs Linde   Yes, yes – but how can you think – ?

Nora   Then you must testify that it isn't true, Christine. I'm not mad – I know exactly what I'm saying – and I'm telling you, no one else knows anything about this. I did it entirely on my own. Remember that.

Mrs Linde   All right. But I simply don't understand –

Nora   Oh, how could you understand? A – miracle – is about to happen.

Mrs Linde   Miracle?

Nora   Yes. A miracle. But it's so frightening, Christine. It mustn't happen, not for anything in the world.

Mrs Linde   I'll go over and talk to Krogstad.

Nora   Don't go near him. He'll only do something to hurt you.

Mrs Linde   Once upon a time he'd have done anything for my sake.

Nora   He?

Mrs Linde   Where does he live?

Nora   Oh, how should I know – ? Oh yes, wait a moment – ! (*Feels in her pocket.*) Here's his card. But the letter, the letter – !

Helmer (*from his study, knocks on the door*)   Nora!

Nora (*cries in alarm*)   What is it?

Helmer   Now, now, don't get alarmed. We're not coming in – you've closed the door. Are you trying on your costume?

Nora   Yes, yes – I'm trying on my costume. I'm going to look so pretty for you, Torvald.

Mrs Linde (*who has been reading the card*)   Why, he lives just round the corner.

Nora   Yes; but it's no use. There's nothing to be done now. The letter's lying there in the box.

Mrs Linde   And your husband has the key?

Nora   Yes, he always keeps it.

Mrs Linde   Krogstad must ask him to send the letter back unread. He must find some excuse –

Nora   But Torvald always opens the box at just about this time –

Mrs Linde   You must stop him. Go in and keep him talking. I'll be back as quickly as I can.

She hurries out through the hall.

Nora (*goes over to* **Helmer**'s *door, opens it and peeps in*)   Torvald!

Helmer (*offstage*)   Well, may a man enter his own drawing-room again? Come on, Rank, now we'll see what – (*In the doorway.*) But what's this?

Nora   What, Torvald dear?

Helmer   Rank's been preparing me for some great transformation scene.

Rank (*in the doorway*)   So I understood. But I seem to have been mistaken.

Nora   Yes, no one's to be allowed to see me before tomorrow night.

Helmer   But, my dear Nora, you look quite worn out. Have you been practising too hard?

Nora   No, I haven't practised at all yet.

Helmer   Well, you must.

Nora   Yes, Torvald, I must, I know. But I can't get anywhere without your help. I've completely forgotten everything.

Helmer   Oh, we'll soon put that to rights.

Nora   Yes, help me, Torvald. Promise me you will? Oh, I'm so nervous. All those people – ! You must forget everything except me this evening. You mustn't think of business – I won't even let you touch a pen. Promise me, Torvald?

Helmer   I promise. This evening I shall think of nothing but you – my poor, helpless little darling. Oh, there's just one thing I must see to – (*Goes towards the hall door.*)

Nora   What do you want out there?

Helmer   I'm only going to see if any letters have come.

Nora   No, Torvald, no!

Helmer   Why what's the matter?

Nora   Torvald, I beg you. There's nothing there.

Helmer   Well, I'll just make sure.

He moves towards the door. **Nora** *runs to the piano and plays the first bars of the* Tarantella.

Helmer (*at the door, turns*)   Aha!

Nora   I can't dance tomorrow if I don't practise with you now.

Helmer (*goes over to her*)   Are you really so frightened, Nora dear?

Nora   Yes terribly frightened. Let me start practising now, at once – we've still time before dinner. Oh, do sit down and play for me, Torvald dear. Correct me, lead me, the way you always do.

Helmer   Very well, my dear, if you wish it.

He sits down at the piano, **Nora** *seizes the tambourine and a long multi-coloured shawl from the cardboard box, wraps the shawl hastily around her, then takes a quick leap into the centre of the room and cries.*

Nora   Play for me! I want to dance!

Helmer *plays and* **Nora** *dances.* **Dr Rank** *stands behind* **Helmer** *at the piano and watches her.*

Helmer (*as he plays*)   Slower, slower!

Nora   I can't!

Helmer   Not so violently, Nora.

Nora   I must!

Helmer (*stops playing*)   No, no, this won't do at all.

Nora (*laughs and swings her tambourine*)   Isn't that what I told you?

Rank   Let me play for her.

Helmer (*gets up*)   Yes, would you? Then it'll be easier for me to show her.

Rank *sits down at the piano and plays.* **Nora** *dances more and more wildly.* **Helmer** *has stationed himself by the stove and tries repeatedly to correct her, but she seems not to hear him. Her hair works loose and falls over her shoulders; she ignores it and continues to dance.* **Mrs Linde** *enters.*

Mrs Linde (*stands in the doorway as though tongue-tied*)   Ah – !

Nora (*as she dances*)   Oh, Christine, we're having such fun!

Helmer   But, Nora darling, you're dancing as if your life depended on it.

Nora   It does.

Helmer   Rank, stop it! This is sheer lunacy. Stop it, I say!

Rank *ceases playing.* **Nora** *suddenly stops dancing.*

Helmer (*goes over to her*)   I'd never have believed it. You've forgotten everything I taught you.

Nora (*throws away the tambourine*)   You see!

Helmer   I'll have to show you every step.

Nora   You see how much I need you! You must show me every step of the way. Right to the end of the dance. Promise me you will, Torvald?

Helmer   Never fear. I will.

Nora   You mustn't think about anything but me – today or tomorrow. Don't open any letters – don't even open the letterbox –

Helmer   Aha, you're still worried about that fellow –

Nora   Oh, yes, yes, him too.

Helmer   Nora, I can tell from the way you're behaving, there's a letter from him already lying there.

Nora   I don't know. I think so. But you mustn't read it now. I don't want anything ugly to come between us till it's all over.

Rank (*quietly to* **Helmer**)   Better give her her way.

Helmer (*puts his arm round her*)   My child shall have her way. But tomorrow night, when your dance is over –

Nora   Then you will be free.

Maid (*appears in the doorway, right*)   Dinner is served, madam.

Nora   Put out some champagne, Helen.

Maid   Very good, madam. (*Goes.*)

Helmer   I say! What's this, a banquet?

Nora   We'll drink champagne until dawn! (*Calls.*) And, Helen! Put out some macaroons! Lots of macaroons – for once!

Helmer (*takes her hands in his*)   Now, now, now. Don't get so excited. Where's my little songbird, the one I know?

Nora   All right. Go and sit down – and you, too, Dr Rank. I'll be with you in a minute. Christine, you must help me put my hair up.

Rank (*quietly, as they go*)   There's nothing wrong, is there? I mean, she isn't – er – expecting – ?

Helmer   Good heavens no, my dear chap. She just gets scared like a child sometimes – I told you before –

They go out, right.

Nora   Well?

Mrs Linde   He's left town.

Nora   I saw it from your face.

Mrs Linde   He'll be back tomorrow evening. I left a note for him.

Nora   You needn't have bothered. You can't stop anything now. Anyway, it's wonderful really, in a way – sitting here and waiting for the miracle to happen.

Mrs Linde   Waiting for what?

Nora   Oh, you wouldn't understand. Go in and join them. I'll be with you in a moment.

Mrs Linde *goes into the dining-room.*

Nora (*stands for a moment as though collecting herself. Then she looks at her watch.*)   Five o'clock. Seven hours till midnight. Then another twenty-four hours till midnight tomorrow. And then the tarantella will be finished. Twenty-four and seven? Thirty-one hours to live.

Helmer (*appears in the doorway, right*)   What's happened to my little songbird?

Nora (*runs to him with her arms wide*)   Your songbird is here!

Act Three

The same room. The table which was formerly by the sofa has been moved into the centre of the room; the chairs surround it as before. A lamp is burning on the table. The door to the hall stands open. Dance music can be heard from the floor above. **Mrs Linde** *is seated at the table, absent-mindedly glancing through a book. She is trying to read, but seems unable to keep her mind on it. More than once she turns and listens anxiously towards the front door.*

Mrs Linde (*looks at her watch*) Not here yet. There's not much time left. Please God he hasn't – ! (*Listens again.*) Ah, here he is.

Goes out into the hall and cautiously opens the front door. Footsteps can be heard softly ascending the stairs.

Mrs Linde (*whispers*) Come in. There's no one here.

Krogstad (*in the doorway*) I found a note from you at my lodgings. What does this mean?

Mrs Linde I must speak with you.

Krogstad Oh? And must our conversation take place in this house?

Mrs Linde We couldn't meet at my place; my room has no separate entrance. Come in. We're quite alone. The maid's asleep, and the Helmers are at the dance upstairs.

Krogstad (*comes into the room*) Well, well! So the Helmers are dancing this evening? Are they indeed?

Mrs Linde Yes, why not?

Krogstad True enough. Why not?

Mrs Linde Well, Krogstad. You and I must have a talk together.

Krogstad Have we two anything further to discuss?

Mrs Linde We have a great deal to discuss.

Krogstad I wasn't aware of it.

Mrs Linde   That's because you've never really understood me.

Krogstad   Was there anything to understand? It's the old story, isn't it – a woman chucking a man because something better turns up?

Mrs Linde   Do you really think I'm so utterly heartless? You think it was easy for me to give you up?

Krogstad   Wasn't it?

Mrs Linde   Oh, Nils, did you really believe that?

Krogstad   Then why did you write to me the way you did?

Mrs Linde   I had to. Since I had to break with you, I thought it my duty to destroy all the feelings you had for me.

Krogstad (*clenches his fists*)   So that was it. And you did this for money!

Mrs Linde   You mustn't forget I had a helpless mother to take care of, and two little brothers. We couldn't wait for you, Nils. It would have been so long before you'd have had enough to support us.

Krogstad   Maybe. But you had no right to cast me off for someone else.

Mrs Linde   Perhaps not. I've often asked myself that.

Krogstad (*more quietly*)   When I lost you, it was just as though all solid ground had been swept from under my feet. Look at me. Now I'm a shipwrecked man, clinging to a spar.

Mrs Linde   Help may be near at hand.

Krogstad   It was near. But then you came, and stood between it and me.

Mrs Linde   I didn't know, Nils. No one told me till today that this job I'd found was yours.

Krogstad   I believe you, since you say so. But now you know, won't you give it up?

Mrs Linde   No – because it wouldn't help you even if I did.

Krogstad   Wouldn't it? I'd do it all the same.

Mrs Linde   I've learned to look at things practically. Life and poverty have taught me that.

Krogstad   And life has taught me to distrust fine words.

Mrs Linde   Then it has taught you a useful lesson. But surely you still believe in actions?

Krogstad   What do you mean?

Mrs Linde   You said you were like a shipwrecked man clinging to a spar.

Krogstad   I have good reason to say it.

Mrs Linde   I'm in the same position as you. No one to care about, no one to care for.

Krogstad   You made your own choice.

Mrs Linde   I had no choice – then.

Krogstad   Well?

Mrs Linde   Nils, suppose we two shipwrecked souls could join hands?

Krogstad   What are you saying?

Mrs Linde   Castaways have a better chance of survival together than on their own.

Krogstad   Christine!

Mrs Linde   Why do you suppose I came to this town?

Krogstad   You mean – you came because of me?

Mrs Linde   I must work if I'm to find life worth living. I've always worked, for as long as I can remember. It's been the greatest joy of my life – my only joy. But now I'm alone in the world, and I feel so dreadfully lost and empty. There's no joy in working just for oneself. Oh, Nils, give me something – someone – to work for.

Krogstad   I don't believe all that. You're just being hysterical and romantic. You want to find an excuse for self-sacrifice.

Mrs Linde   Have you ever known me to be hysterical?

Krogstad   You mean you really – ? Is it possible? Tell me – you know all about my past?

Mrs Linde   Yes.

Krogstad   And you know what people think of me here?

Mrs Linde   You said just now that with me you might have become a different person.

Krogstad   I know I could have.

Mrs Linde   Couldn't it still happen?

Krogstad   Christine – do you really mean this? Yes – you do – I see it in your face. Have you really the courage – ?

Mrs Linde   I need someone to be a mother to; and your children need a mother. And you and I need each other. I believe in you, Nils. I am afraid of nothing – with you.

Krogstad (*clasps her hands*)   Thank you, Christine – thank you! Now I shall make the world believe in me as you do! Oh – but I'd forgotten –

Mrs Linde (*listens*)   Ssh! The tarantella! Go quickly, go!

Krogstad   Why? What is it?

Mrs Linde   You hear that dance? As soon as it's finished, they'll be coming down.

Krogstad   All right, I'll go. It's no good, Christine. I'd forgotten – you don't know what I've just done to the Helmers.

Mrs Linde   Yes, Nils. I know.

Krogstad   And yet you'd still have the courage to – ?

Mrs Linde   I know what despair can drive a man like you to.

Krogstad   Oh, if only I could undo this!

Mrs Linde   You can. Your letter is still lying in the box.

Krogstad   Are you sure?

Mrs Linde   Quite sure. But –

Krogstad (*looks searchingly at her*)   Is that why you're doing this? You want to save your friend at any price? Tell me the truth. Is that the reason?

Mrs Linde   Nils, a woman who has sold herself once for the sake of others doesn't make the same mistake again.

Krogstad   I shall demand my letter back.

Mrs Linde   No, no.

Krogstad   Of course I shall. I shall stay here till Helmer comes down. I'll tell him he must give me back my letter – I'll say it was only to do with my dismissal, and that I don't want him to read it –

Mrs Linde   No, Nils, you mustn't ask for that letter back.

Krogstad   But – tell me – wasn't that the real reason you asked me to come here?

Mrs Linde   Yes – at first, when I was frightened. But a day has passed since then, and in that time I've seen incredible things happen in this house. Helmer must know the truth. This unhappy secret of Nora's must be revealed. They must come to a full understanding. There must be an end of all these shiftings and evasions.

Krogstad   Very well. If you're prepared to risk it. But one thing I can do – and at once –

Mrs Linde (*listens*)   Hurry! Go, go! The dance is over. We aren't safe here another moment.

Krogstad   I'll wait for you downstairs.

Mrs Linde   Yes, do. You can see me home.

Krogstad   I've never been so happy in my life before!

He goes out through the front door. The door leading from the room into the hall remains open.

Mrs Linde (*tidies the room a little and gets her hat and coat*)   What a change! Oh, what a change! Someone to work for – to live for! A home to bring joy into! I won't let this chance of happiness slip through my fingers. Oh, why don't they come? (*Listens.*) Ah, here they are. I must get my coat on.

She takes her hat and coat, **Helmer***'s and* **Nora***'s voices become audible outside. A key is turned in the lock and* **Helmer** *leads* **Nora** *almost forcibly into the hall. She is dressed in an Italian costume with a large black shawl. He is in evening dress, with a black coat.*

Nora (*still in the doorway, resisting him*)   No, no, no – not in here! I want to go back upstairs. I don't want to leave so early.

Helmer   But my dearest Nora –

Nora   Oh, please, Torvald, please! Just another hour!

Helmer   Not another minute, Nora, my sweet. You know what we agreed. Come along, now. Into the drawing-room. You'll catch cold if you stay out here.

He leads her, despite her efforts to resist him, gently into the room.

Mrs Linde   Good evening.

Nora   Christine!

Helmer   Oh, hullo, Mrs Linde. You still here?

Mrs Linde   Please forgive me. I did so want to see Nora in her costume.

Nora   Have you been sitting here waiting for me?

Mrs Linde   Yes. I got here too late, I'm afraid. You'd already gone up. And I felt I really couldn't go home without seeing you.

Helmer (*takes off* **Nora***'s shawl*)   Well, take a good look at her. She's worth looking at, don't you think? Isn't she beautiful, Mrs Linde?

Mrs Linde   Oh, yes, indeed –

Helmer   Isn't she unbelievably beautiful? Everyone at the party said so. But dreadfully stubborn she is, bless her pretty little heart. What's to be done about that? Would you believe it, I practically had to use force to get her away!

Nora   Oh, Torvald, you're going to regret not letting me stay – just half an hour longer.

Helmer   Hear that, Mrs Linde? She dances her tarantella – makes a roaring success – and very well deserved – though possibly a trifle too realistic – more so than was aesthetically necessary, strictly speaking. But never mind that. Main thing is – she had a success – roaring success. Was I going to let her stay on after that and spoil the impression? No, thank you! I took my beautiful little Capri signorina – my capricious little Capricienne, what? – under my arm – a swift round of the ballroom, a curtsy to the company, and, as they say in novels, the beautiful apparition disappeared! An exit should always be dramatic, Mrs Linde. But unfortunately that's just what I can't get Nora to realize. I say, it's hot in here. (*Throws his cloak on a chair and opens the door to his study.*) What's this? It's dark in here. Ah, yes, of course – excuse me. (*Goes in and lights a couple of candles.*)

Nora (*whispers softly, breathlessly*)   Well?

Mrs Linde (*quietly*)   I've spoken to him.

Nora   Yes?

Mrs Linde   Nora – you must tell your husband everything.

Nora (*dully*)   I knew it.

Mrs Linde   You have nothing to fear from Krogstad. But you must tell him.

Nora   I shan't tell him anything.

Mrs Linde   Then the letter will.

Nora   Thank you, Christine. Now I know what I must do. Ssh!

Helmer (*returns*)   Well, Mrs Linde, finished admiring her?

Mrs Linde   Yes. Now I must say good night.

Helmer   Oh, already? Does this knitting belong to you?

Mrs Linde (*takes it*)   Thank you, yes. I nearly forgot it.

Helmer   You knit, then?

Mrs Linde Why, yes.

Helmer Know what? You ought to take up embroidery.

Mrs Linde Oh? Why?

Helmer It's much prettier. Watch me, now. You hold the embroidery in your left hand, like this, and then you take the needle in your right hand and go in and out in a slow, easy movement – like this. I am right, aren't I?

Mrs Linde Yes, I'm sure –

Helmer But knitting, now – that's an ugly business – can't help it. Look – arms all huddled up – great clumsy needles going up and down – makes you look like a damned Chinaman. I say that really was a magnificent champagne they served us.

Mrs Linde Well, good night, Nora. And stop being stubborn! Remember!

Helmer Quite right, Mrs Linde!

Mrs Linde Good night, Mr Helmer.

Helmer (*accompanies her to the door*) Good night, good night! I hope you'll manage to get home all right? I'd gladly – but you haven't far to go, have you? Good night, good night.

She goes. He closes the door behind her and returns.

Helmer Well, we've got rid of her at last. Dreadful bore that woman is!

Nora Aren't you very tired, Torvald?

Helmer No, not in the least.

Nora Aren't you sleepy?

Helmer Not a bit. On the contrary, I feel extraordinary exhila-rated. But what about you? Yes, you look very sleepy and tired.

Nora Yes, I am very tired. Soon I shall sleep.

Helmer You see, you see! How right I was not to let you stay longer!

Nora   Oh, you're always right, whatever you do.

Helmer (*kisses her on the forehead*)   Now my little songbird's talking just like a real big human being. I say, did you notice how cheerful Rank was this evening?

Nora   Oh? Was he? I didn't have a chance to speak with him.

Helmer   I hardly did. But I haven't seen him in such a jolly mood for ages. (*Looks at her for a moment, then comes closer.*) I say, it's nice to get back to one's home again, and be all alone with you. Upon my word, you're a distractingly beautiful young woman.

Nora   Don't look at me like that, Torvald!

Helmer   What, not look at my most treasured possession? At all this wonderful beauty that's mine, mine alone, all mine.

Nora (*goes round to the other side of the table*)   You mustn't talk to me like that tonight.

Helmer (*follows her*)   You've still the tarantella in your blood, I see. And that makes you even more desirable. Listen! Now the other guests are beginning to go. (*More quietly.*) Nora – soon the whole house will be absolutely quiet.

Nora   Yes, I hope so.

Helmer   Yes, my beloved Nora, of course you do! You know – when I'm out with you among other people like we were tonight, do you know why I say so little to you, why I keep so aloof from you, and just throw you an occasional glance? Do you know why I do that? It's because I pretend to myself that you're my secret mistress, my clandestine little sweetheart, and that nobody knows there's anything at all between us.

Nora   Oh, yes, yes, yes – I know you never think of anything but me.

Helmer   And then when we're about to go, and I wrap the shawl round your lovely young shoulders, over this wonderful curve of your neck – then I pretend to myself that you are my young bride, that we've just come from the wedding, that I'm taking you to my house for the first time – that, for the first time, I am alone with you – quite alone with you, as you stand there young and trembling and beautiful. All evening I've had no eyes for anyone but you. When I saw you dance the tarantella, like a huntress, a temptress, my blood grew hot, I couldn't stand it any longer! That was why I seized you and dragged you down here with me –

Nora   Leave me, Torvald! Get away from me! I don't want all this.

Helmer   What? Now, Nora, you're joking with me. Don't want, don't want – ? Aren't I your husband?

There is a knock on the front door.

Nora (*starts*)   What was that?

Helmer (*goes towards the hall*)   Who is it?

Dr Rank (*outside*)   It's me. May I come in for a moment?

Helmer (*quietly, annoyed*)   Oh, what does he want now? (*Calls.*) Wait a moment. (*Walks over and opens the door.*) Well! Nice of you not to go by without looking in.

Rank   I thought I heard your voice, so I felt I had to say goodbye. (*His eyes travel swiftly around the room.*) Ah, yes – these dear rooms, how well I know them. What a happy, peaceful home you two have.

Helmer   You seemed to be having a pretty happy time yourself upstairs.

Rank   Indeed I did. Why not? Why shouldn't one make the most of this world? As much as one can, and for as long as one can. The wine was excellent –

Helmer   Especially the champagne.

Rank   You noticed that too? It's almost incredible how much I managed to get down.

Nora   Torvald drank a lot of champagne too, this evening.

Rank   Oh?

Nora   Yes. It always makes him merry afterwards.

Rank   Well, why shouldn't a man have a merry evening after a well-spent day?

Helmer   Well-spent? Oh, I don't know that I can claim that.

Rank (*slaps him across the back*)   I can, though, my dear fellow!

Nora   Yes, of course, Dr Rank – you've been carrying out a scientific experiment today, haven't you?

Rank   Exactly.

Helmer   Scientific experiment! Those are big words for my little Nora to use!

Nora   And may I congratulate you on the finding?

Rank   You may indeed.

Nora   It was good then?

Rank   The best possible finding – both for the doctor and the patient. Certainty.

Nora (*quickly*)   Certainty?

Rank   Absolute certainty. So aren't I entitled to have a merry evening after that?

Nora   Yes, Dr Rank. You were quite right to.

Helmer   I agree. Provided you don't have to regret it tomorrow.

Rank   Well, you never get anything in this life without paying for it.

Nora   Dr Rank – you like masquerades, don't you?

Rank   Yes, if the disguises are sufficiently amusing.

Nora   Tell me. What shall we two wear at the next masquerade?

Helmer   You little gadabout! Are you thinking about the next one already?

Rank   We two? Yes, I'll tell you. You must go as the Spirit of Happiness –

Helmer   You try to think of a costume that'll convey that.

Rank   Your wife need only appear as her normal, everyday self –

Helmer   Quite right! Well said! But what are you going to be? Have you decided that?

Rank   Yes, my dear friend. I have decided that.

Helmer   Well?

Rank   At the next masquerade, I shall be invisible.

Helmer   Well, that's a funny idea.

Rank   There's a big, black hat – haven't you heard of the invisible hat? Once it's over your head, no one can see you any more.

Helmer (*represses a smile*)   Ah yes, of course.

Rank   But I'm forgetting what I came for. Helmer, give me a cigar. One of your black Havanas.

Helmer   With the greatest pleasure. (*Offers him the box.*)

Rank (*takes one and cuts off the tip*)   Thank you.

Nora (*strikes a match*)   Let me give you a light.

Rank   Thank you. (*She holds out the match for him. He lights his cigar.*) And now – goodbye.

Helmer   Goodbye, my dear chap, goodbye.

Nora   Sleep well, Dr Rank.

Rank   Thank you for that kind wish.

Nora   Wish me the same.

Rank   You? Very well – since you ask. Sleep well. And thank you for the light. (*He nods to them both and goes.*)

Helmer (*quietly*)   He's been drinking too much.

Nora (*abstractedly*)   Perhaps.

Helmer *takes his bunch of keys from his pocket and goes out into the hall.*

Nora   Torvald, what do you want out there?

Helmer   I must empty the letter-box. It's absolutely full. There'll be no room for the newspapers in the morning.

Nora   Are you going to work tonight?

Helmer   You know very well I'm not. Hullo, what's this?
Someone's been at the lock.

Nora   At the lock –

Helmer   Yes, I'm sure of it. Who on earth – ? Surely not one
of the maids? Here's a broken hairpin. Nora, it's yours –

Nora (*quickly*)   Then it must have been the children.

Helmer   Well, you'll have to break them of that habit. Hm,
hm. Ah, that's done it. (*Takes out the contents of the box and calls
into the kitchen.*) Helen! Helen! Put out the light on the staircase.
(*Comes back into the drawing-room and closes the door to the hall.*)

Helmer (*with the letters in his hand*)   Look at this! You see how
they've piled up? (*Glances through them.*) What on earth's this?

Nora (*at the window*)   The letter! Oh no, Torvald, no!

Helmer   Two visiting cards – from Rank.

Nora   From Dr Rank?

Helmer (*looks at them*)   Peter Rank, M.D. They were on top. He
must have dropped them in as he left.

Nora   Has he written anything on them?

Helmer   There's a black cross above his name. Rather grue-
some, isn't it? It looks just as thought he was announcing his
death.

Nora   He is.

Helmer   What? Do you know something? Has he told you
anything?

Nora   Yes. When these cards come, it means he's said goodbye
to us. He wants to shut himself up in his house and die.

Helmer   Ah, poor fellow. I knew I wouldn't be seeing him for
much longer. But so soon – ! And now he's going to slink away
and hide like a wounded beast.

Nora   When the time comes, it's best to go silently. Don't you think so, Torvald?

Helmer (*walks up and down*)   He was so much a part of our life. I can't realize that he's gone. His suffering and loneliness seemed to provide a kind of dark background to the happy sunlight of our marriage. Well, perhaps it's best this way. For him, anyway. (*Stops walking.*) And perhaps for us too, Nora. Now we have only each other. (*Embraces her.*) Oh, my beloved wife – I feel as though I could never hold you close enough. Do you know, Nora, often I wish some terrible danger might threaten you, so that I could offer my life and my blood, everything, for your sake.

Nora (*tears herself loose and says in a clear, firm voice*)   Read your letters now, Torvald.

Helmer   No, no. Not tonight. Tonight I want to be with you, my darling wife –

Nora   When your friend is about to die – ?

Helmer   You're right. This news has upset us both. An ugliness has come between us; thoughts of death and dissolution. We must try to forget them. Until then – you go to your room; I shall go to mine.

Nora (*throws her arms round his neck*)   Good night, Torvald! Good night!

Helmer (*kisses her on the forehead*)   Good night, my darling little songbird. Sleep well, Nora. I'll go and read my letters.

He goes into the study with the letters in his hand, and closes the door.

Nora (*wild-eyed, fumbles around, seizes* **Helmer***'s cloak, throws it round herself and whispers quickly, hoarsely*)   Never see him again. Never. Never. Never. (*Throws the shawl over her head.*) Never see the children again. Them, too. Never. Never. Oh – the icy black water! Oh – that bottomless – that – ! Oh, if only it were all over! Now he's got it – he's reading it. Oh no, no! Not yet! Goodbye Torvald! Goodbye my darlings!

She turns to run into the hall. As she does so, **Helmer** *throws open his door and stands there with an open letter in his hand.*

Helmer Nora!

Nora (*shrieks*) Ah – !

Helmer What is this? Do you know what is in this letter?

Nora Yes, I know. Let me go! Let me go!

Helmer (*holding her back*) Go? Where?

Nora (*tries to tear herself loose*) You mustn't try to save me, Torvald!

Helmer (*staggers back*) Is it true? Is it true, what he writes? Oh, my God! No, no – it's impossible, it can't be true!

Nora It *is* true. I've loved you more than anything else in the world.

Helmer Oh, don't try to make silly excuses.

Nora (*takes a step towards him*) Torvald –

Helmer Wretched woman! What have you done?

Nora Let me go! You're not going to suffer for my sake. I won't let you!

Helmer Stop being theatrical. (*Locks the front door.*) You're going to stay here and explain yourself. Do you understand what you've done? Answer me! Do you understand?

Nora (*looks unflinchingly at him and, her expression growing colder, says*) Yes. Now I am beginning to understand.

Helmer (*walking round the room*) Oh, what a dreadful awakening! For eight whole years – she who was my joy and pride – a hypocrite, a liar – worse, worse – a criminal! Oh, the hideousness of it! Shame on you, shame!

Nora *is silent and stares unblinkingly at him.*

Helmer (*stops in front of her*) I ought to have guessed that something of this sort would happen. I should have foreseen it. All your father's recklessness and instability – be quiet! – I repeat, all your father's recklessness and instability he has handed on to you! No religion, no morals, no sense of duty! Oh, how I have been punished for closing my eyes to his faults! I did it for your sake. And now you reward me like this.

Nora   Yes. Like this.

Helmer   Now you have destroyed all my happiness. You have ruined my whole future. Oh, it's too dreadful to contemplate! I am in the power of a man who is completely without scruples. He can do what he likes with me, demand what he pleases, order me to do anything – I dare not disobey him. I am condemned to humiliation and ruin simply for the weakness of a woman.

Nora   When I am gone from this world, you will be free.

Helmer   Oh, don't be melodramatic. Your father was always ready with that kind of remark. How would it help me if you were 'gone from this world', as you put it? It wouldn't assist me in the slightest. He can still make all the facts public; and if he does, I may quite easily be suspected of having been an accomplice in your crime. People may think that I was behind it – that it was I who encouraged you! And for all this I have to thank you, you whom I have carried on my hands through all the years of our marriage! Now do you realize what you've done to me?

Nora (*coldly calm*)   Yes.

Helmer   It's so unbelievable I can hardly credit it. But we must try to find some way out. Take off that shawl. Take it off, I say! I must try to buy him off somehow. This thing must be hushed up at any price. As regards our relationship – we must appear to be living together just as before. Only *appear*, of course. You will therefore continue to reside here. That is understood. But the children shall be taken out of your hands. I dare no longer entrust them to you. Oh, to have to say this to the woman I once loved so dearly – and whom I still – ! Well, all that must be finished. Henceforth there can be no question of happiness; we must merely strive to save what shreds and tatters –

The front door bell rings, **Helmer** *starts.*

Helmer   What can that be? At this hour? Surely not – ? He wouldn't – ? Hide yourself, Nora. Say you're ill.

Nora *does not move.* **Helmer** *goes to the door of the room and opens it. The* **Maid** *is standing half-dressed in the hall.*

Maid   A letter for madam.

Helmer   Give it me. (*Seizes the letter and shuts the door.*) Yes, it's from him. You're not having it. I'll read this myself.

Nora   Read it.

Helmer (*by the lamp*)   I hardly dare to. This may mean the end for us both. No. I must know. (*Tears open the letter hastily; reads a few lines; looks at a piece of paper which is enclosed with it; utters a cry of joy.*) Nora! (*She looks at him questioningly.*) Nora! No – I must read it once more. Yes, yes, it's true! I am saved! Nora, I am saved!

Nora   What about me?

Helmer   You too, of course. We're both saved, you and I. Look! He's returning your I.O.U. He writes that he is sorry for what has happened – a happy accident has changed his life – oh, what does it matter what he writes? We are saved, Nora! No one can harm you now. Oh, Nora, Nora – no, first let me destroy this filthy thing. Let me see – ! (*Glances at the I.O.U.*) No, I don't want to look at it. I shall merely regard the whole business as a dream. (*He tears the I.O.U. and both letters into pieces, throws them into the stove and watches them burn.*) There. Now they're destroyed. He wrote that ever since Christmas Eve you've been – oh, these must have been three dreadful days for you, Nora.

Nora   Yes. It's been a hard fight.

Helmer   It must have been terrible – seeing no way out except – no, we'll forget the whole sordid business. We'll just be happy and go on telling ourselves over and over again: 'It's over! It's over!' Listen to me, Nora. You don't seem to realize. It's over! Why are you looking so pale? Ah, my poor little Nora, I understand. You can't believe that I have forgiven you. But I have, Nora. I swear it to you. I have forgiven you everything. I know that what you did you did for your love of me.

Nora   That is true.

Helmer   You have loved me as a wife should love her husband. It was simply that in your inexperience you chose the wrong means. But do you think I love you any the less because you don't know how to act on your own initiative? No, no. Just lean on me. I shall counsel you. I shall guide you. I would not be a true man if your feminine helplessness did not make you doubly attractive in my eyes. You mustn't mind the hard words I said to you in those first dreadful moments when my whole world seemed to be tumbling about my ears. I have forgiven you, Nora I swear it to you; I have forgiven you.

Nora   Thank you for your forgiveness. (*She goes out through the door, right.*)

Helmer   No, don't go – (*Looks in.*) What are you doing there?

Nora (*offstage*)   Taking off my fancy dress.

Helmer (*by the open door*)   Yes, do that. Try to calm yourself and get your balance again, my frightened little songbird. Don't be afraid. I have broad wings to shield you. (*Begins to walk around near the door.*) How lovely and peaceful this little home of ours is, Nora. You are safe here; I shall watch over you like a hunted dove which I have snatched unharmed from the claws of the falcon. Your wildly beating little heart shall find peace with me. It will happen, Nora; it will take time, but it will happen, believe me. Tomorrow all this will seem quite different. Soon everything will be as it was before. I shall no longer need to remind you that I have forgiven you; your own heart will tell you that it is true. Do you really think I could ever bring myself to disown you, or even to reproach you? Ah, Nora, you don't understand what goes on in a husband's heart. There is something indescribably wonderful and satisfying for a husband in knowing that he has forgiven his wife – forgiven her unreservedly, from the bottom of his heart. It means that she has become his property in a double sense; he has, as it were, brought her into the world anew; she is now not only his wife but also his child. From now on that is what you shall be to me, my poor, help-less, bewildered little creature. Never be frightened of anything again, Nora. Just open your heart to me. I shall be both your will and your conscience. What's this? Not in bed? Have you changed?

Nora (*in her everyday dress*)   Yes, Torvald. I've changed.

Helmer   But why now – so late – ?

Nora   I shall not sleep tonight.

Helmer   But, my dear Nora –

Nora (*looks at her watch*)   It isn't that late. Sit down there, Torvald. You and I have a lot to talk about.

She sits down on one side of the table.

Helmer   Nora, what does this mean? You look quite drawn –

Nora   Sit down. It's going to take a long time. I've a lot to say to you.

Helmer (*sits down on the other side of the table*)   You alarm me, Nora. I don't understand you.

Nora   No, that's just it. You don't understand me. And I've never understood you – until this evening. No, don't interrupt me. Just listen to what I have to say. You and I have got to face facts, Torvald.

Helmer   What do you mean by that?

Nora (*after a short silence*)   Doesn't anything strike you about the way we're sitting here?

Helmer   What?

Nora   We've been married for eight years. Does it occur to you that this is the first time we two, you and I, man and wife, have ever had a serious talk together?

Helmer   Serious? What do you mean, serious?

Nora   In eight whole years – no, longer – ever since we first met – we have never exchanged a serious word on a serious subject.

Helmer   Did you expect me to drag you into all my worries – worries you couldn't possibly have helped me with?

Nora   I'm not talking about worries. I'm simply saying that we have never sat down seriously to try to get to the bottom of anything.

Helmer   But, my dear Nora, what on earth has that got to do with you?

Nora   That's just the point. You have never understood me.
A great wrong has been done to me, Torvald. First by papa, and
then by you.

Helmer   What? But we two have loved you more than anyone
in the world!

Nora (*shakes her head*)   You have never loved me. You just thought
it was fun to be in love with me.

Helmer   Nora, what kind of a way is this to talk?

Nora   It's the truth, Torvald. When I lived with papa, he used
to tell me what he thought about everything, so that I never had
any opinions but his. And if I did have any of my own, I kept them
quiet, because he wouldn't have liked them. He called me his little
doll, and he played with me just the way I played with my dolls.
Then I came here to live in your house –

Helmer   What kind of a way is that to describe our marriage?

Nora (*undisturbed*)   I mean, then I passed from papa's hands
into yours. You arranged everything the way you wanted it, so
that I simply took over your taste in everything – or pretended
I did – I don't really know – I think it was a little of both – first
one and then the other. Now I look back on it, it's as if I've been
living here like a pauper, from hand to mouth. I performed tricks
for you, and you gave me food and drink. But that was how you
wanted it. You and papa have done me a great wrong. It's your
fault that I have done nothing with my life.

Helmer   Nora, how can you be so unreasonable and
ungrateful? Haven't you been happy here?

Nora   No; never. I used to think I was. But I haven't ever been
happy.

Helmer   Not – not happy?

Nora   No. I've just had fun. You've always been very kind to
me. But our home has never been anything but a playroom. I've
been your doll-wife, just as I used to be papa's doll-child. And the
children have been my dolls. I used to think it was fun when you
came in and played with me, just as they think it's fun when I go

in and play games with them. That's all our marriage has been, Torvald.

Helmer　There may be a little truth in what you say, though you exaggerate and romanticize. But from now on it'll be different. Playtime is over. Now the time has come for education.

Nora　Whose education? Mine or the children's?

Helmer　Both yours and the children's, my dearest Nora.

Nora　Oh, Torvald, you're not the man to educate me into being the right wife for you.

Helmer　How can you say that?

Nora　And what about me? Am I fit to educate the children?

Helmer　Nora!

Nora　Didn't you say yourself a few minutes ago that you dare not leave them in my charge?

Helmer　In a moment of excitement. Surely you don't think I meant it seriously?

Nora　Yes. You were perfectly right. I'm not fitted to educate them. There's something else I must do first. I must educate myself. And you can't help me with that. It's something I must do by myself. That's why I'm leaving you.

Helmer (*jumps up*)　What did you say?

Nora　I must stand on my own feet if I am to find out the truth about myself and about life. So I can't go on living here with you any longer.

Helmer　Nora, Nora!

Nora　I'm leaving you now, at once. Christine will put me up for tonight –

Helmer　You're out of your mind! You can't do this! I forbid you!

Nora　It's no use your trying to forbid me any more. I shall take with me nothing but what is mine. I don't want anything from you, now or ever.

Helmer   What kind of madness is this?

Nora   Tomorrow I shall go home – I mean, to where I was born. It'll be easiest for me to find some kind of a job there.

Helmer   But you're blind! You've no experience of the world –

Nora   I must try to get some, Torvald.

Helmer   But to leave your home, your husband, your children! Have you thought what people will say?

Nora   I can't help that. I only know that I must do this.

Helmer   But this is monstrous! Can you neglect your most sacred duties?

Nora   What do you call my most sacred duties?

Helmer   Do I have to tell you? Your duties towards your husband, and your children.

Nora   I have another duty which is equally sacred.

Helmer   You have not. What on earth could that be?

Nora   My duty towards myself.

Helmer   First and foremost you are a wife and mother.

Nora   I don't believe that any longer. I believe that I am first and foremost a human being, like you – or anyway, that I must try to become one. I know most people think as you do, Torvald, and I know there's something of the sort to be found in books. But I'm no longer prepared to accept what people say and what's written in books. I must think things out for myself, and try to find my own answer.

Helmer   Do you need to ask where your duty lies in your own home? Haven't you an infallible guide in such matters – your religion?

Nora   Oh, Torvald, I don't really know what religion means.

Helmer   What are you saying?

Nora   I only know what Pastor Hansen told me when I went to confirmation. He explained that religion meant this and that.

When I get away from all this and can think things out on my
own, that's one of the questions I want to look into. I want to
find out whether what Pastor Hansen said was right – or anyway,
whether it is right for me.

Helmer   But it's unheard of for so young a woman to behave
like this! If religion cannot guide you, let me at least appeal to
your conscience. I presume you have some moral feelings left?
Or – perhaps you haven't? Well, answer me.

Nora   Oh, Torvald, that isn't an easy question to answer. I simply
don't know. I don't know where I am in these matters. I only know
that these things mean something quite different to me from what
they do to you. I've learned now that certain laws are different
from what I'd imagined them to be; but I can't accept that such
laws can be right. Has a woman really not the right to spare her
dying father pain, or save her husband's life? I can't believe that.

Helmer   You're talking like a child. You don't understand how
society works.

Nora   No, I don't. But now I intend to learn. I must try to
satisfy myself which is right, society or I.

Helmer   Nora, you're ill. You're feverish. I almost believe
you're out of your mind.

Nora   I've never felt so sane and sure in my life.

Helmer   You feel sure that it is right to leave your husband and
your children?

Nora   Yes. I do.

Helmer   Then there is only one possible explanation.

Nora   What?

Helmer   That you don't love me any longer.

Nora   No, that's exactly it.

Helmer   Nora! How can you say this to me?

Nora   Oh, Torvald, it hurts me terribly to have to say it,
because you've always been so kind to me. But I can't help it.
I don't love you any longer.

Helmer (*controlling his emotions with difficulty*)   And you feel quite sure about this, too?

Nora   Yes, absolutely sure. That's why I can't go on living here any longer.

Helmer   Can you also explain why I have lost your love?

Nora   Yes, I can. It happened this evening, when the miracle failed to happen. It was then that I realized you weren't the man I'd thought you to be.

Helmer   Explain more clearly. I don't understand, you.

Nora   I've waited so patiently, for eight whole years – well, good heavens, I'm not such a fool as to suppose that miracles occur every day. Then this dreadful thing happened to me, and then I *knew:* 'Now the miracle will take place!' When Krogstad's letter was lying out there, it never occurred to me for a moment that you would let that man trample over you. I *knew* that you would say to him: 'Publish the facts to the world!' And when he had done this –

Helmer   Yes, what then? When I'd exposed my wife's name to shame and scandal –

Nora   Then I was certain that you would step forward and take all the blame on yourself, and say: 'I am the one who is guilty!'

Helmer   Nora!

Nora   You're thinking I wouldn't have accepted such a sacrifice from you? No, of course I wouldn't! But what would my word have counted for against yours? That was the miracle I was hoping for, and dreading. And it was to prevent it happening that I wanted to end my life.

Helmer   Nora, I would gladly work for you night and day, and endure sorrow and hardship for your sake. But no man can be expected to sacrifice his honour, even for the person he loves.

Nora   Millions of women have done it.

Helmer   Oh, you think and talk like a stupid child.

Nora   That may be. But you neither think nor talk like the man I could share my life with. Once you'd got over your fright – and you weren't frightened of what might threaten me, but only of what threatened you – once the danger was past, then as far as you were concerned it was exactly as though nothing had happened. I was your little songbird just as before – your doll whom henceforth you would take particular care to protect from the world because she was so weak and fragile. (*Gets up.*) Torvald, in that moment I realized that for eight years I had been living here with a complete stranger, and had borne him three children – ! Oh, I can't bear to think of it! I could tear myself to pieces!

Helmer (*sadly*)   I see it, I see it. A gulf has indeed opened between us. Oh, but Nora – couldn't it be bridged?

Nora   As I am now, I am no wife for you.

Helmer   I have the strength to change.

Nora   Perhaps – if your doll is taken from you.

Helmer   But to be parted – to be parted from you! No, no, Nora, I can't conceive of it happening!

Nora (*goes into the room, right*)   All the more necessary that it should happen.

She comes back with her outdoor things and a small travelling-bag, which she puts down on a chair by the table.

Helmer   Nora, Nora, not now! Wait till tomorrow!

Nora (*puts on her coat*)   I can't spend the night in a strange man's house.

Helmer   But can't we live here as brother and sister, then – ?

Nora (*fastens her hat*)   You know quite well it wouldn't last. (*Puts on her shawl.*) Goodbye, Torvald. I don't want to see the children. I know they're in better hands than mine. As I am now, I can be nothing to them.

Helmer   But some time, Nora – some time – ?

Nora   How can I tell? I've no idea what will happen to me.

Helmer   But you are my wife, both as you are and as you will be.

Nora   Listen, Torvald. When a wife leaves her husband's house, as I'm doing now, I'm told that according to the law he is freed of any obligations towards her. In any case, I release you from any such obligations. You mustn't feel bound to me in any way however small, just as I shall not feel bound to you. We must both be quite free. Here is your ring back. Give me mine.

Helmer   That too?

Nora   That too.

Helmer   Here it is.

Nora   Good. Well, now it's over. I'll leave the keys here. The servants know about everything to do with the house – much better than I do. Tomorrow, when I have left town, Christine will come to pack the things I brought here from home. I'll have them sent on after me.

Helmer   This is the end, then! Nora, will you never think of me anymore?

Nora   Yes, of course. I shall often think of you and the children and this house.

Helmer   May I write to you, Nora?

Nora   No. Never. You mustn't do that.

Helmer   But at least you must let me send you –

Nora   Nothing. Nothing.

Helmer   But if you should need help – ?

Nora   I tell you, no. I don't accept things from strangers.

Helmer   Nora – can I never be anything but a stranger to you?

Nora (*picks up her bag*)   Oh, Torvald! Then the miracle of miracles would have to happen.

Helmer   The miracle of miracles!

Nora   You and I would both have to change so much that – oh, Torvald, I don't believe in miracles any longer.

Helmer   But I want to believe in them. Tell me. We should have to change so much that − !

Nora   That life together between us two could become a marriage. Goodbye.

She goes out through the hall.

Helmer (*sinks down on a chair by the door and buries his face in his hands*)   Nora! Nora! (*Looks round and gets up.*) Empty! She's gone! (*A hope strikes him.*) The miracle of miracles − ?

The street door is slammed shut downstairs.

AUGUST STRINDBERG

Miss Julie

A Naturalistic Tragedy

translated by Michael Meyer

Characters

Miss Julie
Jean, *her father's valet*
Christine, *her father's cook*
Other servants

A large kitchen, the roof and side walls of which are concealed by drapes and borders. The rear wall rises at an angle from the left; on it, to the left, are two shelves with utensils of copper, iron and pewter. The shelves are lined with scalloped paper. Over to the right we can see three-quarters of a big, arched exit porch, with twin glass doors, through which can be seen a fountain with a statue of Cupid, lilac bushes in bloom, and tall Lombardy poplars. On the left of the stage is visible the corner of a big tiled stove, with a section of an overhead hood to draw away fumes. To the right, one end of the kitchen table, of white pine, with some chairs. The stove is decorated with birch-leaves; the floor is strewn with juniper twigs. On the end of the table is a big Japanese spice-jar containing flowering lilacs. An ice-box, a scullery table, a sink. Above the door is a big old-fashioned bell, of the alarm type. To the left of this emerges a speaking-tube.

Christine *is standing at the stove, frying in a pan. She is dressed in a light cotton dress, with apron.* **Jean** *enters, dressed in livery and carrying a pair of big riding boots, with spurs. He puts them down on the floor where we can see them.*

Jean   Miss Julie's gone mad again tonight, completely mad!

Christine   Oh, you're here at last?

Jean   I went with his lordship to the station, and on the way back I just popped into the barn to watch the dancing, and who do I see but Miss Julie leading the dance with the gamekeeper? But as soon as she sees me, she rushes across and offers her arm for the ladies' waltz. And then she danced like – I've never known the like! She's mad.

Christine   She always has been. Especially this last fortnight, since the engagement got broken off.

Jean   Yes, what about that? He was a gentleman, even if he wasn't rich. Ach, they don't know their own minds. (*He sits down at the end of the table.*) It's odd, though, that a young lady should choose to stay at home with the servants, on Midsummer Eve, eh? rather than go off to her relations with her father.

Christine   Oh, I expect she doesn't feel like seeing anyone after that hullaballoo she had with her young man.

Jean   Very likely! He knew how to stand up for himself, though. Know how it happened, Christine? I saw it, you know, though I took care not to let on I had.

Christine   No! You saw it?

Jean   Indeed I did. They were down at the stable yard one evening, and Miss Julie was putting him through his paces, as she called it – do you know what that meant? She made him leap over her riding whip, the way you teach a dog to jump. He leaped twice, and each time she gave him a cut; but the third time, he snatched the whip out of her hand and broke it across his knee. And that was the last we saw of him.

Christine   Was that what happened? You can't mean it.

Jean   Yes, that's the way it was. Now, what have you got to tempt me with this evening, Christine?

Christine (*serves from the pan and lays a place*)   Oh, just a bit of kidney I cut from the joint.

Jean (*smells the food*)   Lovely! *Ceci est mon grand délice!* (*He feels the plate.*) You might have warmed the plate, though.

Christine   You're fussier than his lordship himself, once you start. (*She pulls his hair affectionately.*)

Jean (*angrily*)   Don't pull my hair. You know how sensitive I am.

Christine   Now, now. It's only love.

Jean eats. **Christine** brings a bottle of beer.

Jean   Beer – on Midsummer Eve? No, thank you. I can do better than that. (*He opens a drawer in the table and takes out a bottle of red wine with yellow sealing-wax on the cork.*) See that? Yellow seal!

Give me a glass, now. A wine glass, I'm drinking this *pur*.

Christine (*goes back to the stove and puts a small saucepan on*)   God have mercy on whoever gets you for a husband. I never met such a fusspot.

Jean   Oh, rubbish. You'd be jolly pleased to get a gentleman like me. And I don't think you've lost anything through people calling you my fiancée. (*He tastes the wine.*) Good! Very good! Just not quite sufficiently *chambré*. (*He warms the glass with his hand.*) We bought this one in Dijon. Four francs a litre it cost – and then there was the bottling – and the duty. What are you cooking now? The smell's infernal.

Christine   Oh, some filthy muck Miss Julie wants for Diana.

Jean   Please express yourself more delicately, Christine. But why should you have to cook for that confounded dog on Midsummer Eve? Is it ill?

Christine   It's ill all right! It managed to slip out with the gatekeeper's pug, and now it's in trouble – and *that* Miss Julie won't allow.

Jean   Miss Julie is stuck-up about some things, in others she demeans herself, exactly like her ladyship when she was alive. She was most at home in the kitchen or the stables, but one horse wasn't enough to pull her carriage. She went around with dirty cuffs, but there had to be a crest on every button. Miss Julie, now, to return to her – she doesn't bother about herself and her person. To my mind, she is not what one would call a lady. Just now, when she was dancing in the barn, she grabbed the gamekeeper from Anna and made him dance with her. We'd never do that – but that's how it is when the gentry try to act common – they become really common. But she's a magnificent creature! What a figure! Ah! What shoulders! and – et cetera!

Christine   No need to overdo it. I've heard what Clara says, and she dresses her.

Jean   Oh, Clara! You women are always jealous of each other. I've been out riding with her – and the way she dances – !

Christine   Well, aren't you going to dance with me, when I'm ready?

Jean   Yes, of course.

Christine   Promise?

Jean   Promise? When I say I'll do a thing, I do it. Thank you for that, it was very nice. (*He corks the bottle.*)

Miss Julie (*in the doorway, talking to someone outside*)   I'll be back immediately. Don't wait for me.

Jean *hides the bottle in the drawer of the table and gets up respectfully.*

Miss Julie (*enters and goes up to* **Christine** *by the stove*)   Well, is it ready?

Christine *indicates that* **Jean** *is present.*

Jean (*gallantly*)   Have you ladies secrets to discuss?

Miss Julie (*flips him in the face with her handkerchief*)   Don't be inquisitive!

Jean   Ah! Charming, that smell of violets.

Miss Julie (*coquettishly*)   Impertinent! So you know about perfumes, too? You certainly know how to dance – stop looking, now, go away!

Jean (*boldly, yet respectfully*)   Is this some magic brew you ladies are preparing on Midsummer Eve, which will reveal the future and show whom fate has in store for you?

Miss Julie (*sharply*)   You'd need sharp eyes to see him. (*To* **Christine**.) Pour it into a bottle, and cork it well. Come now, and dance a schottische with me, Jean.

Jean (*slowly*)   I don't wish to seem disrespectful, but this dance I had promised to Christine –

Miss Julie   Well, she can have another dance with you, can't you, Christine? Won't you lend me Jean?

Christine   That's hardly up to me. If Miss Julie condescends, it's not his place to refuse. Go ahead, Jean, and thank madam for the honour.

Jean   To be frank, without wishing to offend, I wonder if it would be wise for Miss Julie to dance twice in succession with the same partner. These people soon start talking –

Miss Julie (*flares up*)   Talking? What kind of talk? What do you mean?

Jean (*politely*)   If madam doesn't understand, I must speak more plainly. It looks bad if you show a preference for one of your servants while others are waiting to be similarly honoured –

Miss Julie   Preference! What an idea! I am astounded. I, the lady of the house, honour my servants by attending their dance, and when I take the floor I want to dance with someone who knows how to lead. I don't want to be made ridiculous –

Jean   As madam commands. I am at your service.

Miss Julie (*softly*)   Don't regard it as a command. Tonight we are ordinary people trying to be happy, and all rank is laid aside. Come, give me your arm! Don't worry, Christine! I won't steal your lover!

Jean *offers* **Miss Julie** *his arm, and escorts her out.*

Pantomime

This should be played as though the actress were actually alone. When the occasion calls for it she should turn her back on the audience. She does not look towards them; and must not hasten her movements as though afraid lest they should grow impatient.

Christine *alone. A violin can be faintly heard in the distance, playing a schottische.* **Christine** *hums in time with the music; clears up after* **Jean***, washes the plate at the sink, dries it and puts it away in a cupboard. Then she removes her apron, takes a small mirror from a drawer, props it against the pot of lilac on the table; lights a candle and warms a curling-iron, with which she then crisps the hair over her forehead. Goes out into the doorway and listens. Returns to the table. Finds* **Miss Julie***'s handkerchief, which the latter has forgotten; picks it up and smells it; then, spreads it out, as though thinking of something else, stretches it, smooths it, folds it into quarters, etc.*

Jean (*enters alone*)   No, she really *is* mad! What a way to dance! Everyone was grinning at her from behind the doors. What do you make of it, Christine?

Christine   Oh, she's got her monthly coming on, and then she always acts strange. Well, are you going to dance with me now?

Jean   You're not angry with me for leaving you like that – ?

Christine   No, a little thing like that doesn't bother me. Besides, I know my place –

Jean (*puts his arm round her waist*)   You're a sensible girl, Christine. You'd make a good wife –

Miss Julie (*enters; is disagreeably surprised; speaks with forced lightness*) Well, you're a fine gentleman, running away from your partner like that!

Jean   On the contrary, Miss Julie. As you see, I have hastened to return to the partner I forsook!

Miss Julie (*changes her tone*)   Do you know, you dance magnificently. But why are you wearing uniform on Midsummer Eve? Take it off at once.

Jean   Then I must ask your ladyship to step outside for a moment. I have my black coat here – (*Gestures right.*)

Miss Julie   Does my presence embarrass you? Can't you change a coat with me here? You'd better go into your room, then. Or stay, and I'll turn my back.

Jean   With your ladyship's permission.

He goes right. We see his arm as he changes his coat.

Miss Julie (*to* **Christine**)   Christine, Jean is very familiar with you. Are you engaged to him?

Christine   Engaged? If you like. We call it that.

Miss Julie   Call – ?

Christine   Well, you've been engaged yourself, madam –

Miss Julie   We were properly engaged.

Christine   Didn't come to anything, though, did it?

Jean *enters in black tails and a black bowler hat.*

Miss Julie   *Très gentil, monsieur Jean! Très gentil!*

Jean   *Vous voulez plaisanter, madame!*

Miss Julie   *Et vous voulez parler français!* Where did you learn that?

Jean   In Switzerland. I was wine waiter at the biggest hotel in Lucerne.

Miss Julie   You look quite the gentleman in those tails.

Charmant! (*She sits at the table.*)

Jean   Oh, you're flattering me.

Miss Julie (*haughtily*)   Flattering *you*?

Jean   My natural modesty forbids me to suppose that you would pay a truthful compliment to one so humble as myself, so I assumed you were exaggerating, for which I believe the polite word is flattering.

Miss Julie   Where did you learn to talk like that? You must have spent a lot of your time at the theatre.

Jean   Yes. And I've been around a bit, too.

Miss Julie   But you were born here, weren't you?

Jean   My father worked on the next farm to yours. I used to see you when I was a child, though you wouldn't remember me.

Miss Julie   No, really?

Jean   Yes. I remember one time especially – no, I oughtn't to mention that.

Miss Julie   Oh yes! Tell me. Come on! Just this once.

Jean   No, I really couldn't now. Some other time, perhaps.

Miss Julie   Some other time means never. Is it so dangerous to tell it now?

Jean   It isn't dangerous, but I'd rather not. Look at her! (*He indicates* **Christine**, *who has fallen asleep in a chair by the stove.*)

Miss Julie   A charming wife she'll make. Does she snore too?

Jean   She doesn't do that, but she talks in her sleep.

Miss Julie (*cynically*)   How do you know?

Jean (*coolly*)   I've heard her.

Pause. They look at each other.

Miss Julie Why don't you sit?

Jean Wouldn't permit myself to do that in your presence.

Miss Julie But if I order you to?

Jean Then I shall obey.

Miss Julie Sit, then. No, wait. Can you give me something to drink first?

Jean I don't know what we have in the ice-cabinet. Only beer, I think.

Miss Julie What do you mean, only beer? My taste is very simple. I prefer it to wine.

Jean *takes a bottle of beer from the ice-cabinet; opens it, gets a glass and plate from the cupboard and serves her.*

Jean Mademoiselle!

Miss Julie Thank you. Won't you have something yourself?

Jean I'm not much of a beer drinker, but if madam orders me –

Miss Julie Orders? Surely you know that a gentleman should never allow a lady to drink alone.

Jean That's perfectly true. (*He opens another bottle and pours a glass.*)

Miss Julie Drink my health, now! (**Jean** *hesitates.*) Are you shy?

Jean (*kneels in a parody of a romantic attitude, and raises his glass*) To my mistress's health!

Miss Julie Bravo! Now kiss my shoe, and the ceremony is complete.

Jean *hesitates, then boldly takes her foot in his hands and kisses it lightly.*

Miss Julie Excellent. You ought to have been an actor.

Jean (*gets up*) We mustn't go on like this, Miss Julie. Someone might come in and see us.

Miss Julie What then?

Jean   People would talk, that's all. And if you knew how their tongues were wagging up there just now –

Miss Julie   What kind of thing were they saying? Tell me. Sit down.

Jean (*sits*)   I don't want to hurt you, but they were using expressions which – which hinted that – well, you can guess! You aren't a child, and when people see a lady drinking alone with a man – let alone a servant – on Midsummer Eve – then –

Miss Julie   Then what? Anyway, we're not alone. Christine is here.

Jean   Asleep.

Miss Julie   Then I shall wake her. (*She gets up.*) Christine! Christine! Are you asleep?

Christine *mumbles to herself in her sleep.*

Miss Julie   Christine! My God, she is asleep!

Christine (*in her sleep*)   Are his lordship's boots brushed? Put on the coffee. Quickly, quickly, quickly! (*She laughs, then grunts.*)

Miss Julie (*takes her by the nose*)   Will you wake up?

Jean (*sharply*)   Leave her alone!

Miss Julie (*haughtily*)   What!

Jean   People who stand at a stove all day get tired when night comes. And sleep is something to be respected –

Miss Julie (*changes tack*)   A gallant thought, and one that does you honour. (*She holds out her hand to* **Jean**.) Come outside then, and pick some lilac for me.

During the following dialogue, **Christine** *wakes and wanders drowsily right to go to bed.*

Jean   With you?

Miss Julie   With me.

Jean   Impossible. I couldn't.

Miss Julie   I don't understand. Surely you don't imagine – ?

Jean   I don't, but other people might.

Miss Julie   What? That I should have an *amour* with a servant?

Jean   I'm not being conceited, but such things have happened – and to these people, nothing is sacred.

Miss Julie   Quite the little aristocrat, aren't you?

Jean   Yes, I am.

Miss Julie   If I choose to step down –

Jean   Don't step down, Miss Julie, take my advice. No one will believe you did it freely. People will always say you fell –

Miss Julie   I have a higher opinion of people than you. Come and see! Come.

She fixes him with her eyes.

Jean   You know, you're strange.

Miss Julie   Perhaps. But so are you. Everything is strange. Life, people, everything, is a scum which drifts, drifts on and on across the water until it sinks, sinks. I have a dream which recurs from time to time, and I'm reminded of it now. I've climbed to the top of a pillar, and am sitting there, and I can see no way to descend. When I look down, I become dizzy, but I must come down – but I haven't the courage to jump. I can't stay up there, and I long to fall, but I don't fall. And yet I know I shall find no peace till I come down, no rest till I come down, down to the ground. And if I could get down, I should want to burrow my way deep into the earth . . . Have you ever felt anything like that?

Jean   No. I dream that I'm lying under a high tree in a dark wood. I want to climb, up, up to the top, and look round over the bright landscape where the sun is shining – plunder the bird's nest up there where the gold eggs lie. And I climb and climb, but the trunk is so thick and slippery, and it's so far to the first branch. But I know that if I could only get to that first branch, I'd climb my way to the top as though up a ladder. I haven't reached it yet, but I shall reach it, even if it's only in a dream.

Miss Julie   Why do we stand here talking about dreams? Come, now! Just into the park!

She offers him her arm, and they go.

Jean   We must sleep with nine midsummer flowers under our pillows tonight, Miss Julie, and our dreams will come true!

They turn in the doorway. **Jean** *puts a hand to one of his eyes.*

Miss Julie   Have you something in your eye?

Jean   It's nothing. Only a speck of dust. It'll be all right soon.

Miss Julie   My sleeve must have brushed it. Sit down and I'll take it out. (*She takes him by the arm, makes him sit, takes his head and pushes it backwards, and tries to remove the dust with the corner of her handkerchief.*) Sit still now, quite still! (*She slaps his hands.*) Come, obey me! I believe you're trembling, you great, strong lout! (*She feels his bicep.*) What muscles you have!

Jean (*warningly*)   Miss Julie!

Miss Julie   Yes, monsieur Jean?

Jean   *Attention! Je ne suis qu'un homme!*

Miss Julie   Sit still, will you! There! Now it's gone. Kiss my hand and thank me.

Jean (*gets up*)   Miss Julie, listen to me. Christine's gone to bed now – will you listen to me!

Miss Julie   Kiss my hand first.

Jean   Listen to me!

Miss Julie   Kiss my hand first.

Jean   All right. But you've only yourself to blame.

Miss Julie   For what?

Jean   For what? Are you a child? You're twenty-five. Don't you know it's dangerous to play with fire?

Miss Julie   Not for me. I am insured.

Jean (*boldly*)   No, you're not. And if you are, there's inflammable material around that isn't.

Miss Julie   Meaning you?

Jean   Yes. Not because I'm me, but because I'm a young man –

Miss Julie   Of handsome appearance! What incredible conceit! A Don Juan, perhaps? Or a Joseph! Yes, upon my word, I do believe you're a Joseph!

Jean   Do you?

Miss Julie   I almost fear it.

Jean *moves boldly forward and tries to take her round the waist to kiss her.*

Miss Julie (*slaps him*)   Stop it!

Jean   Are you joking or serious?

Miss Julie   Serious.

Jean   Then you were being serious just now too. You play games too seriously, and that's dangerous. Well, now I'm tired of this game and with your permission I'll get back to my work. His lordship's boots must be ready in time, and it's long past midnight.

Miss Julie   Forget the boots.

Jean   No. They're part of my job, which doesn't include being your playmate. And never will. I flatter myself I'm above that.

Miss Julie   Aren't we proud!

Jean   In some respects. In others, not.

Miss Julie   Have you ever been in love?

Jean   We don't use that word. But I've been fond of a lot of girls, and once I was sick because I couldn't get the one I wanted. Yes, sick, do you hear, like those princes in the *Arabian Nights*, who couldn't eat or sleep because of love.

Miss Julie   Who was she? (**Jean** *is silent.*) Who was she?

Jean   You cannot order me to answer that.

Miss Julie   If I ask you as an equal? As a friend! Who was she?

Jean You.

Miss Julie (*sits*) How absurd!

Jean Yes, if you like. It was absurd. Look, this was the story I didn't want to tell you just now – but now I will tell you. Do you know how the world looks from down there? No, you don't. Like hawks and eagles, whose backs one seldom sees because most of the time they hover above you! I lived in a hut with seven brothers and sisters and a pig, out in the grey fields where never a tree grew. But from the window I could see the wall of his lordship's park, with apple trees rising above it. It was the Garden of Paradise, and there stood many evil angels with flaming swords to guard it. But despite them I and other boys found a way in to the tree of life – You despise me now?

Miss Julie Oh, I suppose all boys steal apples.

Jean You can say that now, but you do despise me. However. One day I entered the garden with my mother, to weed the onion beds. On one side of the garden stood a Turkish pavilion in the shadow of jasmine trees and overgrown with honeysuckle. I'd never seen such a building. I wondered what it could be for. People went in and came out again; and, one day, the door was left open. I crept in and saw the walls hung with pictures of kings and emperors, and there were red velvet curtains on the windows with tassels – ah, now you understand! It was the lavatory. I – (*He breaks a flower from the lilac and holds it beneath* **Miss Julie**'s *nose.*) I'd never been inside the palace, never seen anything except the church – but this was more beautiful – and however my thoughts might stray, they always returned there. And gradually I began to long just once to experience the full ecstasy of actually – *enfin,* I tip-toed inside, saw and marvelled. But then – someone's coming! There was only one exit – for the lords and ladies. But for me – there was another – and I had no choice but to take it. (**Miss Julie**, *who has taken the lilac blossom, lets it fall on the table.*) Then I ran, broke through a raspberry hedge, charged across a strawberry patch, and found myself on a terrace with a rose garden. There I saw a pink dress and a pair of white stockings. You. I hid under a pile of weeds – *under,* can you imagine that? under thistles that pricked me and wet earth that stank like me. And I looked at you as you walked among the roses, and I thought: 'If it is true that a thief can enter heaven and dwell with the angels, then it's strange that a peasant's child here on earth cannot enter the great park and play with the Count's daughter.'

Miss Julie (*romantically*)   Do you suppose all poor children have had the same ideas as you?

Jean (*at first hesitant, then with conviction*)   Have *all* poor – ? Yes! Of course! Of course!

Miss Julie   It must be a terrible misfortune to be poor.

Jean (*deeply cut, speaks with strong emotion*)   Oh, Miss Julie! Oh! A dog may lie on the Countess's sofa, a horse may have its nose patted by a young lady's hand, but a servant – ! (*He changes his tone.*) Oh, now and then a man has strength enough to hoist himself up in the world, but how often does it happen? But do you know what I did? I ran down into the millstream with my clothes on. They dragged me out and beat me. But the following Sunday, when my father and all the others had gone to visit my grandmother, I managed to fix things so that I stayed at home. And then I scrubbed myself with soap and hot water, put on my best clothes, and went to church, in order that I might see you. I saw you, and returned home, determined to die. But I wanted to die beautifully, and pleasantly, without pain. Then I remembered it was dangerous to sleep under an elder bush. We had a big one, in flower. I stripped it of everything it held, and then I lay down in the oat-bin. Have you ever noticed how beautiful oats are? Soft to the touch like human skin. Well, I shut the lid and closed my eyes. I fell asleep, and woke up feeling really very ill. But I didn't die, as you can see. What did I want? I don't know. I had no hope of winning you, of course – but you were a symbol to me of the hopelessness of my ever climbing out of the class in which I was born.

Miss Julie   Do you know you're quite a *raconteur*? Did you ever go to school?

Jean   A bit. But I've read a lot of novels, and gone to theatres. And I've heard gentry talk. That's where I've learned most.

Miss Julie   Do you listen to what we say?

Jean   Certainly! And I've heard plenty, too, sitting on the coachman's box or rowing the boat. One time I heard you and a lady friend –

Miss Julie   Indeed? What did you hear?

Jean   Oh, I wouldn't care to repeat it. But it surprised me a little. I couldn't imagine where you'd learned all those words. Maybe at bottom there isn't as big a difference as people suppose between people and – people.

Miss Julie   Oh, nonsense. We don't act like you do when we're engaged.

Jean (*looks at her*)   Are you sure? Come, Miss Julie, you don't have to play the innocent with me –

Miss Julie   The man to whom I offered my love was a bastard.

Jean   That's what they always say – afterwards.

Miss Julie   Always?

Jean   I've heard the expression several times before on similar occasions.

Miss Julie   What occasions?

Jean   Like the one in question. The last time I actually slept with a woman –

Miss Julie (*rises*)   Be quiet! I don't wish to hear any more.

Jean   *She* didn't want to, either. Strange. Well, have I your permission to go to bed?

Miss Julie (*softly*)   Go to bed? On Midsummer Eve?

Jean   Yes. Dancing with that pack up there doesn't greatly amuse me.

Miss Julie   Get the key of the boat and row me out on the lake, I want to see the sun rise.

Jean   Is that wise?

Miss Julie   You speak as though you were frightened of your reputation.

Jean   Why not? I don't want to make myself a laughing-stock and maybe get sacked without a reference, now that I'm beginning to make my way. And I think I have a certain responsibility towards Christine.

Miss Julie   Oh, I see, it's Christine now –

Jean   Yes, but you too. Take my advice. Go back to your room and go to bed.

Miss Julie   Am *I* to obey *you*?

Jean   For once. For your own sake, I beg you! It's late, drowsiness makes one drunk, one's head grows dizzy. Go to bed. Besides – if my ears don't deceive me – the other servants are coming here to look for me. And if they find us together, you are lost!

Approaching voices are heard, singing.

Voices
   One young girl in a big dark wood!
   Tridiridi-ralla, tridiridi-ra!
   Met a boy she never should!
   Tridiridi-ralla-ra!

   Oh, lay me on the grass so soft!
   Tridiridi-ralla, tridiridi-ra!
   So her mm-mm-mm she lost!
   Tridiridi-ralla-ra!

   Oh, thank you dear, but I must go!
   Tridiridi-ralla, tridiridi-ra!
   Another loves me now . . . oh!
   Tridiridi-ralla-ra!

Miss Julie   I know these people, and I love them, as I know they love me. Let them come here, and I'll prove it to you.

Jean   No, Miss Julie, they don't love you. They take your food, but once you've turned your back they spit at you. Believe me! Listen to them, listen to what they're singing! No, don't listen!

Miss Julie (*listens*)   What are they singing?

Jean   It's a filthy song. About you and me.

Miss Julie   How dare they! The traitors – !

Jean   Yes, but that's what they're like. One can't fight them. One can only run away.

Miss Julie   Run away? But where? We can't go out – or into Christine's room!

Jean   No. Into my room, then. We can't bother about conventions now. And you can trust me. I am your true, loyal and respectful – friend.

Miss Julie   But suppose – suppose they look for you in there?

Jean   I'll bolt the door. And if anyone tries to break in, I'll shoot. Come! (*He drops to his knees.*) Please! Come!

Miss Julie (*urgently*)   You promise –

Jean   I swear.

Miss Julie *runs out right,* **Jean** *hastens after her.*

Ballet

The peasants stream in, wearing their best clothes, with flowers in their hats and a fiddler at their head. A barrel of beer and a keg of schnapps decorated with greenery are set on the table, glasses are produced, and they drink. They form a ring and dance and mime, singing: 'One young girl in a big dark wood!' When this is finished, they go out singing.

Miss Julie *enters, alone. She sees the chaos in the kitchen, clasps her hands, then takes out a powder puff and powders her face.*

Jean (*enters, agitated*)   There – you see! And you heard. Do you think you can possibly stay here now?

Miss Julie   No. I don't. But what can we do?

Jean   Go away – travel – far away from here –

Miss Julie   Travel? Yes, but where?

Jean   To Switzerland, to the Italian lakes! Have you never been there?

Miss Julie   No. Is it beautiful there?

Jean   Ah! An eternal summer! Oranges, laurel trees – ah!

Miss Julie   But what shall we do there?

Jean   I'll start a hotel. *De luxe* – for *de luxe* people.

Miss Julie   Hotel?

Jean   Ah, that's a life, believe me! New faces all the time, new languages! Never a minute for worry or nerves, or wondering what to do. There's work to be done every minute, bells ringing night and day, trains whistling, carriages coming and going, and all the time the golden sovereigns roll into the till. Yes, that's the life!

Miss Julie   It sounds exciting. But – I – ?

Jean   Shall be the mistress of the house; the pearl of the establishment. With your looks – and your style – why, we're made! It'll be terrific! You'll sit at your desk like a queen, setting your slaves in motion by pressing an electric bell. The guests will file before your throne, humbly laying their tribute upon your table – you've no idea how people tremble when they get a bill in their hand. I shall salt the bills, and you shall sugar them with your prettiest smile! Oh, let's get away from here! (*He takes a timetable from his pocket.*) Now, at once, by the next train! We'll be in Malmö by 6.30, Hamburg 8.40 tomorrow morning, Frankfurt to Basel will take a day, through the Gothard Pass – we'll be in Como in, let me see, three days. Three days!

Miss Julie   It sounds wonderful. But, Jean – you must give me courage. Tell me you love me. Come and kiss me.

Jean (*hesitates*)   I'd like to – but I daren't. Not in this house – not again. Of course I love you – can you doubt it, Miss Julie?

Miss Julie (*shy, feminine*)   *Miss!* Call me Julie! There are no barriers between us now. Call me Julie!

Jean (*tormented*)   I can't! There are still barriers between us – there always will be, as long as we're in this house. There's the past, there's his lordship – I've never met anyone I respected as I do him – I only have to see his gloves on a chair and I feel like a small boy – I only have to hear that bell ring and I jump like a frightened horse – and when I see his boots standing there, so straight and proud, I cringe. (*He kicks the boots.*) Superstition – ideas shoved into our heads when we're children – but we can escape them. Come to another country, a republic, and others will cringe before my porter's livery – yes, they'll cringe, I tell you, but I shan't! I wasn't born to cringe – I'm a man, I've got character, just let me get my fingers on that first branch and watch me climb! Today I'm a servant, but next year I'll own my own hotel, in ten years I'll be a landed gentleman! Then I'll go to Romania, get a decoration – why, I might – might, mind you – end up with a title.

Miss Julie   How wonderful!

Jean   Oh, in Romania I could buy myself a title. I'd be a count, and you'd be a countess. My countess!

Miss Julie   What do I care about all that? That's what I'm giving up now. Tell me you love me, otherwise – yes, otherwise – what am I?

Jean   I'll tell you a thousand times – later. Only – not here. Above all, no emotional scenes, or it'll be all up with us. We must think this over coolly, like sensible people. (*He takes a cigar, cuts and lights it.*) Sit down there now, and I'll sit here and we'll talk as though nothing had happened.

Miss Julie (*desperately*)   Oh, my God! Have you no feelings?

Jean   I? No one has more feelings than I. But I can control them.

Miss Julie   A moment ago you could kiss my shoe – and now – !

Jean (*harshly*)   That was a moment ago. Now we've something else to think about.

Miss Julie   Don't speak so harshly to me.

Jean   I'm not speaking harshly. I'm talking sense. One folly has been committed, don't let's commit any more. His lordship may be here any moment, and by then we've got to decide what we're going to do with our lives. What do you think of my plans for our future? Do you approve of them?

Miss Julie   They seem to me quite sensible but – just one question. A big project like that needs a lot of capital. Have you that?

Jean (*chews his cigar*)   I? Certainly. I have my professional expertise, my experience, my knowledge of languages. We've adequate capital, I should say.

Miss Julie   But all that doesn't add up to the price of a railway ticket.

Jean   That's perfectly true; which is why I need a backer to advance me the money.

Miss Julie   Where are you going to find one quickly?

Jean   You'll find one, if you come with me.

Miss Julie   I couldn't. And I haven't any money of my own.

Pause.

Jean   Then our whole plan collapses.

Miss Julie   And – ?

Jean   Things must stay as they are.

Miss Julie   Do you suppose I'm going to remain under this roof as your whore? With *them* sniggering at me behind their fingers? Do you think I can look my father in the face after this? No! Take me away from here, from the shame and the dishonour – oh, what have I done, my God, my God! (*Sobs.*)

Jean   Come, don't start that. What have you done? The same as many others before you.

Miss Julie (*screams convulsively*)   Oh, now you despise me! I'm falling – I'm falling – !

Jean   Fall down to me, and I'll lift you up again.

Miss Julie   What dreadful power drew me to you? The attraction of the weak to the strong? Of the faller to the climber? Or was it love? Was this love? Do you know what love is?

Jean   I? Yes, of course. Do you think I've never had a woman before?

Miss Julie   How can you think and talk like that?

Jean   That's life as I've learned it, And that's me. Now calm down and stop acting the lady. We're both in the same boat now. Come here, my girl, and I'll give you a glass of wine. (*He opens the drawer, takes out the bottle of wine and fills two used glasses.*)

Miss Julie   Where did you get that wine from?

Jean   The cellar.

Miss Julie   My father's burgundy!

Jean   Is it too good for his son-in-law?

Miss Julie   And I drink beer! I!

Jean   That only proves you have an inferior palate to mine.

Miss Julie   Thief!

Jean   Going to tell?

Miss Julie   Oh, oh! Accomplice to a sneakthief! Was I drunk, was I dreaming? Midsummer Night! The night of innocent happiness –

Jean   Innocent? Hm!

Miss Julie (*paces to and fro*)   Is there anyone on this earth as miserable as I?

Jean   Why should you be miserable after such a conquest? Think of Christine in there. Don't you suppose she has feelings too?

Miss Julie   I thought so just now, but I don't any longer. Servants are servants –

Jean   And whores are whores.

Miss Julie (*kneels and clasps her hands*)   Oh, God in Heaven, end my miserable life! Save me from this mire into which I'm sinking! Save me, save me!

Jean   I can't deny I feel sorry for you. When I lay in the onion bed and saw you in the rose garden – I might as well tell you now – I had the same dirty thoughts as any small boy.

Miss Julie   You – who wanted to die for me?

Jean   The oat-bin? Oh, that was just talk.

Miss Julie   A lie?

Jean (*begins to get sleepy*)   More or less. I once read a story in a paper about a sweep who curled up in a wood-chest with some lilacs because he'd had a paternity order brought against him –

Miss Julie   I see. You're the kind who –

Jean   Well, I had to think up something. Women always fall for pretty stories.

Miss Julie   Swine!

Jean   *Merde!*

Miss Julie   And now you've managed to see the eagle's back –

Jean   Not exactly its back.

Miss Julie   And I was to be the first branch –

Jean   But the branch was rotten –

Miss Julie   I was to be the signboard of the hotel –

Jean   And I the hotel –

Miss Julie   I was to sit at your desk, attract your customers, fiddle your bills –

Jean   No, I'd have done that –

Miss Julie   Can a human soul become so foul?

Jean   Wash it, then!

Miss Julie   Servant, lackey, stand up when I speak!

Jean   Servant's whore, lackey's bitch, shut your mouth and get out of here. You dare to stand there and call me foul? Not one of my class ever behaved the way you've done tonight. Do you think any kitchen-maid would accost a man like you did? Have you ever seen any girl of my class offer her body like that? I've only seen it among animals and prostitutes.

Miss Julie (*crushed*)   You're right. Hit me, trample on me, I've deserved nothing better. I'm worthless – but help me, help me out of this – if there is a way out.

Jean (*more gently*)   I don't want to disclaim my share in the honour of having seduced you, but do you imagine a man in my position would have dared to so much as glance at you if you hadn't invited him? I'm still dumbfounded –

Miss Julie   And proud.

Jean   Why not? Though I must confess I found the conquest a little too easy to be really exciting.

Miss Julie   Hurt me more.

Jean (*gets up*)   No. Forgive me for what I've said. I don't hit defenceless people, least of all women. I can't deny it gratifies me to have found that it was only a gilt veneer that dazzled our humble eyes, that the eagle's back was as scabbed as our own, that the whiteness of those cheeks was only powder, that those polished fingernails had black edges, that that handkerchief was dirty though it smelt of perfume – But on the other hand, it hurts me to have discovered that what I was aspiring towards was not something worthier and more solid. It hurts me to see you sunk so low, to find that deep down you are a kitchen slut. It hurts me, like seeing the autumn flowers whipped to tatters by the rain and trodden into the mud.

Miss Julie   You speak as though you were already above me.

Jean   I am. You see, I could make you into a countess, but you could never make me into a count.

Miss Julie   But I am of noble blood, and you can never be that.

Jean   That's true. But my children could be noblemen, if –

Miss Julie   But you're a thief. That's something I am not.

Jean   There are worse things than being a thief. Besides, when I work in a house I regard myself more or less as a member of the family, a child of the house, and people don't call it stealing when a child takes a berry from a bush heavy with fruit. (*His passion rises again.*) Miss Julie, you're a fine woman, much too good for someone like me. You've been the victim of a drunken folly, and you want to cover it up by pretending to yourself that you love me. You don't, unless perhaps physically – and then your love is no better than mine – but I can never be content with being just your animal, and I can never make you love me.

Miss Julie   Are you sure of that?

Jean   You mean it might happen? Yes, I could love you easily – you're beautiful, you're refined – (*He approaches her and takes her hand.*) Educated, lovable when you want to be, and once you have awoken a man's passion, it could never die. (*He puts his arm round her waist.*) You are like hot wine, strongly spiced, and a kiss from you – ! (*He tries to lead her out but she slowly tears herself free.*)

Miss Julie   Let me go! You won't win me like that!

Jean   How, then? Not like that. Not by caresses and fine words. Not by thinking of your future, rescuing you from what you've done. How, then?

Miss Julie   How? How? I don't know. There is no way. I detest you as I detest rats, but I cannot run away from you.

Jean   Run away with me!

Miss Julie (*straightens herself*)   Run away? Yes, we must run away. But I'm so tired. Give me a glass of wine. I'm so tired. (**Jean** *pours her some. She looks at her watch.*) But we must talk first. We have a little time. (*She drains the glass and holds it out for more.*)

Jean   Don't drink so much, you'll get drunk.

Miss Julie   What does that matter?

Jean   What does it matter? It's stupid to get drunk. What were you going to say to me just now?

Miss Julie   We must run away! But first we must talk – that is, I must talk – so far you've been doing all the talking. You've told me about your life, now I must tell you about myself, so that we know all about each other before we go away together.

Jean   One moment. Forgive me, but – consider – you may later regret having revealed your private secrets to me.

Miss Julie   Aren't you my friend?

Jean   Yes – sometimes. But don't rely on me.

Miss Julie   You're only saying that. Anyway, everyone else knows. You see, my mother was a commoner, of quite humble birth. She was brought up with ideas about equality, freedom for women and all that. And she had a decided aversion to marriage. So when my father proposed to her, she replied that she would never become his wife, but that he could become her lover. My father told her that he had no desire to see the woman he loved enjoy less respect than himself. When she explained that the world's respect did not concern her, he agreed to her conditions. But now he was cut off from his social circle and confined to his domestic life, which could not satisfy him. And then? I came into the world, against my mother's wish as far as I can gather. She wanted to bring me up as a child of nature, and into the bargain I was to learn everything that a boy has to learn, so that I might stand as an example of how a woman can be as good as a man. I had to wear boy's clothes, and learn to look after horses – though I was never allowed to enter the cowshed. I had to groom and saddle them, and hunt – even learn to slaughter animals. That was horrible. Meanwhile, on the estate, all the men were set to perform the women's tasks, and the women the men's – so that it began to fail, and we became the laughing-stock of the district. In the end my father put his foot down, and everything was changed back to the way he wanted it. That was when they married. Then my mother fell ill – what illness, I don't know – but she often had convulsions, hid herself, in the attic and the garden, and sometimes stayed out all night. Then there was the great fire which you have heard about. The house, the stables and the cowshed were all burned down, under circumstances suggesting arson – for the accident happened the very day our quarterly insurance had expired, and the premium my father sent had been delayed through the inefficiency of the servant carrying it, so that it hadn't arrived in time. (*She fills her glass and drinks.*)

Jean   Don't drink so much.

Miss Julie   Oh, what does it matter? So we were left penniless, and had to sleep in the carriages. My father couldn't think where he would be able to find the money to rebuild the house, as he'd cut himself off from his old friends. Then mother advised him to ask for a loan from an old friend of hers, a brick merchant who lived in the neighbourhood. Father got the money, free of interest, which rather surprised him. So the house was rebuilt. (*She drinks again.*) Do you know who burned the house down?

Jean   Your mother!

Miss Julie   Do you know who the brick merchant was?

Jean   Your mother's lover!

Miss Julie   Do you know whose the money was?

Jean   Wait a moment. No, that I don't know.

Miss Julie   It was my mother's.

Jean   His lordship's too, then. Unless he'd made a marriage settlement.

Miss Julie   No, there wasn't any marriage settlement. My mother had had a little money of her own, which she didn't want my father to have control of. So she entrusted it to her – friend.

Jean   Who kept it!

Miss Julie   Exactly. He kept it. All this came to my father's knowledge – but he couldn't start an action, repay his wife's lover, or prove that the money was his wife's. It was my mother's revenge on him, for taking control of the house out of her hands. He was on the verge of shooting himself – the rumour was that he had done so, but had failed to kill himself. Well, he lived; and he made my mother pay for what she had done. Those five years were dreadful for me, I can tell you. I was sorry for my father, but I took my mother's side, because I didn't know the circumstances. I'd learned from her to distrust and hate men – she hated men. And I swore to her that I would never be a slave to any man.

Jean   But then you got engaged to that young lawyer?

Miss Julie   So that he should be my slave.

Jean   And he wasn't willing?

Miss Julie   He was willing enough, but he didn't get the chance. I tired of him.

Jean   I saw it. In the stable.

Miss Julie   Saw what?

Jean   How he broke off the engagement.

Miss Julie   That's a lie! It was I who broke it off! Has he been saying he did it, the little liar?

Jean   He wasn't a liar. You hate men, Miss Julie.

Miss Julie   Yes. Most of the time. But sometimes – when nature burns – ! Oh, God! Will the fire never die?

Jean   You hate me too?

Miss Julie   Immeasurably! I'd like to shoot you like an animal –

Jean   'The offender gets two years' penal servitude and the animal is shot.' That's the law for bestiality, isn't it? But you've nothing to shoot with. So what shall we do?

Miss Julie   Go away!

Jean   To torment each other to death?

Miss Julie   No. To be happy – for two days – a week – as long as one can be happy – and then – die –

Jean   Die? Don't be stupid. I'd rather start the hotel than do that.

Miss Julie (*not hearing him*)   – on the Lake of Como, where the sun always shines, where the laurels are green at Christmas, and the orange-trees flame!

Jean   Actually, it's always raining on the Lake of Como, and I never saw any oranges there except in the grocers' shops. But it's a good spot for tourists, there are a lot of villas to hire out to loving couples, and that's a profitable industry – you know why?

Because they lease them for six months, and then leave after three weeks.

Miss Julie (*naively*)   Why after three weeks?

Jean   They quarrel, of course! But they have to pay the full rent, and then you hire it out again. So it goes on, couple after couple. For love must go on, if not for very long.

Miss Julie   You don't want to die with me?

Jean   I don't want to die at all. Partly because I like life, and partly because I regard suicide as a crime against the Providence which gave us life.

Miss Julie   You believe in God – *you?*

Jean   Certainly I do. And I go to church every other Sunday. Quite frankly now, I'm tired of all this, and I'm going to bed.

Miss Julie   I see. And you think I'm going to rest content with that? Don't you know what a man owes to a woman he has shamed?

Jean (*takes out his purse and throws a silver coin on the table*)   Here. I always pay my debts.

Miss Julie (*pretends not to notice the insult*)   Do you know what the law says – ?

Jean   Unfortunately the law doesn't demand any penalty from a woman who seduces a man.

Miss Julie   Can you see any other solution than that we should go away, marry, and part?

Jean   And if I refuse to enter into this *mésalliance?*

Miss Julie   *Mésalliance?*

Jean   Yes – for me! I've got a better heritage than you. None of my ancestors committed arson.

Miss Julie   How do you know?

Jean   You couldn't prove it, because we don't have any family records – except with the police. But I've studied your pedigree in a book I found on the table in the drawing room. Do you know who the first of your ancestors to get a title was? He was a miller who let the king sleep with his wife one night during the Danish war. I haven't any noble ancestors like that – I haven't any noble ancestors at all. But I could become one myself.

Miss Julie   This is my reward for opening my heart to a servant, for giving my family's honour – !

Jean   Honour? Don't say I didn't tell you. One shouldn't drink, it loosens the tongue. And that's bad.

Miss Julie   Oh God, how I regret it, how I regret it! If you at least loved me – !

Jean   For the last time – what do you want? Shall I burst into tears, shall I jump over your riding crop, shall I kiss you, trick you down to Lake Como for three weeks, and then – what? What shall I do? What do you want me to do? This is beginning to get tiresome. It's always like this when one gets involved with women. Miss Julie! I see you are unhappy, I know you are suffering, but I do not understand you! We don't fool around like you do – we don't hate – love is a game we play when we have a little time free from work, but we aren't free all day and all night like you! I think you must be ill. Yes, undoubtedly, you're ill.

Miss Julie   Speak kindly to me, Jean. Treat me like a human being.

Jean   Act like one yourself, then. You spit at me, and won't let me wipe it off – on you.

Miss Julie   Help me, help me! Just tell me what to do. Where shall I go?

Jean   For God's sake! If I only knew!

Miss Julie   I've been mad, I know I've been mad, but isn't there some way out?

Jean   Stay here, and keep calm. No one knows.

Miss Julie   Impossible. The servants know. And Christine.

Jean   They don't know for sure. They wouldn't really believe it could happen.

Miss Julie (*hesitantly*)   But – it could happen again.

Jean   That is true.

Miss Julie   And – then?

Jean (*frightened*)   Then? My God, why didn't I think of that? Yes, there's only one answer – you must go away. At once. I can't come with you – then we'd be finished – you must go alone – far away – anywhere.

Miss Julie   Alone? Where? I can't!

Jean   You must! And before his lordship returns. If you stay, you know what'll happen. Once one has made a mistake one wants to go on, because the damage has already been done. Then one gets more and more careless and – in the end one gets found out. So go! You can write to his lordship later and tell him everything – except that it was me! He'll never guess that. And I don't suppose he'll be over-keen to find out who it was.

Miss Julie   I'll go, if you'll come with me.

Jean   Are you mad, woman? Miss Julie run away with her servant! It'd be in the newspapers in a couple of days, and his lordship'd never live that down.

Miss Julie   I can't go. I can't stay. Help me! I'm so tired, so dreadfully tired. Order me! Make me do something! I can't think, I can't act –

Jean   Now you see what a contemptible creature you are! Why do you prink yourselves up and stick your noses in the air as though you were the lords of creation? Very well, I shall order you. Go up to your room, get dressed, get some money for the journey and come back here.

Miss Julie (*half-whispers*)   Come with me.

Jean   To your room? Now you're being crazy again. (*He hesitates for a moment.*) No! Go, at once! (*He takes her hand and leads her out.*)

Miss Julie (*as she goes*)   Speak kindly to me, Jean!

Jean   An order always sounds unkind. Now you know how it feels!

Jean, *left alone, heaves a sigh of relief, sits at the table, takes out a notebook and pencil, and makes some calculations muttering occasionally to himself.*

Dumb mime, until **Christine** *enters, dressed for church, with a man's dickey and white tie in her hand.*

Christine   Blessed Jesus, what a mess! What on earth have you been up to?

Jean   Oh, it was Miss Julie – she brought the servants in. You must have been fast asleep – didn't you hear anything?

Christine   I slept like a log.

Jean   Dressed for church already?

Christine   Yes. You promised to come with me to Communion this morning.

Jean   So I did. And I see you've brought the uniform. OK, then.

He sits. **Christine** *dresses him in his dickey and white tie. Pause.*

Jean (*sleepily*)   What's the lesson today?

Christine   Execution of John the Baptist, I expect.

Jean   Oh God, that's a long one. Hi, you're strangling me! Oh, I'm so tired, so tired.

Christine   Well, what have you been doing, up all night? You're quite green in the face.

Jean   Sitting here, talking with Miss Julie.

Christine   She doesn't know what's right and proper, that one.

Pause.

Jean   I say, Christine.

Christine   Mm?

Jean   It's strange, you know, when you think of it. Her.

Christine   What's strange?

Jean   Everything.

Pause.

Christine (*sees the glasses, half empty, on the table*)   Have you been drinking together, too?

Jean   Yes.

Christine   For shame! Look me in the eyes!

Jean   Yes?

Christine   Is it possible? Is it *possible?*

Jean (*after a moment*)   Yes.

Christine   Ugh! *That* I'd never have believed! No! Shame on you, shame!

Jean   You aren't jealous of her, are you?

Christine   No, not of her! If it had been Clara or Sophie – then I'd have torn your eyes out. But her – no – I don't know why. Ah, but it's disgusting!

Jean   Are you angry with her, then?

Christine   No, with you! It's a wicked thing to have done, wicked! Poor lass! No, I don't care who hears it, I don't want to stay any longer in a house where people can't respect their employers.

Jean   Why should one respect them?

Christine   Yes, you're so clever, you tell me! But you don't want to work for people who lower themselves, do you? Eh? You lower yourself by it, that's my opinion.

Jean   Yes, but it's a comfort for us to know they aren't any better than us.

Christine   Not to my mind. If they're no better than we are there's no point our trying to improve ourselves. And think of his lordship! Think of him and all the misery he's had in his time! No, I don't want to stay in this house any longer. Blessed Jesus! And with someone like you! If it'd been that young lawyer fellow – if it'd been a gentleman –

Jean   What's wrong with me?

Christine   Oh, you're all right in your way, but there's a difference between people and people. No, I'll never be able to forget this. Miss Julie, who was always so proud, so cool with men – I never thought she'd go and give herself to someone – and to someone like you! She, who all but had poor Diana shot for running after the gatekeeper's pug! Yes, I'm not afraid to say it! I won't stay here any longer. On the 24th of October I go!

Jean   And then?

Christine   Yes, since you've raised the subject, it's time you started looking round for something, seeing as we're going to get married.

Jean   What kind of thing? I can't have a job like this once I'm married.

Christine   No, of course not. Still, you might get something as a porter, or maybe a caretaker in some government office. A bird in the hand's worth two in the bush; and there'll be a pension for your wife and children.

Jean (*grimaces*)   Yes, that's all very fine, but I don't intend to die to oblige my wife and children just yet, thank you very much. I've higher ambitions than that.

Christine   Ambitions? What about your responsibilities? Think of them.

Jean   Oh, shut up about responsibilities, I know my duty. (*He listens towards the door.*) But we've plenty of time to think about that. Go inside now and get yourself ready, and we'll go to church.

Christine   Who's that walking about upstairs?

Jean   I don't know. Probably Clara.

Christine (*going*)   It surely can't be his lordship. He couldn't have come back without our hearing him.

Jean (*frightened*)   His lordship? No, it can't be, he'd have rung.

Christine (*goes*)   Well, God help us. I've never been mixed up in the likes of this before.

The sun has now risen and is shining on the tops of the trees in the park. Its beams move gradually until they fall at an angle through the windows. **Jean** *goes to the door and makes a sign.*

Miss Julie (*enters in travelling clothes with a small birdcage, covered with a cloth, which she places on a chair*)   I'm ready now.

Jean   Ssh! Christine is awake!

Miss Julie (*very nervous throughout this dialogue*)   Does she suspect anything?

Jean   She knows nothing. But, my God – what a sight you look!

Miss Julie   What's wrong – ?

Jean   You're as white as a corpse, and – forgive me, but your face is dirty.

Miss Julie   Let me wash, then. Here. (*She goes to the washbasin and washes her face and hands.*) Give me a towel. Oh – the sun's rising!

Jean   And then the Devil loses his power.

Miss Julie   Yes, the Devil's been at work tonight. But Jean, listen. Come with me! I've got some money now.

Jean (*doubtfully*)   Enough?

Miss Julie   Enough to start with! Come with me! I can't go alone, not today. Think – Midsummer Day, on a stuffy train, squashed among crowds of people staring at me – having to stand still on stations, when one longs to be flying away! No, I can't, I can't! And then – memories – memories of midsummers in child-hood, the church garlanded with birch-leaves and lilac, dinner at the long table, the family, friends – the afternoons in the park, dancing, music, flowers, games! Oh, one runs, one runs away, but memories follow in the baggage-wagon – and remorse – and guilt!

Jean   I'll come with you – but it must be now, at once, before it's too late. Now, this minute!

Miss Julie   Get dressed, then. (*She picks up the birdcage.*)

Jean   No luggage, though. That'd give us away.

Miss Julie   No, nothing. Only what we can have in the compartment with us.

Jean (*has taken his hat*)   What have you got there? What is it?

Miss Julie   It's only my greenfinch. I don't want to leave her.

Jean   For heaven's sake! We can't take a birdcage with us now. You're crazy. Put that cage down.

Miss Julie   My one memory of home – the only living thing that loves me, since Diana was unfaithful to me. Don't be cruel! Let me take her with me!

Jean   Put that cage down, I tell you. And don't talk so loud, Christine will hear us.

Miss Julie   No I won't leave her for strangers to have. I'd rather you killed her.

Jean   Bring the little beast here then, and I will.

Miss Julie   All right – but don't hurt her. Don't – no, I can't!

Jean   Bring it here. I can.

Miss Julie (*takes the bird out of its cage and kisses it*)   Ah, poor little Serina, are you going to die now and leave your mistress?

Jean   Please don't make a scene. Your life and your happiness are at stake. Here, quickly! (*He snatches the bird from her, takes it to the chopping block and picks up the kitchen axe.* **Miss Julie** *turns away*.) You ought to have learned how to wring chickens' necks instead of how to fire a pistol. (*He brings down the axe*.) Then you wouldn't have been frightened of a drop of blood.

Miss Julie (*screams*)   Kill me too! Kill me! You, who can slaughter an innocent creature without a tremor! Oh, I hate and detest you! There is blood between us now! I curse the moment I set eyes on you, I curse the moment I was conceived in my mother's womb!

Jean   What's the good of cursing? Come!

Miss Julie (*goes towards the chopping block, as though drawn against her will*)   No, I don't want to go yet. I can't – I must see – ssh!

There's a carriage outside! (*She listens, but keeps her eyes fixed all the while on the chopping block and the axe.*) Do you think I can't bear the sight of blood? You think I'm so weak – oh, I should like to see your blood, your brains, on a chopping block – I'd like to see all your sex swimming in a lake of blood – I think I could drink from your skull, I'd like to bathe my feet in your guts, I could eat your heart, roasted! You think I'm weak – you think I loved you, because my womb wanted your seed, you think I want to carry your embryo under my heart and feed it with my blood, bear your child and take your name! By the way, what is your surname! I've never heard it – you probably haven't any. I'd have to be 'Mrs Kitchen-boy', or 'Mrs Lavatory man' – you dog, who wear my collar, you lackey who carry my crest on your buttons – am I to share with my own cook, compete with a scullery slut? Oh, oh, oh! You think I'm a coward and want to run away? No, now I shall stay. Let the storm break! My father will come home – find his desk broken open – his money gone! He'll ring – this bell – twice, for his lackey – then he'll send for the police – and I shall tell everything. Everything. Oh, it'll be good to end it all – if only it could be the end. And then he'll have a stroke and die. Then we shall all be finished, and there'll be peace – peace – eternal rest! And the coat of arms will be broken over the coffin – the title extinct – and the lackey's line will be carried on in an orphanage, win laurels in the gutter, and end in a prison!

Jean   That's the blue blood talking! Bravo, Miss Julie! Just give the miller a rest, now – !

Christine *enters, dressed for church, with a prayer-book in her hand.*
Miss Julie *runs towards her and falls into her arms, as though seeking shelter.*

Miss Julie   Help me, Christine! Help me against this man!

Christine (*motionless, cold*)   What kind of a spectacle's this on a Sunday morning? (*She looks at the chopping block.*) And what a pigsty you've made here. What does all this mean? I never heard such shouting and bawling.

Miss Julie   Christine! Christine, listen to me and I'll explain everything.

Jean (*somewhat timid and embarrassed*)   While you ladies discuss the matter, I'll go inside and shave. (*He slips out right.*)

Miss Julie   You must try to understand! You must listen to me!

Christine   No, this kind of thing I don't understand. Where are you going in those clothes? And what's he doing with his hat on – eh? – eh?

Miss Julie   Listen to me, Christine. Listen, and I'll explain everything –

Christine   I don't want to know anything –

Miss Julie   You must listen to me –

Christine   About what? What you've done with Jean? That doesn't bother me – that's between you and him. But if you're thinking of trying to fool him into running away, we'll soon put a stop to that.

Miss Julie (*very nervous*)   Now try to be calm, Christine, and listen to me. I can't stay here, and Jean can't stay here – so we have to go –

Christine   Hm, hm!

Miss Julie (*becoming brighter*)   Listen, I've just had an idea – why don't we all three go away – abroad – to Switzerland – and start a hotel together – I've money, you see – and Jean and I could run it – and you, I thought you might take charge of the kitchen – isn't that a good idea? Say yes, now! And come with us, and then everything'll be settled! Say yes, now!

Christine (*coldly, thoughtfully*)   Hm, hm!

Miss Julie (*speaks very rapidly*)   You've never been abroad, Christine – you must get away from here and see the world. You've no idea what fun it is to travel by train – new people all the time – new countries – we'll go through Hamburg and look at the zoo – you'll like that – and then we'll go to the theatre and listen to the opera – and when we get to Munich there'll be all the museums, Christine, and Rubens and Raphael, those great painters, you know – you've heard of Munich – where King Ludwig lived, you know, the King who went mad. And we'll see his palaces – they've still got palaces there, just like in the fairy tales – and from there it isn't far to Switzerland – and the Alps, Christine – fancy, the Alps, with snow on them in the middle of summer – and oranges grow there, and laurel trees that are green all the year round –

Jean *can be seen in the wings right, whetting his razor on a strop which he holds between his teeth and his left hand. He listens contentedly to what is being said, every now and then nodding his approval.*

Miss Julie (*more rapidly still*)   And we'll start a hotel there – I'll sit at the desk while Jean stands in the doorway and receives the guests – I'll go out and do the shopping – and write the letters – oh Christine, what a life it'll be! The trains will whistle, and then the buses'll arrive, and bells will ring on all the floors and in the restaurant – and I'll write out the bills – and salt them, too – you can't imagine how timid tourists are when they have to pay the bill! And you – you'll be in charge of the kitchen – you won't have to do any cooking yourself, of course – and you'll wear fine clothes, for the guests to see you in – and you, with your looks, I'm not flattering you, Christine, you'll get yourself a husband one fine day, a rich Englishman, you'll see – English people are so easy to – (*slowing down*) – catch – and we'll become rich – and build ourselves a villa on Lake Como – it rains there sometimes, of course, but – (*slows right down*) – the sun must shine there too, sometimes – though it looks dark – and – so – if it doesn't we can come home again – back to – (*Pause.*) Back here – or somewhere –

Christine   Now listen. Do you believe all this?

Miss Julie (*crushed*)   Do I believe it?

Christine   Yes.

Miss Julie (*wearily*)   I don't know. I don't believe in anything any longer. (*She falls on to the bench and puts her head on the table between her hands.*) Nothing. Nothing at all.

Christine (*turns right to where* **Jean** *is standing*)   So! You were thinking of running away!

Jean (*crestfallen, puts his razor down on the table*)   Running away? Oh now, that's exaggerating. You heard Miss Julie's plan and although she's tired now after being up all night I think it's a very practical proposition.

Christine   Listen to him! Did you expect me to act as cook to that – ?

Jean (*sharply*)   Kindly express yourself respectfully when you refer to your mistress. Understand?

Christine   Mistress!

Jean   Yes.

Christine   Listen to him, listen to him!

Jean   Yes, listen to me, and talk a little less. Miss Julie is your mistress, and what you despise in her you should despise in yourself too.

Christine   I've always had sufficient respect for myself –

Jean   To be able to turn up your nose at others.

Christine   To stop me from demeaning myself. You tell me when you've seen his lordship's cook mucking around with the groom or the pigman! Just you tell me!

Jean   Yes, you managed to get hold of a gentleman for yourself. You were lucky.

Christine   Yes, a gentleman who sells his lordship's oats, which he steals from the stables –

Jean   You should talk! You take a percentage on all the groceries, and a rake-off from the butcher –

Christine   What!

Jean   And you say you can't respect your employers! You, you, you!

Christine   Are you coming with me to church now? You need a good sermon after what you've done.

Jean   No, I'm not going to church today. You can go by yourself, and confess what you've been up to.

Christine   Yes, I will, and I'll come home with my sins forgiven, and yours too. The blessed Saviour suffered and died on the cross for all our sins, and if we turn to Him with a loyal and humble heart He'll take all our sins upon Him.

Jean   Including the groceries?

Miss Julie   Do you believe that, Christine?

Christine   With all my heart, as surely as I stand here. I learned it as a child, Miss Julie, and I've believed it ever since. And where the sin is exceeding great, there His mercy shall overflow.

Miss Julie   Oh, if only I had your faith! Oh, if – !

Christine   Ah, but you can't have that except by God's special grace, and that isn't granted to everyone –

Miss Julie   Who has it, then?

Christine   That's God's great secret, Miss Julie. And the Lord's no respecter of persons. There shall the last be first –

Miss Julie   Then He has respect for the last?

Christine (*continues*)   And it is easier for a camel to pass through the eye of a needle than for a rich man to enter the Kingdom of Heaven. That's how it is, Miss Julie. Well, I'll be going – and as I pass the stable I'll tell the groom not to let any of the horses be taken out before his lordship comes home, just in case. Goodbye. (*She goes.*)

Jean   Damned bitch! And all for a greenfinch!

Miss Julie (*dully*)   Never mind the greenfinch. Can you see any way out of this, any end to it?

Jean (*thinks*)   No.

Miss Julie   What would you do in my place?

Jean   In your place? Wait, now. If I was a lady – of noble birth – who'd fallen – ? I don't know. Yes. I do know.

Miss Julie (*picks up the razor and makes a gesture*)   This?

Jean   Yes. But *I* wouldn't do it, mind. There's a difference between us.

Miss Julie   Because you're a man and I am a woman? What difference does that make?

Jean   The difference – between a man and a woman.

Miss Julie (*holding the razor*)   I want to do it – but I can't. My father couldn't do it, either, the time he should have.

Jean   No, he was right. He had to be revenged first.

Miss Julie   And now my mother will be revenged again, through me.

Jean   Have you never loved your father, Miss Julie?

Miss Julie   Yes – enormously – but I've hated him too. I must have done so without realising it. But it was he who brought me up to despise my own sex, made me half woman and half man. Who is to blame for what has happened – my father, my mother, myself? Myself? I have no self. I haven't a thought I didn't get from my father, not an emotion I didn't get from my mother – and this last idea – that all people are equal – I got that from him, my fiancé whom I called a wretched little fool because of it. How can the blame be mine, then? Put it all on to Jesus, as Christine did – no, I'm too proud to do that, and too clever – thanks to my learned father. And that about a rich person not being able to get into heaven, that's a lie, and Christine has money in the savings bank so she won't get there either. Whose fault is it all? What does it matter to us whose fault it is? I shall have to bear the blame, carry the consequences –

Jean   Yes, but –

There are two sharp rings on the bell. **Miss Julie** *jumps up.* **Jean** *changes his coat.*

Jean   His lordship's home! Good God, do you suppose Christine – ? (*Goes to the speaking-tube, knocks on it, and listens.*)

Miss Julie   Has he been to his desk?

Jean It's Jean, milord. (*He listens. The audience cannot hear what is said to him.*) Yes, milord. (*He listens.*) Yes, milord. Immediately. (*He listens.*) At once, milord. (*Listens.*) Very good, my lord. In half an hour.

Miss Julie (*desperately frightened*) What does he say? For God's sake, what does he say?

Jean He wants his boots and his coffee in half an hour.

Miss Julie In half an hour, then – ! Oh, I'm so tired! I can't feel anything, I can't repent, can't run away, can't stay, can't live – can't die. Help me! Order me, and I'll obey you like a dog. Do me this last service, save my honour, save his name! You know what I ought to will myself to do, but I can't. Will me to, Jean, order me!

Jean I don't know – now I can't either – I don't understand – it's just as though this coat made me – I *can't* order you – and now, since his lordship spoke to me – I can't explain it properly, but – oh, it's this damned lackey that sits on my back – I think if his lordship came down now and ordered me to cut my throat, I'd do it on the spot.

Miss Julie Then pretend that you are he, and I am you. You acted so well just now, when you went down on your knees – then you were an aristocrat – or – haven't you ever been to the theatre and seen a hypnotist? (**Jean** *nods.*) He says to his subject: 'Take the broom!' and he takes it. He says: 'Sweep!' and he sweeps –

Jean But the subject has to be asleep.

Miss Julie (*in an ecstasy*) I am already asleep – the whole room is like smoke around me – and you look like an iron stove – which resembles a man dressed in black, with a tall hat – and your eyes shine like coals, when the fire is dying – and your face is a white smear, like ash – (*The sun's rays have now reached the floor and are shining on* **Jean**.) It's so warm and good – ! (*She rubs her hands as though warming them before a fire.*) And so bright – and so peaceful – !

Jean (*takes the razor and places it in her hand*) Here's the broom. Go now – while it's light – out to the barn – and – (*He whispers in her ear.*)

Miss Julie (*awake*)   Thank you. Now I am going to rest. But just tell me this – those who are first – they too can receive grace? Say it to me – even if you don't believe it.

Jean   Those who are first? No, I can't! But, wait – Miss Julie – now I see it! You are no longer among the first. You are – among the last!

Miss Julie   That's true. I am among the last of all. I am the last. Oh! But now I can't go! Tell me once more – say I must go!

Jean   No, now I can't either. I can't!

Miss Julie   And the first shall be last.

Jean   Don't think, don't think! You take all my strength from me, you make me a coward. What? I thought the bell moved! No. Shall we stuff paper in it? To be so afraid of a bell! Yes, but it isn't only a bell – there's someone sitting behind it – a hand sets it in motion – and something else sets the hand in motion – you've only got to close your ears, close your ears! Yes, but now he's ringing louder! He'll ring till someone answers – and then it'll be too late. The police will come – and then – !

Two loud rings on the bell.

Jean (*cringes, then straightens himself up*)   It's horrible. But it's the only possible ending. Go!

Miss Julie *walks firmly out through the door.*

GERHART HAUPTMANN

The Weavers

translated by Frank Marcus

Characters

Dreissiger, *a manufacturer*
Frau Dreissiger, *his wife*
In **Dreissiger**'s *service:*
Pfeifer, *a manager*
Neumann, *a cashier*
An **Office Boy**
Johann, *a coachman*
A **Servant Girl**
Weinhold, *tutor to* **Dreissiger**'s *sons*
Pastor Kittelhaus
Frau Pastor Kittelhaus, *his wife*
Heide, *Police Superintendent*
Kutsche, *a policeman*
Welzel, *an innkeeper*
Frau Welzel, *his wife*
Anna Welzel, *their daughter*
Wiegand, *a joiner*
A **Travelling Salesman**
A **Peasant**
A **Forester**
Schmidt, *a surgeon*
Hornig, *a ragpicker*
Old Wittig, *a blacksmith*
Baecker
Moritz Jaeger
Old Baumert
Mother Baumert, *his wife*
Bertha Baumert, *their daughter*
Emma Baumert, *another daughter*
Fritz, **Emma**'s *son, four years old*
August Baumert, **Old Baumert**'s *son*
Old Ansorge
Frau Heinrich
Old Hilse
Frau Helse, *his wife*
Gottlieb Hilse, *their son*
Luise I-Hilse, *his wife*

Mielchen, *their daughter, seven years old*
Reimann
Heiber
A **Boy**, *eight years old*
Dyeworkers
A large crowd of **Young** *and* **Old Weavers** *and* **Weaver Women**

The events described in this play take place in the 1840s in Kaschbach in the Eulengebirge, as well as in Peterswaldau and Langenbielau at the foot of the Eulengebirge.

Act One

*A spacious, grey-tinted room in **Dreisiger**'s house at Peterswaldau. It is the room where the weavers have to deliver the finished articles. On the left, windows without curtains, in the back wall a glass door, on the right an identical glass door, through which a continuous stream of weavers, weavers' wives and children come and go. Along the right wall, which is covered like the others mostly with wooden shelves for storage, stretches a bench on which the arriving weavers lay out their wares. They step forward in order of arrival and submit their wares for inspection. **Manager Pfeifer** stands behind the big table on which the wares to be inspected are laid down. He uses a pair of dividers and a magnifying glass to help with the scrutiny. When he has finished the examination, the weaver puts his products on the scale where an **Office Boy** checks their weight. The same boy pushes the accepted products into a repository. The price to be paid is called out by **Manager Pfeifer** to **Cashier Neumann** who sits behind a small table.*

It is a sultry day towards the end of May. The clock registers twelve. Most of the waiting weavers resemble people standing behind the bars of a court-room where they await decisions of life and death with tortured anxiety. There is something of the oppressed about them, something of the receiver of charity who, going from humiliation to humiliation, is merely tolerated and expected to make himself as inconspicuous as possible. In addition, there is an inflexible feature of harassed irresolute brooding in their expressions. The men, who have much in common with each other, half dwarfish, half schoolmasterly, are predominantly sunken-chested, coughing, poverty-stricken people with dirty, pale complexions: creatures of the loom, whose knees have become bent as a result of excessive sitting. Their women look less typical at first glance; they're broken, harassed, exhausted – whereas the men still show a certain pitiful gravity – and ragged, whereas the men's clothes are patched. The young girls are nonetheless not unattractive; waxen pallor, tender shapes and large, protruding melancholy eyes are typical of them.

Cashier Neumann (*counting money*)   That leaves sixteen silver groschen, two pfennigs.

1st Weaver Woman (*thirty, very emaciated, holds the money in trembling fingers*)   Thank you.

Neumann (*when the woman fails to move on*)   Well? Is something wrong again?

1st Weaver Woman (*imploring excitedly*)   I badly need a few pfennigs in advance.

Neumann   And I need a few hundred thalers. If it's a question of need – ! (*Curtly, already busy with paying another weaver.*) Herr Dreissiger himself decides about advances.

1st Weaver Woman   Could I perhaps speak with Herr Dreissiger himself?

Manager Pfeifer (*a former weaver, his characteristics are unmistakable, except that he is well-nourished, decently dressed, clean-shaven and a vigorous taker of snuff. He shouts across harshly.*) God knows, Herr Dreissiger would be kept busy if he had to decide on every little thing himself; that's our job. (*He measures and examines with the magnifying-glass.*) Damn! There's a draught. (*He wraps a thick scarf around his neck.*) Close the door, whoever comes in.

Office Boy (*loudly to* **Pfeifer**)   It's like talking to a brick wall.

Pfeifer   All right, finished! – Scales!

The **Weaver** *puts his product on the scales.*

If you were better at your work. Full of lumps again . . . I don't even have to look.

Baecker *has entered. A young, exceptionally strong weaver, his demeanour is unconstrained, almost impudent.* **Pfeifer**, **Neumann** *and the* **Office Boy** *exchange knowing looks when be enters.*

Baecker   Hell! I'm sweating like a pig.

Old Weaver (*quietly*)   Looks like rain.

Old Baumert *pushes himself through the glass door on the right. Behind the door one notices the waiting* **Weavers** *crowded together shoulder-to-shoulder. The old man has hobbled to the front and put his pack on the bench near* **Baecker**'s. *He sits next to it and wipes the sweat off his face.*

Old Baumert   I've earned a rest.

Baecker (*ironically*)   Rest in peace.

Old Baumert   That'll be the day. How's it going, Baecker?

Baecker   Same as usual, Father Baumert. Looks like another long wait!

Old Weaver   Who cares. A weaver can wait an hour or a day.

Pfeifer   Quiet there at the back! Can't hear myself speak.

Baecker (*quietly*)   He's on form today.

Pfeifer (*to the weaver standing before him*)   How often have I said it! You've got to clean the webs properly. What kind of mess is this? Clots of dirt in here as long as my finger, and straw and all this filth.

Weaver Reimann   It might be those new carders.

Office Boy (*having weighed the webs*)   It's short of weight too.

Pfeifer   The weavers these days – waste of good material. Jesus, in my time! My master would have had something to say, In those days weaving was different. You had to know what you were doing. Today it's not necessary. Reimann, ten silver groschen.

Weaver Reimann   But a pound of waste is always allowed for . . .

Pfeifer   I haven't got the time. That's done with. What have you got?

Weaver Heiber (*spreading out his work. While* **Pfeifer** *examines it, he goes up to him and speaks to him quietly and urgently.*)   You'll forgive me, Herr Pfeifer, I wanted to ask you a favour, sir, if maybe you'd be so kind and do me a good turn, sir, and not have my advance pay come off my money this time.

Pfeifer (*measuring and examining, sarcastically*)   Well, well! Let's take a good look then. Looks like half of it got left at home.

Weaver Heiber (*continuing as before*)   I'll gladly make up for it next week. Last week I only had two full working days. My wife's lying sick at home.

Pfeifer (*putting the weave on the scales*)   That's what I call a right mess. (*Already giving his attention to a new lot of work.*) Look at the selvedge, broad at one end, narrow at the other. Loose here, pulled together there and barely seventy threads. What do you call this – decent work? A fine effort, I must say.

Weaver Heiber *suppresses tears, stands humiliated and helpless.*

Baecker (*in a low voice to* **Baumert**)   Bastard! He'd charge us for the yarn if he could.

1st Weaver Woman (*having only stepped back a little from the cash desk and helplessly looking around with staring eyes, without moving, musters courage and turns again pleading to the cashier*)   I can soon . . . I don't know, if you don't give me an advance . . . oh Jesus, Jesus.

Pfeifer (*calling across*)   All this calling on Jesus. Leave Lord Jesus in peace. You don't bother with Lord Jesus the rest of the time, Better look after your husband, then we wouldn't see him all the time sitting in the tavern window. We can't give any advance. We have to account for everything here – it's not our money. We have to meet our demands as well. If you work hard and know what you're doing and do your duty in the fear of God, then you'll never need an advance. That's all there is to it.

Neumann   And if a weaver from Bielau earned four times as much as he'd waste four times as much and still get into debt.

1st Weaver Woman (*loudly, as if appealing to everybody's sense of justice*)   I'm really not lazy but I can't carry on like this. I've had two miscarriages. And as for my husband, he can only do half a work-load; he went to the shepherd in Zerlau but he couldn't help him with his trouble either, . . . you can't force things . . . we do all the work we can. For weeks I haven't slept a wink but I expect it'll be all right when I feel some strength in my bones again. (*Imploring him.*) You'll be in my prayers; allow me a few groschen just this once.

Pfelfer (*undisturbed*)   Fiedler – eleven silver groschen.

1st Weaver Woman   Only a few groschen to buy some bread. The farmer won't lend me any more. We've all our children . . .

Neumann (*quietly, with mock seriousness to the* **Office Boy**)   Every year another child Keeps the weaver good and mild.

Office Boy (*completing it*)   Let the cradle be the loom
Living, sitting, dining-room.

Weaver Reimann (*not touching the money which the* **cashier** *has counted out for him*)   We always get thirteen and a half groschen for a web.

Pfeifer   If you don't like it, Reimann, just say the word, There are plenty of weavers. Especially those like you. You get full pay for a full load.

Weaver Reimann   How can it be short of weight?

Pfeifer   Bring a perfect piece of linen and you won't be short of pay.

Weaver Reimann   It is perfect; it's impossible that there are too many flaws.

Pfeifer (*while examining*)   He who weaves well, lives well.

Weaver Heiber *has stayed near* **Pfeifer** *to await a favourable opportunity. He smiled over* **Pfeifer**'s *remark and now approaches him and speaks to him as before.*

Weaver Heiber   I wanted to kindly ask you, Herr Pfeifer, if perhaps you could see your way to have pity and not deduct the five groschen advance today. My old woman's been in bed with cramp ever since Lent. She can't do a stroke of work. So I have to pay a girl to clean the spools. That's why . . .

Pfeifer (*taking snuff*)   Heiber, you're not the only one I've got to deal with today. The others want their turn too.

Weaver Reimann   That's how I got the warp – so that's how I wound it up and took it off again. I can't bring back better than I get.

Pfeifer   If it doesn't suit you, you needn't collect any more yarn. There are people who'd give their right arm for it.

Neumann (*to* **Reimann**)   You don't want to take the money?

Weaver Reimann   I really can't accept it.

Neumann (*without bothering with* **Reimann**)   Heiber – ten silver groschen. Deduct five silver groschen advance. That leaves five silver groschen.

Weaver Heiber (*steps forward, looks at the money, shakes his head incredulously and slowly and awkwardly takes it*)   Oh dear, oh dear! (*Sighing.*) Oh well . . . !

Old Baumert (*to* **Heiber**)   That's life for you, Franz! Nothing but sighing.

Weaver Heiber (*speaks with an effort*)   You see I've a sick girl at home. I need a bottle of medicine.

Old Baumert   What's wrong with her?

Weaver Heiber   You see, she's been poorly ever since she was little. I don't really know . . . well, I can tell you, she was born with it. She's always getting ill, it's in her blood.

Old Baumert   Everybody's got troubles. Where there's poverty, misfortune follows misfortune. There's no end to it and no salvation.

Weaver Heiber   What have you got wrapped in that cloth?

Old Baumert   We had nothing to eat at home. So I had to kill our dog. There wasn't much of him, he was half-starved himself. He was a nice little dog. I didn't want to kill him myself, I didn't have the heart to do it.

Pfeifer (*having examined* **Baecker***'s web, calls*)   Baecker – thirteen and a half silver groschen.

Baecker   I call that alms, not pay. And mean alms at that.

Pfeifer   Will those who have been dealt with leave as quickly as possible. We can't move here as it is.

Baecker (*to those standing near him, without lowering his voice*)   It's a shabby tip, nothing more. And for this we're supposed to work our treadle from early morning to late at night. And when you've worked the loom for eighteen days, night after night, drained, and half dead with the dust and the burning heat, then you're lucky if you've made thirteen and a half silver groschen.

Pfeifer   No complaints here!

Baecker   Don't tell *me* to shut my mouth.

Pfeifer (*jumps up shouting*)   We'll see about that! (*He goes to the glass door and calls into the office.*) Herr Dreissiger, Herr Dreissiger, would you be so kind.

Dreissiger *enters. Early forties. Obese, asthmatic. With a stern look.*

Dreissiger   What's the matter, Pfeifer?

Pfeifer (*angrily*)   Baecker won't keep his mouth shut.

Dreissiger (*squares his shoulders, throws back his head and looks at* **Baecker** *with quivering nostrils*)   I see – Baecker! (*To* **Pfeifer**:) Is that the one?

The employees nod.

Baecker (*impudently*)   That's it, Herr Dreissiger. (*Pointing to himself.*) That is the one – (*Pointing at* **Dreissiger**.) and that's another one.

Dreissiger (*indignantly*)   Who does this man think he is!?

Pfeifer   He's too well off! He'll dance on thin ice once too often.

Baecker (*brutally*)   Keep you mouth shut, you little crawler. His mother must have slept with Lucifer to produce a devil like him.

Dreissiger (*losing his temper, shouts*)   Hold your tongue this instant, or else . . . (*He trembles and advances a few steps.*)

Baecker (*standing his ground*)   I'm not deaf.

Dreissiger (*controls himself, and asks in an apparently business-like manner*)   Isn't this boy one of those . . . ?

Pfeifer   He's a weaver from Bielau. You'll find them wherever there's trouble.

Dreissiger (*trembling*)   Just let me tell you: if it happens once more that a gang of half-drunk, juvenile delinquents pass my house as they did last night – with that disgusting song . . .

Baecker   You mean 'The Song of Blood and Justice'?

Dreissiger   You know quite well which song I mean. Let me tell you: if I hear that once again, I'll get hold of one of you and – I swear I'm not joking – and hand him over to the

State Prosecutor. And when I discover who's responsible for this wretched, so-called song . . .

Baecker   It's a good song!

Dreissiger   One more word and I'll send for the police – immediately. – I don't mess about. – I can deal with louts like you. I've dealt with bigger fish in my time.

Baecker   I can believe it. A true factory owner can eat two or three hundred weavers before breakfast. He won't even leave a a few rotten bones. A man like that has four stomachs, like a cow, and a set of teeth like a wolf. No, it's nothing for him!

Dreissiger (*to his employees*)   This man gets no more work from us.

Baecker   Whether I starve to death at the loom or in a ditch, that's all the same to me.

Dreissiger   Get out! Get out this instant!

Baecker (*firmly*)   First I want my pay.

Dreissiger   How much is due to him, Neumann?

Neumann   Twelve silver groschen, five pfennigs.

Dreissiger (*hastily takes the money from the cashier and throws it on the table, so that some of the coins roll on the floor*)   There! And now quickly! Out of my sight!

Baecker   First I want my pay.

Dreissiger   There's your pay; and if you don't get out at once . . . It's twelve o'clock, my dyers are going off to lunch . . . !

Baecker   I want my pay given to me. This is where it belongs. (*He indicates the palm of his hand.*)

Dreissiger (*to the* **Office Boy**)   Pick it up, Tildner.

The **Office Boy** *picks it up and puts the money in* **Baecker**'*s hand.*

Baecker   Everything's got to be done properly. (*Without hurrying, he deposits the money in an old bag.*)

Dreissiger   Well? (*Impatiently, as* **Baecker** *still hasn't gone.*) Want any help?

Movement breaks out amongst the tightly-packed weavers. Someone lets out a long, deep sigh. Suddenly somebody falls. All interest turns to the new event.

Dreissiger   What's going on there?

Various weavers and weaver women say, 'Someone's fallen down', 'It's a sick little boy' and 'Has be fainted or what?'

Dreissiger   Now what's the matter? Fallen down? (*He approaches.*)

Old Weaver   He's lying there.

They make room. An eight-year-old child can be seen lying on the ground, as if dead.

Dreissiger   Does anyone know the child?

Old Weaver   He's not from our village.

Old Baumert   He looks like one of the Heinrichs. (*He looks at him carefully.*) That's right! He's Heinrich's kid.

Dreissiger   Where do these people live?

Old Baumert   Up near us in Kaschbach, Herr Dreissiger. He's a musician, and during the day he weaves. They've got nine children and a tenth is on the way.

Various weavers and weaver women: 'They're very badly off', 'The rain comes through their roof', 'The mother hasn't got two shirts to share among her nine boys'.

Old Baumert (*touching the child*)   Come on, child, what's the matter with you? Wake up!

Dreissiger   Come and get hold of him. We'll lift him up. It's scandalous to let such a weak child come this long way. Get some water, Pfeifer.

1st Weaver Woman (*helping to lift him up*)   Now don't do anything silly and die on us, child!

Dreissiger   Or brandy, Pfeifer. Brandy is better.

Baecker (*forgotten, has been standing and watching. Now, with one hand on the door-handle, he calls across loudly and mockingly.*)   Try giving him something to eat, then he'll soon come to. (*He goes out.*)

Dreissiger   That man will come to a bad end. Take him under the arm, Neumann. Slowly . . . slowly . . . there . . . there . . . we'll take him to my room. What do you want?

Neumann   He said something, Herr Dreissiger. He moved his lips.

Dreissiger   What do you want, child?

Child (*whispering*)   I'm hungry!

Dreissiger (*turning pale*)   One can't hear what he's saying.

1st Weaver Woman   I think he meant . . .

Dreissiger   We'll soon see. No need to hold things up. – He can lie down on my sofa. We'll hear what the doctor says.

Dreissiger, **Neumann** and **1st Weaver Woman** *take the* **Child** *into the office.*

A movement begins among the weavers like that of school-children when the teacher has left the class-room. They stretch and straighten themselves, they whisper, step from one foot to the other, and in a few seconds there is loud and general conversation.

Old Baumert   I think Baecker is right.

Various weavers and weaver women:
'It's as he said.'
'It's nothing new here that people faint from hunger.'
'God knows what'll happen in the winter if they go on cutting our pay.'
'It's a bad year for potatoes.'
'Nothing will change until we are all flat on our backs.'

Old Baumert   The best thing to do is what the weaver in Nentwich did; put a noose round his neck, and tied himself to the loom. Here, take a pinch, I was in Neurode, my brother-in-law works in the factory there where they make snuff. He gave me a few grains. What are you carrying in your handkerchief?

Old Weaver   A little bit of pearl-barley. Ullbrichmiller's cart drove in front of me. There was a small slit in one of the sacks. I made the most of it.

Old Baumert   There are twenty-two mills in Peterswaldau and for people like us there's nothing.

Old Weaver   You mustn't lose your courage. Something always turn up and helps us carry on.

Weaver Heiber   When we get hungry we must pray to the Fourteen Saints and if that doesn't satisfy us we must put a stone in our mouth and suck it. Isn't that so, Baumert?

Dreissiger, **Pfeifer** *and* **Neumann** *return.*

Dreissiger   It was nothing serious. The child is quite bright again. (*Excited, walking about, puffing.*) But it's still a disgrace. The child is like a blade of grass waiting to be blown over. It's inconceivable how people . . . how parents can be so irrespon-sible. Burdening him with two bundles of cotton on a good one and a half mile walk – it's really hard to credit. I'll simply have to make it a rule that no products will be accepted from children. (*He paces about again in silence.*) Anyway I shall insist that such a thing doesn't happen again. Who gets blamed for it in the end? The factory owners, of course. It's always our fault. If some poor little boy gets trapped in the snow in the winter and falls asleep, some hack will come running and two days later we'll read a horror-story in all the papers. The father, the parents who sent out such a child . . . it's never their fault! Oh no, it's the factory owner who's the scapegoat. The weavers are always handled with velvet gloves, but it's the factory owner who gets it in the neck: he's a man with a heart of stone, a dangerous fellow who's fair game for any press-hound that wants to take a bite. He lives in luxury and pleasure and pays the poor weavers starvation wages. It never occurs to them that such a man has also got worries and sleepless nights; that he runs great risks undreamt of by the workers; that he sometimes doesn't know whether he's coming or going with all that addition, division and multiplication; doing his calculations again and again; that he's got to think of a hundred different things and always, as it were, fighting matters of life and death; he has so much competition that not a day passes without aggravation and loss: they don't make a song-and-dance about that. And who doesn't depend on the factory-owner, who doesn't suck him dry and want to live off him! No, no! You should be in his shoes sometimes, you'd soon get fed up. (*After some reflection.*) Remember how that ruffian, that lout Baecker, carried on just now! Now he'll go and trumpet that I'm God knows how pitiless. How I kick the weavers out over any little thing. Is that true? Am I so heartless?

Several voices: 'No, Herr Dreissiger!'

That's what I think too. And then these scabs march around singing nasty songs about us factory-owners; they talk about hunger but have enough to drink their liquor by the quart. They ought to stick their noses in somewhere else and smell the conditions of the linen-weavers. They can talk about hardship. But you people, you cotton-weavers, the way things are with you, you should quietly thank God. And I ask the old, industrious and efficient weavers who are here: can a worker who knows his trade make a living with me or not?

Very many voices: 'Yes, Herr Dreissiger'.

You see! – A man like Baecker wouldn't understand this. But I advise you, keep those louts in check. If things get too hot I'll quit. I'll give up the business and then you'll see what's what. Then you'll see who gives you work. Certainly not the honourable Baecker.

1st Weaver Woman *has gone up to* **Dreissiger** *and, with obsequious humility, brushes the dust off his coat.*

1st Weaver Woman   You've got a spot on your coat, Herr Dreissiger, sir.

Dreissiger   Business is lousy, you know that yourselves. I keep putting money in instead of earning it. But in spite of that I make sure that my weavers always keep in work, then I expect this to be recognised. The goods lie there in thousands of bundles and I don't know whether I'll ever be able to sell them. I've just heard that a lot of weavers in this district have no work at all, and therefore . . . well, Pfeifer can explain the rest to you. The thing is: so that you can see the good-will . . . naturally, I can't hand out charity,

I'm not rich enough for that, but up to a certain point I can give the unemployed an opportunity to earn at least a little. That this involves me in immense risks is my affair. The way I look at it is if someone can work enough to buy himself a cheese sandwich every day, that's better than having nothing at all. Am I right?

Several voices: 'Yes, yes, Herr Dreissiger!'

I'm quite ready to employ another two hundred weavers. Under what conditions, Pfeifer will explain to you. (*He is about to go.*)

1st Weaver Woman (*stands in his way, breathless, imploring and urgent*) Dear Herr Dreissiger, what I wanted to ask you very kindly, whether perhaps . . . I've had two miscarriages.

Dreissiger (*hurriedly*) Talk to Pfeifer, my good woman. I'm late as it is. (*He leaves her standing.*)

Weaver Reimann (*also stands in his way, in an injured and accusing tone*) Herr Dreissiger, I really must complain. Herr Pfeifer gave me . . . I've always got twelve and a half groschen for my webs . . .

Dreissiger (*interrupting him*) There's the manager – ask him. He's the one in charge.

Weaver Heiber (*stopping* **Dreissiger**) Herr Dreissiger, sir – (*Stuttering and incoherent.*) I'd like to beg you most kindly whether perhaps you could see your way . . . whether perhaps Herr Pfeifer could . . . could perhaps . . .

Dreissiger What do you want?

Weaver Heiber The advance I had last time, I mean, had . . .

Dreissiger I don't know what you're talking about.

Weaver Heiber I was in some difficulty because . . .

Dreissiger Pfeifer's business, Pfeifer's business. I really can't . . . settle your business with Pfeifer.

He escapes into the office. The supplicants look at each other helplessly. One after the other, they retreat, sighing deeply.

Pfeifer (*resuming the inspection*) Well, Anna, what have you brought?

Old Baumert How much were you thinking of paying for a web, Herr Pfeifer?

Pfeifer For a web, ten silver groschen.

Old Baumert That's what I thought.

Movement among the weavers, whispering and grumbling.

End of Act One.

Act Two

A room in the house of Wilhelm Ansorge in Kaschbach in the Eulengebirge. It is a narrow room, not six feet high, the floor is rotting away and the rafters are black with soot. In the room are two young girls: **Emma** *and* **Bertha Baumert**, *sitting at their looms. In front of a spooling wheel sits* **Mother Baumert**, *a bent old woman. Her son* **August**, *who is an idiot with a small body and head and long, spidery limbs, is sitting on a stool by another spooling wheel; he is about twenty years old.*

The weak, rose-coloured evening light forces its way through two small windows, holes in the left wall which are partially stuffed with paper and straw. It falls onto the loose, light blonde hair of the girls, onto their thin, bare shoulders and thin waxen necks and onto the folds of their coarse blouses, which, except for short skirts of rough linen, constitutes their clothing. The warm glow falls fully upon the face, neck and chest of the old woman: a face emaciated to a skeleton, with folds and wrinkles in its bloodless skin. Her sunken eyes are inflamed and watery as a result of the lint, the smoke, and from working by lamplight; a long goitre neck with folds and sinews. Her sunken chest is packed with cloths and scarfs.

Part of the right wall, together with the stone and stove bench, the bedstead and several brightly tinted holy pictures, are still getting some light. On the bar of the stove rags are hanging up to dry, while behind it is piled with old rubbish. Old pots and cooking utensils stand on the stow hench, potato peelings are laid out on a piece of paper to dry. From the rafters hang skeins and reels of yarn. Baskets with spools stand beside the looms. In the back wall there is a door without a lock. Leaning against the wall beside it is a bundle of willow switches. Several damaged quarter-bushel baskets lie about near them. The room is filled with the sound of the looms, the rhythmic movement of the lathe which shakes both floor and walls, the shuffle and clicking of the rapid shuttle moving backwards and forwards. Amongst this is the deep constant whirring of the spooling wheels, which sounds like the humming of bumblebees.

Mother Baumert (*in a whining, exhausted voice, as the girls stop weaving and lean over the web*) Do you have to knot it again?

Emma (*the older of the girls, she is twenty-two, as she knots the torn yarn*) Call this yarn?

Bertha (*fifteen years old*)   There's something wrong with the warp.

Emma   Where has he got to? He's been gone since 9 o'clock.

Mother Baumert   I know, I know! Where do you think he could be?

Bertha   Don't worry, mother!

Mother Baumert   It's always a worry!

Emma *continues to weave.*

Bertha   Wait, Emma!

Emma   What is it?

Bertha   I thought I heard someone coming.

Emma   It'll be Ansorge coming home.

Fritz (*a small, barefoot, ragged boy of four runs in crying*)   Mother, I'm hungry . . .

Emma   Wait, Fritzy, wait a bit! Grandfather's coming soon. He'll bring some bread and some beans.

Fritz   I'm so hungry, mother!

Emma   I told you. Don't be so stupid. He'll be coming any minute. Hell bring a nice loaf of bread and some beans to make soup . . . and when we stop work mother will take the potato peelings to the farmer and he'll give us a nice pitcher of buttermilk for our little boy.

Fritz   But where is grandfather?

Emma   At the factory, delivering a web, Fritzy.

Fritz   At the factory?

Emma   Yes, Fritzy, yes! Down to Dreissiger's in Peterswaldau.

Fritz   Does he get bread there?

Emma   Yes, of course. He gives him money so that he can buy bread.

Fritz   Does grandfather get a lot of money?

Emma (*impatiently*)   Oh stop it boy, all these questions! (*She continues to weave, so does* **Bertha**.)

After a few moments they stop again.

Bertha   August, go and ask Ansorge if we could have a little light.

August *goes, accompanied by* **Fritz**.

Mother Baumert (*whining with childish fear*)   Children, children, what's happened to him?

Bertha   I expect he'll have gone to see Hauffern.

Mother Baumert (*crying*)   As long as he hasn't gone to the tavern!

Emma   Don't cry mother! Father's not like that.

Mother Baumert (*beside herself with fear*)   Oh dear, oh dear, what will become of us? If he . . . if he comes home . . . if he's drunk and doesn't bring anything? There's not so much as a handful of salt in the house, not a crumb of bread, not a shovel of coal for the fire . . .

Bertha   Let it be, mother! The moon's out tonight. We'll take August with us and collect some firewood.

Mother Baumert   Then the forester will catch you!

Ansorge, *an Old Weaver of gigantic build, who has to duck to get into the room, sticks his head and shoulders through the door. His hair and beard are wild.*

Ansorge   What is it?

Bertha   Can we have some light?

Ansorge (*in a low voice, as though in the presence of someone sick*)   It's still light enough.

Mother Baumert   Now you want us to sit in the dark.

Ansorge   I have to be careful. (*He withdraws.*)

Bertha   You see how stingy he is?

Emma   So now we have to wait till it suits him.

Frau Heinrich *enters. A woman of thirty. She is pregnant. Her tired face expresses tortured anxiety and fearful tension.*

Frau Heinrich   Evening everyone.

Mother Baumert   Well, Frau Heinrich, what have you got for us?

Frau Heinrich (*limping*)   I've trodden on a splinter.

Bertha   Come and sit down. I'll see if I can get it out for you.

Frau Heinrich *sits down,* **Bertha** *kneels in front of her and busies herself with her foot.*

Mother Baumert   How are things at home, Frau Heinrich?

Frau Heinrich (*desperately*)   It can't go on like this. (*She fights in vain against tears; she is silently crying*).

Mother Baumert   The best thing that could happen would be if the good Lord had pity on people like us and took us from this world.

Frau Heinrich (*no longer in control of herself*)   My poor children are starving! (*She sobs and moans.*) I don't know what to do any more, whatever you do, you run around till you drop. I'm more dead than alive, and yet it makes no difference. Nine hungry mouths and I'm supposed to feed them. What with? Last night I had a crust of bread which wasn't even enough for the two little ones. Which one should I have given it to? All of them cried 'Me, mother! Me, mother!'. . . And this is while I can still get about. What will happen when I'm confined? Our last few potatoes were lost in the flood. We haven't a scrap of anything.

Bertha (*has removed the splinter and washed the wound*)   I'll tie a rag round it – (*To* **Emma**.) – see if you can find one!

Mother Baumert   We're no better off, Frau Heinrich.

Frau Heinrich   At least you've got your girls. You have a husband who can work, but mine was laid low again last week. He carried on so! I was frightened to death and didn't know what to do with him. When he gets these fits he just has to lie in bed for a week.

Mother Baumert   Mine isn't much better. He's just about to collapse too – it's his chest and his back, and we're down to the last pfennig. If he doesn't come back with a few groschen today I don't know how we'll carry on.

Emma   That's no more than the truth, Frau Heinrich, we've got to the point . . . Father had to take our little dog to be slaughtered so that we could have some solid food in our stomachs.

Frau Heinrich   You haven't got just a handful of flour to spare?

Mother Baumert   Not even that, Frau Heinrich; there's not even a grain of salt left.

Frau Heinrich   Well I don't know what to do!

She rises, stands still, thinking.

I really don't know! – there's no help for it. (*Crying in anger and fear.*) I'd be satisfied with pig swill! I just can't go home empty-handed. I just can't. May God forgive me, I don't know what else I can do. (*She limps off quickly.*)

Mother Baumert (*calls after her warningly*)   Frau Heinrich. Frau Heinrich! Don't do anything silly!

Bertha   She won't harm herself, don't you worry about that.

Emma   She always carries on like that. (*She sits down again on her stool and weaves for a few seconds.*)

August comes in, lighting the way for his father, **Old Baumert**, who is dragging a bundle of yarn.

Mother Baumert   God in heaven, where have you been all this time?

Old Baumert   Don't bite my head off. First let me get my breath back. Why don't you look who's come with me.

Moritz Jaeger *ducks under the door as he comes in. A sturdy, red-cheeked Reservist of medium height. His Hussar's cap is set at a jaunty angle and he wears a smart uniform, polished boots, and a clean, collarless shirt. Having entered, he stands to attention and gives a military salute.*

Moritz Jaeger (*briskly*)   Good evening, Aunt Baumert!

Mother Baumert   Well, well! You're home again? So you haven't forgotten us after all? Come and sit down here.

Emma (*wipes a wooden stool with her skirt and slides it towards him*)   Good evening, Moritz! Have you come to see how poor people live?

Jaeger   Tell me, Emma, I wouldn't believe it. You've got a boy nearly old enough to be a soldier? Where did you find him?

Bertha (*taking the few bits of food her father is carrying, puts the meat in the pan and pushes it in the oven while* **August** *lights the fire*)   Do you remember a weaver called Finger?

Mother Baumert   He used to live here with us. He wanted to marry her, but his lungs were already going. I warned the girl often enough. Did she listen to me? Now he's been dead and gone a long time and she has to try to raise the boy. Now tell me, Moritz, how have things been with you?

Old Baumert   Leave him alone, mother. You can see he's well fed, anyway. He can laugh at all of us. He's got clothes like a Prince and a silver watch. And on top of that, ten thalers in cash.

Jaeger (*swaggering, with a triumphant smile on his face*)   I can't complain. I've never been badly off as a soldier.

Old Baumert   He's been a batman to a cavalry officer. Listen to him, he talks like a gentleman!

Jaeger   I got so used to their posh talk I can't stop myself!

Mother Baumert   Well, would you believe it! Such a good-for-nothing as he was, and he comes into all this money! You were no use for anything; you couldn't spool one bobbin without getting it tangled. Always running away – setting traps for mice and snares for robins was what you really liked; well isn't that so?

Jaeger   It's true, Aunt. But I never caught any robins, only swallows.

Emma   It was no good telling him that swallows are poisonous.

Jaeger   It was all the same to me. So how have things been with you, Aunt Baumert?

Mother Baumert   Oh, Jesus, it's been very, very bad these last four years. I have these pains, you see. See my fingers, I don't know if it's rheumatics or what it is. I'm in so much misery! I can hardly move a limb. Nobody would believe what pain I suffer.

Old Baumert   It's bad with her. She won't last long.

Bertha   In the morning we have to dress her; in the evening we undress her. We have to feed her like a small child.

Mother Baumert (*in a plaintive, whining voice*)   They have to do everything for me. I'm more than sick, I'm a burden. How often I've prayed to the good Lord to take me away. Oh Jesus, Jesus, it's too much for me. I just don't know . . . people might think . . . but I've been used to working since I was a child . . . I always pulled my weight and now all of a sudden – (*She tries in vain to rise.*) – I just can't do it any longer. – I have a good husband and good children, but all I can do is sit by and watch them . . . ! Look at the girls! No blood in them – they're as pale as a linen sheet. The treadle can never stop no matter how the girl feels. What sort of life is it for them? The whole year they can't get off the bench. They haven't even a dress to show for all their work. Nothing to wear to go out amongst people or to set foot in the church for a bit of comfort. They look as if they'd been cut off the gallows, young girls of fifteen and twenty.

Bertha (*by the oven*)   It's beginning to smoke again!

Old Baumert   Look at that smoke. You'd think something could be done about it – it's falling to pieces, that stove. We can't mend it – we just have to swallow the soot. We are all coughing, one worse than the other. If we cough we cough, and if we choke to death, who'll care?

Jaeger   That's Ansorge's job. He's got to repair it.

Bertha   I'd like to see what he'd say if we asked. He grumbles enough as it is.

Mother Baumert   We take up too much room for his liking.

Old Baumert   And if we said anything, we'd be kicked out. He hasn't had any rent from us for nearly six months.

Mother Baumert   A man like him, on his own, could be a bit more helpful.

Old Baumert   He's got nothing either, mother. Things are bad enough for him, even if he doesn't make much of it.

Mother Baumert   He's got his house.

Old Baumert   No, Mother, what are you talking about! There's hardly a floorboard he can call his own.

Jaeger *has sat down. He takes a small pipe out of one coat pocket and a small bottle of brandy from the other.*

Jaeger   It can't go on like this. I've been amazed to see how people live here. Dogs live better than you in the towns.

Old Baumert (*eagerly*)   That's right! You've noticed it too? And if we say anything they say that times are bad.

Ansorge *enters with an earthenware bowl of soup in one hand and a half-finished basket in the other.*

Ansorge   Welcome, Moritz! So you're back again?

Jaeger   Thank you, Father Ansorge.

Ansorge (*pushing his bowl in the oven*)   Just look at you! You look like a Count!

Old Baumert   Show him the lovely watch. He's brought a new suit and ten thalers cash!

Ansorge (*shaking his head*)   Well, well, would you believe it! –

Emma (*filling a small sack with potato peelings*)   I'm going to take the peelings now. Perhaps it'll be enough for a little milk. (*She goes.*)

Jaeger (*while they watch him admiringly*)   Remember how often you made things hot for me. They'll show Moritz, you used to say, just wait till he gets in the army! Well, as you can see, things have gone pretty well for me. I got my stripe after six months. You've got to show willing, that's the main thing. I polished the sergeant's boots, I groomed his horse, I fetched his beer, I was as sharp as a weasel, always there: cleaned the cannons till they shone; first in the stable, first at roll-call, first in the saddle; and when the time came to attack, quick march – hell and damnation!! – kept watch like a guard dog. I thought to myself, you'll get no help from anyone, you're on your own. I kept my head and it worked. And one day the Captain said in front of the whole squadron, this is how a Hussar ought to be!

Silence. He lights his pipe.

Ansorge (*shaking his head*)   So you've been lucky. Well, well, would you believe it.

He *sits on the floor with the can beside him and works on the basket, holding it between his knees.*

Old Baumert   Let's hope you've brought some of that luck with you. – What about a drink?

Jaeger   Of course, Father Baumert. And when it's finished, there's more.

He throws a coin on the table.

Ansorge (*with a stupid grin of surprise*)   Well, well, such goings on! . . . A roast in the oven, a quart of brandy – (*He drinks from the bottle*) – your health, Moritz! Well, well, well!

From now on the brandy bottle is passed round.

Old Baumert   If we could just have a bit of roast now and again, even if it was only on Holy Days, instead of never seeing meat for months on end. Now we'll have to wait till another little dog comes by, like this one, four weeks ago. But things like that don't happen very often.

Ansorge   Did you have him killed?

Old Baumert   He would have starved to death anyway . . .

Ansorge   Well, well, well . . .

Mother Baumert   He was such a nice, friendly dog.

Jaeger   You still haven't lost your taste for roast dog?

Old Baumert   If only we had enough!

Mother Baumert   A bit of meat does you good.

Old Baumert   Why, have you lost your taste for it? Stay with us for a while, Moritz, and you'll soon get it back!

Ansorge (*sniffing*)   Well, well, well . . . It smells good . . . I'll wager it tastes good.

Old Baumert (*sniffing*)   It's the real thing all right.

Ansorge   Tell us what you think, Moritz. You know about the outside world. Will things change for us weavers or what?

Jaeger   I should hope so!

Ansorge   Up here we can't live and we can't die. Believe you me, things are bad for us. You can fight to the last, but in the end you have to give in. Poverty gnaws at the roof over your head and the floor under your feet. In the old days, when you could still get work at the factory, you could just about carry on in spite of the worry and hardship. But I haven't been able to get any work for more than a year. Basket-weaving is finished too, you can barely scrape a living at it. I weave into the night and when I fall into bed I've earned a groschen and six pfennigs. You've got education, you tell me, is that enough with everything going up? I have to throw three thalers away in house tax, one thaler in ground rent, and three in interest. I can count on earning fourteen thalers; that leaves me with seven thalers for the whole year. With that I have to cook, eat, dress myself, get shoes and keep my clothes repaired. I have to have a place to live in and God knows what else. Is it surprising when there isn't enough to go round?

Old Baumert   Someone ought to go to Berlin and tell the King what state we're in.

Jaeger   That wouldn't be much good, Father Baumert. The papers are full of it. But the rich, they twist and turn . . . they can outwit the best Christians.

Old Baumert (*shaking his head*)   So they can't even do anything in Berlin!

Ansorge   Tell me Moritz, is that really true? Is there no law against it? If I work my fingers to the bone and can't even pay the rent, can the farmer still take my house away? The farmer wants his money so I don't know what'll happen. If I have to leave this house . . . (*Through tears.*) I was born here, my father sat at his loom here for over forty years. How often he used to say to mother: 'Mother, when I've gone, hold on to the house. I've earned this house,' he said. 'Every nail is a sleepless night, every beam a year of dry bread.' You would have thought . . .

Jaeger   They take the last thing you've got – they've the right.

Ansorge   Well, well, well! If it comes to that it would be better if they carried me out rather than I should spend my last days without a home. What's death? My father was glad to die. Only right at the end he got a bit frightened. But when I crawled into bed with him, he was quiet again. – When I think of it – I was a boy of thirteen at the time. I was tired and went to sleep next to him – I didn't know any better – and when I woke up he was already cold.

Mother Baumert (*after a pause*)   Give Ansorge his soup, Bertha, out of the oven.

Bertha   Eat this, Father Ansorge!

Ansorge (*eating while crying*)   Well, well, well . . .

Old Baumert *has begun to eat the meat from the pan.*

Mother Baumert   Wait, Father, wait till Bertha's set the table.

Old Baumert (*chewing*)   It's two years since I last had a proper dinner. Soon after I sold my Sunday clothes we bought a piece of pork with the money. I've had no meat from that day to this.

Jaeger   The likes of us don't need meat. The factory owners eat it for us. They wade about in fat up to here. If you don't believe me, go down to Bielau or to Peterswaldau and see for yourselves. It's like Fairyland! One factory owner's castle after another. Palace next to palace! With glass in the windows and turrets and iron fences. None of them feels the pinch. They can afford roasts and cakes, carriages and coaches, governesses and God knows what else. There's no end to their greed! They don't know what to do with all that wealth and pleasure.

Ansorge   In the old days things were different. The factory owners allowed the weavers to live too. Today they keep it all to themselves. And what I say is that it's because the upper class doesn't believe any more, neither in God nor the Devil. They don't know about Commandments and punishments. So they steal our last crust of bread so we lose the little strength we've got. It's them that's to blame for all our troubles. If our factory owners were better men, we wouldn't be having such bad times.

Jaeger   Listen, and I'll read you something. (*He pulls some pieces of paper from his pocket.*) Here, August, run down to the tavern and get another quart. What's so funny, you never stop laughing?

Mother Baumert   I don't know what's the matter with the boy. He's always happy. He laughs and laughs, come what may. (*To* **August**.) Go on, run along!

August goes *off with the empty bottle*.

Well, Father, you know a good thing when you taste it!

Old Baumert (*still eating, stimulated by the food and drink*)   Moritz, you're the man for us! You can read and write; you know how things are in our trade; you feel for us poor weavers; you should take charge of things here.

Jaeger   You think so? Well, I'm game! There's nothing I'd like more than to take on those old factory bosses and make them jump, I wouldn't mind at all. I'm an easy-going bloke, but when I'm rubbed up the wrong way and lose my temper, watch out! I'll take Dreissiger in one hand and Dietrich in the other and knock their heads together till the sparks fly! – If we stood together we could really make things hot for those factory owners . . . we don't need the King or the Government for that. We could just say we want this and that or this and not that and they'd soon whistle another tune. If they saw us sticking together they'd soon show us the white flag. I know those pious brothers – they're a lot of cowardly bastards.

Mother Baumert   It's no more than the truth. No one can say I'm a bad woman. I've always said there's room for the rich people too, but when it comes to this . . .

Jaeger   As for me, the devil take them all – they don't deserve any better.

Bertha   Where's Father?

Old Baumert *has quietly disappeared.*

Mother Baumert   I don't know where he's gone.

Bertha   Maybe he's not used to the meat?

Mother Baumert (*beside herself, crying*)   You see? You see? He can't keep it down!

Old Baumert (*returns, crying with despair*)   I must be near my end! They've nearly got me! You manage to get something good to eat and you can't keep it down. (*He sits by the stove, still crying.*)

Jaeger (*in a sudden fanatical outburst*)   And there are people not far from here, lawyers and the like, with big fat bellies, with nothing better to do than to watch the days go by. They're the ones who say the weavers would be all right, if they weren't so lazy.

Ansorge   They're not human beings. They're monsters.

Jaeger   Don't worry. They'll get what they deserve. Me and Red Baecker, we had a few drinks and before we left we sang them the Song of Blood and Justice.

Ansorge   Oh Jesus, is that that song?

Jaeger   Yes, yes, I've got it here.

Ansorge   I think it's called Dreissiger's song or something, isn't it?

Jaeger   I'll read it to you.

Mother Baumert   Who wrote it?

Jaeger   Nobody knows. Now listen –
He reads, haltingly, like a schoolboy, with wrong emphasis, but with unmistakable passion. Everything is in his voice: pain, anger, hate and thirst for vengeance.

'This is a place which has a Court
Worse than the Inquisition;
No sentence is pronounced, instead
Immediate perdition.

Your torture will be long and slow,
And painful every breath,
Your screams will count as witnesses
Until relieved by death.'

Old Baumert, *captured by the words of the song and deeply stirred, has several times resisted the temptation to interrupt* **Jaeger**. *Now he can contain himself no longer.*

Old Baumert (*stammering, amid laughter and tears to his wife*)   This is the torture chamber. The man who wrote this, Mother, told the truth. You know that, all right . . . how did it go? 'Your screams will count as witnesses'?

Jaeger   'Witnesses, until relieved by death.'

Old Baumert   That's just how it is with us, every single day. From morning till night . . .

While **Ansorge**, *who has stopped his work, listens with deep emotion and* **Mother Baumert** *and* **Bertha** *continually wipe their eyes,* **Jaeger** *goes on.*

Jaeger   'The hangman's name is Dreissiger
Assisted by his clerks.
They strap you tightly to the rack
And snap at you like sharks.
You scroundrels all,
You Satan's brood . . .'

Old Baumert (*stamping and shaking with anger*)   Yes, Satan's brood!!!

Jaeger (*reading*)   '. . . You denizens of Hell,
You feed upon the helpless poor
And make your stomachs swell.'

Ansorge   Yes, that's just how it is.

Old Baumert (*clenching his fist, threateningly*)   'You feed upon the helpless poor − '!

Jaeger (*reading*)   'No use to plead with them or beg,
They're deaf to all appeals.
"If you don't like it, go and gnaw
Rotten potato peels." '

Old Baumert   How did it go? 'No use to plead with them or beg'? Every word . . . every word is as true as the Bible! 'No use to plead with them or beg!'

Ansorge   That's it. 'No use to plead . . .'

Jaeger (*reading*)   'Who wants to live in misery
Without a crust of bread?
You'd think they would be merciful –
They'd rather we were dead.
Now pity is a fine old word
To cannibals unknown.
They've but a single aim in life:
To reap what we have sown.'

Old Baumert (*jumps up, excited to the point of frenzy*)   'To reap what we have sown.' That's right! We sow and they reap. Here I am, Robert Baumert, master weaver of Kaschbach. Who can stand up and say . . . I've been an honest man all my life and now look at me! What have I got to show for it? Look at me! What have they done to me? 'Your torture will be long and slow.' (*He stretches out his arms.*) Here, feel them, skin and bone. 'You scroundrels all, you Satan's brood!' (*He collapses into a chair, weeping with despair and anger.*)

Ansorge (*hurls the basket into the corner, rises, trembling with anger from head to foot and stammers*)   And it's got to change, that's what I say – NOW! We won't stand for it any longer, we won't stand for it I tell you, come what may!

End of Act Two.

Act Three

The bar of a tavern in Peterswaldau. It is a large room with a beamed ceiling supported by a wooden column in the middle, which is surrounded by a table. To the right of the column, which obscures the door jamb in the back wall, is the entrance to the tavern. Through the door can be seen a large room containing barrels and brewing implements. In the corner, to the right of the door, is the bar counter – a wooden partition, five to six feet in height, with shelves for bar utensils. Against the wall beside it is a cupboard containing rows of bottles; between the partition and the cupboard is a small space for the barman. In front of the bar counter is a table with a colourful cloth on it. A pretty lamp hangs above it, several wicker chairs surround it. To the right is a door marked 'Weinstube', which leads into the exclusive saloon. Downstage right is an old grandfather clock. On the left of the entrance along the back wall stands a table with bottles and glasses and further in the corner a large tiled stove. The left wall has three small windows. Beneath them is a bench and under each window is a large wooden table at right angles to the wall. There are benches with backs standing behind and in front of each table. At each end under the window is a wooden chair. The entire room is painted blue with posters, coloured prints and reproductions of oil paintings, including a portrait of Frederick William IV on the walls.

Scholz Welzel, *a good-natured giant of more than fifty, is drawing beer from a barrel into a glass.* **Frau Welzel** *is ironing near the stove. She is a sturdy, cleanly clad woman of barely thirty-five years.* **Anna Welzel**, *a pretty seventeen-year-old girl with lovely red-gold hair, sits behind the table embroidering. She is neatly dressed. She stops work for a moment and listens as from the distance comes the sound of schoolchildren singing funeral hymns.*

Master Wiegand, *the carpenter, sits at the same table in his working clothes with a glass of Bavarian beer. He is a man one can't help noticing. He knows what it takes to get on in the world: cunning, quick-wittedness and ruthless ambition. A travelling salesman sitting at the column table is eating a steak with enjoyment. He is of medium height, well-fed, inclined to cheerfulness. He is fashionably dressed. His luggage – valise, sample-case, umbrella, overcoat, and travelling rug – are on the chairs beside him.*

Welzel (*aside to* **Wiegand**, *as he serves the travelling salesman with a glass of beer*)   All hell's let loose in Peterswaldau today.

Wiegand (*he has a sharp, trumpeting voice*)   Well it's delivery day up at Dreissiger's.

Frau Welzel   It's not usually so lively.

Wiegand   Maybe it's because he's taking on two hundred new weavers today.

Frau Welzel (*still ironing*)   Yes, that'll be why. If he asks for two hundred, six hundred will have turned up. We've got enough of them.

Wiegand   Jesus, more than enough. Even when they're starving they don't die. They just keen putting more children into the world than we can use.

The hymns become louder.

What with the funeral on top of everything. Weaver Fabish died.

Welzel   He took his time over it. He'd been looking like a ghost for years.

Wiegand   Believe me, Welzel, I've never glued together such a tiny coffin. That corpse weighed less than ninety pounds.

Salesman (*eating*)   I can't understand it . . . wherever you look in every paper, you read the most horrifying stories about the weavers' hardships. You get the impression that everybody around here is three-quarters dead. And then you see a funeral like this. I'd just arrived in the village. Brass band, teachers, schoolchildren, the pastor and a procession of people behind – God, it's as if the Emperor of China were being buried! If they have enough money to pay for that . . . ! (*He drinks his beer. After putting down the glass, lightly.*) Isn't that so, Miss? Aren't I right?

Anna *smiles with embarrassment and continues her embroidery.*

Salesman   A pair of slippers for father, eh?

Welzel   Oh, I wouldn't wear things like that on my feet.

Salesman   Come, come! I'd give half my fortune if the slippers were for me!

Frau Welzel   He doesn't appreciate things like that.

Wiegand (*having cleared his throat several times, he moves the chair in an attempt to attract attention*)   This gentleman has expressed surprise about the funeral. Wouldn't you say, young lady, that this was, in fact, a small funeral?

Salesman   Yes, but what I say is that it must have cost an enormous lot of money. Where do they get the money from?

Wiegand   Excuse me, sir, I don't think you understand the ways of our poorer classes. Let me tell you they have very exaggerated notions about the respect due and the duty owed to their dear departed. If it happens to be a parent, it's a matter of superstition to scrape together every penny from wherever they can. And if the children haven't got it, they borrow from the nearest man who has. And that's how they get up to their ears in debt. The Reverend Pastor is owed money, the Sexton and everybody else. And the drink and the food and things like that . . . I've nothing against filial piety, but not if the bereaved have to spend the rest of their lives trying to meet their obligations.

Salesman   If I may say so, surely the pastor should talk them out of such foolishness?

Wiegand   I beg your pardon, sir, but I must say something in their defence. Every little parish must maintain its place of worship and the shepherd of its flock. In the case of these big funerals, the clergy receives more than its share. The more the burial costs, the more there is in the plate. If you know how things are, you'll understand why the priests don't like small funerals.

Hornig *enters. He is a small, bow-legged old man with a rope round his shoulders and chest. He is a rag-and-bone man.*

Hornig   Greetings, all! Can I have a drink? Well, young lady, have you got any rags for me? (*Seeing* **Anna**.) Ah, young. Anna! Pretty hair ribbons! Shirt tapes! . . . garters, lovely pins! Hairpins, hooks and eyes, all for a few rags. (*In a changed tone:*) The rags will be turned into lovely white paper, and your sweetheart can write you a letter on it.

Anna   Thank you, but I haven't got a sweetheart.

Frau Welzel (*busying herself with the iron*)   That's her. Won't hear of marrying.

Salesman (*jumps up looking pleasantly surprised, goes to the table and holds out his hand to* **Anna**) You're quite right, Miss! Do as I have done. Come on, shake hands on it! We'll both stay single!

Anna (*blushing, gives him her hand*)   But you're married already?

Salesman   God forbid! I only pretend to be. You thought because I was wearing this ring . . .? I only wear it to prevent unsolicited attacks on my irresistible charms! But I'm not afraid of you! (*He puts the ring in his pocket.*) Tell me seriously, Miss, wouldn't you like to get just a little bit married?

Anna (*shaking her head*)   Get away with you!

Frau Welzel   She'll stay single unless someone very special turns up.

Salesman   Well why not? There was a rich Silesian businessman who married his mother's chambermaid and the rich factory-owner Dreissiger married an inn-keeper's daughter. She isn't half as pretty as you, Miss, and she drives around in a carriage with liveried servants. So why not? (*He walks about, stretching his legs.*) I'll have a cup of coffee.

Ansorge and **Old Baumert** enter. *Each with a pack, they sit quietly and humbly with* **Hornig** *at the table downstage left.*

Welzel   Welcome! Nice to see you again, Father Ansorge!

Hornig   So you've come crawling out from under your stone?

Ansorge (*awkwardly and visibly embarrassed*)   I've been to collect another web.

Old Baumert   He wants to work for ten groschen.

Ansorge   I would never have done it but basket-making has come to an end.

Wiegand   It's better than nothing. He's doing it to spread the work around. I'm on very good terms with Dreissiger, A week ago, I took out his double windows, and we had a chat. He's only doing it from the goodness of his heart.

Ansorge   Well, well, well.

Welzel (*serving the weavers their drinks*)   Here you are. Tell me Ansorge: how long is it since you had a shave? – This gentleman wants to know.

Salesman (*calling over to them*)   Shame on you Herr Welzel, I never said that. I only noticed the master-weaver on account of his dignified appearance. You don't often see such giants.

Ansorge (*scratching his head with embarassment*)   Well. well, well.

Salesman   Such figures of strength are very rarely seen these days. We've been weakened by civilization, I'm always pleased to see an example of natural man. Look at his bushy eyebrows and his wild beard.

Hornig   You see, sir, it's like this; these people can't afford a barber and a razor is even more out of the question. What grows, grows. There's no way of keeping up appearances.

Salesman   My apologies, sir, I never intended . . . (*Quietly to the* **Inn-Keeper**:) Dare one offer the hairy monster a glass of beer?

Welzel   I don't think he'd take it, he's got funny ideas.

Salesman   Well I won't try then. Permit me, Miss? (*He sits at* **Anna**'s *table.*) Ever since I came in, I've been blinded by the glory of your hair: its gentle brilliance, its soft curves, its fullness! (*Enraptured, he kisses the tips of his fingers.*) And the colour . . . like ripening corn. If you came to Berlin with that hair you'd create a sensation. Parole d'honneur. You could even be presented at Court . . . (*He leans back to admire her hair.*) Magnificent! Absolutely magnificent!

Wiegand   That's how she came by her nick-name.

Salesman   What's that?

Anna (*giggling to herself*)   Oh stop it!

Hornig   They call you 'The Little Vixen' don't they?

Welzel   Now stop it! You'll turn the girl's head. She's full of silly ideas as it is. Today she wants a Count, tomorrow it'll be a Duke.

Frau Welzel   Leave the girl alone, Father. It's no crime to want to get on in life. Not everyone thinks as you do, It's just as well or nobody would move an inch – we'd all stop where we are. If Dreissiger's grandfather had thought as you do, he'd have stayed a poor weaver all his life. Now he's worth a fortune. And old Tromtra was only a poor weaver and now he's got twelve estates and he's been ennobled.

Wiegand   She's right, Welzel. In this case, your wife knows what she's talking about. I can vouch for that. If I'd thought the way you do what would have happened to my seven apprentices?

Hornig   You know what's what. We've got to admit that. The weaver may be alive and kicking but you're already busy varnishing his coffin.

Wiegand   If you want to get on in the world you've got to keep your eyes open.

Hornig   That's more than can be said for your customers. You know better than any doctor when a weaver's child is about to die.

Wiegand (*scarcely smiling, suddenly angry*)   And you know better than the police who the weavers are who help themselves to a bit of extra yarn every week. You come for the rags but you are quite happy to pick up the extras.

Hornig   And the flowers bloom in the churchyard. The more of us go to sleep in our wooden suits, the better the tailor likes it. You look at all these children's graves, pat yourself on the belly and say, 'It's been a good year again. The little darlings have dropped like ladybirds from the trees. Now I can afford another drink every week.'

Wiegand   At least that doesn't make me a receiver of stolen goods.

Hornig   The most you do is to double-charge the rich manufacturers or to help yourself to some timber from Dreissiger's new house on a dark night.

Wiegand (*turning his back on him*)   Gabble on if you want to but leave me out of it. (*Suddenly:*) Hornig the Big-Mouth!

Hornig   Wiegand the Vulture!

Wiegand (*to the others*)   He can put a curse on cattle.

Hornig   Be careful! I might put my curse on you.
Wiegand *turns pale.*

Frau Welzel (*having gone out, returns with coffee for the*
Salesman)   Would you prefer to have your coffee in the
saloon?

Salesman   What gave you that idea! (*With a yearning look at*
Anna). I shall sit here until I die.

A young **Forester** *and a* **Peasant** *enter, the latter carrying a whip.*

Forester ⎫
Peasant ⎬   Afternoon.

They stand at the bar.

Peasant   Two gingers for me.

Welzel   Welcome to both of you.

*He pours the gingers; both take their glasses and clink them, sip and put them
down.*

Salesman   Had a nice walk, forester?

Forester   All right. I've come from Steinseifersdorf.

Two **Old Weavers** *enter and sit with* **Ansorge**, **Baumert** *and*
Hornig.

Salesman   Excuse me. Aren't you the forester on the estate of
Count Hocheim?

Forester   I'm from Count Keil's.

Salesman   Of course, that's what I meant. There are so many
Counts and Barons and Squires, you need a memory like an
elephant. May I ask why you're carrying an axe?

Forester   I took it off some timber-thieves.

Old Baumert   These gentlemen are particular about every
piece of fire-wood.

Salesman   It would be a nice thing if everyone just helped
themselves.

Old Baumert   If I may say so, it's the same here as everywhere: there are small thieves and big thieves. There are timber-merchants who get rich off their stolen wood but if a poor weaver . . .

1st Old Weaver (*interrupting* **Baumert**)   We mustn't help ourselves to a twig or our lords and masters will get hold of us and skin us alive. We've got to pay protection-money, spinning-money, rates and taxes, we've got to run in circles whether we want to or not.

Ansorge   That's bow it is. What the factory-owners leave us, their lordships steal from our pockets.

2nd Old Weaver (*having sat down at the next table*)   I said so myself to his lordship, 'You'll pardon me, my lord, but this year I can't manage so many days on the land. I just can't do it! And why not? Because, begging your pardon, the floods have spoiled it all. The little land I owned has been ruined by the water. I've got to work day and night if I'm going to stay alive. This terrible weather . . . God help me, all I could do was stand and wring my hands. That lovely soil came rushing down the mountain and into my hut. And all those good seeds . . . 'Oh Jesus, Jesus', I kept shouting at the clouds. For a whole week I cried until I couldn't see in front of my eyes. And afterwards it took eighty journeys up and down the mountain to get the soil back.

Peasant (*brutally*)   You're making a terrible meal of all this. Whatever Heaven sends us, we must put up with. And if you're badly off, whose fault is it but your own? When business was good what did you do? Gambled and drank it all away. If you'd saved a bit then you'd have something to fall back on now, you wouldn't need to steal yarn and wood.

1st Young Weaver (*with some friends in the entrance ball, calls loudly from the door-way*)   A peasant stays a peasant even if he sleeps 'til nine.

1st Old Weaver   That's how things are nowadays. The peasant and the nobility pull at the same rope. If a weaver wants a home the peasant says, 'I'll give you a small hole to live in. You'll pay me a good rent and help me bring in my hay and my corn, and if you don't like the idea, see where it gets you.' If you go to another one he'll tell you the same as the first.

Old Baumert (*grimly*)   A weaver is like an apple – everyone takes their bite.

Peasant (*flaring up*)   You miserable bastards, you're no good to anybody. Can you handle a plough? Can you draw a straight furrow? Or pitch a bale of hay onto the wagon? You're good for nothing except lazing about and serving your women. You're a lot of shits, you're no good to anybody.

Meanwhile he has paid and gone, followed by the **Forester** *laughing.* **Welzel**, **Wiegand** *and* **Frau Welzel** *laugh loudly, the* **Salesman** *to himself. When the laughter subsides, there is silence.*

Hornig   A peasant like that is as dumb as his ox. If I didn't know what misery there is here . . . the things you see in the villages! Four or five of them lying naked on a sack of straw.

Salesman (*in a mildly reproving tone*)   If you permit me, my dear fellow, there are widely differing opinions about the hardship in the mountains. If you read the papers . . .

Hornig   Oh, I can read the papers as well as you. I know what I've seen, I've been amongst these people a long time. When a man's been pulling a cart for forty years he knows what's what. Remember the Fullers? The children looking for scraps in the dung-heap with the neighbour's geese? All dead – found stark naked on the floor of their house – fear of starving made them eat stinking glue – Death cut them down by the hundreds.

Salesman   If you can read then you'll know that the government ordered a searching enquiry and that . . .

Hornig   We know all about that. A man from the government arrives, knows better than all of us, acts as though he'd seen it all himself, walks a bit round the village where the stream runs and where the nicest houses are – doesn't want to get dirt on his nice, shiny shoes – and so he thinks it's as nice everywhere, climbs into his carriage and drives home again. And so he writes to Berlin, 'There is no poverty here'. If he'd had a little patience and climbed up to the villages near the source of the stream and across the stream on the far end or even off the road where the little, single huts are, and the dirty old hovels on the mountainside, some of which are so black and ruined that it wouldn't be worth putting a match to them and setting them alight, maybe then he'd have written differently to Berlin. They should have come to me, those gentlemen from the government who didn't want to believe that there's hardship here, I could have shown them something, I could have opened their eyes to these filthy holes.

The 'Weavers' Song' is heard from outside.

Welzel   They're singing that devil's song again.

Wiegand   They're turning the whole village upside down.

Frau Welzel   It's as if there was something in the air.

Jaeger and **Baecker** *arm-in-arm noisily enter the bar from the saloon at the head of a group of young weavers.*

Jaeger   Company halt! At ease!

They sit at the various tables, joining the other weavers, and engage them in conversation.

Hornig (*calling to* **Baecker**)   What's going on? What are you all up to?

Baecker (*with emphasis*)   Maybe something is going to happen. Right, Moritz?

Hornig   That'd be a change. Don't do anything rash.

Baecker   Blood's started to flow. Want to see it?

He rolls up his sleeve and shows him a bloody tattoo on his bare upper arm. Several of the other young weavers at different tables do the same.

Baecker   We've been at Schmidt's getting tattooed.

Hornig   I see what you mean. It's no surprise that there's such excitement in the streets. With you lot running all over the village . . .

Jaeger (*showing off, in a loud voice*)   Two quarts here, Welzel! I'm paying. Maybe you think I haven't got the cash? Well, wait and see! If I felt like it I could drink schnapps and sip coffee 'til tomorrow morning, just like a travelling salesman.

Laughter among the young weavers.

Salesman (*with mock surprise*)   Do you mean me or do you mean me?

Laughter from the **Welzels** *and* **Wiegand**.

Jaeger   If the cap fits . . .

Salesman   If I may say so, young man, your business seems to be flourishing.

Jaeger   I can't complain. I'm in textiles, I go halves with the manufacturers. The hungrier the weaver, the fatter I get. The greater their need, the more I feed.

Baecker   Well said, Moritz, well said.

Welzel *has brought the schnapps. On the way back to the bar he stops and slowly turns to the weavers with all his natural authority.*

Welzel (*with quiet emphasis*)   Leave that gentleman alone, he's done you no harm.

1st Young Weaver   We're not doing him any harm either.

Frau Welzel *and the* **Salesman** *have exchanged words.*

She takes his coffee-cup and carries it through to the saloon. The **Salesman** *follows her amid much laughter from the weavers.*

Young Weavers (*singing*)   'The hangman's name is Dreissiger, Assisted by his clerks . . .'

Welzel   Ssh, ssh. You can sing that song where you like, but I don't allow it in my house.

1st Old Weaver   He's quite right – stop your singing.

Baecker (*shouts*)   We'll be paying Dreissiger another visit so that he gets a chance to hear it again.

Wiegand   Don't get too wild or he might misunderstand you.

Laughter.

Old Wittig *has entered. He is a grey-haired smith without a cap, with a leather apron and clogs, still sooty from his forge. He stops at the bar waiting for his brandy.*

Old Wittig   Let them make a bit of a show. Dogs that bark, don't bite.

1st Old Weaver
2nd Old Weaver } Wittig, Wittig!

Wittig   At your service. What's up?

1st Old Weaver } Wittig's here – Wittig, Wittig – come here,
2nd Old Weaver } Wittig, sit with us! Over here, Wittig!

Wittig   I'd better be careful sitting with old devils like you.

Jaeger   Come on, have a drink with us.

Wittig   You can keep your brandy. When I drink I pay for myself.

He takes his glass of schnapps and sits with **Old Baumert** *and* **Ansorge**. *He pats* **Ansorge**'s *stomach.*

What do weavers eat these days? Boiled cabbage and lice?

Old Baumert (*ecstatically*)   And what if I said that's not good enough any more?

Wittig (*with feigned surprise, looks dumbly at him*)   Is it really you, Heimi? (*Laughing uncontrollably.*) You people kill me. Old Baumert wants to make a revolution. It'll be the tailors next, then the baa-lambs and then the mice and rats. My goodness! What a to-do that'll be! (*He is shaking with laughter.*)

Old Baumert   Don't get me wrong, Wittig, I'm the same as before. And I still say if you can do it peacefully, it's better.

Wittig   It'll be dirty, not peaceful. When has it ever been peaceful? Was it peaceful in France? Did Robespierre pat the heads of the rich? Off with it was the rule! To the guillotine! That's how it was – (*Sings:*) 'Allons enfants de la patrie . . . ' Did you ever see a roast goose fly straight into your mouth?

Old Baumert   If I had half of what I need . . .

1st Old Weaver   We're in it up to our necks already, Wittig.

2nd Old Weaver   There's no point in going home now.
Whether you work or whether you sleep, you starve either way.

1st Old Weaver   You can go mad at home.

Ansorge   I don't care any more, it just gets worse.

1st Old Weaver (*with mounting excitement*)   No peace any more –
no spirit to work. Up in Steinkunzendorf there's a man sitting by
the river washing himself day and night, naked as God created him.
He's gone soft in the head.

3rd Old Weaver (*rises, driven by the spirit, starts to speak 'with the
Tongues' raising a threatening finger*)   The Last Judgement is nigh! Cast
off the rich and mighty! Judgement is at hand. The Lord God . . .

Some laughter as he is pushed back into his seat.

Welzel   One drink and he loses his head.

3rd Old Weaver (*jumping up again*)   Alas! They believe not in
God, nor Hell nor Heaven! Religion is a mockery . . .

1st Old Weaver   All right, all right. Calm down.

Baecker   Let the man have his say. Maybe someone will take
his prayers to heart.

Weavers (*tumultuously*)   Let him speak! Let him!

3rd Old Weaver (*with a raised voice*)   And then did Hell open
wide its soul and its jaws gaped without measure so that all who
deny the right of the poor and use force upon them in their
wretchedness, shall descend into it – thus spake the Lord.

Commotion.

3rd Old Weaver (*suddenly declaims like a schoolboy*)

'How wondrous to relate
The linen-weaver's fate
His work ignored, there's nothing on his place.'

Baecker   But we're fustian weavers.

Laughter.

Hornig   The linen-weavers are even worse off. They haunt the mountains like ghosts. At least you still speak up for yourselves.

Wittig   Do you think the worst is over? The factory-owners will soon drive out the little strength that's left in your bodies.

Baecker   He said it himself, 'The weavers will work for bread and cheese'.

Commotion.

Weavers   Who said that?

Baecker   That's what Dreissiger said about us.

1st Young Weaver   That bastard should be strung up by his arse.

Jaeger   Listen, Wittig, you're always on about the French Revolution, you've always got a lot to say for yourself. Well maybe you'll soon have a chance to show what you're made of – a big mouth or a man of his word.

Wittig (*exploding with rage*)   One more word out of you, boy . . . have you heard the whistle of bullets? Have you seen action on enemy soil?

Jaeger   I never said you were a coward. We're comrades, aren't we?

Wittig   I spit on your comradeship, you jumped-up little beggar!

Policeman Kutsche *enters.*

Weavers   Quiet! The police!

There is prolonged hissing until total silence ensues.

Kutsche (*taking his place at the bar amid total silence from the others*)   Small brandy please. (*Again, total silence.*)

Wittig   Well, Kutsche, come to check that all's well here?

Kutsche (*ignoring him*)   Good day to you, Herr Wiegand.

Wiegand (*who is still in the corner, by the bar*)   Good day, Kutsche.

Kutsche   How's business?

Wiegand   Fine, thanks.

Baecker   The superintendent's afraid we're ruining our stomachs with all the pay we're getting.

Laughter.

Jaeger   That's right, isn't it Welzel? We've all had roast pork and dumplings and cabbage, and we're just about to open the champagne.

Laughter.

Welzel   And pigs might fly.

Kutsche   Even if you had had champagne and roast, you still wouldn't be satisfied. I haven't had champagne and I manage somehow.

Baecker (*referring to* **Kutsche**'s *nose*)   Yes, he dips *his* nose in beer and brandy. That's why it's so red and glowing.

Laughter.

Wittig   It's a hard life for a policeman: first, he's got to lock up some starving beggar-boy, then a pretty weaver's girl needs his protection, then he drinks himself stupid to beat up his wife, so she runs to the neighbours in fear and terror. What with parading around on horseback and snoring in his feather-bed 'til nine – I tell you, it's not easy.

Kutsche   Say what you like! You'll talk yourself into a noose one of these days. We know your kind, your trouble-making's well-known, even to the magistrate. I know someone whose wife and child turn up in the poor-house as regular as clock-work thanks to his beer-swilling. And when he lands in jail he won't stop stirring 'til he comes to a sticky end.

Wittig (*laughing bitterly*)   Who knows what's coming. You might be right about the last bit. (*Angrily.*) But if it comes to it, I'll know who to thank, who it was told tales about me to the factory-owners and on the estates and who slandered me and blackened my name, so that I couldn't get work any more – who put the peasants at my throat and the millers, so that week in, week out, not a single horse was brought in for shoeing or a wheel for repair.

I know who it is. One day, I had to pull this wicked brute off his horse because he was beating some poor little brat with a bull-whip for helping himself to a couple of unripe pears. But let me tell you this: you know me, if you get thrown in jail, you can start writing your will and if I hear even a whisper, I'll grab anything that's handy – a horse-shoe, a hammer, the spoke of a wheel or a bucket, and I'll come for you even if I have to drag you out of bed off your wife – I'll pull you out and break your skull as me as my name is Wittig. (*He has jumped up, wanting to attack* **Kutsche**.)

Weavers (*restraining him*)   Wittig, Wittig, be reasonable.

Kutsche *has risen involuntarily. His face is pale. During the following, he retreats: the nearer he gets to the door, the braver he becomes. He delivers the last words from the threshold so that he can disappear immediately.*

Kutsche   What do you want of me? I've never had anything to do with you. I had something to say to the weavers, it's got nothing to do with you, I've got no business with you. But I've a message for you weavers: the Chief of Police forbids you to sing that song – that Dreissiger Song, or whatever you call it. And if the singing in the street doesn't cease forthwith, he'll see to it you have plenty of time to sing it in jail. You can sing it with your bread and water as long as you like.

He goes out.

Wittig (*shouting after him*)   You can't tell us what to do, if we shout loud enough to rattle the windows and if you can hear us all the way to Reichenbach and if we sing so that factory-owners' houses collapse on their heads and make the policemen's helmets dance on their skulls – that's still nobody's business.

Baecker *has meanwhile risen and given the signal to sing. He begins himself and the others all join in.*

	'This is a place which has a court.
Baecker ⎫	Worse than the Inquisition;
The Others ⎭	No sentence is pronounced, instead
	Immediate perdition.'

Welzel *tries to calm them down but nobody listens to him.* **Wiegand** *covers his ears and runs off.*

The **Weavers** *rise and, during the following verse, follow* **Wittig** *and* **Baecker**, *who with nods and signs, have given the signal for action.*

Baecker ⎫   'Your torture will be long and slow.
The Other ⎬   And painful every breath;
                ⎭   Your screams will count as witnesses
                     Until relieved by Death.'

Most of the weavers are already in the street when they sing the following verse, only a few young boys are still in the bar, paying for their drinks. By the end of the next verse, the room is empty except for **Welzel**, *his wife, his daughter,* **Hornig** *and* **Old Baumert**.

'You scoundrels all, you Satan's brood
You denizens of Hell –
You feed upon the helpless poor
And make your stomachs swell.'

Welzel (*calmly collects the glasses*)   They're being very stupid today.

Old Baumert *is about to leave.*

Hornig   For God's sake, Baumert, what's going on?

Old Baumert   They want to go to Dreissiger's to see if he'll put up their wages.

Welzel   And you go along with this nonsense?

Old Baumert   It's not up to me, Welzel. If you're young you have a choice, if you're old you must go. (*He goes off, slightly embarrassed.*)

Hornig (*rises*)   I wouldn't be surprised if there's trouble ahead.

Welzel   Who would have thought the old boys would lose their heads.

Hornig   Well, every man must have a dream.

End of Act Three.

Act Four

Peterswaldau. A private room in the house of the textile manufacturer, **Dreissiger**. *The room is decorated luxuriously in the frosty manner of the first half of the nineteenth century. The ceiling, the stove and the doors are white; the wallpaper is patterned in straight lines of small flowers in a cold, blue-grey tone. The furniture is covered in red upholstery, richly decorated and carved – cupboards and chairs are in the same material and distributed as follows; on the right, between two windows with cherry-red damask curtains, is the writing-desk, a bureau with a drop-front. Opposite, a sofa, close to an iron safe and in front of the sofa are a table, armchairs and chairs, against the back wall, a cupboard for firearms. The walls are partly covered by bad pictures in gold frames. Above the sofa hangs a mirror in a heavy Rococo frame, heavily gilded. A door on the left leads into the passage, an open double-door in the back wall leads into a salon over-decorated with the same tasteless splendour. In the salon one sees two ladies,* **Frau Dreissiger** *and* **Frau Kittelhaus**, *busy looking at the pictures – furthermore* **Pastor Kittelhaus** *in conversation with the tutor and student* **Weinhold**.*

Kittelhaus, *a small, friendly man, enters the front room chatting and smoking with the tutor, who is also smoking. He looks around and shakes his head in surprise as there is nobody there.*

Kittelhaus   It's not at all surprising, Herr Weinhold, you are young. When we were your age we held views which were not, perhaps, identical but certainly similar. And there's something marvellous about being young – all those wonderful ideals, Herr Weinhold. Unfortunately, they are fleeting, fleeting like April sunshine. Wait until you are my age. When one has preached from the pulpit for thirty years, fifty-two times a year, not counting the Holy days and Festivals, one becomes, of necessity, more balanced. Think of me, Herr Weinhold, when you've reached that point.

Weinhold *is nineteen, pale, thin and gangling, with long, blond hair. He is very nervous and restless in his movements.*

Weinhold   With all due respect Pastor . . . I don't know, there are great differences of character.

Kittelhaus   My dear young man, you may be a restless spirit – (*Reprovingly.*) – Oh, yes, you are – however strong your views and however impatiently you attack the status quo now, you'll mellow in due course. Oh yes, I admit some of our brethren of fairly advanced age still get up to rather juvenile pranks. One preaches against the evils of drink and founds temperance societies, another composes manifestos which make undeniably stirring reading. But what has he achieved by that? The hardship among the weavers, where they exist, are not ameliorated. But social harmony is undermined. One can truly say, 'Cobbler, stick to your last!' Guardians of the soul should not become guardians of the flesh. Preach the Word of God purely and simply and leave it to Him to provide shelter and food for the birds. He will not suffer the lily of the field to perish. – Now I'd really like to know where our charming host has disappeared to so suddenly.

Frau Dreissiger *enters, followed by* **Frau Kittelhaus**. *She is a pretty woman of thirty of a robust type. There is a certain ambivalence between her manner of speech and her movements. She is dressed with ostentatious elegance.*

Frau Dreissiger   You are quite right, Pastor, Wilhelm's always disappearing like this. He gets an idea, rushes off, and leaves me standing. I've told him again and again but he takes no notice.

Kittelhaus   That's why he is a businessman, my dear lady.

Weinhold   If I'm not mistaken there's something going on downstairs.

Dreissiger *enters. He is hot and bothered.*

Dreissiger   Well, Rosa, is coffee being served?

Frau Dreissiger (*sulking*)   You're always running away.

Dreissiger (*lightly*)   What are you talking about!

Kittelhaus   I beg your pardon, Herr Dreissiger, but has there been any trouble?

Dreissiger   There's always trouble, every day in the good Lord's calendar, my dear Pastor. I've got used to it. Well Rosa, everything under control?

Frau Dreissiger *goes grumpily to the bell-pull and pulls it violently several times.*

(*Striding about.*)   I wish you could have been there just now, Herr Weinhold, it would have been good experience for you. And besides . . . right, what about a game of Whist?

Kittelhaus   Yes, yes and yes again! Shake the cares of the day from your shoulders and let us look after you.

Dreissiger (*has gone to the window, pulls a curtain aside and looks out. Involuntarily:*)   Hooligans! Come here a minute, Rosa.

She comes.

Can you see that tall, red-haired man?

Kittelhaus   That's the one they call Red Baecker.

Dreissiger   Is he, by any chance, the one who insulted you two days ago? Do you remember telling me – Johann was helping you into the carriage.

Frau Dreissiger   Oh, stop sulking. I must know. I've had enough of this insolence. If he was the one, I can do something about it.

The 'Weavers' Song' is heard.

Do you hear that, do you hear that?

Kittelhaus (*indignantly*)   Is there no end to this nonsense? I have to say it – I think it's high time the police stepped in. Allow me! (*He goes to the window.*) Have a look, Herr Weinhold. It's not only the young ones, the decent, old weavers are amongst them, men who for years I've known to be highly respectable and God-fearing, they're taking part in this unheard-of nonsense. They are trampling God's Law under-foot. Don't tell me you are prepared to defend them.

Weinhold   Of course not, Pastor. I mean . . . cum grano salis . . . they are hungry, ignorant people, they show their discontent in the only way they know. I wouldn't expect such people . . .

Frau Kittelhaus, *small, thin, faded, looks more like an old spinster than a wife.*

Frau Kittelhaus   Really, Herr Weinhold, I'm surprised at you.

Dreissiger   I'm sorry, Herr Weinhold, I didn't take you into my house to listen to your lectures on humanity. I must ask you to confine yourself to the education of my sons. Don't concern yourself in my affairs. Do I make myself clear?

Weinhold (*stands rigid and pale, bows, with a forced smile. Softly:*)   Perfectly, I fully understand. I could see it coming; in any case, I would not have wished to remain here.

He goes.

Dreissiger (*brutally*)   Then go as soon as possible, we need the room.

Frau Dreissiger   But Wilhelm!

Dreissiger   Are you out of your mind? You are taking the part of a man who's prepared to defend such outrageous slander as this song.

Frau Dreissiger   But, sweetheart, he didn't. . .

Dreissiger   Did he or did he not defend that song, Pastor?

Kittelhaus   One must consider his youth, Herr Dreissiger.

Frau Kittelhaus   I can't understand it, this young man comes from such a good and respectable family. His father was a civil servant for forty years and was never guilty of the slightest misdemeanour. His mother was overjoyed that he found such an excellent position here, and now . . . now he fails to make the most of it.

Pfeifer (*tears open the hall-door and shouts*)   Herr Dreissiger, Herr Dreissiger! They've got him. They want you to come, they've caught him.

Dreissiger (*anxiously*)   Did someone get the police?

Pfeifer   The Superintendent's just coming up.

Dreissiger (*in the doorway*)   I'm much obliged to you, Superintendent. I'm glad you've come.

Kittelhaus *indicates by gesture that it might be better for the ladies to retire. He, his wife and* **Frau Dreissiger** *disappear into the salon.*

(*In a state of great excitement.*) My dye-workers have caught one of the leaders. I couldn't stand it any longer. Their impudence goes beyond a joke. It's disgraceful! I had guests here and these scoundrels dared to . . . they insult my wife whenever she goes out; my sons' lives aren't safe. There's a risk that my guests could be subjected to physical violence. If ordered society tolerates that innocent people like me and my family arc continually and openly insulted, then . . . then all I can say is I'm sorry, but my idea of law and order is somewhat different.

Superintendent (*a man of about fifty, medium height, corpulent, red-faced. He wears cavalry uniform with a long sabre and spurs*)   Of course not . . . no, of course not, Herr Dreissiger! – I'm at your disposal. Be calm, I'm entirely at your disposal, it's perfectly in order . . . in fact I'm delighted that you've caught one of the chief culprits. I'm glad that the matter has finally come to a head. There are some disruptive elements here that I've had my eye on for a long time.

Dreissiger   That's right. Some youths who are afraid of work, lazy louts who lead revolting lives, sit around the taverns all day 'til all their money has disappeared down their throats. But I'm determined to put an end to it, I'll show these professional foul-mouths – I'll teach them a lesson they won't forget in a hurry. It's in everybody's interest, not just my own.

Superintendent   Quite right, absolutely, Herr Dreissiger. No-one could possibly blame you. As far as it's within my powers . . .

Dreissiger   These louts deserve to be bull-whipped!

Superintendent   Quite right, quite right, we must make an example of them.

Kutsche *enters and stands at attention. Through the hall-door heavy footsteps are heard, clomping up the stairs.*

Kutsche   Beg to report sir, we've arrested a man.

Dreissiger   Do you want to see the man, Superintendent?

Superintendent   Of course, of course, we need to examine him at close quarters first. Would you oblige me, Herr Dreissiger, by not speaking to him. I promise you every satisfaction or my name is not Heide.

Dreissiger   I can't agree to that, I'm afraid. The man should come before the magistrate without delay.

Jaeger *is led by five dye-workers, whose faces, hands and clothes are covered with dye, having come directly from work. The prisoner, his cap set cockily on his head, behaves with impudent gaiety and is in high spirits as a result of his earlier consumption of brandy.*

Jaeger   You miserable lot! Call yourselves workers? Comrades? Before I did a thing like that – I'd rather my arm dropped off than lay hands on a work-mate.

At a sign from the **Superintendent**, **Kutsche** *indicates to the dye-workers to release their captive.* **Jaeger** *stands free and defiant while around him, all the doors are guarded.*

Superintendent (*shouting at* **Jaeger**)   Hat off, lout!

Jaeger *takes off his cap, but very slowly without relinquishing his ironic smile.*

Name?

Jaeger   Who do you think I am, your swineherd?

There is a reaction to his words from among those present.

Dreissiger   Insolence!

Superintendent (*grows pale, struggles to control himself*) We'll see about that. – I asked your name! (*Wildly, as he receives no reply.*) Answer, you scum, or I'll have you whipped!

Jaeger, *with unflinching jollity, calls over the heads of those present to a pretty* **Servant Girl** *who is about to serve coffee and has stopped in open-mothed amazement at the unexpected scene.*

Jaeger   Hey, Emily. What are you doing among this lot? If I were you I'd get out quick. There's a storm blowing that'll blow everything away by the morning.

The **Servant Girl** *realises she is being spoken to, blushes with embarrassment, covers her face with her hands and runs out, leaving the coffee-tray behind.*

Superintendent (*to* **Dreissiger**, *almost struck dumb*)   In all my days . . . I've never come across such total disrespect . . .

Jaeger *spits on the floor.*

Dreissiger   You are not in a pig-sty. Do you understand?

Superintendent   I've reached the end of my patience. For the last time, your name?

Kittelhaus, *who has been listening through a partly-opened door, now enters the fray, shaking with emotion.*

Kittelhaus   His name is Jaeger, Superintendent. Moritz . . . isn't it . . . Moritz Jaeger. (*To* **Jaeger**:) Tell me, Jaeger, don't you recognise me any more?

Jaeger (*seriously*)   You are Pastor Kittelhaus.

Kittelhaus   Yes, Jaeger, the guardian of your soul, who took you into the Community of Saints when you were but a babe in swaddling-clothes, the same from whose hands you first received Holy Communion, can't you remember? I've tried and tried to instil the Word of God in your heart. Is this the thanks I get?

Jaeger (*darkly, like a beaten schoolboy*)   I put a thaler in the plate.

Kittelhaus   Money, money! Do you really think that a miserable coin . . . keep your money . . . I'd rather you did. What nonsense this is! Be good, be a Christian, remember your faith. Keep God's commandments, be virtuous and be pious. Money, money . . .

Jaeger   I'm a Quaker, Pastor, I don't believe in anything more.

Kittelhaus   Quaker! What are you talking about! Try to be a better man, and don't pronounce these undigested words! The Quakers are pious people, not heathens like you. Quaker, indeed.

Superintendent   If you'll allow me, Pastor – (*He steps between* **Kittelhaus** *and* **Jaeger**.) Kutsche! Tie up his hands.

Voices from outside are heard yelling: 'Jaeger! Let him out!'

Dreissiger (*slightly shocked, has made his way to the window*)   What is the meaning of this?

Superintendent   Oh, I know what it means. They want to have the scoundrel back with them, but we shan't do them that favour. Do you understand, Kutsche? He goes to jail.

Kutsche (*with the rope in his hand, hesitating*)   With respect, sir, we may have some difficulty, there's a hell of a crowd out there, a really nasty bunch, sir. There's Baecker, there's the blacksmith . . .

Kittelhaus   With your permission, Superintendent, to prevent aggravating things, might it not be more suitable to try and settle it peacefully? Perhaps Jaeger will promise to come along quietly, or . . .

Superintendent   Do you know what you're saying! This is my responsibility. I can't possibly agree to that. Get on with it Kutsche! Don't waste time.

Jaeger (*putting his hands together and holding them out, laughing*)   Make it tight. As tight as you can, it won't be for long.

Kutsche *helped by the others, ties his hands.*

Superintendent   All right, move! (*To* **Dreissiger**:) If you're worried, let the dye-workers go with him. They can form a guard round him. I'll ride in front and Kutsche will follow, anyone who tries to stop us will be hacked down.

Voices (*from below*)   Cock-a-doodle-doo! Bow-wow-wow!

Superintendent (*shaking his fist at the window*)   Rabble! I'll teach you to cock-a-doodle-doo and bow-wow. Forward march!

He strides out with sabre drawn, the others follow with **Jaeger**.

Jaeger (*shouting as he goes*)   Look at Frau Dreissiger acting like a lady. She's no better than the rest of us, she served my father with three pfennigs' worth of schnapps hundreds of times. Squadron – left! Quick march! (*He goes out laughing.*)

Dreissiger (*after a pause, apparently calm*)   What do you think, Pastor? Shall we get on with our game of Whist? I don't think anything will interrupt us now. (*He lights a cigar, giving a staccato laugh.*) I'm beginning to find the whole thing rather funny. That rascal! (*Amid nervous laughter.*) It's unbelievably ridiculous, first, that row with Weinhold with him leaving five minutes later, never to return, then this business! I think we deserve a game of Whist.

Kittelhaus   Yes, but . . . (*Shouting is heard from below.*) yes, but . . . those people are still making a terrible noise.

Dreissiger   Then let's go back into the other room. They won't disturb us there.

Kittelhaus (*shaking his head*)   If only I knew what's got into them. I'm afraid I must agree with Herr Weinhold, at least to this extent: until recently I too was of the opinion that the weavers were a humble, patient, and easily handled type of people. Don't you agree, Herr Dreissiger?

Dreissiger   Of course they were patient and easily handled, of course they were docile and orderly people – as long as the do-gooders left them alone. They've taken a lot of trouble to convince them they live in appalling squalor. Just think of it: all those societies and committees for the relief of hardship among the weavers. I wish someone would put their thinking straight. Now they're in full flow. Now they complain constantly; this doesn't suit them and that doesn't suit them – now only the best will do.

Suddenly a loud cheer is heard.

Kittelhaus   So all they've achieved with their humanitarianism is to turn sheep into wolves overnight.

Dreissiger   No, no, considered rationally, Pastor, something good might yet come of it. Such occurrences might not pass unnoticed in higher circles. Perhaps they might realise things can't go on like this, that something must be done unless our local industry is to be completely destroyed.

Kittelhaus   But what would you say is the reason for this huge decline?

Dreissiger   Foreign markets have barricaded themselves against us by means of heavy import duties so we're cut off from our best customers, and at home we're forced to compete for our very existence because we've been totally abandoned.

Pfeifer (*staggers in, pale and out of breath*)   Herr Dreissiger, Herr Dreissiger!

Dreissiger (*already in the doorway of the salon about to leave, turns, irritated*)   What is it now, Pfeifer?

Pfeifer   No . . . no . . . leave me alone.

Dreissiger   What's happened?

Kittelhaus   You're frightening us, say something!

Pfeifer (*still hysterical*)   Leave me alone! Who'd have thought . . . I don't believe it! The authorities . . . they're really in trouble this time.

Dreissiger   For heaven's sake, what's the matter with you? Has someone broken his neck?

Pfeifer (*almost crying with fear, shouts*)   They've only freed Moritz Jaeger, beaten up the Superintendent and chased him away, beaten up the policeman and chased *him* away. Without his helmet . . . the sabre broken . . . no, no!

Dreissiger   Pfeifer, you've gone mad!

Kittelhaus   This could mean a revolution.

Pfeifer (*sits on a chair, his whole body trembling, whimpering*)   It's serious, Herr Dreissiger, it's serious.

Dreissiger   In that case, the whole police-force . . .

Pfeifer   Herr Dreissiger, it's serious!

Dreissiger   Shut up, Pfeifer! For heaven's sake!

Frau Dreissiger *enters the salon with* **Frau Kittelhaus**.

Frau Dreissiger   This is really disgraceful, Wilhelm. Our whole evening has been spoiled, and now Frau Kittelhaus has said she wants to go home.

Kittelhaus   My dear Frau Dreissiger, it might really be better . . .

Frau Dreissiger   Couldn't you have stopped them, Wilhelm?

Dreissiger   Go on, go on! You go and tell them! (*Standing helplessly in front of the* **Pastor**.) Am I a tyrant? *Am* I a slave-driver?

Johann *the coachman enters.*

Johann   I've harnessed the horses, Madam. Herr Weinhold's put Jurgen and Karl in the carriage already. If it gets worse we're ready to go.

Frau Dreissiger   If what gets worse?

Johann   Well, I don't know. I just thought . . . there are more and more people . . . they've driven off the Superintendent and the policeman too.

Pfeifer   It's serious, Herr Dreissiger, it's serious!

Frau Dreissiger (*with mounting fear*)   What's going to happen? What do they want, these people? Surely they won't attack us, Johann?

Johann   Some of them are like mad dogs.

Pfeifer   It's getting serious, really serious!

Dreissiger   Shut up, fool! Are the doors barred?

Kittelhaus   Do me a favour . . . please, just one favour I've made a decision . . . do me just this one favour. (*To* **Johann**:) What do these people want?

Johann (*embarrassed*)   They want more pay, the stupid bastards.

Kittelhaus   Right, good. I shall go out and do my duty. I shall have a serious word with them.

Johann   I shouldn't, sir. There's no point in talking to them.

Kittelhaus   My dear Herr Dreissiger, one last request. Station some people behind the door and as soon as I've gone out let them lock it.

Frau Kettelhaus   Do you really want to do this, Joseph?

Kittelhaus   I must. I must. I know what must be done. Have no fear, the Good Lord will protect me.

Frau Kittelhaus *presses his hand, steps back wiping tears from her eyes.*

Kittelhaus (*while from below a dull rumble can be heard uninterruptedly*)   I shall pretend . . . I shall pretend that I'm on my way home. I want to see whether a man of the cloth . . . whether I still command enough respect . . . I want to see for myself . . . (*He takes his hat and his stick.*) Forward then in the name of God!

He goes out accompanied by **Dreissiger**, **Pfeifer** *and* **Johann**.

Frau Kittelhaus   Dear Frau Dreissiger — (*She bursts into tears and embraces her.*) — As long as he comes to no harm!

Frau Dreissiger (*as if in a trance*)   I really don't know, Frau Kittelhaus, I feel as if . . . I don't know how I feel. Is this really happening? If it's true . . . it's as though wealth was a crime. If anyone had told me — I don't know, Frau Kittelhaus — it might have been better if I'd stayed with my own kind.

Frau Kittelhaus   Dear Frau Dreissiger, you find disappointment and trouble everywhere.

Frau Dreissiger   Exactly, that's just what I was thinking. But just because we have more than other people, we haven't stolen it, God knows, every bit of it was earned honestly. It's incredible that people should want to attack you. Is it my husband's fault that business is bad?

A tumultuous roar is heard from below. As the two women look at each other pale and frightened, **Dreissiger** *storms in.*

Dreissiger   Quick, Rosa! Throw something over your shoulders and get into the carriage, I'll join you!

He rushes to the safe, opens it and removes several valuables.

Johann (*entering*)   Everything's ready. Quick! Before they get to the back!

Frau Dreissiger (*embracing* **Johann**, *terrified*)   Johann, my dearest Johann! Save us, dearest Johann! Save my little ones, please . . .

Dreissiger   Control yourself! Let go of Johann!

Johann   Don't worry, ma'am. No-one will catch us, the horses are in good shape. If anyone gets in our way, he'll be run over. (*He goes.*)

Frau Kittelhaus (*helpless with fear*)   My husband! What about my husband? Where is he, Herr Dreissiger?

Dreissiger   He's all right, Frau Kittelhaus, calm yourself, he's all right.

Frau Kittelhaus   Something terrible's happened to him — you're not telling me, you're not telling me!

Dreissiger   Don't worry, they'll regret it. I know exactly who's responsible. Such shameless behaviour will not go unpunished. A congregation that manhandles its own Pastor – my God! Mad dogs, that's what they are, vicious animals who must be handled accordingly. (*To* **Frau Dreissiger**, *who again is standing as if entranced:*) Go on, move yourself! (*Pounding is heard on the front door.*) Can't you hear? They've gone mad! (*The sound of breaking glass is heard from downstairs.*) Insanity! We have no choice, we must get out of here.

Voices (*calling in unison*)   We want Pfeifer! We want Pfeifer!

Frau Dreissiger   Pfeifer, they want Pfeifer.

Pfeifer (*rushing in*)   Herr Dreissiger! There are people at the back-door and the front door will be smashed in in three minutes. Wittig keeps hitting it with a pail like a madman.

Voices (*from below getting louder and clearer*)   Pfeifer, Pfeifer! We want Pfeifer!

Frau Dreissiger *runs away in terror, followed by* **Frau Kittelhaus**.

Pfeifer *listens, growing pale as the shouting registers. He is gripped by panic. The following is delivered frantically as he cries, whimpers, begs and whines. He gets hold of* **Dreissiger**, *overwhelming him with hysterical affection, stroking his arms and cheeks, kissing his hands and clinging to him like a drowning man, effectively pinioning him and not letting go.*

Pfeifer   Oh dearest, kindest, most noble Herr Dreissiger, don't leave me behind! I've always served you faithfully; and I've always been good to the weavers. I couldn't give them more pay because it wasn't up to me – don't leave me, they'll kill me! If they find me, they'll beat me to death! Oh God, oh God! My wife, my children . . .

Dreissiger (*as he tries in vain to free himself from* **Pfeifer**)   Let go of me, man! It's all right – everything will be all right. (*He goes out with* **Pfeifer**.)

The room stays empty for a few seconds. A window is shattered. Noise echoes through the house. There is a shout of 'Hurrah', followed by silence. A few seconds pass then the sound of quiet, careful footsteps is heard on the stairs leading to the first floor accompanied by restrained and timid exclamation.

Voices   On the left! – Upstairs! – Ssh! – Careful, careful! – Don't move anything! – Look what I've got! – Put that down! – We're going to a wedding! – In there! – Go on, try in there!

Young Weavers and **Weaver Girls** *appear in the doorway. They don't dare enter, they prod each other, trying not to be the one to make the first move. After a few seconds, they overcome their shyness and the thin, sickly, ragged figures spread themselves around* **Dreissiger**'s *room and salon; at first curious they look at things shyly then, a little more bravely, they start to pick things up and examine them. The* **Weaver Girls** *try the sofas; groups form to admire themselves in the mirrors. Some climb on the chairs in order to look more closely at the pictures and take them down. Meanwhile more and more of the miserable figures stream in from the hall.*

Old Weaver (*enters*)   No, no, leave me out of it! Things are already being torn apart downstairs. It's all mad, there's no rhyme nor season to it – it'll come to a bad end. No one with any sense would do a thing like this. I'll take good care not to join in with this madness.

Jaeger, **Baecker**, **Wittig**, *carrying a wooden pail,* **Old Baumert** *and a number of other* **Weavers** *come rushing in as though after a quarry. They call to each other hoarsely.*

Jaeger   Where's he gone?

Baecker   Where's the slave-driver?

Old Baumert   If we can eat grass, he can eat saw-dust.

Wittig   When we catch him, we'll string him up.

1st Young Weaver   We'll grab his legs and throw him out of the window onto the stones – he won't move in a hurry.

2nd Young Weaver (*enters*)   He's done a bunk.

All   Who?

2nd Young Weaver   Dreissiger.

Baecker   Pfeifer too?

Voices   Get Pfeifer! Let's find him.

Old Baumert   Out you come, little Pfeifer. There's a weaverman out here you can starve. (*Laughter.*)

Jaeger   Even if we don't get that bastard Dreissiger, we can make a poor man of him.

Old Baumert   He'll be poor as a church-mouse. We'll make a poor man of him.

Thay all rush toward the salon in order to demolish it.

Baecker (*runs ahead, turns and stops the others*)   Stop! Listen to me! When we've finished here we'll start the real business. From here we'll go down to Bielau, to Dietrich who uses mechanical looms. It's the factories that cause all the misery.

Ansorge *enters from the hall-way. After a few steps, he stands still, looks around him with incredulity, shakes his head, slaps his forehead.*

Ansorge   Who am I? Anton Ansorge, weaver. This Ansorge, has he gone mad? I must be, my head's spinning like a top. What's he doing here? He's joining in the fun and games. This Ansorge, where is he? (*Slaps his head repeatedly.*) I've gone crazy! I don't know what's going on, I'm not right in the head. Go away, go away! Get out, you rebels! Heads out, legs out, hands out! You take my little house, I'll take your little house. Come on, let's go!

With a cry, he goes into the salon. Those present follow him cheering and laughing.

End of Act Four.

Act Five

Langenbielau. The weaving-room of **Old Hilse**. *To the left, a small window, in front of it, a loom; to the right, a bed with a table pushed up against it. In the right corner, a stove with a bench. Sitting around the table on a foot-stool on a bed, and on a wooden-stool are* **Old Hilse**, *his equally old, blind and nearly deaf wife, his son* **Gottlieb** *and his wife* **Luise** *at their morning devotions. A spooling-wheel with bobbins stand between the table and the loom. All kinds of spinning, weaving and spooling implements are kept on the top of the browned ceiling-beams, long strands of yarn hang down. All sorts of rubbish is scattered around the room, the very narrow, low and shallow room has a door in the back wall leading to the rest of the 'house'. Opposite this door, at the other end of the house, is another door which is open and through which we can see into a similar work-room. The 'house' is paved with stone and the plaster is cracked; a flight of rickety wooden stairs leads up into the attic, a wash-tub on a stool is partly visible; ragged clothes and a few, scrappy domestic implements lie scattered about. Light from the left illuminates all the rooms.*

Old Hilse, *a bearded, strong-boned man, bent and wasted as the result of age, work, illness and hardship. A war-veteran, he has only one arm. He has a pointed nose, pale face, trembles. He appears to consist only of skin, bone and sinews. He has the deep-set characteristically sore eyes of the weaver. He, his son and daughter-in-law rise; be prays:*

Old Hilse   Dear Lord, we cannot thank you enough that in your goodness and graciousness, you have taken pity on us this night. So on this night, again we have come to no harm. Lord, your goodness is so great that we poor, sinful children are not worthy that your foot should stamp on us, so sinful and corrupt are we. But you, dear Father, want to see us and accept us for the sake of your dear Son, our Lord and Saviour, Jesus Christ, Jesus's blood and righteousness we my jewels and my cost of honour. And if at times we are too much cast down by your chastisement – if the furnace that is to purify us burns with too strong a heat – then don't take it too amiss; forgive us our sins. Grant us patience, Holy Father, so that after all this suffering we can participate in your eternal bliss. Amen.

Mother Hilse (*having listened, strenuously, bent forward, crying*)   You always make up such beautiful prayers, father.

Luise *goes to the wash-tub,* **Gottlieb** *into the room opposite.*

Old Hilse   Where's the girl?

Luise   Over at Petterswaldau – at Dreissiger's. She spooled a few more bobbins last night.

Old Hilse (*speaking very loudly*)   I'd better bring you your wheel, Mother.

Mother Hilse   Well, bring it, Bring it, father.

Old Hilse (*putting the wheel down in front of her*)   I wanted to do it myself . . .

Mother Hilse   No . . . no . . . what would I do with all that time.

Old Hilse   I'll give your fingers a bit of a wipe so the yarn doesn't get greasy – all right? (*He wipes her hands with a rag.*)

Luise (*from the wash-tub*)   Where would we have got the grease from?

Old Hilse   If there's no grease we eat dry bread – if there's no bread we eat potatoes – if there's no potatoes any more we eat dry bran.

Old Hilse (*irritated*)   And when there's no black flour, we'll do what the Wenglers did – we'll search where a tanner's buried a dead horse. Then we'll dig it up and live on rotten meat for a few weeks – that's what we'll do, isn't it?

Gottlieb (*from the back room*)   Is that a vulture I hear?

Old Hilse   You should watch yourself with that Godless talk! (*He goes to the loom and calls.*) Will you give me a hand, Gottlieb? There's still a few threads to pull through.

Luise (*from the wash-tub*)   Gottlieb, come and help your father!

Gottlieb *enters. The old man and his son begin the arduous task of putting up the threads. The threads of the warp are pulled through the eyes of the comb or the shaft of the loom. They have scarcely begun when* **Hornig** *appears in the 'house'.*

Hornig (*from the threshold*)   Good luck with your work.

Old Hilse   Thank you Hornig. Tell me, when do you get any sleep? During the day you do your rounds, and at night you stand guard.

Hornig   I don't sleep any more.

Luise   Welcome, Hornig.

Old Hilse   Well, what's the good news?

Hornig   It is good news too. The weavers in Peterswaldau have risked hell and damnation and chased the factory-owner Dreissiger away – and the whole of his family.

Luise (*with a trace of excitement*)   Hornig's telling stories again.

Hornig   Not this time, young woman, not this time. – I've got some nice children's aprons on the cart – no, honestly, I'm telling you no more than the truth. They've chased them away. Last night, they arrived in Reichenbach, and as God's my witness they wouldn't keep them there at first from fear of the weavers, so he had to move on again in a hurry – to Schweidnitz this time.

Old Hilse *carefully takes up the threads of the warp and brings them near the shaft, while from the other side* **Gottlieb** *uses a wire hook to pull them through one of the eyes.*

Old Hilse   It's about time you stopped, Hornig.

Hornig   May I be struck dead – every child knows as much.

Old Hilse   Tell me, have I gone mad or have you?

Hornig   Honest, what I told you is the God's truth. I wouldn't have said anything if I hadn't seen it myself. I saw it with my own eyes, as true as I can see you now, Gottlieb. They've wrecked the factory owner's house from top to bottom. They threw his china from the attic windows – right over the roof. I wonder how much linen's lying in the river. The water's stopped up, believe me, it's flooding the banks. It looked blue as sulphur from all the indigo dye they chucked out of the window. Blue dust-clouds kept shooting down. They've done over that house good and proper. Not only the living-quarters, the dye-works too – and the

warehouse. The staircase is smashed to pieces, the floor-boards
torn up, windows broken, the sofa, the chairs, smashed and
slashed, cut and torn, trampled on and hacked to pieces. You've
no idea – it's worse than the war.

Old Hilse   And they were supposed to be weavers from here?
(*Slowly and incredulously he shakes his head. Tenants, curious, have gathered
outside the door.*)

Hornig   Where else? I could give you all their names. I took a
Councillor through the house, I spoke to a lot of them. They were
as helpful as ever. They went about their business very carefully
but they made a thorough job of it. The Councillor spoke to
them too – they were their usual humble selves. They wouldn't be
stopped though. The finest pieces of furniture, they were smashed
by the weavers as though they were being paid for it.

Old Hilse   You took a Councillor through the house?

Hornig   Why not? I had nothing to be afraid of, they all know
me – I've no quarrel with them, I'm on good terms with everybody.
I went through that house as sure as my name's Hornig and believe
me, I went weak at the knees – and the Councillor too – it really
touched him. And do you know why? You didn't hear a single
word – it was all done in silence. It really touched your heart to see
the way those poor, hungry beggars took their revenge.

Luise (*trembling with excitement, rubbing her eyes with her apron*)   It's
right! It had to come.

Voices (*of the neighbours*)   There are enough slave-drivers around
here – there's one across the street – he's got four horses and six
carriages in his stables but his weavers die of starvation.

Old Hilse (*still unbelieving*)   How is it supposed to have started?

Hornig   Who knows? Who can tell? One says one thing,
another tells you something else.

Old Hilse   What did they say?

Hornig   As God's my witness, Dreissiger's supposed to have
said, 'If the weavers are hungry, they can graze on grass, like the
other animals!' – that's all I know.

There is movement among the **Neighbours** *as one tells the other with angry gestures.*

Old Hilse   Now listen to me, Hornig. You can say to me, 'Father Hilse, tomorrow you must die', and I'll answer, 'That's all right by me, I don't mind'. – If you said to me, 'Father Hilse, tomorrow the King of Prussia will pay you a visit', I'd say, 'I believe you', but to tell me that weavers, people like me and my son, should have done things like that – never! No, I will never believe that!

Mielchen, *a pretty seven-year old girl with long, loose flaxen hair, carrying a little basket on her arm comes jumping in. She holds a silver table-spoon towards her mother.*

Mielchen   Mama, Mama, look what I've got. You can buy me a dress with this.

Luise   What is it now, child? (*With increasing excitement and tension.*) What have you got there? You're all out of breath, and the bobbins are still in your basket. What does it mean?

Old Hilse   Where did you get the spoon from, child?

Luise   Maybe she found it.

Hornig   Could be worth two or three thaler.

Old Hilse (*beside himself*)   Get out, girl, get out! – I said go – quickly! Will you do as I say or must I beat you? You'll take that spoon right back where you found it. Go on! Do you want to make thieves of all of us? Eh? You little brat, I'll teach you to steal! (*He looks for something to hit her with.*)

Mielchen (*clings to her mother's skirt, cries*)   Grandpa, don't hit me! – we – have – all – got – them. The – bobbin children – all – have them.

Luise (*with a mixture of fear and anxiety, bursts out*)   You see, she found it. Where did you find it?

Mielchen (*sobbing*)   In Peters – waldau – we found it – in front of Dreissiger's – house.

Old Hilse   That's all I wanted to hear. Now get out or I'll kick you out!

Mother Hilse   What's going on?

Hornig   I'll tell you what, Father Hilse, let Gottlieb put on a coat and take the spoon over to the police-station.

Old Hilse   Gottlieb, put your coat on!

Gottlieb (*already putting it on, eagerly*)   I'll go to the station and tell them not to make too much of it, she's only a child and she doesn't understand – I'll give them the spoon. Stop crying, girl.

The crying child is taken by her mother into the back room, she closes the door and then returns.

Hornig   That could easily be worth three thaler.

Gottlieb   Give me a cloth, Luke, so it doesn't get damaged. Would you believe it, so valuable. (*He has tears in his eyes as he wraps the spoon.*)

Luise   If we sold it, we could eat for weeks.

Old Hilse   Go on, hurry up! Go as quickly as you can. – Sell it, indeed. Go on, get this devil's spoon out of here!

Gottlieb *leaves with the spoon.*

Hornig   Time for me to be on my way. (*He goes, talks for a few seconds with the neighbours, then goes out.*)

Surgeon Schmidt (*enters. He is a mercurial, rotund little man with a ruddy, sly face.*)   Good morning, everyone. A nice business this is. You be careful. (*Wagging his finger.*) You're a sly bunch, you are. (*He stands in the doorway.*) Good morning, Father Hilse. (*To one of the women neighbours:*) Well, Mother, how's the pain? Better, eh? There, you see? I thought I'd better see how you're getting on, Father Hilse.

Father Hilse   What's the trouble with mother?

Luise   The veins in her eyes have dried up, Doctor. She can't see anything any more.

Schmidt   That's because of the dust and working by candle-light. Now tell me, do any of you know what's going on here? It seems the whole of Peterswaldau is on its way here. I sit in my carriage this morning, thinking about nothing in particular, suddenly I hear extraordinary stories. What in the devil's name has got hold of these people, Father Hilse? They're rampaging like a pack of wolves – revolution, rebellion – they're totally out of control – plundering and marauding . . . Where's Mielchen?

Mielchen, *her eyes still red from crying, is pushed in by her mother.*

Have a look in my coat-pocket, Mielchen.

She does so.

The ginger-nuts are for you – now, now, not all at once. Good girl. First, a song: – 'Foxy, leave our . . . ' – come on, 'Foxy, leave our goose alone' . . . you bad girl, I've been hearing stories about you. You called the sparrows on the rectory garden fence a bad name and they've gone and reported it to the Pastor. (*To the others:*) Now somebody tell me, are there really fifteen hundred people on the march?

Bells are heard ringing in the distance.

Do you hear that? In Reichenbach, they're ringing a storm-warning. Fifteen hundred people. Like the end of the world. Frightening!

Old Hilse   Are they really on the way to Bielau?

Schmidt   Of course. I've just driven through them, right through the whole mob. I'd like to have got out and given each one of them a sleeping-draught. They were trotting along, one behind the other, looking like death warmed up and singing and making a terrible din, enough to turn one's stomach – it made me want to be sick. Friedrich, my driver, up on the box, howled like an old woman. As soon as we got through them we had to stop off for a good, stiff drink. I wouldn't be a factory-owner for anything in the world.

Singing is heard in the distance.

Do you hear that? Sounds like someone banging on an old frying-pan. They'll be here within five minutes. Goodbye, my friends, don't do anything stupid. The soldiers are right on their tails. Don't lose your heads, like that crowd from Peterswaldau.

Bells are starting to toll from a nearby church.

God in Heaven! Now our bells have started ringing – that'll drive them completely insane. (*He goes upstairs.*)

Gottlieb (*returns breathlessly*)   I've seen them, I've seen them. (*To a woman neighbour:*) They're here, mother. (*In the doorway.*) Father, they're here! They've bean-poles, hooks and axes. They're already up at Dietrich's making a terrible row, I think he's giving them money to get rid of them. Oh God, what'll become of us? I don't want to know. All these people, all this crowd – once they get started, oh God, our factory-owners will really be up against it.

Old Hilse   Why did you have to run? You'll get your old chest trouble and then you'll be flat on your back again.

Gottlieb (*half exhilarated*)   I had to run or they'd have dragged me along with them. They were all shouting at me to join them as it was. Godfather Baumert was one of them. He said to me, 'Go and get your five groschen. You're a starving weaver like the rest of us'. He even said, 'Go and tell your father'. I'm supposed to tell you, Father, to come and help pay back the factory-owners for cutting our wages. (*With passion.*) 'Times are changing,' he said, 'things are going to change for us weavers, we should all come and do our bit. Then we'll all get our half-pound of meat on Sundays, and on Holy Days blood-sausage and cabbage, 'It's all going to change,' that's what he told me.

Old Hilse (*with suppressed indignation*)   Call himself your Godfather! And he wants you to take part in such criminal activities? Have nothing to do with it, Gottlieb, this is the devil's work.

Luise (*overcome with passion and excitement, vehemently*)   That's right, Gottlieb, go and crawl behind the stove. Help yourself to a spoon and put a bowl of butter-milk on your knees, change into a dress and say your prayers – then you'll be what your father wants – call yourself a man!

Laughter from the neighbours.

Old Hilse (*shaking with fury*)   And you call yourself a woman? I'll tell you something – you may be a mother but you've got a wicked tongue. You set yourself up as an example to your child and then you push your husband into crime and lawlessness.

Luise (*beside herself*)   You and your fine speeches . . . they won't
feed my child! Thanks to that, all four of them went ragged and
filthy – your words haven't dried a single nappy. Yes, I call myself
a mother if you want to know and if you want to know something
else I hope a plague falls on these factory-owners, I wish them
to hell! Just because I am a mother – how was I to keep the poor
little creatures alive? I've cried without stopping from the moment
one of the poor things came into the world to when death took
pity on it. You didn't care two hoots, you prayed and sang while I
worked my fingers to the bone to buy a single bowl of butter-milk.
All those hundreds of nights I racked my brain, wondering how
I could save just one of them from the churchyard. What crime
has a child committed to deserve such a miserable end – and over
at Dietrich's they bathed in wine and washed in milk – no, no,
when things get going here, no power on earth will hold me back.
And I tell you this; if they storm Dietrich's castle – I'll be the first,
and heaven help anyone who tries to stop me! – I've had enough.
That's all there is to it.

Old Hilse   You're a lost soul, no-one can help you.

Luise (*in a rage*)   It's you that can't be helped. Crawlers – that's
what you are, insects, but not men. You're worse than the beggars
they spit at in the street, cowards that run away when they hear
a baby's rattle, fools that thank their masters for giving them a
beating. They've bled you so white you can't even get red in the
face any more. Someone should take a whip to you and beat some
life into your rotten bones. (*She goes off quickly.*)

An embarrassed pause.

Mother Hilse   What's the matter with Luise, Father?

Old Hilse   Nothing, Mother, what should be the matter?

Mother Hilse   Tell me, Father, am I imagining it or are they
ringing the bells?

Old Hilse   I expect they're burying somebody, Mother.

Mother Hilse   I wish it was me. Why can't I die?

Pause.

Old Hilse (*puts down his work and rises solemnly*)   Gotdieb! – Your wife said some hurtful things. Look at this, Gottlieb! (*He bares his chest.*) There was a bullet in here the size of a thimble and the King knows where I lost my arm. It wasn't nibbled away by mice. (*He walks back and forth.*) Your wife wasn't even thought of when I was spilling my blood by the quart for the Fatherland. Let her shout as much she wants, that's all right by me, to me it's just flea-bite. Afraid? Me, afraid? What am I supposed to be afraid of, tell me? A few soldiers who might be coming after the rioters? Jesus, if that was all, it would be nothing. Maybe I'm getting a little weak in the back but if it came to it my bones are as strong as ivory, I could take on a couple of lousy bayonets. And if it got worse? Oh, how glad I'd be to make an end of it, I wouldn't need much persuading to die – rather today than tomorrow, I'd be only too glad. What am I leaving behind? Who'd shed a tear over this old heap of misery, that pile of fears and tortures that we call life? I'd be glad to leave it behind. But then, Gottlieb, there comes something else. – And if we throw that away, there's nothing.

Gottlieb   Who knows what happens when you're dead? Nobody's ever seen it.

Old Hilse   I tell you, Gottlieb, don't throw doubt on the only thing we poor people have. Why have I sat here working this treadle for forty years or more until it almost killed me? Why have I watched them over there wallowing in luxury – making gold out of my hunger and misery? For what? Because I had hope. In all my misery and hardship I still had something. (*Pointing out of the window.*) They've got their share in this world, I thought to myself, I've got mine in the other. You can hack me into little pieces but you can't take away my faith, it is ordained. The Day of Judgement is coming but we will not be the judges; 'vengeance is mine' sayeth the Lord, Our God.

A Voice (*through the window*)   Weavers, out!

Old Hilse   Do as you like. (*He climbs into the weaving-stool.*) You won't get me outside.

Gottlieb (*after a short hesitation*)   I'm going to work come what may. (*He goes out.*)

The 'Weavers' Song' is heard, sung by several hundred voices, close by; it sound like a dull, monotonous lament.

Neighbours' Voices   Christ, they're coming like ants! – Where do they all come from. – Stop pushing, I want to see too. – Look at that bean-pole walking in front. – My God! They're all over the place!

Hornig (*steps in among the* **Neighbours**)   How's that for a show? You don't see that every day. You should come up to Dietrich's, things are really happening there, he's lost his house, he's lost his factory – his wine cellar's gone, everything. They're emptying the bottles so fast, they're not even bothering to pull out the corks. Bang bang bang and the necks are broken – they don't even care if they cut their mouths on the splinters. Some of them are running about, bleeding like pigs – they'll do the same to Dietrich.

The singing has stopped.

Neighbours' Voices   They don't look all that angry.

Hornig   Give them some time, they're having a good look at the place. Can you see, they're watching that palace from all sides. You see that little, fat man – he's brought a horse-bucket with him, he's the blacksmith from Peterswaldau – he's a feared man. He can break down the strongest doors like they were pretzels. I'm not exaggerating. When he gets his hands on the factory-owner, he'll have had it!

Neighbours' Voices   Look at that! – A stone's just come through the window! – I bet old Dietrich's scared now. – He's hanging out a sign. – Why a sign? – What does it say? – Can you read it? – I'd be in trouble if I couldn't read. – Well, read it! – 'You – will – all – get – satis – faction – you will all get satisfaction.'

Hornig   He might as well not have bothered, it won't help him now. The brothers have their own ideas, they've got their eyes on the factory – it's the mechanical looms they want to get rid of, it's them that's ruining the hand-weavers: a blind man can see that, There's nothing he can do – the Christians are on the march! No magistrate or governor will bring them back to reason let alone that sign. Anyone who's seen their handiwork will know that the time has come.

Neighbours' Voices   All those people, what a crowd! – What do you want? – (*Excitedly:*) They're coming over the bridge! – (*Frightened:*) They're coming this way! – (*With the utmost surprise and fear:*) They're coming towards us! They're coming here! – They'll drag the weavers from their houses!

They all flee. The house is empty. A crowd of rebels, dirty, dusty, their faces reddened by alcohol and effort, wild, looking as if they'd been up all night, rumpled, surge into the house crying 'Weavers out' and disperse into all the rooms. **Baecker** *and several young weavers, armed with truncheons and sticks, enter* **Old Hilse**'s *room. When they recognise him, they stop, slightly sobered.*

Baecker   Stop working, Father Hilse, let others slave away at the treadle, you've suffered enough – all this will be taken care of.

1st Young Weaver   You shan't go to sleep hungry one more day.

2nd Young Weaver   Every weaver shall have a roof over his head again and a shirt on his back.

Old Hilse   What devil has brought you here with sticks and axes?

Baecker   We'll break them on Dietrich's back.

2nd Young Weaver   We'll heat them 'til they're red-hot then stuff them down these factory-owners' throats, so that they can feel how hunger burns.

1st Young Weaver   Come with us, Father Hilse! We'll show no mercy.

2nd Young Weaver   No-one took pity on us. Neither God nor man. Now we'll give justice to ourselves.

Old Baumert (*enters, already somewhat unsteady on his feet. He holds a slaughtered chicken under his arm. He holds out his arms*)   Brothers – now we're all brothers! Come to my arms, brothers!

Laughter.

Old Hilse   What a sight you are, Wilhelm.

Old Baumert   Gustav! Gustav, you poor, starving wretch – come to my arms! (*He is very moved.*)

Old Hilse (*growls*)   Leave me in peace.

Old Baumert   That's how it is, Gustav, a man must have luck. Look at me – how do I look? A man must have luck! Do I look like a Count? (*Slapping his stomach.*) Guess what's in this belly? A nobleman's feast is in this belly. If a man's lucky he gets champagne and roast hare – I'll tell you something; we've been making a mistake, we must help ourselves.

All (*not in unison*)   We must help ourselves. Hooray!

Old Baumert   When you have your first bite of good food inside you, you soon feel alive again. (*He hiccups.*) Jesus! It makes you feel as strong as an ox, there's so much strength in your limbs, you don't care who you're hitting, it's a great feeling!

Jaeger (*in the doorway, armed with an old cavalry-sabre*)   We've made some tremendous attacks.

Baecker   We're well organised now. We're inside their houses before you can count to three, then we spread like wildfire – we make things crackle and shake until the sparks fly like in a blacksmith's forge.

1st Young Weaver   We ought to start a little fire.

2nd Young Weaver   Yes! We'll march to Reichenbach and set the roofs of the rich people alight!

Jaeger   They wouldn't mind – think of all the fire insurance they'd collect.

Laughter.

Baecker   From here we march to Freiburg, to Trumtra's.

Jaeger   We should visit some of the government officials – I read somewhere that all our misfortune comes from the hureaucrats.

2nd Young Weaver   We'll soon march on Breslau, more people are joining us all the time.

Old Eaumert (*to* **Hilse**)   Have a drink, Gustav.

Old Hilse   I never drink schnapps.

Old Baumert   That was in the old days, today it's a different world, Gustav.

2nd Young Weaver   Christmas doesn't come every day.

Laughter.

Old Hilse (*impatiently*)   You hounds of hell! What do you want from me?

Old Baumert (*slightly intimidated, excessively friendly*)   I wanted to bring you a chicken – look. You can make Mother some soup.

Old Hilse (*touched, more friendly*)   You go and tell Mother.

Mother Hilse (*her hand cupped to her ear, has strained to listen. She waves them away*)   Leave me alone, I don't want any chicken soup.

Old Hilse   You're right, Mother, I don't want any either. Especially not this. As for you, Baumert, let me tell you something. When the old start behaving like children, the Devil jumps for joy. And just so you're in no doubt, I want you all to know – me and you, we've got nothing in common. You're here against my will – you have no right to be here!

Voice   He who's not with us is against us.

Jaeger (*brutally threatening*)   You've got it all wrong, old man. We're not thieves.

Voice   We're hungry – nothing more.

1st Young Weaver   We want to live and nothing more, so we cut the rope from round our necks.

Jaeger   And we were right to do it! (*Holding his fist in front of* **Hilse**'s *face.*) Another word out of you and you'll get this in the face.

Baecker   Stop it! Calm down. Leave the old man alone – we thought as you did once, Father Hilse, – better dead than live like this.

Old Hilse   I've lived for sixty years or more.

Baecker   That doesn't matter – things have got to change.

Old Hilse   That'll be the day.

Baecker   What we can't get peacefully, we'll take by force.

Old Hilse   By force? (*Laughs.*) You're digging your own graves. They'll show you who's got force, just you wait, boy!

Jaeger   You mean because of the soldiers? We were soldiers too. We can tackle a few Companies.

Old Hilse   With your mouth perhaps. And even if you do, you'll chase away two and ten will come back.

Voices (*through the window*)   The soldiers are coming! Take cover!

Sudden silence. For a moment, the dim sound of fife and drum is heard. In the silence, a sudden, involuntary cry.

To hell with it, I'm getting out of here!

General laughter.

Baecker   Who's talking about getting out? Who was that?

Jaeger   Who's afraid of a few lousy Prussians? I'll take charge, I was in the army, I know their game.

Old Hilse   What are you going to shoot with? Your truncheons.

1st Young Weaver   Take no notice of the old fool, he's not quite right in the head.

2nd Young Weaver   He's certainly a bit gone.

Gottlieb (*has entered unnoticed, he gets hold of the* **1st Young Weaver**)   Is that how you speak to an old man?

1st Young Weaver   Leave me alone, I didn't say anything.

Old Hilse (*interceding*)   Let him jabber. Don't provoke him, Gottlieb. He'll soon see which of us isn't right in the head.

Baecker   Coming with us, Gottlieb?

Old Hilse   No, he's not!

Luise (*calling as she enters*)   Don't waste your time with these church-mice, they're no good to anybody. Come to the square! Come on, the square! Father Baumert, quickly! The Major's speaking to people from his horse. He's telling them to go home. If we don't hurry, we've lost the game!

Jaeger (*as he leaves*)   You've got yourself a brave husband.

Luise   Who says I've got a husband?

Voices (*singing* in *the hallway*)
'Once there was a little man,
Ha! Ha! Ha!
Whose wife had an enormous span
Ho! Ho! Ho!'

Wittig (*his horse-bucket in his hand, has come from the upper floor. He stops for a moment on his way out*)   Anyone who's not a coward, follow me!
He storms out, followed by a cheering group including **Luise** *and* **Jaeger**.

Baecker   Keep well, Father Hilse, we'll speak again. (*About to go.*)

Old Hilse   I doubt that. I won't live another five years, and you won't get out before that.

Baecker (*stops, surprised*)   Get out of what, Father Hilse?

Old Hilse   Out of prison, what else?

Baecker (*laughing wildly*)   That's what I've been waiting for. At least you get bread there, Father Hilse. (*He goes out.*)

Old Baumert (*has been sitting on a stool, brooding. He now rises*)   You were right, Gustav, I am a little bit drunk, but I'm still clear in my head. You've got your view of things and I've got mine. I say Baecker is right – if it ends in ropes and chains, it'll still be better in prison than home. You're looked after there, you don't have to go hungry. I'd have preferred not to join them but you see, Gustav, a man must breathe fresh air just once in his life. (*Walks slowly to the door.*) Keep well, Gustav. If anything should happen, say a little prayer for me, won't you? (*He goes out.*)

The rioters have all gone now and the hallway gradually fills up again with curious neighbours. **Old Hilse** *knots at his web.* **Gottlieb** *has taken the axe from behind the stove and tests the blade sub-consciously. Both of them are shaken but silent. From outside the burn and roar of a great mass of people is heard.*

Mother Hilse   Look, Father, the floor is shaking in such a funny way. What's happening? What's going on?

Pause.

Old Hilse   Gottlieb?

Gottlieb   What is it?

Old Hilse   Put that axe down!

Gottlieb   Then who'll cut the fire-wood? (*He leans the axe against the stove.*)

Pause.

Mother Hilse   Listen to what your father tells you, Gottlieb.

Voice (*Singing in front of the window*)
'Stay at home my little man
Ha! Ha! Ha!
Clean the plates and scrape the pan
Ho! Ho! Ho!'

Gottlieb (*jumps up and shouts out through the window with fist clenched*)   Bastard! You dare provoke me!

A volley of rifle-fire is heard.

Mother Hilse (*shocked*)   Oh Jesus Christ, now it's starting to thunder!

Old Hilse (*his hand on his heart praying*)   Oh God in heaven, protect the poor weavers, protect my poor brothers.

A brief silence.

Old Hilse (*shattered, to himself*)   Now the blood is flowing.

Gottlieb *has jumped up at the sound of the salvo. He grips the axe firmly. He is pale and almost unable to control his deep, inner emotion.*

Gottlieb   Am I still supposed to hide here?

Weaver Girl (*calling from the hallway*)   Father Hilse, Father Hilse! Get away from the window! A bullet flew through our window upstairs. (*She disappears.*)

Mielchen (*sticks her face through the window, laughing*)   Grandpa, Grandpa! They shot with their guns! Some of them fell down! One of them keeps rolling around like a wheel and one of them's twitching like a sparrow with its head pulled off! Oh and *so* much blood's coming out! (*She disappears.*)

Weaver Woman   They've killed a few.

Old Weaver (*in the hallway*)   They'll take on the soldiers now, mark my words.

Another Weaver (*dazed*)   Look at the women – just look at the women! Lifting up their skirts, spitting at the soldiers.

Weaver Woman (*calling from outside*)   Look, Gottlieb! Look at your wife! She's got more guts than you, she's jumping in front of those bayonets as if she was dancing.

Four men carry a wounded man through the hallway. Silence. Then a voice is heard clearly.

Voice   It's Weaver Ulbrich. (*A few seconds silence.*) Not a chance, he got a bullet right through the ear.

Men are heard climbing the wooden staircase. Suddenly from outside, cheering is heard.

Voices (*in the hallway*)   Where did they get the stones from? – From the road they're building. – The soldiers have had it. – It's raining paving-stones.

Sceams of terror and shouting from outside spreads into the hallway. The door is slammed shut with a cry of terror.

Voices (*from the hallway*)   They're re-loading. – They'll soon be more shooting. – Father Hilse, get away from the window.

Gottlieb (*runs for his axe*)   My God! My God! Are we animals? Do they want us to eat bullets instead of bread? (*Axe in hand, he hesitates for a moment, they says to* **Old Hilse**.) Shall I let them shoot my wife? I won't allow it! (*As he storms out.*) Look out, I'm coming! (*He goes.*)

Old Hilse   Gottlieb, Gottlieb!

Mother Hilse   Where is Gottlieb?

Old Hilse   He's gone to the Devil.

Voice (*from the hallway*)   Get away from the window, Father Hilse!

Old Hilse   I won't! Not even if you all go mad. (*To* **Mother Hilse**, *with growing ecstasy*:) This is where we'll stay and do our duty, even if the snow catches fire. (*He starts to weave.*)

There is a loud volley. **Old Hilse** *is struck. He rises up and falls forward across his loom, dead. At the same moment, there is a resounding cry of 'Hooray'. Cheering, the people hitherto in the hallway storm outside.*

Mother Hilse (*asking several times*)   Father, Father, what's the matter with you?

The uninterrupted cheering gradually fades into the distance. Suddenly, in a great hurry, **Mielchen** *runs into the room.*

Mielchen   Grandpa, Grandpa! They're chasing the soldiers out of the village! They've stormed Dietrich's house, the same way they did over at Dreissiger's. Grandpa?

She is suddenly frightened, becoming aware of what has happened. She sticks her finger in her mouth and carefully approaches the dead man.

Grandpa!

Mother Hilse   Why don't you say something, Father? You're frightening me.

The End.

BERNARD SHAW

Mrs Warren's Profession

Characters

Mr Praed
Vivie Warren
Mrs Warren
Sir George Crofts
Frank Gardner
The Rev. Samuel Gardner

Act One

Summer afternoon in a cottage garden on the eastern slope of a hill a little south of Haslemere in Surrey. Looking up the hill, the cottage is seen in the left hand corner of the garden, with its thatched roof and porch, and a large latticed window to the left of the porch. A paling completely shuts in the garden, except for a gate on the right. The common rises uphill beyond the paling to the sky line. Some folded canvas garden chairs are leaning against the side bench in the porch. A lady's bicycle is propped against the wall, under the window. A little to the right of the porch a hammock is slung from two posts. A big canvas umbrella, stuck in the ground, keeps the sun off the hammock, in which a young lady lies reading and making notes, her head towards the cottage and her feet towards the gate. In front of the hammock, and within reach of her hand, is a common kitchen chair, with a pile of serious-looking books and a supply of writing paper on it.

A gentleman walking on the common comes into sight from behind the cottage. He is hardly past middle age, with something of the artist about him, unconventionally but carefully dressed, and clean-shaven except for a moustache, with an eager susceptible face and very amiable and considerate manners. He has silky black hair, with waves of grey and white in it. His eyebrows are white, his moustache black. He seems not certain of his way. He looks over the paling; takes stock of the place; and sees the young lady.

The Gentleman (*taking off his hat*)   I beg your pardon. Can you direct me to Hindhead View – Mrs Alison's?

The Young Lady (*glancing up from her book*)   This is Mrs Alison's. (*She resumes her work.*)

The Gentleman   Indeed! Perhaps – may I ask are you Miss Vivie Warren?

The Young Lady (*sharply, as she turns on her elbow to get a good look at him*)   Yes.

The Gentleman (*daunted and conciliatory*)   I'm afraid I appear intrusive. My name is Praed. (**Vivie** *at once throws her books upon the chair, and gets out of the hammock.*) Oh, pray dont let me disturb you.

Vivie (*striding to the gate and opening it for him*)   Come in, Mr Praed. (*He comes in.*) Glad to see you. (*She proffers her hand and takes his with a resolute and hearty grip. She is an attractive specimen of the sensible, able, highly-educated young middle-class Englishwoman. Age 22. Prompt, strong, confident, self-possessed. Plain business-like dress, but not dowdy. She wears a chatelaine at her belt, with a fountain pen and a paper knife among its pendants.*)

Praed   Very kind of you indeed, Miss Warren. (*She shuts the gate with a vigorous slam. He passes in to the middle of the garden, exercising his fingers, which are slightly numbed by her greeting.*) Has your mother arrived?

Vivie (*quickly, evidently scenting aggression*)   Is she coming?

Praed (*surprised*)   Didnt you expect us?

Vivie   No.

Praed   Now, goodness me, I hope Ive not mistaken the day. That would be just like me, you know. Your mother arranged that she was to come down from London and that I was to come over from Horsham to be introduced to you.

Vivie (*not at all pleased.*)   Did she? Hm! My mother has rather a trick of taking me by surprise – to see how I behave myself when she's away, I suppose. I fancy I shall take my mother very much by surprise one of these days, if she makes arrangements that concern me without consulting me beforehand. She hasnt come.

Praed (*embarrassed*)   I'm really very sorry.

Vivie (*throwing off her displeasure*)   It's not your fault, Mr Praed, is it? And I'm very glad youve come. You are the only one of my mother's friends I have ever asked her to bring to see me.

Praed (*relieved and delighted*)   Oh, now this is really very good of you, Miss Warren!

Vivie   Will you come indoors; or would you rather sit out here and talk?

Praed   It will be nicer out here, dont you think?

Vivie   Then I'll go and get you a chair. (*She goes to the porch for a garden chair.*)

Praed (*following her*)   Oh, pray, pray! Allow me. (*He lays hands on the chair.*)

Vivie (*letting him take it*)   Take care of your fingers: theyre rather dodgy things, those chairs. (*She goes across to the chair with the books on it; pitches them into the hammock; and brings the chair forward with one swing.*)

Praed (*who has just unfolded his chair*)   Oh, now do let me take that hard chair. I like hard chairs.

Vivie   So do I. Sit down, Mr Praed. (*This invitation she gives with genial peremptoriness, his anxiety to please her clearly striking her as a sign of weakness of character on his part. But he does not immediately obey.*)

Praed   By the way, though, hadnt we better go to the station to meet your mother?

Vivie (*coolly*)   Why? She knows the way.

Praed (*disconcerted*)   Er − I suppose she does. (*He sits down.*)

Vivie   Do you know, you are just like what I expected. I hope you are disposed to be friends with me.

Praed (*again beaming*)   Thank you, my dear Miss Warren: thank you. Dear me! I'm so glad your mother hasnt spoilt you!

Vivie   How?

Praed   Well, in making you too conventional. You know, my dear Miss Warren, I am a born anarchist. I hate authority. It spoils the relations between parent and child: even between mother and daughter. Now I was always afraid that your mother would strain her authority to make you very conventional. It's such a relief to find that she hasnt.

Vivie   Oh! have I been behaving unconventionally?

Praed   Oh no: oh dear no. At least not conventionally unconventionally, you understand. (*She nods and sits down. He goes on, with a cordial outburst.*) But it was so charming of you to say that you were disposed to be friends with me! You modern young ladies are splendid: perfectly splendid!

Vivie (*dubiously*)   Eh? (*Watching him with dawning disappointment as to the quality of his brains and character.*)

Praed   When I was your age, young men and women were afraid of each other: there was no good fellowship. Nothing real. Only gallantry copied out of novels, and as vulgar and affected as it could be. Maidenly reserve! gentlemanly chivalry! always saying no when you meant yes! simple purgatory for shy and sincere souls.

Vivie   Yes, I imagine there must have been a frightful waste of time. Especially women's time.

Praed   Oh, waste of life, waste of everything. But things are improving. Do you know, I have been in a positive state of excitement about meeting you ever since your magnificent achievements at Cambridge: a thing unheard of in my day. It was perfectly splendid, your tieing with the third wrangler. Just the right place, you know. The first wrangler is always a dreamy, morbid fellow, in whom the thing is pushed to the length of a disease.

Vivie   It doesnt pay. I wouldnt do it again for the same money!

Praed (*aghast*)   The same money!

Vivie   I did it for £50.

Praed   Fifty pounds!

Vivie   Yes. Fifty pounds. Perhaps you dont know how it was. Mrs Latham, my tutor at Newnham, told my mother that I could distinguish myself in the mathematical tripos if I went in for it in earnest. The papers were full just then of Phillipa Summers beating the senior wrangler. You remember about it, of course.

Praed (*shakes his head energetically*)   ! ! !

Vivie   Well anyhow she did: and nothing would please my mother but that I should do the same thing. I said flatly it was not worth my while to face the grind since I was not going in for teaching; but I offered to try for fourth wrangler or thereabouts for £50. She closed with me at that, after a little grumbling; and I was better than my bargain. But I wouldnt do it again for that. £200 would have been nearer the mark.

Praed (*much damped*)   Lord bless me! Thats a very practical way of looking at it.

Vivie   Did you expect to find me an unpractical person?

Praed   But surely it's practical to consider not only the work these honors cost, but also the culture they bring.

Vivie   Culture! My dear Mr Praed: do you know what the mathematical tripos means? It means grind, grind, grind for six to eight hours a day at mathematics, and nothing but mathematics. I'm supposed to know something about science; but I know nothing except the mathematics it involves. I can make calculations for engineers, electricians, insurance companies, and so on; but I know next to nothing about engineering or electricity or insurance. I dont even know arithmetic well. Outside mathematics, lawn tennis, eating, sleeping, cycling, and walking, I'm a more ignorant barbarian than any woman could possibly be who hadnt gone in for the tripos.

Praed (*revolted*)   What a monstrous, wicked, rascally system! I knew it! I felt at once that it meant destroying all that makes womanhood beautiful.

Vivie   I dont object to it on that score in the least. I shall turn it to very good account, I assure you.

Praed   Pooh! in what way?

Vivie   I shall set up chambers in the City, and work at actuarial calculations and conveyancing. Under cover of that I shall do some law, with one eye on the Stock Exchange all the time. Ive come down here by myself to read law: not for a holiday, as my mother imagines. I hate holidays.

Praed   You make my blood run cold. Are you to have no romance, no beauty in your life?

Vivie   I dont care for either, I assure you.

Praed   You cant mean that.

Vivie   Oh yes I do. I like working and getting paid for it. When I'm tired of working, I like a comfortable chair, a cigar, a little whisky, and a novel with a good detective story in it.

Praed (*rising in a frenzy of repudiation*)   I dont believe it. I am an artist; and I cant believe it: I refuse to believe it. It's only that you havnt discovered yet what a wonderful world art can open up to you.

Vivie   Yes I have. Last May I spent six weeks in London with Honoria Fraser. Mamma thought we were doing a round of sightseeing together; but I was really at Honoria's chambers in Chancery Lane every day, working away at actuarial calculations for her, and helping her as well as a greenhorn could. In the evenings we smoked and talked, and never dreamt of going out except for exercise. And I never enjoyed myself more in my life. I cleared all my expenses, and got initiated into the business without a fee into the bargain.

Praed   But bless my heart and soul, Miss Warren, do you call that discovering art?

Vivie   Wait a bit. That wasnt the beginning. I went up to town on an invitation from some artistic people in Fitz-john's Avenue: one of the girls was a Newnham chum. They took me to the National Gallery –

Praed (*approving*)   Ah! ! (*He sits down, much relieved.*)

Vivie (*continuing*)   – to the Opera –

Praed (*still more pleased*)   Good!

Vivie   – and to a concert where the band played all the evening: Beethoven and Wagner and so on. I wouldnt go through that experience again for anything you could offer me. I held out for civility's sake until the third day; and then I said, plump out, that I couldnt stand any more of it, and went off to Chancery Lane. Now you know the sort of perfectly splendid modern young lady I am. How do you think I shall get on with my mother?

Praed (*startled*)   Well, I hope – er –

Vivie   It's not so much what you hope as what you believe, that I want to know.

Praed   Well, frankly, I am afraid your mother will be a little disappointed. Not from any shortcoming on your part, you know: I dont mean that. But you are so different from her ideal.

Vivie   Her what?!

Praed   Her ideal.

Vivie   Do you mean her ideal of ME?

Praed   Yes.

Vivie   What on earth is it like?

Praed   Well, you must have observed, Miss Warren, that people who are dissatisfied with their own bringing-up generally think that the world would be all right if everybody were to be brought up quite differently. Now your mother's life has been – er – I suppose you know –

Vivie   Dont suppose anything, Mr Praed. I hardly know my mother. Since I was a child I have lived in England, at school or college, or with people paid to take charge of me. I have been boarded out all my life. My mother has lived in Brussels or Vienna and never let me go to her. I only see her when she visits England for a few days. I dont complain: it's been very pleasant; for people have been very good to me; and there has always been plenty of money to make things smooth. But dont imagine I know anything about my mother. I know far less than you do.

Praed (*very ill at ease*)   In that case – (*He stops, quite at a loss. Then, with a forced attempt at gaiety.*) But what nonsense we are talking! Of course you and your mother will get on capitally. (*He rises, and looks abroad at the view.*) What a charming little place you have here!

Vivie (*unmoved*)   Rather a violent change of subject, Mr Praed. Why wont my mother's life bear being talked about?

Praed   Oh, you really mustnt say that. Isnt it natural that I should have a certain delicacy in talking to my old friend's daughter about her behind her back? You and she will have plenty of opportunity of talking about it when she comes.

Vivie   No: she wont talk about it either. (*Rising.*) However, I daresay you have good reasons for telling me nothing. Only, mind this, Mr Praed. I expect there will be a battle royal when my mother hears of my Chancery Lane project.

Praed (*ruefully*)   I'm afraid there will.

Vivie   Well, I shall win, because I want nothing but my fare to London to start there to-morrow earning my own living by devil-ling for Honoria. Besides, I have no mysteries to keep up; and it seems she has. I shall use that advantage over her if necessary.

Praed (*greatly shocked*)   Oh no! No, pray. Youd not do such a thing.

Vivie   Then tell me why not.

Praed   I really cannot. I appeal to your good feeling. (*She smiles at his sentimentality.*) Besides, you may be too bold. Your mother is not to be trifled with when she's angry.

Vivie   You cant frighten me, Mr Praed. In that month at Chancery Lane I had opportunities of taking the measure of one or two women very like my mother. You may back me to win. But if I hit harder in my ignorance than I need, remember that it is you who refuse to enlighten me. Now, let us drop the subject. (*She takes her chair and replaces it near the hammock with the same vigorous swing as before.*)

Praed (*taking a desperate resolution*)   One word, Miss Warren. I had better tell you. It's very difficult; but –

Mrs Warren *and* **Sir George Crofts** *arrive at the gate.* **Mrs Warren** *is between 40 and 50, formerly pretty, showily dressed in a brilliant hat and a gay blouse fitting tightly over her bust and flanked by fashionable sleeves. Rather spoilt and domineering, and decidedly vulgar, but, on the whole, a genial and fairly presentable old blackguard of a woman.*

Crofts *is a tall powerfully-built man of about 50, fashionably dressed in the style of a young man. Nasal voice, reedier than might be expected from his strong frame. Clean-shaven bulldog jaws, large flat ears, and thick neck: gentlemanly combination of the most brutal types of city man, sporting man, and man about town.*

Vivie   Here they are. (*Coming to them as they enter the garden.*) How do, mater? Mr Praed's been here this half hour waiting for you.

Mrs Warren   Well, if youve been waiting, Praddy, it's your own fault: I thought youd have had the gumption to know I was coming by the 3.10 train. Vivie: put your hat on, dear: youll get sunburnt. Oh, I forgot to introduce you. Sir George Crofts: my little Vivie.

Crofts *advances to* **Vivie** *with his most courtly manner. She nods, but makes no motion to shake hands.*

Crofts   May I shake hands with a young lady whom I have known by reputation very long as the daughter of one of my oldest friends?

Vivie (*who has been looking him up and down sharply*)   If you like. (*She takes his tenderly proffered hand and gives it a squeeze that makes him open his eyes; then turns away and says to her mother:*) Will you come in, or shall I get a couple more chairs? (*She goes into the porch for the chairs.*)

Mrs Warren   Well, George, what do you think of her?

Crofts (*ruefully*)   She has a powerful fist. Did you shake hands with her, Praed?

Praed   Yes: it will pass off presently.

Crofts   I hope so. (**Vivie** *reappears with two more chairs. He hurries to her assistance.*) Allow me.

Mrs Warren (*patronizingly*)   Let Sir George help you with the chairs, dear.

Vivie (*pitching them into his arms*)   Here you are. (*She dusts her hands and turns to* **Mrs Warren**.) Youd like some tea, wouldnt you?

Mrs Warren (*sitting in* **Praed**'s *chair and fanning herself*)   I'm dying for a drop to drink.

Vivie   I'll see about it. (*She goes into the cottage.*)

Sir George *has by this time managed to unfold a chair and plant it beside* **Mrs Warren**, *on her left. He throws the other on the grass and sits down, looking dejected and rather foolish, with the handle of his stick in his mouth.* **Praed**, *still very uneasy, fidgets about the garden on their right.*

Mrs Warren (*to* **Praed**, *looking at* **Crofts**)   Just look at him, Praddy: he looks cheerful, dont he? He's been worrying my life out these three years to have that little girl of mine shewn to him; and now that Ive done it, he's quite out of countenance. (*Briskly.*) Come! sit up, George; and take your stick out of your mouth. (**Crofts** *sulkily obeys.*)

Praed   I think, you know – if you dont mind my saying so – that we had better get out of the habit of thinking of her as a little girl. You see she has really distinguished herself; and I'm not sure, from what I have seen of her, that she is not older than any of us.

Mrs Warren (*greatly amused*)   Only listen to him, George! Older than any of us! Well, she has been stuffing you nicely with her importance.

Praed   But young people are particularly sensitive about being treated in that way.

Mrs Warren   Yes; and young people have to get all that nonsense taken out of them, and a good deal more besides. Dont you interfere, Praddy: I know how to treat my own child as well as you do. (**Praed**, *with a grave shake of his head, walks up the garden with his hands behind his back.* **Mrs Warren** *pretends to laugh, but looks after him with perceptible concern. Then she whispers to* **Crofts**:) Whats the matter with him? What does he take it like that for?

Crofts (*morosely*)   Youre afraid of Praed.

Mrs Warren   What! Me! Afraid of dear old Praddy! Why, a fly wouldnt be afraid of him.

Crofts   Youre afraid of him.

Mrs Warren (*angry*)   I'll trouble you to mind your own business, and not try any of your sulks on me. I'm not afraid of you, anyhow. If you cant make yourself agreeable, youd better go home. (*She gets up, and, turning her back on him, finds herself face to face with* **Praed**.) Come, Praddy, I know it was only your tender-heartedness. Youre afraid I'll bully her.

Praed   My dear Kitty: you think I'm offended. Dont imagine that: pray dont. But you know I often notice things that escape you; and though you never take my advice, you sometimes admit afterwards that you ought to have taken it.

Mrs Warren   Well, what do you notice now?

Praed   Only that Vivie is a grown woman. Pray, Kitty, treat her with every respect.

Mrs Warren (*with genuine amazement*)   Respect! Treat my own daughter with respect! What next, pray!

Vivie (*appearing at the cottage door and calling to* **Mrs Warren**)

Mother: will you come to my room before tea?

Mrs Warren   Yes, dearie. (*She laughs indulgently at* **Praed***'s gravity, and pats him on the cheek as she passes him on her way to the porch.*) Dont be cross, Praddy. (*She follows* **Vivie** *in to the cottage.*)

Crofts (*furtively*)   I say, Praed.

Praed   Yes.

Crofts   I want to ask you a rather particular question.

Praed   Certainly. (*He takes* **Mrs Warren***'s chair and sits close to* **Crofts***.*)

Crofts   Thats right: they might hear us from the window. Look here: did Kitty ever tell you who that girl's father is?

Praed   Never.

Crofts   Have you any suspicion of who it might be?

Praed   None.

Crofts (*not believing him*)   I know, of course, that you perhaps might feel bound not to tell if she had said anything to you. But it's very awkward to be uncertain about it now that we shall be meeting the girl every day. We wont exactly know how we ought to feel towards her.

Praed   What difference can that make? We take her on her own merits. What does it matter who her father was?

Crofts (*suspiciously*)   Then you know who he was?

Praed (*with a touch of temper*)   I said no just now. Did you not hear me?

Crofts   Look here, Praed. I ask you as a particular favor. If you do know (*movement of protest from* **Praed**) – I only say, if you know, you might at least set my mind at rest about her. The fact is, I feel attracted.

Praed (*sternly*)   What do you mean?

Crofts   Oh, dont be alarmed: it's quite an innocent feeling. Thats what puzzles me about it. Why, for all I know *I* might be her father.

Praed   You! Impossible!

Crofts (*catching him up cunningly*)   You know for certain that I'm not?

Praed   I know nothing about it, I tell you, any more than you. But really, Crofts – oh no, it's out of the question. Theres not the least resemblance.

Crofts   As to that, theres no resemblance between her and her mother that I can see. I suppose she's not your daughter, is she?

Praed (*rising indignantly*)   Really, Crofts – !

Crofts   No offence, Praed. Quite allowable as between two men of the world.

Praed (*recovering himself with an effort and speaking gently and gravely*)   Now listen to me, my dear Crofts. (*He sits down again.*) I have nothing to do with that side of Mrs Warren's life, and never had. She has never spoken to me about it; and of course I have never spoken to her about it. Your delicacy will tell you that a handsome woman needs some friends who are not – well, not on that footing with her. The effect of her own beauty would become a torment to her if she could not escape from it occasionally. You are probably on much more confidential terms with Kitty than I am. Surely you can ask her the question yourself.

Crofts   I have asked her, often enough. But she's so determined to keep the child all to herself that she would deny that it ever had a father if she could. (*Rising.*) I'm thoroughly uncomfortable about it, Praed.

Praed (*rising also*)   Well, as you are, at all events, old enough to be her father, I dont mind agreeing that we both regard Miss Vivie in a parental way, as a young girl whom we are bound to protect and help. What do you say?

Crofts (*aggressively*)   I'm no older than you, if you come to that.

Praed   Yes you are, my dear fellow: you were born old. I was born a boy: Ive never been able to feel the assurance of a grown-up man in my life. (*He folds his chair and carries it to the porch.*)

Mrs Warren (*calling from within the cottage*)   Prad-dee!

George! Tea-ea-ea-ea!

Crofts (*hastily*)   She's calling us. (*He hurries in.*)

Praed *shakes his head bodingly, and is following* **Crofts** *when he is hailed by a young gentleman who has just appeared on the common, and is making for the gate. He is pleasant, pretty, smartly dressed, cleverly good-for-nothing, not long turned 20, with a charming voice and agreeably disrespectful manners. He carries a light sporting magazine rifle.*

The Young Gentleman   Hallo! Praed!

Praed   Why, Frank Gardner! (*Frank comes in and shakes hands cordially.*) What on earth are you doing here?

Frank   Staying with my father.

Praed   The Roman father?

Frank   He's rector here. I'm living with my people this autumn for the sake of economy. Things came to a crisis in July: the Roman father had to pay my debts. He's stony broke in consequence; and so am I. What are you up to in these parts? Do you know the people here?

Praed   Yes: I'm spending the day with a Miss Warren.

Frank (*enthusiastically*)   What! Do you know Vivie? Isnt she a jolly girl? I'm teaching her to shoot with this. (*Putting down the rifle.*) I'm so glad she knows you: youre just the sort of fellow she ought to know. (*He smiles, and raises the charming voice almost to a singing tone as he exclaims:*) It's ever so jolly to find you here, Praed.

Praed   I'm an old friend of her mother. Mrs Warren brought me over to make her daughter's acquaintance.

Frank   The mother! Is she here?

Praed   Yes: inside, at tea.

Mrs Warren (*calling from within*)   Prad-dee-ee-ee-eee! The tea-cake'll be cold.

Praed (*calling*)   Yes, Mrs Warren. In a moment. Ive just met a friend here.

Mrs Warren   A what?

Praed (*louder*)   A friend.

Mrs Warren   Bring him in.

Praed   All right. (*To* **Frank**:) Will you accept the invitation?

Frank (*incredulous, but immensely amused*)   Is that Vivie's mother?

Praed   Yes.

Frank   By Jove! What a lark! Do you think she'll like me?

Praed   Ive no doubt youll make yourself popular, as usual. Come in and try (*moving towards the house.*)

Frank   Stop a bit. (*Seriously.*) I want to take you into my confidence.

Praed   Pray dont. It's only some fresh folly, like the barmaid at Redhill.

Frank   It's ever so much more serious than that. You say youve only just met Vivie for the first time?

Praed   Yes.

Frank (*rhapsodically*)   Then you can have no idea what a girl she is. Such character! Such sense! And her cleverness! Oh, my eye, Praed, but I can tell you she is clever! And – need I add? – she loves me.

Crofts (*putting his head out of the window*)   I say, Praed: what are you about? Do come along. (*He disappears.*)

Frank   Hallo! Sort of chap that would take a prize at a dog show, aint he? Who's he?

Praed   Sir George Crofts, an old friend of Mrs Warren's. I think we had better come in.

On their way to the porch they are interrupted by a call from the gate. Turning, they see an elderly clergyman looking over it.

The Clergyman (*calling*)   Frank!

Frank   Hallo! (*To* **Praed**:) The Roman father. (*To* **The Clergyman**:) Yes, gov'nor: all right: presently. (*To* **Praed**:) Look here, Praed: youd better go in to tea. I'll join you directly.

Praed   Very good. (*He goes into the cottage.*)

The Clergyman *remains outside the gate, with his hands on the top of it. The* **Rev. Samuel Gardner***, a beneficed clergyman of the Established Church, is over 50. Externally he is pretentious, booming, noisy, important. Really he is that obsolescent social phenomenon the fool of the family dumped on the Church by his father the patron, clamorously asserting himself as father and clergyman without being able to command respect in either capacity.*

Rev. S   Well, sir. Who are your friends here, if I may ask?

Frank   Oh, it's all right, gov'nor! Come in.

Rev. S   No, sir; not until I know whose garden I am entering.

Frank   It's all right. It's Miss Warren's.

Rev. S   I have not seen her at church since she came.

Frank   Of course not: she's a third wrangler. Ever so intellectual. Took a higher degree than you did; so why should she go to hear you preach?

Rev. S   Dont be disrespectful, sir.

Frank   Oh, it dont matter: nobody hears us. Come in. (*He opens the gate, unceremoniously pulling his father with it into the garden.*) I want to introduce you to her. Do you remember the advice you gave me last July, gov'nor?

Rev. S (*severely*)   Yes. I advised you to conquer your idleness and flippancy, and to work your way into an honorable profession and live on it and not upon me.

Frank   No: thats what you thought of afterwards. What you actually said was that since I had neither brains nor money, I'd better turn my good looks to account by marrying somebody with both. Well, look here, Miss Warren has brains: you cant deny that.

Rev. S   Brains are not everything.

Frank   No, of course not: theres the money –

Rev. S (*interrupting him austerely*)   I was not thinking of money sir. I was speaking of higher things. Social position, for instance.

Frank   I dont care a rap about that.

Rev. S   But I do, sir.

Frank   Well, nobody wants you to marry her. Anyhow she has what amounts to a high Cambridge degree; and she seems to have as much money as she wants.

Rev. S (*sinking into a feeble vein of humor*)   I greatly doubt whether she has as much money as you will want.

Frank   Oh, come: I havnt been so very extravagant. I live ever so quietly; I dont drink; I dont bet much; and I never go regularly on the razzle-dazzle as you did when you were my age.

Rev. S (*booming hollowly*)   Silence, sir.

Frank   Well, you told me yourself, when I was making ever such an ass of myself about the barmaid at Redhill, that you once offered a woman £50 for the letters you wrote to her when –

Rev. S (*terrified*)   Sh-sh-sh, Frank, for Heaven's sake! (*He looks round apprehensively. Seeing no one within earshot he plucks up courage to boom again, but more subduedly.*) You are taking an ungentlemanly advantage of what I confided to you for your own good, to save you from an error you would have repented all your life long. Take warning by your father's follies, sir; and dont make them an excuse for your own.

Frank   Did you ever hear the story of the Duke of Wellington and his letters?

Rev. S   No, sir; and I dont want to hear it.

Frank   The old Iron Duke didnt throw away £50: not he. He just wrote: 'Dear Jenny: publish and be damned! Yours affectionately, Wellington.' Thats what you should have done.

Rev. S (*piteously*)   Frank, my boy: when I wrote those letters I put myself into that woman's power. When I told you about them I put myself, to some extent, I am sorry to say, in your power. She refused my money with these words, which I shall never forget. 'Knowledge is power,' she said; 'and I never sell power'. Thats more than twenty years ago; and she has never made use of her power or caused me a moment's uneasiness. You are behaving worse to me than she did, Frank.

Frank   Oh yes I dare say! Did you ever preach at her the way you preach at me every day?

Rev. S (*wounded almost to tears*)   I leave you, sir. You are incorrigible. (*He turns towards the gate.*)

Frank (*utterly unmoved*)   Tell them I shant be home to tea, will you, gov'nor, like a good fellow? (*He moves towards the cottage door and is met by* **Praed** *and* **Vivie** *coming out.*)

Vivie (*to* **Frank**)   Is that your father, Frank? I do so want to meet him.

Frank   Certainly. (*Calling after his father*) Gov'nor. Youre wanted. (*The parson turns at the gate, fumbling nervously at his hat.* **Praed** *crosses the garden to the opposite side, beaming in anticipation of civilities.*) My father: Miss Warren.

Vivie (*going to the clergyman and shaking his hand*)   Very glad to see you here, Mr Gardner. (*Calling to the cottage:*) Mother: come along: youre wanted.

Mrs Warren *appears on the threshold, and is immediately transfixed recognizing the clergyman.*

Vivie (*continuing*)   Let me introduce –

Mrs Warren (*swooping on the* **Reverend Samuel**)   Why, it's Sam Gardner, gone into the Church! Well, I never! Dont you know us, Sam? This is George Crofts, as large as life and twice as natural. Dont you remember me?

Rev. S (*very red*)   I really – er –

Mrs Warren   Of course you do. Why, I have a whole album of your letters still: I came across them only the other day.

Rev. S (*miserably confused*)   Miss Vavasour, I believe.

Mrs Warren (*correcting him quickly in a loud whisper*)   Tch! Nonsense! Mrs Warren: dont you see my daughter there?

Act Two

Inside the cottage after nightfall. Looking eastward from within instead of westward from without, the latticed window, with its curtains drawn, is now seen in the middle of the front wall of the cottage, with the porch door to the left of it. In the left-hand side wall is the door leading to the kitchen. Farther back against the same wall is a dresser with a candle and matches on it, and **Frank**'s *rifle standing beside them, with the barrel resting in the plate-rack. In the centre a table stands with a lighted lamp on it.* **Vivie**'s *books and writing materials are on a table to the right of the window, against the wall. The fireplace is on the right, with a settle: there is no fire. Two of the chairs are set right and left of the table.*

The cottage door opens, shewing a fine starlit night without; and **Mrs Warren**, *her shoulders mapped in a shawl borrowed from* **Vivie**, *enters, followed by* **Frank**, *who throws his cap on the window seat. She has had enough of walking, and gives a gasp of relief as she unpins her hat; takes it off; sticks the pin through the crown; and puts it on the table.*

Mrs Warren   O Lord! I dont know which is the worst of the country, the walking or the sitting at home with nothing to do. I could do with a whisky and soda now very well, if only they had such a thing in this place.

Frank   Perhaps Vivie's got some.

Mrs Warren   Nonsense! What would a young girl like her be doing with such things! Never mind: it dont matter. I wonder how she passes her time here! I'd a good deal rather be in Vienna.

Frank   Let me take you there. (*He helps her to take off her shawl, gallantly giving her shoulders a very perceptible squeeze as he does so.*)

Mrs Warren   Ah! would you? I'm beginning to think youre a chip of the old block.

Frank   Like the gov'nor, eh? (*He hangs the shawl on the nearest chair and sits down.*)

Mrs Warren   Never you mind. What do you know about such things? Youre only a boy. (*She goes to the hearth, to be farther from temptation.*)

Frank Do come to Vienna with me? It'd be ever such larks.

Mrs Warren No, thank you. Vienna is no place for you – at least not until youre a little older. (*She nods at him to emphasize this piece of advice. He makes a mock-piteous face, belied by his laughing eyes. She looks at him; then comes back to him.*) Now, look here, little boy (*taking his face in her hands and turning it up to her*): I know you through and through by your likeness to your father, better than you know yourself. Dont you go taking any silly ideas into your head about me. Do you hear?

Frank (*gallantly wooing her with his voice*) Cant help it, my dear Mrs Warren: it runs in the family.

She pretends to box his ears; then looks at the pretty laughing upturned face for a moment, tempted. At last she kisses him, and immediately turns away, out of patience with herself.

Mrs Warren There! I shouldnt have done that. I am wicked. Never mind, my dear: it's only a motherly kiss. Go and make love to Vivie.

Frank So I have.

Mrs Warren (*turning on him with a sharp note of alarm in her voice*) What!

Frank Vivie and I are ever such chums.

Mrs Warren What do you mean? Now see here: I wont have any young scamp tampering with my little girl. Do you hear? I wont have it.

Frank (*quite unabashed*) My dear Mrs Warren: dont you be alarmed. My intentions are honorable: ever so honorable; and your little girl is jolly well able to take care of herself. She dont need looking after half so much as her mother. She aint so handsome, you know.

Mrs Warren (*taken aback by his assurance*) Well, you have got a nice healthy two inches thick of cheek all over you. I dont know where you got it. Not from your father, anyhow.

Crofts (*in the garden*) The gipsies, I suppose?

Rev. S (*replying*) The broomsquires are far worse.

Mrs Warren (*to* **Frank**)   S-sh! Remember! youve had your warning.

Crofts *and the* **Reverend Samuel** *come in from the garden, the clergyman continuing his conversation as he enters.*

Rev. S   The perjury at the Winchester assizes is deplorable.

Mrs Warren   Well? what became of you two? And wheres Praddy and Vivie?

Crofts (*putting his hat on the settle and his stick in the chimney corner*)   They went up the hill. We went to the village. I wanted a drink. (*He sits down on the settle, putting his legs up along the seat.*)

Mrs Warren   Well, she oughtnt go off like that without telling me. (*To* **Frank**:) Get your father a chair, Frank: where are your manners? (**Frank** *springs up and gracefully offers his father his chair; then takes another from the wall and sits down at the table, in the middle, with his father on his right and* **Mrs Warren** *on his left.*) George: where are you going to stay tonight? You cant stay here. And whats Praddy going to do?

Crofts   Gardner'll put me up.

Mrs Warren   Oh, no doubt youve taken care of yourself! But what about Praddy?

Crofts   Dont know. I suppose he can sleep at the inn.

Mrs Warren   Havnt you room for him, Sam?

Rev. S   Well – er – you see, as rector here, I am not free to do as I like. Er – what is Mr Praed's social position?

Mrs Warren   Oh, he's all right: he's an architect. What an old stick-in-the-mud you are, Sam!

Frank   Yes, it's all right, gov'nor. He built that place down in Wales for the Duke. Caernarvon Castle they call it. You must have heard of it. (*He winks with lightning smartness at* **Mrs Warren**, *and regards his father blandly.*)

Rev. S   Oh, in that case, of course we shall only be too happy. I suppose he knows the Duke personally.

Frank   Oh, ever so intimately! We can stick him in Georgina's old room.

Mrs Warren   Well, thats settled. Now if those two would only come in and let us have supper. Theyve no right to stay out after dark like this.

Crofts (*aggressively*)   What harm are they doing you?

Mrs Warren   Well, harm or not, I dont like it.

Frank   Better not wait for them, Mrs Warren. Praed will stay out as long as possible. He has never known before what it is to stray over the heath on a summer night with my Vivie.

Crofts (*sitting up in some consternation*)   I say, you know! Come!

Rev. S (*rising, startled out of his professional manner into real force and sincerity*)   Frank, once for all, it's out of the question. Mrs Warren will tell you that it's not to be thought of.

Crofts   Of course not.

Frank (*with enchanting placidity*)   Is that so, Mrs Warren?

Mrs Warren (*reflectively*)   Well, Sam, I dont know. If the girl wants to get married, no good can come of keeping her unmarried.

Rev. S (*astounded*)   But married to him! – your daughter to my son! Only think: it's impossible.

Crofts   Of course it's impossible. Dont be a fool, Kitty.

Mrs Warren (*nettled*)   Why not? Isnt my daughter good enough for your son?

Rev. S   But surely, my dear Mrs Warren, you know the reasons –

Mrs Warren (*defiantly*)   I know no reasons. If you know any, you can tell them to the lad, or to the girl, or to your congregation, if you like.

Rev. S (*collapsing helplessly into his chair*)   You know very well that I couldnt tell anyone the reasons. But my boy will believe me when I tell him there are reasons.

Frank   Quite right, Dad: he will. But has your boy's conduct ever been influenced by your reasons?

Crofts   You cant marry her; and thats all about it. (*He gets up and stands on the hearth, with his back to the fireplace, frowning determinedly.*)

Mrs Warren (*turning on him sharply*)   What have you got to do with it, pray?

Frank (*with his prettiest lyrical cadence*)   Precisely what I was going to ask myself, in my own graceful fashion.

Crofts (*to* **Mrs Warren**)   I suppose you dont want to marry the girl to a man younger than herself and without either a profession or twopence to keep her on. Ask Sam, if you dont believe me. (*To the parson:*) How much more money are you going to give him?

Rev. S   Not another penny. He has had his patrimony and he spent the last of it in July. (**Mrs Warren**'s *face falls.*)

Crofts (*watching her*)   There! I told you. (*He resumes his place on the settle and puts up his legs on the seat again, as if the matter were finally disposed of.*)

Frank (*plaintively*)   This is ever so mercenary. Do you suppose Miss Warren's going to marry for money? If we love one another –

Mrs Warren   Thank you. Your love's a pretty cheap commodity, my lad. If you have no means of keeping a wife, that settles it: you cant have Vivie.

Frank (*much amused*)   What do you say, gov'nor, eh?

Rev. S   I agree with Mrs Warren.

Frank   And good old Crofts has already expressed his opinion.

Crofts (*turning angrily on his elbow*)   Look here: I want none of your cheek.

Frank (*pointedly*)   I'm ever so sorry to surprise you, Crofts, but you allowed yourself the liberty of speaking to me like a father a moment ago. One father is enough, thank you.

Crofts (*contemptuously*)   Yah! (*He turns away again.*)

Frank (*rising*)   Mrs Warren: I cannot give my Vivie up, even for your sake.

Mrs Warren (*muttering*)   Young scamp!

Frank (*continuing*)   And as you no doubt intend to hold out other prospects to her, I shall lose no time in placing my case before her. (*They stare at him, and he begins to declaim gracefully.*)

> He either fears his fate too much,
> Or his deserts are small,
> That dares not put it to the touch
> To gain or lose it all.

The cottage door opens whilst he is reciting; and **Vivie** *and* **Praed** *come in. He breaks off.* **Praed** *puts his hat on the dresser. There is an immediate improvement in the company's behavior.* **Crofts** *takes down his legs from the settle and pulls himself together as* **Praed** *joins him at the fireplace.* **Mrs Warren** *loses her ease of manner and takes refuge in querulousness.*

Mrs Warren   Wherever have you been, Vivie?

Vivie (*taking off her hat and throwing it carelessly on the table.*)   On the hill.

Mrs Warren   Well, you shouldnt go off like that without letting me know. How could I tell what had become of you? And night coming on too!

Vivie (*going to the door of the kitchen and opening it, ignoring her mother.*)   Now, about supper? (*All rise except* **Mrs Warren**.) We shall be rather crowded in here, I'm afraid.

Mrs Warren   Did you hear what I said, Vivie?

Vivie (*quietly*)   Yes, mother. (*Reverting to the supper difficulty*) How many are we? (*Counting.*) One, two, three, four, five, six. Well, two will have to wait until the rest are done: Mrs Alison has only plates and knives for four.

Praed   Oh, it doesnt matter about me. I –

Vivie   You have had a long walk and are hungry, Mr Praed: you shall have your supper at once. I can wait myself. I want one person to wait with me. Frank: are you hungry?

Frank   Not the least in the world. Completely off my peck, in fact.

Mrs Warren (*to* **Crofts**)   Neither are you, George. You can wait.

Crofts   Oh, hang it, Ive eaten nothing since tea-time. Cant Sam do it?

Frank   Would you starve my poor father?

Rev. S (*testily*)   Allow me to speak for myself, sir. I am perfectly willing to wait.

Vivie (*decisively*)   Theres no need. Only two are wanted. (*She opens the door of the kitchen.*) Will you take my mother in, Mr Gardner. (*The parson takes* **Mrs Warren***; and they pass into the kitchen.* **Praed** *and* **Crofts** *follow. All except* **Praed** *clearly disapprove of the arrangement, but do not know how to resist it.* **Vivie** *stands at the door looking in at them.*) Can you squeeze past to that corner, Mr Praed: it's rather a tight fit. Take care of your coat against the white-wash: thats right. Now, are you all comfortable?

Praed (*within*)   Quite, thank you.

Mrs Warren (*within*)   Leave the door open, dearie. (**Vivie** *frowns; but* **Frank** *checks her with a gesture, and steals to the cottage door, which he softly sets wide open.*) Oh Lor, what a draught! Youd better shut it, dear.

Vivie *shuts it with a slam, and then, noting with disgust that her mother's hat and shawl are lying about, takes them tidily to the window seat, whilst* **Frank** *noiselessly shuts the cottage door.*

Frank (*exulting*)   Aha! Got rid of em. Well, Vivvums: what do you think of my governor?

Vivie (*preoccupied and serious*)   Ive hardly spoken to him. He doesnt strike me as being a particularly able person.

Frank   Well, you know, the old man is not altogether such a fool as he looks. You see, he was shoved into the Church rather;

and in trying to live up to it he makes a much bigger ass of himself than he really is. I dont dislike him as much as you might expect. He means well. How do you think youll get on with him?

Vivie (*rather grimly*)   I dont think my future life will be much concerned with him, or with any of that old circle of my mother's, except perhaps Praed. (*She sits down on the settle.*) What do you think of my mother?

Frank   Really and truly?

Vivie   Yes, really and truly.

Frank   Well, she's ever so jolly. But she's rather a caution, isnt she? And Crofts! oh, my eye, Crofts! (*He sits beside her.*)

Vivie   What a lot, Frank!

Frank   What a crew!

Vivie (*with intense contempt for them*)   If I thought that *I* was like that – that I was going to be a waster, shifting along from one meal to another with no purpose, and no character, and no grit in me, I'd open an artery and bleed to death without one moment's hesitation.

Frank   Oh no, you wouldnt. Why should they take any grind when they can afford not to? I wish I had their luck. No: what I object to is their form. It isnt the thing: it's slovenly, ever so slovenly.

Vivie   Do you think your form will be any better when youre as old as Crofts, if you dont work?

Frank   Of course I do. Ever so much better. Vivvums mustnt lecture: her little boy's incorrigible. (*He attempts to take her face caressingly in his hands.*)

Vivie (*striking kis hands down sharply*)   Off with you: Vivvums is not in a humor for petting her little boy this evening. (*She rises and comes forward to the other side of the room.*)

Frank (*following her*)   How unkind!

Vivie (*stamping at him*)   Be serious. I'm serious.

Frank   Good. Let us talk learnedly. Miss Warren: do you know that all the most advanced thinkers are agreed that half the diseases of modern civilization are due to starvation of the affections in the young. Now, *I* –

Vivie (*cutting him short*)   You are very tiresome. (*She opens the inner door.*) Have you room for Frank there? He's complaining of starvation.

Mrs Warren (*within*)   Of course there is. (*Clatter of knives and glasses as she moves the things on the table.*) Here! theres room now beside me. Come along, Mr Frank.

Frank   Her little boy will be ever so even with his Vivvums for this. (*He passes into the kitchen.*)

Mrs Warren (*within*)   Here, Vivie: come on you too, child. You must be famished. (*She enters, followed by* **Crofts**, *who holds the door open for* **Vivie** *with marked deference. She goes out without looking at him; and shuts the door after her.*) Why, George, you cant be done: youve eaten nothing. Is there anything wrong with you?

Crofts   Oh, all I wanted was a drink. (*He thrusts his hands in his pockets, and begins prowling about the room, restless and sulky.*)

Mrs Warren   Well, I like enough to eat. But a little of that cold beef and cheese and lettuce goes a long way. (*With a sigh of only half repletion she sits down lazily on the settle.*)

Crofts   What do you go encouraging that young pup for?

Mrs Warren (*on the alert at once*)   Now see here, George: what are you up to about that girl? Ive been watching your way of looking at her. Remember: I know you and what your looks mean.

Crofts   Theres no harm in looking at her, is there?

Mrs Warren   I'd put you out and pack you back to London pretty soon if I saw any of your nonsense. My girl's little finger is more to me than your whole body and soul. (**Crofts** *receives this with a sneering grin.* **Mrs Warren**, *flushing a little at her failure to impose on him in the character of a theatrically devoted mother, adds in a lower key.*) Make your mind easy: the young pup has no more chance than you have.

Crofts   Maynt a man take an interest in a girl?

Mrs Warren   Not a man like you.

Crofts   How old is she?

Mrs Warren   Never you mind how old she is.

Crofts   Why do you make such a secret of it?

Mrs Warren   Because I choose.

Crofts   Well, I'm not fifty yet; and my property is as good as ever it was −

Mrs Warren (*interrupting him*)   Yes; because youre as stingy as youre vicious.

Crofts (*continuing*)   And a baronet isnt to be picked up every day. No other man in my position would put up with you for a mother-in-law. Why shouldnt she marry me?

Mrs Warren   You!

Crofts   We three could live together quite comfortably: I'd die before her and leave her a bouncing widow with plenty of money. Why not? It's been growing in my mind all the time Ive been walking with that fool inside there.

Mrs Warren (*revolted*)   Yes: it's the sort of thing that would grow in your mind.

He halts in his prowling; and the two look at one another, she steadfastly, with a sort of awe behind her contemptuous disgust: he stealthily, with a carnal gleam in his eye and a loose grin.

Crofts (*suddenly becoming anxious and urgent as he sees no sign of sympathy in her*)   Look here, Kitty: youre a sensible woman: you neednt put on any moral airs. I'll ask no more questions; and you need answer none. I'll settle the whole property on her; and if you want a cheque for yourself on the wedding day, you can name any figure you like − in reason.

Mrs Warren   So it's come to that with you, George, like all the other worn-out old creatures!

Crofts (*savagely*)   Damn you!

Before she can retort the door of the kitchen is opened; and the voices of the others are heard returning. **Crofts**, *unable to recover his presence of mind, hurries out of the cottage.* **The Clergyman** *appears at the kitchen door.*

Rev. S (*looking round*)   Where is Sir George?

Mrs Warren   Gone out to have a pipe. (**The Clergyman** *takes his hat from the table, and joins* **Mrs Warren** *at the fireside. Meanwhile* **Vivie** *comes in, followed by* **Frank**, *who collapses into the nearest chair with an air of extreme exhaustion.* **Mrs Warren** *looks round at* **Vivie** *and says, with her affection of maternal patronage even more forced than usual:*) Well, dearie: have you had a good supper?

Vivie   You know what Mrs Alison's suppers are. (*She turns to* **Frank** *and pets him.*) Poor Frank! was all the beef gone? did it get nothing but bread and cheese and ginger beer? (*Seriously, as if she had done quite enough trifling for one evening:*) Her butter is really awful. I must get some down from the stores.

Frank   Do, in Heaven's name!

Vivie *goes to the writing-table and makes a memorandum to order the butter.* **Praed** *comes in from the kitchen, putting up his handkerchief which he has been using as a napkin.*

Rev. S   Frank, my boy: it is time for us to be thinking of home. Your mother does not know yet that we have visitors.

Praed   I'm afraid we're giving trouble.

Frank (*rising*)   Not the least in the world: my mother will be delighted to see you. She's a genuinely intellectual artistic woman; and she sees nobody here from one year's end to another except the gov'nor; so you can imagine how jolly dull it pans out for her. (*To his father:*) Youre not intellectual or artistic: are you, pater? So take Praed home at once; and I'll stay here and entertain Mrs Warren. Youll pick up Crofts in the garden. He'll be excellent company for the bull-pup.

Praed (*taking his hat from the dresser, and coming close to* **Frank**)   Come with us, Frank. Mrs Warren has not seen Miss Vivie for a long time; and we have prevented them from having a moment together yet.

Frank (*quite softened and looking at* **Praed** *with romantic admiration*)   Of course. I forgot. Ever so thanks for reminding me. Perfect gentleman, Praddy. Always were. My ideal through life. (*He rises to go, but pauses a moment between the two older men, and puts his hand on* **Praed**'s *shoulder*.) Ah, if you had only been my father instead of this unworthy old man! (*He puts his other hand on his father's shoulder.*)

Rev. S (*blustering*)   Silence, sir, silence: you are profane.

Mrs Warren (*laughing heartily*)   You should keep him in better order, Sam. Goodnight. Here: take George his hat and stick with my compliments.

Rev. S (*taking them*)   Goodnight. (*They shake hands. As he passes* **Vivie** *he shakes hands with her also and bids her goodnight. Then, in booming command, to* **Frank**:) Come along, sir, at once. (*He goes out.*)

Mrs Warren   Byebye, Praddy.

Praed   Byebye, Kitty.

They shake hands affectionately and go out together, she accompanying him to the garden gate.

Frank (*to* **Vivie**)   Kissums?

Vivie (*fiercely*)   No. I hate you. (*She takes a couple of books and some paper from the writing-table, and sits down with them at the middle table, at the end next the fireplace.*)

Frank (*grimacing*)   Sorry. (*He goes for his cap and rifle.* **Mrs Warren** *returns. He takes her hand.*) Goodnight, dear Mrs Warren. (*He kisses her hand. She snatches it away, her lips tightening, and looks more than half disposed to box his ears. He laughs mischievously and runs off, clapping-to the door behind him.*)

Mrs Warren (*resigning herself to an evening of boredom now that the men are gone*)   Did you ever in your life hear anyone rattle on so? Isnt he a tease? (*She sits at the table.*) Now that I think of it, dearie, dont you go encouraging him. I'm sure he's a regular good-for-nothing.

Vivie (*rising to fetch more books*)   I'm afraid so. Poor Frank! I shall have to get rid of him; but I shall feel sorry for him, though he's not worth it. That man Crofts does not seem to me to be good for much either: is he? (*She throws the books on the table rather roughly.*)

Mrs Warren (*galled by* **Vivie**'s *indifference*)   What do you know of men, child, to talk that way about them? Youll have to make up your mind to see a good deal of Sir George Crofts, as he's a friend of mine.

Vivie (*quite unmoved*)   Why? (*She sits down and opens a book.*) Do you expect that we shall be much together? You and I, I mean?

Mrs Warren (*staring at her*)   Of course: until youre married. Youre not going back to college again.

Vivie   Do you think my way of life would suit you? I doubt it.

Mrs Warren   Your way of life! What do you mean?

Vivie (*cutting a page of her book with the paper knife on her chatelaine*)   Has it really never occurred to you, mother, that I have a way of life like other people?

Mrs Warren   What nonsense is this youre trying to talk? Do you want to shew your independence, now that youre a great little person at school? Dont be a fool, child.

Vivie (*indulgently*)   Thats all you have to say on the subject, is it, mother?

Mrs Warren (*puzzled, then angry*)   Dont you keep on asking me questions like that. (*Violently.*) Hold your tongue. (**Vivie** *works on, losing no time, and saying nothing.*) You and your way of life, indeed! What next? (*She looks at* **Vivie** *again. No reply.*) Your way of life will be what I please, so it will. (*Another pause.*) Ive been noticing these airs in you ever since you got that tripos or whatever you call it. If you think I'm going to put up with them youre mistaken; and the sooner you find it out, the better. (*Muttering.*) All I have to say on the subject, indeed! (*Again raising her voice angrily.*) Do you know who youre speaking to, Miss?

Vivie (*looking across at her without raising her head from her book*)   No. Who are you? What are you?

Mrs Warren (*rising breathless*)   You young imp!

Vivie   Everybody knows my reputation, my social standing, and the profession I intend to pursue. I know nothing about you. What is that way of life which you invite me to share with you and Sir George Crofts, pray?

Mrs Warren   Take care. I shall do something I'll be sorry for after, and you too.

Vivie (*putting aside her books with cool decision*)   Well, let us drop the subject until you are better able to face it. (*Looking critically at her mother.*) You want some good walks and a little lawn tennis to set you up. You are shockingly out of condition: you were not able to manage twenty yards uphill today without stopping to pant; and your wrists are mere rolls of fat. Look at mine. (*She holds out her wrists.*)

Mrs Warren (*after looking at her helplessly, begins to whimper*)   Vivie –

Vivie (*springing up sharply*)   Now pray dont begin to cry. Anything but that. I really cannot stand whimpering. I will go out of the room if you do.

Mrs Warren (*piteously*)   Oh, my darling, how can you be so hard on me? Have I no rights over you as your mother?

Vivie   Are you my mother?

Mrs Warren (*appalled*)   Am I your mother! Oh, Vivie!

Vivie   Then where are our relatives? my father? our family friends? You claim the rights of a mother: the right to call me fool and child; to speak to me as no woman in authority over me at college dare speak to me; to dictate my way of life; and to force on me the acquaintance of a brute whom any one can see to be the most vicious sort of London man about town. Before I give myself the trouble to resist such claims, I may as well find out whether they have any real existence.

Mrs Warren (*distracted, throwing herself on her knees*)   Oh no, no. Stop, stop. I am your mother: I swear it. Oh, you cant mean to turn on me – my own child! it's not natural. You believe me, dont you? Say you believe me.

Vivie   Who was my father?

Mrs Warren   You dont know what youre asking. I cant tell you.

Vivie (*determinedly*)   Oh yes you can, if you like. I have a right to know; and you know very well that I have that right. You can refuse to tell me, if you please; but if you do, you will see the last of me tomorrow morning.

Mrs Warren   Oh, it's too horrible to hear you talk like that. You wouldnt – you couldnt leave me.

Vivie (*ruthlessly*)   Yes, without a moment's hesitation, if you trifle with me about this. (*Shivering with disgust.*) How can I feel sure that I may not have the contaminated blood of that brutal waster in my veins?

Mrs Warren   No, no. On my oath it's not he, nor any of the rest that you have ever met. I'm certain of that, at least.

Vivie's *eyes fasten sternly on her mother as the significance of this flashes on her.*

Vivie (*slowly*)   You are certain of that, at least. Ah! You mean that that is all you are certain of. (*Thoughtfully.*) I see. (**Mrs Warren** *buries her face in her hands.*) Dont do that, mother: you know you dont feel it a bit. (**Mrs Warren** *takes down her hands and looks up deplorably at* **Vivie**, *who takes out her watch and says:*) Well, that is enough for tonight. At what hour would you like breakfast? Is half-past eight too early for you?

Mrs Warren (*wildly*)   My God, what sort of woman are you?

Vivie (*coolly*)   The sort the world is mostly made of, I should hope. Otherwise I dont understand how it gets its business done. Come: (*Taking her mother by the wrist, and pulling her up pretty resolutely.*) pull yourself together. Thats right.

Mrs Warren (*querulously*)   Youre very rough with me, Vivie.

Vivie   Nonsense. What about bed? It's past ten.

Mrs Warren (*passionately*)   Whats the use of my going to bed? Do you think I could sleep?

Vivie   Why not? I shall.

Mrs Warren   You! youve no heart. (*She suddenly breaks out vehemently in her natural tongue – the dialect of a woman of the people – with* *all her affectations of maternal authority and conventional manners gone, and an overwhelming inspiration of true conviction and scorn in her.*) Oh, I wont bear it: I wont put up with the injustice of it. What right have you to set yourself up above me like this? You boast of what you are to me – to me, who gave you the chance of being what you are. What chance had I? Shame on you for a bad daughter and a stuck-up prude!

Vivie (*sitting down with a shrug, no longer confident; for her replies, which have sounded sensible and strong to her so far, now begin to ring rather woodenly and even priggishly against the new tone of her mother*)   Dont think for a moment I set myself above you in any way. You attacked me with the conventional authority of a mother: I defended myself with the conventional superiority of a respectable woman. Frankly, I am not going to stand any of your nonsense; and when you drop it I shall not expect you to stand any of mine. I shall always respect your right to your own opinions and your own way of life.

Mrs Warren   My own opinions and my own way of life! Listen to her talking! Do you think I was brought up like you? able to pick and choose my own way of life? Do you think I did what I did because I liked it, or thought it right, or wouldnt rather have gone to college and been a lady if I'd had the chance?

Vivie   Everybody has some choice, mother. The poorest girl alive may not be able to choose between being Queen of England or Principal of Newnham; but she can choose between ragpicking and flowerselling, according to her taste. People are always blaming their circumstances for what they are. I dont believe in circumstances. The people who get on in this world are the people who get up and look for the circumstances they want, and, if they cant find them, make them.

Mrs Warren   Oh, it's easy to talk, very easy, isnt it? Here! would you like to know what my circumstances were?

Vivie   Yes: you had better tell me. Wont you sit down?

Mrs Warren   Oh, I'll sit down: dont you be afraid. (*She plants her chair farther forward with brazen energy, and sits down.* **Vivie** *is impressed in spite of herself.*) D'you know what your gran'mother was?

Vivie   No.

Mrs Warren   No, you dont. I do. She called herself a widow and had a fried-fish shop down by the Mint, and kept herself and four daughters out of it. Two of us were sisters: that was me and Liz; and we were both good-looking and well made. I suppose our father was a well-fed man: mother pretended he was a gentleman; but I dont know. The other two were only half sisters: undersized, ugly, starved looking, hard working, honest poor creatures: Liz and I would have half-murdered them if mother hadnt half-murdered us to keep our hands off them. They were the respectable ones. Well, what did they get by their respectability? I'll tell you. One of them worked in a whitelead factory twelve hours a day for nine shillings a week until she died of lead poisoning. She only expected to get her hands a little paralyzed; but she died. The other was always held up to us as a model because she married a Government laborer in the Deptford victualling yard, and kept his room and the three children neat and tidy on eighteen shillings a week – until he took to drink. That was worth being respectable for, wasnt it?

Vivie (*now thoughtfully attentive*)   Did you and your sister think so?

Mrs Warren   Liz didnt, I can tell you: she had more spirit. We both went to a church school – that was part of the ladylike airs we gave ourselves to be superior to the children that knew nothing and went nowhere – and we stayed there until Liz went out one night and never came back. I know the schoolmistress thought I'd soon follow her example; for the clergyman was always warning me that Lizzie'd end by jumping off Waterloo Bridge. Poor fool: that was all he knew about it! But I was more afraid of the whitelead factory than I was of the river; and so would you have been in my place. That clergyman got me a situation as scullery maid in a temperance restaurant where they sent out for anything you liked. Then I was waitress; and then I went to the bar at Waterloo station: fourteen hours a day serving drinks and washing glasses for four shillings a week and my board. That was considered a great promotion for me. Well, one cold, wretched night, when I was so tired I could hardly keep myself awake, who should come up for a half of Scotch but Lizzie, in a long fur cloak, elegant and comfortable, with a lot of sovereigns in her purse.

Vivie (*grimly*)   My aunt Lizzie!

Mrs Warren   Yes; and a very good aunt to have, too. She's living down at Winchester now, close to the cathedral, one of the most respectable ladies there. Chaperones girls at the county ball, if you please. No river for Liz, thank you! You remind me of Liz a little: she was a first-rate business woman – saved money from the beginning – never let herself look too like what she was – never lost her head or threw away a chance. When she saw I'd grown up good-looking she said to me across the bar 'What are you doing there, you little fool? wearing out your health and your appearance for other people's profit!' Liz was saving money then to take a house for herself in Brussels; and she thought we two could save faster than one. So she lent me some money and gave me a start; and I saved steadily and first paid her back, and then went into business with her as her partner. Why shouldnt I have done it? The house in Brussels was real high class: a much better place for a woman to be in than the factory where Anne Jane got poisoned. None of our girls were ever treated as I was treated in the scullery of that temperance place, or at the Waterloo bar, or at home. Would you have had me stay in them and become a worn out old drudge before I was forty?

Vivie (*intensely interested by this time*)   No; but why did you choose that business? Saving money and good management will succeed in any business.

Mrs Warren   Yes, saving money. But where can a woman get the money to save in any other business? Could you save out of four shillings a week and keep yourself dressed as well? Not you. Of course, if youre a plain woman and cant earn anything more; or if you have a turn for music, or the stage, or newspaper-writing: thats different. But neither Liz nor I had any turn for such things: all we had was our appearance and our turn for pleasing men. Do you think we were such fools as to let other people trade in our good looks by employing us as shopgirls, or barmaids, or waitresses, when we could trade in them ourselves and get all the profits instead of starvation wages? Not likely.

Vivie   You were certainly quite justified – from the business point of view.

Mrs Warren   Yes; or any other point of view. What is any
respectable girl brought up to do but to catch some rich man's
fancy and get the benefit of his money by marrying him? – as if
a marriage ceremony could make any difference in the right or
wrong of the thing! Oh, the hypocrisy of the world makes me
sick! Liz and I had to work and save and calculate just like other
people; elseways we should be as poor as any good-for-nothing
drunken waster of a woman that thinks her luck will last for ever.
(*With great energy.*) I despise such people: theyve no character; and
if theres a thing I hate in a woman, its want of character.

Vivie   Come now, mother: frankly! Isnt it part of what you call
character in a woman that she should greatly dislike such a way
of making money?

Mrs Warren   Why, of course. Everybody dislikes having to
work and make money; but they have to do it all the same. I'm
sure Ive often pitied a poor girl, tired out and in low spirits,
having to try to please some man that she doesnt care two straws
for – some half-drunken fool that thinks he's making himself
agreeable when he's teasing and worrying and disgusting a
woman so that hardly any money could pay her for putting up
with it. But she has to bear with disagreeables and take the rough
with the smooth, just like a nurse in a hospital or anyone else. It's
not work that any woman would do for pleasure, goodness knows;
though to hear the pious people talk you would suppose it was a
bed of roses.

Vivie   Still, you consider it worth while. It pays.

Mrs Warren   Of course it's worth while to a poor girl, if she
can resist temptation and is good-looking and well conducted and
sensible. It's far better than any other employment open to her.
I always thought that oughtnt to be. It cant be right, Vivie, that
there shouldnt be better opportunities for women. I stick to that:
it's wrong. But it's so, right or wrong; and a girl must make the
best of it. But of course it's not worth while for a lady. If you took
to it youd be a fool; but I should have been a fool if I'd taken to
anything else.

Vivie (*more and more deeply moved*)   Mother: suppose we were both
as poor as you were in those wretched old days, are you quite sure

that you wouldnt advise me to try the Waterloo bar, or marry a laborer, or even go into the factory?

Mrs Warren (*indignantly*) Of course not. What sort of mother do you take me for! How could you keep your self-respect in such starvation and slavery? And whats a woman worth? whats life worth? without self-respect! Why am I independent and able to give my daughter a first-rate education, when other women that had just as good opportunities are in the gutter? Because I always knew how to respect myself and control myself. Why is Liz looked up to in a cathedral town? The same reason. Where would we be now if we'd minded the clergyman's foolishness? Scrubbing floors for one and sixpence a day and nothing to look forward to but the workhouse infirmary. Dont you be led astray by people who dont know the world, my girl. The only way for a woman to provide for herself decently is for her to be good to some man that can afford to be good to her. If she's in his own station of life, let her make him marry her; but if she's far beneath him she cant expect it: why should she? it wouldnt be for her own happiness. Ask any lady in London society that has daughters; and she'll tell you the same, except that I tell you straight and she'll tell you crooked. Thats all the difference.

Vivie (*fascinated, gazing at her*) My dear mother: you are a wonderful woman: you are stronger than all England. And are you really and truly not one wee bit doubtful – or – or – ashamed?

Mrs Warren Well, of course, dearie, it's only good manners to be ashamed of it: it's expected from a woman. Women have to pretend to feel a great deal that they dont feel. Liz used to be angry with me for plumping out the truth about it. She used to say that when every woman could learn enough from what was going on in the world before her eyes, there was no need to talk about it to her. But then Liz was such a perfect lady! She had the true instinct of it; while I was always a bit of a vulgarian. I used to be so pleased when you sent me your photos to see that you were growing up like Liz: youve just her ladylike, determined way. But I cant stand saying one thing when everyone knows I mean another. Whats the use in such hypocrisy? If people arrange the world that way for women, theres no good pretending it's arranged the other way. No: I never was a bit ashamed really. I consider I had a right to be proud of how we managed everything so respectably, and never had a word against us, and how the girls were so well taken care of. Some of them did very well: one of them married an ambassador. But of course now I darent talk about such things: whatever would they think of us! (*She yawns.*) Oh dear! I do believe I'm getting sleepy after all. (*She stretches herself lazily, thoroughly relieved by her explosion, and placidly ready for her night's rest.*)

Vivie   I believe it is I who will not be able to sleep now. (*She goes to the dresser and lights the candle. Then she extinguishes the lamp, darkening the room a good deal.*) Better let in some fresh air before locking up. (*She opens the cottage door, and finds that it is broad moonlight.*) What a beautiful night! Look! (*She draws aside the curtains of the window. The landscape is seen bathed in the radiance of the harvest moon rising over Blackdown.*)

Mrs Warren (*with a perfunctory glance at the scene*)   Yes, dear; but take care you dont catch your death of cold from the night air.

Vivie (*contemptuously*)   Nonsense.

Mrs Warren (*querulously*)   Oh yes: everything I say is nonsense, according to you.

Vivie (*turning to her quickly*)   No: really that is not so, mother. You have got completely the better of me tonight, though I intended it to be the other way. Let us be good friends now.

Mrs Warren (*shaking her head a little ruefully*)   So it has been the other way. But I suppose I must give in to it. I always got the worst of it from Liz; and now I suppose it'll be the same with you.

Vivie   Well, never mind. Come: goodnight, dear old mother. (*She takes her mother in her arms.*)

Mrs Warren (*fondly*)   I brought you up well, didnt I, dearie?

Vivie   You did.

Mrs Warren   And youll be good to your poor old mother for it, wont you?

Vivie   I will, dear. (*Kissing her.*) Goodnight.

Mrs Warren (*with unction*)   Blessings on my own dearie darling! a mother's blessing!

She embraces her daughter protectingly, instinctively looking upward for divine sanction.

Act Three

In the Rectory garden next morning, with the sun shining from a cloudless sky. The garden wall has a five-barred wooden gate, wide enough to admit a carriage, in the middle. Beside the gate hangs a bell on a coiled spring, communicating with a pull outside. The carriage drive comes down the middle of the garden and then swerves to its left, where it ends in a little gravelled circus opposite the Rectory porch. Beyond the gate is seen the dusty high road, parallel with the wall, bounded on the farther side by a strip of turf and an unfenced pine wood. On the lawn, between the house and the drive, is a clipped yew tree, with a garden bench in its shade. On the opposite side the garden is shut in by a box hedge; and there is a sundial on the turf, with an iron chair near it. A little path leads off through the box hedge, behind the sundial.

Frank, seated on the chair near the sundial, on which he has placed the morning papers, is reading The Standard. His father comes from the house, red-eyed and shivery, and meets Frank's eye with misgiving.

Frank (*looking at his watch*)   Half-past eleven. Nice hour for a rector to come down to breakfast!

Rev. S   Dont mock, Frank: dont mock. I am a little – er – (*Shivering*) –

Frank   Off color?

Rev. S (*repudiating the expression*)   No, sir: unwell this morning. Wheres your mother?

Frank   Dont be alarmed: she's not here. Gone to town by the 11.13 with Bessie. She left several messages for you. Do you feel equal to receiving them now, or shall I wait til youve breakfasted?

Rev. S   I have breakfasted, sir. I am surprised at your mother going to town when we have people staying with us. Theyll think it very strange.

Frank   Possibly she has considered that. At all events, if Crofts is going to stay here, and you are going to sit up every night with him until four, recalling the incidents of your fiery youth, it is clearly my mother's duty, as a prudent housekeeper, to go up to the stores and order a barrel of whisky and a few hundred siphons.

Rev. S   I did not observe that Sir George drank excessively.

Frank   You were not in a condition to, gov'nor.

Rev. S   Do you mean to say that *I –* ?

Frank (*calmly*)   I never saw a beneficed clergyman less sober. The anecdotes you told about your past career were so awful that I really dont think Praed would have passed the night under your roof if it hadnt been for the way my mother and he took to one another.

Rev. S   Nonsense, sir. I am Sir George Crofts' host. I must talk to him about something; and he has only one subject. Where is Mr Praed now?

Frank   He is driving my mother and Bessie to the station.

Rev. S   Is Crofts up yet?

Frank   Oh, long ago. He hasnt turned a hair: he's in much better practice than you. He has kept it up ever since, probably. He's taken himself off somewhere to smoke.

Frank *resumes his paper. The parson turns disconsolately towards the gate; then comes back irresolutely.*

Rev. S   Er – Frank.

Frank   Yes.

Rev. S   Do you think the Warrens will expect to be asked here after yesterday afternoon?

Frank   Theyve been asked already.

Rev. S (*appalled*)   What ! ! !

Frank   Crofts informed us at breakfast that you told him to bring Mrs Warren and Vivie over here today, and to invite them to make this house their home. My mother then found she must go to town by the 11.13 train.

Rev. S (*with despairing vehemence*)   I never gave any such invitation. I never thought of such a thing.

Frank (*compassionately*)   How do you know, gov'nor, what you said and thought last night?

Praed (*coming in through the hedge*)   Good morning.

Rev. S   Good morning. I must apologise for not having met you at breakfast. I have a touch of − of −

Frank   Clergyman's sore throat, Praed. Fortunately not chronic.

Praed (*changing the subject*)   Well, I must say your house is in a charming spot here. Really most charming.

Rev. S   Yes: it is indeed. Frank will take you for a walk, Mr Praed, if you like. I'll ask you to excuse me: I must take the opportunity to write my sermon while Mrs Gardner is away and you are all amusing yourselves. You wont mind, will you?

Praed   Certainly not. Dont stand on the slightest ceremony with me.

Rev. S   Thank you. I'll − er − er − (*He stammers his way to the porch and vanishes into the house.*)

Praed   Curious thing it must be writing a sermon every week.

Frank   Ever so curious, if he did it. He buys em. He's gone for some soda water.

Praed   My dear boy: I wish you would be more respectful to your father. You know you can be so nice when you like.

Frank   My dear Praddy: you forget that I have to live with the governor. When two people live together − it dont matter whether theyre father and son or husband and wife or brother and sister − they cant keep up the polite humbug thats so easy for ten minutes on an afternoon call. Now the governor, who unites to many admirable domestic qualities the irresoluteness of a sheep and the pompousness and aggressiveness of a jackass −

Praed   No, pray, pray, my dear Frank, remember! He is your father.

Frank   I give him due credit for that. (*Rising and flinging down his paper.*) But just imagine his telling Crofts to bring the Warrens over here! He must have been ever so drunk. You know, my dear Praddy, my mother wouldnt stand Mrs Warren for a moment. Vivie mustnt come here until she's gone back to town.

Praed   But your mother doesnt know anything about Mrs Warren, does she? (*He picks up the paper and sits down to read it.*)

Frank   I dont know. Her journey to town looks as if she did. Not that my mother would mind in the ordinary way: she has stuck like a brick to lots of women who had got into trouble. But they were all nice women. Thats what makes the real difference. Mrs Warren, no doubt, has her merits; but she's ever so rowdy; and my mother simply wouldnt put up with her. So – hallo! (*This exclamation is provoked by the reappearance of the clergyman, who comes out of the house in haste and dismay.*)

Rev. S   Mrs Warren and her daughter are coming across the heath with Crofts: I saw them from the study windows. What am I to say about your mother?

Frank   Stick on your hat and go out and say how delighted you are to see them; and that Frank's in the garden; and that mother and Bessie have been called to the bedside of a sick relative, and were ever so sorry they couldnt stop; and that you hope Mrs Warren slept well; and – and – say any blessed thing except the truth, and leave the rest to Providence.

Rev. S   But how are we to get rid of them afterwards?

Frank   Theres no time to think of that now. Here! (*He bounds into the house.*)

Rev. S   He's so impetuous. I dont know what to do with him, Mr Praed.

Frank (*returning with a clerical felt hat, which he claps on his father's head*)   Now: off with you. (*Rushing him through the gate.*) Praed and I'll wait here, to give the thing an unpremeditated air. (*The clergyman, dazed but obedient, hurries off.*)

Frank   We must get the old girl back to town somehow, Praed. Come! Honestly, dear Praddy, do you like seeing them together?

Praed   Oh, why not?

Frank (*his teeth on edge*)   Dont it make your flesh creep ever so little? that wicked old devil, up to every villainy under the sun, I'll swear, and Vivie – ugh!

Praed   Hush, pray. Theyre coming.

The Clergyman *and* **Crofts** *are seen coming along the road, followed by* **Mrs Warren** *and* **Vivie** *walking affectionately together.*

Frank   Look: she actually has her arm round the old woman's waist. It's her right arm: she began it. She's gone sentimental, by God! Ugh! ugh! Now do you feel the creeps? (*The clergyman opens the gate; and* **Mrs Warren** *and* **Vivie** *pass him and stand in the middle of the garden looking at the house.* **Frank**, *in an ecstasy of dissimulation, turns gaily to* **Mrs Warren**, *exclaiming:*) Ever so delighted to see you, Mrs Warren. This quiet old rectory garden becomes you perfectly.

Mrs Warren   Well, I never! Did you hear that, George? He says I look well in a quiet old rectory garden.

Rev. S (*still holding the gate for* **Crofts**, *who loafs through it, heavily bored*)   You look well everywhere, Mrs Warren.

Frank   Bravo, gov'nor! Now look here: lets have a treat before lunch. First lets see the church. Everyone has to do that. It's a regular old thirteenth century church, you know: the gov'nor's ever so fond of it, because he got up a restoration fund and had it completely rebuilt six years ago. Praed will be able to shew its points.

Praed (*rising*)   Certainly, if the restoration has left any to shew.

Rev. S (*mooning hospitably at them*)   I shall be pleased, I'm sure, if Sir George and Mrs Warren really care about it.

Mrs Warren   Oh, come along and get it over.

Crofts (*turning back towards the gate*)   Ive no objection.

Rev. S   Not that way. We go through the fields, if you dont mind. Round here. (*He leads the way by the little path through the box hedge.*)

Crofts   Oh, all right. (*He goes with the parson.*)

Praed *follows with* **Mrs Warren**. **Vivie** *does not stir: she watches them until they have gone, with all the lines of purpose in her face marking it strongly.*

Frank   Aint you coming?

Vivie   No. I want to give you a warning, Frank. You were making fun of my mother just now when you said that about the rectory garden. That is barred in future. Please treat my mother with as much respect as you treat your own.

Frank   My dear Viv: she wouldnt appreciate it: the two cases require different treatment. But what on earth has happened to you? Last night we were perfectly agreed as to your mother and her set. This morning I find you attitudinizing sentimentally with your arm round your parent's waist.

Vivie (*flushing*)   Attitudinizing!

Frank   That was how it struck me. First time I ever saw you do a second-rate thing.

Vivie (*controlling herself*)   Yes, Frank: there has been a change; but I dont think it a change for the worse. Yesterday I was a little prig.

Frank   And today?

Vivie (*wincing; then looking at him steadily*)   Today I know my mother better than you do.

Frank   Heaven forbid!

Vivie   What do you mean?

Frank   Viv: theres a freemasonry among thoroughly immoral people that you know nothing of. Youve too much character. Thats the bond between your mother and me: thats why I know her better than youll ever know her.

Vivie   You are wrong: you know nothing about her. If you knew the circumstances against which my mother had to struggle –

Frank (*adroitly finishing the sentence for her*)   I should know why she is what she is, shouldnt I? What difference would that make? Circumstances or no circumstances, Viv, you wont be able to stand your mother.

Vivie (*very angrily*)   Why not?

Frank   Because she's an old wretch, Viv. If you ever put your arm round her waist in my presence again, I'll shoot myself there and then as a protest against an exhibition which revolts me.

Vivie   Must I choose between dropping your acquaintance and dropping my mother's?

Frank (*gracefully*)   That would put the old lady at ever such a disadvantage. No, Viv; your infatuated little boy will have to stick to you in any case. But he's all the more anxious that you shouldnt make mistakes. It's no use, Viv: your mother's impossible. She may be a good sort; but she's a bad lot, a very bad lot.

Vivie (*hotly*)   Frank − ! (*He stands his ground. She turns away and sits down on the bench under the yew tree, struggling to recover her self-command. Then she says:*) Is she to be deserted by all the world because she's what you call a bad lot? Has she no right to live?

Frank   No fear of that, Viv: she wont ever be deserted. (*He sits on the bench beside her.*)

Vivie   But I am to desert her, I suppose.

Frank (*babyishly, lulling her and making love to her with his voice*)   Musnt go live with her. Little family group of mother and daughter wouldnt be a success. Spoil our little group.

Vivie (*falling under the spell*)   What little group?

Frank   The babes in the wood: Vivie and little Frank. (*He nestles against her like a weary child.*) Lets go and get covered up with leaves.

Vivie (*rhythmically, rocking him like a nurse*)   Fast asleep, hand in hand, under the trees.

Frank   The wise little girl with her silly little boy.

Vivie   The dear little boy with his dowdy little girl.

Frank   Ever so peaceful, and relieved from the imbecility of the little boy's father and the questionableness of the little girl's −

Vivie (*smothering the word against her breast*)   Sh-sh-sh-sh! little girl wants to forget all about her mother. (*They are silent for some moments,*) *rocking one another. Then* **Vivie** *wakes up with a shock, exclaiming:*) What a pair of fools we are! Come: sit up. Gracious! your hair. (*She smooths it.*), I wonder do all grown up people play in that childish way when nobody is looking. I never did it when I was a child.

Frank   Neither did I. You are my first playmate. (*He catches her hand to kiss it, but checks himself to look round first. Very unexpectedly, he sees Crofts emerging from the box hedge.*) Oh damn!

Vivie   Why damn, dear?

Frank (*whispering*)   Sh! Heres this brute Crofts. (*He sits farther away from her with an unconcerned air.*)

Crofts   Could I have a few words with you, Miss Vivie?

Vivie   Certainly.

Crofts (*to* **Frank**)   Youll excuse me, Gardner. Theyre waiting for you in the church, if you dont mind.

Frank (*rising*)   Anything to oblige you, Crofts – except church. If you should happen to want me, Vivvums, ring the gate bell. (*He goes into the house with unruffled suavity.*)

Crofts (*watching him with a crafty air as he disappears, and speaking to* **Vivie** *with an assumption of being on privileged terms with her*)   Pleasant young fellow that, Miss Vivie. Pity he has no money, isnt it?

Vivie   Do you think so?

Crofts   Well, whats he to do? No profession. No property. Whats he good for?

Vivie   I realize his disadvantages, Sir George.

Crofts (*a little taken aback at being so precisely interpreted*)   Oh, it's not that. But while we're in this world we're in it; and money's money. (**Vivie** *does not answer.*) Nice day, isnt it?

Vivie (*with scarcely veiled contempt for this effort at conversation*)   Very.

Crofts (*with brutal good humor, as if he liked her pluck*)   Well, thats not what I came to say. (*Sitting down beside her.*) Now listen, Miss Vivie. I'm quite aware that I'm not a young lady's man.

Vivie   Indeed, Sir George?

Crofts   No; and to tell you the honest truth I dont want to be either. But when I say a thing I mean it; when I feel a sentiment I feel it in earnest; and what I value I pay hard money for. Thats the sort of man I am.

Vivie   It does you great credit, I'm sure.

Crofts   Oh, I dont mean to praise myself. I have my faults, Heaven knows: no man is more sensible of that than I am. I know I'm not perfect; thats one of the advantages of being a middle-aged man; for I'm not a young man, and I know it. But my code is a simple one, and, I think, a good one. Honor between man and man; fidelity between man and woman; and no cant about this religion or that religion, but an honest belief that things are making for good on the whole.

Vivie (*with biting irony*)   'A power, not ourselves, that makes for righteousness', eh?

Crofts (*taking her seriously*)   Oh certainly. Not ourselves, of course. You understand what I mean. Well, now as to practical matters. You may have an idea that Ive flung my money about; but I havnt: I'm richer today than when I first came into the property. Ive used my knowledge of the world to invest my money in ways that other men have overlooked; and whatever else I may be, I'm a safe man from the money point of view.

Vivie   It's very kind of you to tell me all this.

Crofts   Oh well, come, Miss Vivie: you neednt pretend you dont see what I'm driving at. I want to settle down with a Lady Crofts. I suppose you think me very blunt, eh?

Vivie   Not at all: I am much obliged to you for being so definite and business-like. I quite appreciate the offer: the money, the position, Lady Crofts and so on. But I think I will say no, if you dont mind. I'd rather not. (*She rises, and strolls across to the sundial to get out of his immediate neighborhood.*)

Crofts (*not at all discouraged, and taking advantage of the additional room left him on the seat to spread himself comfortably, as if a few preliminary refusals were part of the inevitable routine of courtship*)   I'm in no hurry. It was only just to let you know in case young Gardner should try to trap you. Leave the question open.

Vivie (*sharply*)   My no is final. I wont go back from it.

Crofts *is not impressed. He grins; leans forward with his elbows on his knees to prod with his stick at some unfortunate insect in the grass; and looks cunningly at her. She turns away impatiently.*

Crofts   I'm a good deal older than you. Twenty-five years: quarter of a century. I shant live for ever; and I'll take care that you shall be well off when I'm gone.

Vivie   I am proof against even that inducement, Sir George. Dont you think youd better take your answer? There is not the slightest chance of my altering it.

Crofts (*rising, after a final slash at a daisy, and coming nearer to her*)   Well, no matter. I could tell you some things that would change your mind fast enough; but I wont, because I'd rather win you by honest affection. I was a good friend to your mother: ask her whether I wasnt. She'd never have made the money that paid for your education if it hadnt been for my advice and help, not to mention the money I advanced her. There are not many men would have stood by her as I have. I put not less than £40,000 into it, from first to last.

Vivie (*staring at him*)   Do you mean to say you were my mother's business partner?

Crofts   Yes. Now just think of all the trouble and the explanations it would save if we were to keep the whole thing in the family, so to speak. Ask your mother whether she'd like to have to explain all her affairs to a perfect stranger.

Vivie   I see no difficulty, since I understand that the business is wound up, and the money invested.

Crofts (*stopping short, amazed*)   Wound up! Wind up a business thats paying 35 per cent in the worst years! Not likely. Who told you that?

Vivie (*her color quite gone*)   Do you mean that it is still – ? (*She stops abruptly, and puts her hand on the sundial to support herself. Then she gets quickly to the iron chair and sits down.*) What business are you talking about?

Crofts Well, the fact is it's not what would be considered exactly a high-class business in my set – the county set, you know – our set it will be if you think better of my offer. Not that theres any mystery about it: dont think that. Of course you know by your mother's being in it that it's perfectly straight and honest. I've known her for many years; and I can say of her that she'd cut off her hands sooner than touch anything that was not what it ought to be. I'll tell you all about it if you like. I dont know whether youve found in travelling how hard it is to find a really comfortable private hotel.

Vivie (*sickened, averting her face*) Yes: go on.

Crofts Well, thats all it is. Your mother has a genius for managing such things. Weve got two in Brussels, one in Ostend, one in Vienna, and two in Budapest. Of course there are others besides ourselves in it: but we hold most of the capital; and your mother's indispensable as managing director. Youve noticed, I daresay, that she travels a good deal. But you see you cant mention such things in society. Once let out the word hotel and everybody says you keep a public-house. You wouldnt like people to say that of your mother, would you? Thats why we're so reserved about it. By the way, youll keep it to yourself, wont you? Since its been a secret so long, it had better remain so.

Vivie And this is the business you invite me to join you in?

Crofts Oh no. My wife shant be troubled with business. Youll not be in it more than youve always been.

Vivie *I* always been! What do you mean?

Crofts Only that youve always lived on it. It paid for your education and the dress you have on your back. Dont turn up your nose at business, Miss Vivie; where would your Newnhams and Girtons be without it?

Vivie (*rising, almost beside herself*) Take care. I know what this business is.

Crofts (*starting, with a suppressed oath*) Who told you?

Vivie Your partner. My mother.

Crofts (*black with rage*)   The old –

Vivie   Just so.

He swallows the epithet and stands for a moment swearing and raging foully to himself. But he knows that his cue is to be sympathetic. He takes refuge in generous indignation.

Crofts   She ought to have had more consideration for you. I'd never have told you.

Vivie   I think you would probably have told me when we were married: it would have been a convenient weapon to break me in with.

Crofts (*quite sincerely*)   I never intended that. On my word as a gentleman I didnt.

Vivie *wonders at him. Her sense of the irony of his protest cools and braces her. She replies with contemptuous self-possession.*

Vivie   It does not matter. I suppose you understand that when we leave here today our acquaintance ceases.

Crofts   Why? Is it for helping your mother?

Vivie   My mother was a very poor woman who had no reasonable choice but to do as she did. You were a rich gentleman; and you did the same for the sake of 35 per cent. You are a pretty common sort of scoundrel, I think. That is my opinion of you.

Crofts (*after a stare: not at all displeased, and much more at his ease on these frank terms than on their former ceremonious ones*)   Ha! ha! ha! ha! Go it, little missie, go it; it doesnt hurt me and it amuses you. Why the devil shouldnt I invest my money that way? I take the interest on my capital like other people: I hope you dont think I dirty my own hands with the work. Come! you wouldnt refuse the acquaintance of my mother's cousin the Duke of Belgravia because some of the rents he gets are earned in queer ways. You wouldnt cut the Archbishop of Canterbury, I suppose, because the Ecclesiastical Commissioners have a few publicans and sinners among their tenants. Do you remember your Crofts scholarship at Newnham? Well, that was founded by my brother the M.P. He gets his 22 per cent out of a factory with 600 girls in it, and not one of them getting wages enough to live on. How d'ye suppose they manage when they have no family to fall back on? Ask your mother. And do you expect me to turn my back on 35 per cent when all the rest are pocketing what they can, like sensible men? No such fool! If youre going to pick and choose your acquaintances on moral principles, youd better clear out of this country, unless you want to cut yourself out of all decent society.

Vivie (*conscience stricken*)   You might go on to point out that I myself never asked where the money I spent came from. I believe I am just as bad as you.

Crofts (*greatly reassured*)   Of course you are; and a very good thing too! What harm does it do after all? (*Rallying her jocularly.*) So you dont think me such a scoundrel now you come to think it over. Eh?

Vivie   I have shared profits with you; and I admitted you just now to the familiarity of knowing what I think of you.

Crofts (*with serious friendliness*)   To be sure you did. You wont find me a bad sort: I dont go in for being superfine intellectually: but Ive plenty of honest human feeling; and the old Crofts breed comes out in a sort of instinctive hatred of anything low, in which I'm sure youll sympathize with me. Believe me, Miss Vivie, the world isnt such a bad place as the croakers make out. As long as you dont fly openly in the face of society, society doesnt ask any inconvenient questions; and it makes precious short work of the cads who do. There are no secrets better kept than the secrets everybody guesses. In the class of people I can introduce you to, no lady or gentleman would so far forget themselves as to discuss my business affairs or your mother's. No man can offer you a safer position.

Vivie (*studying him curiously*)   I suppose you really think youre getting on famously with me.

Crofts   Well, I hope I may flatter myself that you think better of me than you did at first.

Vivie (*quietly*)   I hardly find you worth thinking about at all now. When I think of the society that tolerates you, and the laws that protect you! when I think of how helpless nine out of ten young girls would be in the hands of you and my mother! the unmentionable woman and her capitalist bully –

Crofts (*livid*)   Damn you!

Vivie   You need not. I feel among the damned already.

She raises the latch of the gate to open it and go out. He follows her and puts his hand heavily on the top bar to prevent its opening.

Crofts (*panting with fury*)   Do you think I'll put up with this from you, you young devil?

Vivie (*unmoved*)   Be quiet. Some one will answer the bell. (*Without flinching a step she strikes the bell with the back of her hand. It clangs harshly; and he starts back involuntarily. Almost immediately* **Frank** *appears at the porch with his rifle.*)

Frank (*with cheerful politeness*)   Will you have the rifle, Viv; or shall I operate?

Vivie   Frank: have you been listening?

Frank (*coming down into the garden*)   Only for the bell, I assure you; so that you shouldnt have to wait. I think I shewed great insight into your character, Crofts.

Crofts   For two pins I'd take that gun from you and break it across your head.

Frank (*stalking him cautiously*)   Pray dont. I'm ever so careless in handling firearms. Sure to be a fatal accident, with a reprimand from the coroner's jury for my negligence.

Vivie   Put the rifle away, Frank; it's quite unnecessary.

Frank   Quite right, Viv. Much more sportsmanlike to catch him in a trap. (**Crofts**, *understanding the insult, makes a threatening movement.*) Crofts: there are fifteen cartridges in the magazine here; and I am a dead shot at the present distance and at an object of your size.

Crofts   Oh, you neednt be afraid. I'm not going to touch you.

Frank   Ever so magnanimous of you under the circumstances! Thank you!

Crofts   I'll just tell you this before I go. It may interest you, since youre so fond of one another. Allow me, Mister Frank, to introduce you to your half-sister, the eldest daughter of the Reverend Samuel Gardner. Miss Vivie: your half-brother. Good morning. (*He goes out through the gate along the road.*)

Frank (*after a pause of stupefaction, raising the rifle*)   Youll testify before the coroner that it's an accident, Viv. (*He lakes aim at the retreating figure of* **Crofts**. **Vivie** *seizes the muzzle and pulls it round against her breast.*)

Vivie   Fire now. You may.

Frank (*dropping his end of the rifle hastily*)   Stop! take care. (*She lets it go. It falls on the turf.*) Oh, youve given your little boy such a turn. Suppose it had gone off! ugh! (*He sinks on the garden seat overcome.*)

Vivie   Suppose it had: do you think it would not have been a relief to have some sharp physical pain tearing through me?

Frank (*coaxingly*)   Take it ever so easy, dear Viv. Remember: even if the rifle scared that fellow into telling the truth for the first time in his life, that only makes us the babes in the wood in earnest. (*He holds out his arms to her.*) Come and be covered up with leaves again.

Vivie (*with a cry of disgust*)   Ah, not that, not that. You make all my flesh creep.

Frank   Why, whats the matter?

Vivie   Goodbye. (*She makes for the gate.*)

Frank (*jumping up*)   Hallo! Stop! Viv! Viv! (*She turns in the gateway.*) Where are you going to? Where shall we find you?

Vivie   At Honoria Fraser's chambers, 67 Chancery Lane, for the rest of my life. (*She goes off quickly in the opposite direction to that taken by* **Crofts**.)

Frank   But I say – wait – dash it! (*He runs after her.*)

Act Four

Honoria Fraser's chambers in Chancery Lane. An office at the top of New Stone Buildings, with a plate-glass window, distempered walls, electric light, and a patent stove. Saturday afternoon. The chimneys of Lincoln's Inn and the western sky beyond are seen through the window. There is a double writing table in the middle of the room, with a cigar box, ash pans, and a portable electric reading lamp almost snowed up in heaps of papers and books. This table has knee holes and chairs right and left and is very untidy. The clerk's desk, closed and tidy, with its high stool, is against the wall, near a door communicating with the inner rooms. In the opposite wall is the door leading to the public corridor. Its upper panel is of opaque glass, lettered in black on the outside, **Fraser** *and* **Warren**. *A baize screen hides the corner between this door and the window.*

Frank, *in a fashionable light-colored coaching suit, with his stick, gloves, and white hat in his hands, is pacing up and down the office. Somebody tries the door with a key.*

Frank (*calling*)   Come in. It's not locked.

Vivie *comes in, in her hat and jacket. She stops and stares at him.*

Vivie (*sternly*)   What are you doing here?

Frank   Waiting to see you. Ive been here for hours. Is this the way you attend to your business? (*He puts his hat and stick on the table, and perches himself with a vault on the clerk's stool looking at her with every appearance of being in a specially restless, teasing, flippant mood.*)

Vivie   Ive been away exactly twenty minutes for a cup of tea. (*She takes off her hat and jacket and hangs them up behind the screen.*) How did you get in?

Frank   The staff had not left when I arrived. He's gone to play cricket on Primrose Hill. Why dont you employ a woman, and give your sex a chance?

Vivie   What have you come for?

Frank (*springing off the stool and coming close to her*)   Viv: lets go and enjoy the Saturday half-holiday somewhere, like the staff.

What do you say to Richmond, and then a music hall, and a jolly supper?

Vivie   Cant afford it. I shall put in another six hours work before I go to bed.

Frank   Cant afford it, cant we? Aha! Look here. (*He takes out a handful of sovereigns and makes them chink.*) Gold, Viv: gold!

Vivie   Where did you get it?

Frank   Gambling, Viv: gambling. Poker.

Vivie   Pah! It's meaner than stealing it. No: I'm not coming. (*She sits down to work at the table, with her back to the glass door, and begins turning over the papers.*)

Frank (*remonstrating piteously*)   But, my dear Viv, I want to talk to you ever so seriously.

Vivie   Very well: sit down in Honoria's chair and talk here. I like ten minutes chat after tea. (*He murmurs.*) No use groaning: I'm inexorable. (*He takes the opposite seat disconsolately.*) Pass that cigar box, will you?

Frank (*pushing the cigar box across*)   Nasty womanly habit.

Nice men dont do it any longer.

Vivie   Yes: they object to the smell in the office; and weve had to take to cigarets. See! (*She opens the box and takes out a cigaret, which she lights. She offers him one; but he shakes his head with a wry face. She settles herself comfortably in her chair, smoking.*) Go ahead.

Frank   Well, I want to know what youve done – what arrangements youve made.

Vivie   Everything was settled twenty minutes after I arrived here. Honoria has found the business too much for her this year; and she was on the point of sending for me and proposing a partnership when I walked in and told her I hadnt a farthing in the world. So I installed myself and packed her off for a fortnight's holiday. What happened at Haslemere when I left?

Frank   Nothing at all. I said youd gone to town on particular business.

Vivie   Well?

Frank   Well, either they were too flabbergasted to say anything, or else Crofts had prepared your mother. Anyhow, she didnt say anything; and Crofts didnt say anything; and Praddy only stared. After tea they got up and went; and Ive not seen them since.

Vivie (*nodding placidly with one eye on a wreath of smoke*)   Thats all right.

Frank (*looking round disparagingly*)   Do you intend to stick in this confounded place?

Vivie (*blowing the wreath decisively away, and sitting straight up*)   Yes. These two days have given me back all my strength and self-possession. I will never take a holiday again as long as I live.

Frank (*with a very wry face*)   Mps! You look quite happy. And as hard as nails.

Vivie (*grimly*)   Well for me that I am!

Frank (*rising*)   Look here, Viv: we must have an explanation. We parted the other day under a complete misunderstanding. (*He sits on the table, close to her.*)

Vivie (*putting away the cigaret*)   Well: clear it up.

Frank   You remember what Crofts said?

Vivie   Yes.

Frank   That revelation was supposed to bring about a complete change in the nature of our feeling for one another. It placed us on the footing of brother and sister.

Vivie   Yes.

Frank   Have you ever had a brother?

Vivie   No.

Frank   Then you dont know what being brother and sister feels like? Now I have lots of sisters; and the fraternal feeling is quite familiar to me. I assure you my feeling for you is not the least in the world like it. The girls will go their way; I will go mine; and we shant care if we never see one another again. Thats brother and sister. But as to you, I cant be easy if I have to pass a week without seeing you. Thats not brother and sister. It's exactly what I felt an hour before Crofts made his revelation. In short, dear Viv, it's love's young dream.

Vivie (*bitingly*)   The same feeling, Frank, that brought your father to my mother's feet. Is that it?

Frank (*so revolted that he slips off the table for a moment*)   I very strongly object, Viv, to have my feelings compared to any which the Reverend Samuel is capable of harboring; and I object still more to a comparison of you to your mother. (*Resuming his perch.*) Besides, I dont believe the story. I have taxed my father with it, and obtained from him what I consider tantamount to a denial.

Vivie   What did he say?

Frank   He said he was sure there must be some mistake.

Vivie   Do you believe him?

Frank   I am prepared to take his word as against Crofts'.

Vivie   Does it make any difference? I mean in your imagination or conscience; for of course it makes no real difference.

Frank (*shaking his head*)   None whatever to me.

Vivie   Nor to me.

Frank (*staring*)   But this is ever so surprising! (*He goes back to his chair.*) I thought our whole relations were altered in your imagination and conscience, as you put it, the moment those words were out of that brute's muzzle.

Vivie   No: it was not that. I didnt believe him. I only wish I could.

Frank   Eh?

Vivie   I think brother and sister would be a very suitable relation for us.

Frank   You really mean that?

Vivie   Yes. It's the only relation I care for, even if we could afford any other. I mean that.

Frank (*raising his eyebrows like one on whom a new light has dawned, and rising with quite an effusion of chivalrous sentiment*)   My dear Viv: why didnt you say so before? I am ever so sorry for persecuting you. I understand, of course.

Vivie (*puzzled*)   Understand what?

Frank   Oh, I'm not a fool in the ordinary sense: only in the Scriptural sense of doing all the things the wise man declared to be folly, after trying them himself on the most extensive scale. I see I am no longer Vivvum's little boy. Dont be alarmed: I shall never call you Vivvums again – at least unless you get tired of your new little boy, however he may be.

Vivie   My new little boy!

Frank (*with conviction*)   Must be a new little boy. Always happens that way. No other way, in fact.

Vivie   None that you know of, fortunately for you.

Someone knocks at the door.

Frank   My curse upon yon caller, whoe'er he be!

Vivie   It's Praed. He's going to Italy and wants to say goodbye. I asked him to call this afternoon. Go and let him in.

Frank   We can continue our conversation after his departure for Italy. I'll stay him out. (*He goes to the door and opens it.*) How are you, Praddy? Delighted to see you. Come in.

Praed, *dressed for travelling, comes in, in high spirits.*

Praed   How do you do, Miss Warren? (*She presses his hand cordially, though a certain sentimentality in his high spirits jars on her.*) I start in an hour from Holborn Viaduct. I wish I could persuade you to try Italy.

Vivie   What for?

Praed   Why, to saturate yourself with beauty and romance, of course.

Vivie, *with a shudder, turns her chair to the table, as if the work waiting for her there were a support to her.* **Praed** *sits opposite to her.* **Frank** *places a* *chair near* **Vivie**, *and drops lazily and carelessly into it, talking at her over his shoulder.*

Frank   No use, Praddy. Viv is a little Philistine. She is indifferent to my romance, and insensible to my beauty.

Vivie   Mr Praed: once for all, there is no beauty and no romance in life for me. Life is what it is; and I am prepared to take it as it is.

Praed (*enthusiastically*)   You will not say that if you come with me to Verona and on to Venice. You will cry with delight at living in such a beautiful world.

Frank   This is most eloquent, Praddy. Keep it up.

Praed   Oh, I assure you *I* have cried – I shall cry again, I hope – at fifty! At your age, Miss Warren, you would not need to go so far as Verona. Your spirits would absolutely fly up at the mere sight of Ostend. You would be charmed with the gaiety, the vivacity, the happy air of Brussels.

Vivie (*springing up with an exclamation of loathing*)   Agh!

Praed (*rising*)   Whats the matter?

Frank (*rising*)   Hallo, Viv!

Vivie (*to* **Praed**, *with deep reproach*)   Can you find no better example of your beauty and romance than Brussels to talk to me about?

Praed (*puzzled*)   Of course it's very different from Verona. I dont suggest for a moment that –

Vivie (*bitterly*)   Probably the beauty and romance come to much the same in both places.

Praed (*completely sobered and much concerned*)   My dear Miss Warren: I – (*Looking inquiringly at* **Frank**.) Is anything the matter?

Frank   She thinks your enthusiasm frivolous, Praddy. She's had ever such a serious call.

Vivie (*sharply*)   Hold your tongue, Frank. Dont be silly.

Frank (*sitting down*)   Do you call this good manners, Praed?

Praed (*anxious and considerate*)   Shall I take him away, Miss Warren? I feel sure we have disturbed you at your work.

Vivie   Sit down: I'm not ready to go back to work yet. (**Praed** *sits.*) You both think I have an attack of nerves. Not a bit of it. But there are two subjects I want dropped, if you dont mind. One of them (*to* **Frank**) is love's young dream in any shape or form: the other (*to* **Praed**) is the romance and beauty of life, especially Ostend and the gaiety of Brussels. You are welcome to any illusions you may have left on these subjects: I have none. If we three are to remain friends, I must be treated as a woman of business, permanently single (*to* **Frank**) and permanently unromantic (*to* **Praed**).

Frank   I also shall remain permanently single until you change your mind. Praddy: change the subject. Be eloquent about something else.

Praed (*diffidently*)   I'm afraid theres nothing else in the world that I can talk about. The Gospel of Art is the only one I can preach. I know Miss Warren is a great devotee of the Gospel of Getting on; but we cant discuss that without hurting your feelings, Frank, since you are determined not to get on.

Frank   Oh, dont mind my feelings. Give me some improving advice by all means: it does me ever so much good. Have another try to make a successful man of me, Viv. Come: lets have it all: energy, thrift, foresight, self-respect, character. Dont you hate people who have no character, Viv?

Vivie (*wincing*)   Oh, stop, stop: let us have no more of that horrible cant. Mr Praed: if there are really only those two gospels in the world, we had better all kill ourselves; for the same taint is in both, through and through.

Frank (*looking critically at her*)   There is a touch of poetry about you today, Viv, which has hitherto been lacking.

Praed (*remonstrating*)   My dear Frank: arnt you a little unsympathetic?

Vivie (*merciless to herself*)   No: it's good for me. It keeps me from being sentimental.

Frank (*bantering her*)   Checks your strong natural propensity that way, dont it?

Vivie (*almost hysterically*)   Oh yes: go on: dont spare me. I was sentimental for one moment in my life – beautifully sentimental – by moonlight; and now –

Frank (*quickly*)   I say, Viv: take care. Dont give yourself away.

Vivie   Oh, do you think Mr Praed does not know all about my mother? (*Turning on* **Praed**.) You had better have told me that morning, Mr Praed. You are very old fashioned in your delicacies, after all.

Praed   Surely it is you who are a little old fashioned in your prejudices, Miss Warren. I feel bound to tell you, speaking as an artist, and believing that the most intimate human relationships are far beyond and above the scope of the law, that though I know that your mother is an unmarried woman, I do not respect her the less on that account. I respect her more.

Frank (*airily*)   Hear! Hear!

Vivie (*staring at him*)   Is that all you know?

Praed   Certainly that is all.

Vivie   Then you neither of you know anything. Your guesses are innocence itself compared to the truth.

Praed (*rising, startled and indignant, and preserving his politeness with an effort*)   I hope not. (*More emphatically.*) I hope not, Miss Warren.

Frank (*whistles*)   Whew!

Vivie   You are not making it easy for me to tell you, Mr Praed.

Praed (*his chivalry drooping before their conviction*)   If there is anything worse – that is, anything else – are you sure you are right to tell us, Miss Warren?

Vivie   I am sure that if I had the courage I should spend the rest of my life in telling everybody – stamping and branding it into them until they all felt their part in its abomination as I feel mine. There is nothing I despise more than the wicked convention that protects these things by forbidding a woman to mention them.

And yet I cant tell you. The two infamous words that describe what my mother is are ringing in my ears and struggling on my tongue; but I cant utter them: the shame of them is too horrible for me. (*She buries her face in her hands. The two men, astonished, stare at one another and then at her. She raises her head again desperately and snatches a sheet of paper and a pen.*) Here: let me draft you a prospectus.

Frank   Oh, she's mad. Do you hear, Viv? mad. Come! Pull yourself together.

Vivie   You shall see. (*She writes.*) 'Paid up capital: not less than £40,000 standing in the name of Sir George Crofts, Baronet, the chief shareholder. Premises at Brussels, Ostend, Vienna and Budapest. Managing director: Mrs. Warren'; and now dont let us forget her qualifications: the two words. (*She writes the words and pushes the paper to them.*) There! Oh no: dont read it: dont! (*She snatches it back and tears it to pieces; then seizes her head in her hands and hides her face on the table.*)

Frank, *who has watched the writing over her shoulder, and opened his eyes very widely at it, takes a card from his pocket; scribbles the two words on it; and silently hands it to* **Praed**, *who reads it with amazement, and hides it hastily in his pocket.*

Frank (*whispering tenderly*)   Viv, dear: thats all right. I read what you wrote: so did Praddy. We understand. And we remain, as this leaves us at present, yours ever so devotedly.

Praed   We do indeed, Miss Warren. I declare you are the most splendidly courageous woman I ever met.

This sentimental compliment braces **Vivie**. *She throws it away from her with an impatient shake, and forces herself to stand up, though not without some support from the table.*

Frank   Dont stir, Viv, if you dont want to. Take it easy.

Vivie   Thank you. You can always depend on me for two things: not to cry and not to faint. (*She moves a few steps towards the door of the inner room, and stops close to* **Praed** *to say:*) I shall need much more courage than that when I tell my mother that we have come to the parting of the ways. Now I must go into the next room for a moment to make myself neat again, if you dont mind.

Praed   Shall we go away?

Vivie   No: I'll be back presently. Only for a moment. (*She goes into the other room,* **Praed** *opening the door for her.*)

Praed   What an amazing revelation! I'm extremely disappointed in Crofts: I am indeed.

Frank   I'm not in the least. I feel he's perfectly accounted for at last. But what a facer for me, Praddy! I cant marry her now.

Praed (*sternly*)   Frank! (*The two look at one another,* **Frank** *unruffled,* **Praed** *deeply indignant.*) Let me tell you, Gardner, that if you desert her now you will behave very despicably.

Frank   Good old Praddy! Ever chivalrous! But you mistake: it's not the moral aspect of the case: it's the money aspect. I really cant bring myself to touch the old woman's money now.

Praed   And was that what you were going to marry on?

Frank   What else? *I* havnt any money, not the smallest turn for making it. If I married Viv now she would have to support me; and I should cost her more than I am worth.

Praed   But surely a clever bright fellow like you can make something by your own brains.

Frank   Oh yes, a little (*He takes out his money again.*) I made all that yesterday in an hour and a half. But I made it in a highly speculative business. No, dear Praddy: even if Bessie and Georgina marry millionaires and the governor dies after cutting them off with a shilling, I shall have only four hundred a year. And he wont die until he's three score and ten: he hasnt originality enough. I shall be on short allowance for the next twenty years. No short allowance for Viv, if I can help it. I withdraw gracefully and leave the field to the gilded youth of England. So thats settled. I shant worry her about it: I'll just send her a little note after we're gone. She'll understand.

Praed (*grasping his hand*)   Good fellow, Frank! I heartily beg your pardon. But must you never see her again?

Frank   Never see her again! Hang it all, be reasonable. I shall come along as often as possible, and be her brother. I can not understand the absurd consequences you romantic people expect from the most ordinary transactions. (*A knock at the door.*) I wonder who this is. Would you mind opening the door? If it's a client it will look more respectable than if I appeared.

Praed   Certainly. (*He goes to the door and opens it.* **Frank** *sits down in* **Vivie**'*s chair to scribble a* note.) My dear Kitty: come in: come in.

Mrs Warren *comes in, looking apprehensively round for* **Vivie**. *She has done her best to make herself matronly and dignified. The brilliant hat is replaced by a sober bonnet, and the gay blouse covered by a costly black silk mantle. She is pitiably anxious and ill at ease: evidently panic-stricken.*

Mrs Warren (*to* **Frank**)   What! Youre here, are you?

Frank (*turning in his chair from his writing, but not rising*)   Here, and charmed to see you. You come like a breath of spring.

Mrs Warren   Oh, get out with your nonsense. (*In a low voice.*) Wheres Vivie?

Frank *points expressively to the door of the inner room, but says nothing.*

Mrs Warren (*sitting down suddenly and almost beginning to cry*) Praddy: wont she see me, dont you think?

Praed   My dear Kitty: dont distress yourself. Why should she not?

Mrs Warren   Oh, you never can see why not: youre too innocent. Mr Frank: did she say anything to you?

Frank (*folding his note*)   She must see you, if (*very expressively*) you wait til she comes in.

Mrs Warren (*frightened*)   Why shouldnt I wait?

Frank *looks quizzically at her; puts his note carefully on the inkbottle, so that* **Vivie** *cannot fail to find it when next she dips her pen; then rises and devotes his attention to her.*

Frank   My dear Mrs Warren: suppose you were a sparrow – ever so tiny and pretty a sparrow hopping in the road-way – and you saw a steam roller coming in your direction, would you wait for it?

Mrs Warren   Oh, dont bother me with your sparrows. What did she run away from Haslemere like that for?

Frank   I'm afraid she'll tell you if you rashly await her return.

Mrs Warren   Do you want me to go away?

Frank   No: I always want you to stay. But I advise you to go away.

Mrs Warren   What! And never see her again!

Frank   Precisely.

Mrs Warren (*crying again*)   Praddy: dont let him be cruel to me. (*She hastily checks her tears and wipes her eyes.*) She'll be so angry if she sees Ive been crying.

Frank (*with a touch of real compassion in his airy tenderness*)   You know that Praddy is the soul of kindness, Mrs Warren. Praddy: what do you say? Go or stay?

Praed (*to* **Mrs Warren**)   I really should be very sorry to cause you unnecessary pain; but I think perhaps you had better not wait. The fact is – (**Vivie** *is heard at the inner door.*)

Frank   Sh! Too late. She's coming.

Mrs Warren   Dont tell her I was crying. (**Vivie** *comes in. She stops gravely on seeing* **Mrs Warren**, *who greets her with hysterical cheerfulness.*) Well, dearie. So here you are at last.

Vivie   I am glad you have come: I want to speak to you. You said you were going, Frank, I think.

Frank   Yes. Will you come with me, Mrs Warren? What do you say to a trip to Richmond, and the theatre in the evening? There is safety in Richmond. No steam roller there.

Vivie   Nonsense, Frank. My mother will stay here.

Mrs Warren (*scared*)   I dont know: perhaps I'd better go. We're disturbing you at your work.

Vivie (*with quiet decision*)   Mr Praed: please take Frank away.

Sit down, mother. (**Mrs Warren** *obeys helplessly.*)

Praed Come, Frank. Goodbye, Miss Vivie.

Vivie (*shaking hands*) Goodbye. A pleasant trip.

Praed Thank you: thank you. I hope so.

Frank (*to* **Mrs Warren**) Goodbye: youd ever so much better have taken my advice. (*He shakes hands with her. Then airily to* **Vivie**:) Byebye, Viv.

Vivie Goodbye. (*He goes out gaily without shaking hands with her.*)

Praed (*sadly*) Goodbye, Kitty.

Mrs Warren (*snivelling*) – oobye!

Praed *goes.* **Vivie**, *composed and extremely grave, sits down in Honoria's chair, and waits for her mother to speak.* **Mrs Warren**, *dreading a pause, loses no time in beginning.*

Mrs Warren Well, Vivie, what did you go away like that for without saying a word to me? How could you do such a thing! And what have you done to poor George? I wanted him to come with me; but he shuffled out of it. I could see that he was quite afraid of you. Only fancy: he wanted me not to come. As if (*trembling*) I should be afraid of you, dearie. (**Vivie**'s *gravity deepens.*) But of course I told him it was all settled and comfortable between us, and that we were on the best of terms. (*She breaks down.*) Vivie: whats the meaning of this? (*She produces a commercial envelope, and fumbles at the enclosure with trembling fingers.*) I got it from the bank this morning.

Vivie It is my month's allowance. They sent it to me as usual the other day. I simply sent it back to be placed to your credit, and asked them to send you the lodgment receipt. In future I shall support myself.

Mrs Warren (*not daring to understand*) Wasnt it enough? Why didnt you tell me? (*With a cunning gleam in her eye.*) I'll double it: I was intending to double it. Only let me know how much you want.

Vivie You know very well that that has nothing to do with it. From this time I go my own way in my own business and among my own friends. And you will go yours. (*She rises.*) Goodbye.

Mrs Warren (*rising, appalled*)   Goodbye?

Vivie   Yes: Goodbye. Come: dont let us make a useless scene: you understand perfectly well. Sir George Crofts has told me the whole business.

Mrs Warren (*angrily*)   Silly old − (*She swallows an epithet, and turns white at the narrowness of her escape from uttering it.*)

Vivie   Just so.

Mrs Warren   He ought to have his tongue cut out. But I thought it was ended: you said you didnt mind.

Vivie (*steadfastly*)   Excuse me: I do mind.

Mrs Warren   But I explained −

Vivie   You explained how it came about. You did not tell me that it is still going on. (*She sits.*)

Mrs Warren, *silenced for a moment, looks forlornly at* **Vivie**, *who waits, secretly hoping that the combat is over. But the cunning expression comes back into* **Mrs Warren**'s *face; and she bends across the table, sly and urgent, half whispering.*

Mrs Warren   Vivie: do you know how rich I am?

Vivie   I have no doubt you are very rich.

Mrs Warren   But you dont know all that that means: youre too young. It means a new dress every day; it means theatres and balls every night; it means having the pick of all the gentlemen in Europe at your feet; it means a lovely house and plenty of servants; it means the choicest of eating and drinking; it means everything you like, everything you want, everything you can think of. And what are you here? A mere drudge, toiling and moiling early and late for your bare living and two cheap dresses a year. Think over it. (*Soothingly.*) Youre shocked, I know. I can enter into your feelings; and I think they do you credit; but trust me, nobody will blame you: you may take my word for that. I know what young girls are; and I know youll think better of it when youve turned it over in your mind.

Vivie   So thats how it's done, is it? You must have said all that to many a woman, mother, to have it so pat.

Mrs Warren (*passionately*)   What harm am I asking you to do?
(**Vivie** *turns away contemptuously.* **Mrs Warren** *continues desperately.*)
Vivie: listen to me: you dont understand: youve been taught
wrong on purpose: you dont know what the world is really like.

Vivie (*arrested*)   Taught wrong on purpose! What do you mean?

Mrs Warren   I mean that youre throwing away all your
chances for nothing. You think that people are what they pretend
to be: that the way you were taught at school and college to think
right and proper is the way things really are. But it's not: it's all
only a pretence, to keep the cowardly slavish common run of
people quiet. Do you want to find that out, like other women, at
forty, when youve thrown yourself away and lost your chances;
or wont you take it in good time now from your own mother, that
loves you and swears to you that it's truth: gospel truth? (*Urgently.*)
Vivie: the big people, the clever people, the managing people, all
know it. They do as I do, and think what I think. I know plenty
of them. I know them to speak to, to introduce you to, to make
friends of for you. I dont mean anything wrong: thats what you
dont understand: your head is full of ignorant ideas about me.
What do the people that taught you know about life or about
people like me? When did they ever meet me, or speak to me, or
let anyone tell them about me? the fools! Would they ever have
done anything for you if I hadnt paid them? Havnt I told you
that I want you to be respectable? Havnt I brought you up to be
respectable? And how can you keep it up without my money and
my influence and Lizzie's friends? Cant you see that youre cutting
your own throat as well as breaking my heart in turning your back
on me?

Vivie   I recognize the Crofts philosophy of life, mother. I heard
it all from him that day at the Gardners'.

Mrs Warren   You think I want to force that played-out old sot
on you! I dont, Vivie: on my oath I dont.

Vivie   It would not matter if you did: you would not succeed.
(**Mrs Warren** *winces, deeply hurt by the implied indifference towards
her affectionate intention.* **Vivie**, *neither understanding this nor concerning
herself about it, goes on calmly.*) Mother: you dont at all know the sort
of person I am. I dont object to Crofts more than to any other

coarsely built man of his class. To tell you the truth, I rather
admire him for being strongminded enough to enjoy himself in
his own way and make plenty of money instead of living the usual
shooting, hunting, dining-out, tailoring, loafing life of his set merely
because all the rest do it. And I'm perfectly aware that if I'd been
in the same circumstances as my aunt Liz, I'd have done exactly
what she did. I dont think I'm more prejudiced or straitlaced than
you: I think I'm less. I'm certain I'm less sentimental. I know very
well that fashionable morality is all a pretence, and that if I took
your money and devoted the rest of my life to spending it fashionably, I might be as worthless and vicious as the silliest woman could
possibly want to be without having a word said to me about it. But
I dont want to be worthless. I shouldnt enjoy trotting about the
park to advertise my dressmaker and carriage builder, or being
bored at the opera to shew off a shopwindowful of diamonds.

Mrs Warren (*bewildered*)   But –

Vivie   Wait a moment: Ive not done. Tell me why you continue
your business now that you are independent of it. Your sister, you
told me, has left all that behind her. Why dont you do the same?

Mrs Warren   Oh, it's all very easy for Liz: she likes good
society, and has the air of being a lady. Imagine me in a cathedral
town! Why, the very rooks in the trees would find me out even if
I could stand the dulness of it. I must have work and excitement,
or I should go melancholy mad. And what else is there for me to
do? The life suits me: I'm fit for it and not for anything else. If I
didnt do it somebody else would; so I dont do any real harm by it.
And then it brings in money; and I like making money. No: it's no
use: I cant give it up – not for anybody. But what need you know
about it? I'll never mention it. I'll keep Crofts away. I'll not trouble
you much: you see I have to be constantly running about from one
place to another. Youll be quit of me altogether when I die.

Vivie   No: I am my mother's daughter. I am like you: I must
have work, and must make more money than I spend. But my
work is not your work, and my way not your way. We must part.
It will not make much difference to us: instead of meeting one
another for perhaps a few months in twenty years, we shall never
meet: thats all.

Mrs Warren (*her voice stifled in tears*)   Vivie: I meant to have been more with you: I did indeed.

Vivie   It's no use, mother: I am not to be changed by a few cheap tears and entreaties any more than you are, I daresay.

Mrs Warren (*wildly*)   Oh, you call a mother's tears cheap.

Vivie   They cost you nothing; and you ask me to give you the peace and quietness of my whole life in exchange for them. What use would my company be to you if you could get it? What have we two in common that could make either of us happy together?

Mrs Warren (*lapsing recklessly into her dialect*)   We're mother and daughter. I want my daughter. Ive a right to you. Who is to care for me when I'm old? Plenty of girls have taken to me like daughters and cried at leaving me; but I let them all go because I had you to look forward to. I kept myself lonely for you. Youve no right to turn on me now and refuse to do your duty as a daughter.

Vivie (*jarred and antagonized by the echo of the slums in her mother's voice*)   My duty as a daughter! I thought we should come to that presently. Now once for all, mother, you want a daughter and Frank wants a wife. I dont want a mother; and I dont want a husband. I have spared neither Frank nor myself in sending him about his business. Do you think I will spare you?

Mrs Warren (*violently*)   Oh, I know the sort you are: no mercy for yourself or anyone else. *I* know. My experience has done that for me anyhow: I can tell the pious, canting, hard, selfish woman when I meet her. Well, keep yourself to yourself: *I* dont want you. But listen to this. Do you know what I would do with you if you were a baby again? aye, as sure as theres a Heaven above us.

Vivie   Strangle me, perhaps.

Mrs Warren   No: I'd bring you up to be a real daughter to me, and not what you are now, with your pride and your prejudices and the college education you stole from me: yes, stole: deny it if you can: what was it but stealing? I'd bring you up in my own house, I would.

Vivie (*quietly*)   In one of your own houses.

Mrs Warren (*screaming*)   Listen to her! listen to how she spits on her mother's grey hairs! Oh, may you live to have your own daughter tear and trample on you as you have trampled on me. And you will: you will. No woman ever had luck with a mother's curse on her.

Vivie   I wish you wouldnt rant, mother. It only hardens me. Come: I suppose I am the only young woman you ever had in your power that you did good to. Dont spoil it all now.

Mrs Warren   Yes, Heaven forgive me, it's true; and you are the only one that ever turned on me. Oh, the injustice of it! the injustice! the injustice! I always wanted to be a good woman. I tried honest work; and I was slave-driven until I cursed the day I ever heard of honest work. I was a good mother; and because I made my daughter a good woman she turns me out as if I was a leper. Oh, if I only had my life to live over again! I'd talk to that lying clergyman in the school. From this time forth, so help me Heaven in my last hour, I'll do wrong and nothing but wrong. And I'll prosper on it.

Vivie   Yes: it's better to choose your line and go through with it. If I had been you, mother, I might have done as you did: but I should not have lived one life and believed in another. You are a conventional woman at heart. That is why I am bidding you goodbye now. I am right, am I not?

Mrs Warren (*taken aback*)   Right to throw away all my money?

Vivie   No: right to get rid of you! I should be a fool not to! Isnt that so?

Mrs Warren (*sulkily*)   Oh well, yes, if you come to that, I suppose you are. But Lord help the world if everybody took to doing the right thing! And now I'd better go than stay where I'm not wanted. (*She turns to the door.*)

Vivie (*kindly*)   Wont you shake hands?

Mrs Warren (*after looking at her fiercely for a moment with a savage impulse to strike her*)   No, thank you. Goodbye.

Vivie (*matter-of-factly*)   Goodbye. (**Mrs Warren** *goes out, slamming the door behind her. The strain on* **Vivie**'s *face relaxes; her grave expression* *breaks up into one of joyous content; her breath goes out in a half sob, half laugh of intense relief. She goes buoyantly to her place at the writing-table; pushes the electric lamp out of the way; pulls over a great sheaf of papers; and is in the act of dipping her pen in the ink when she finds* **Frank***'s note. She opens it unconcernedly and reads it quickly, giving a little laugh at some quaint turn of expression in it.*) And goodbye, Frank. (*She tears the note up and tosses the pieces into the wastepaper basket without a second thought. Then she goes at her work with a plunge, and soon becomes absorbed in its figures.*)

ANTON CHEKHOV

Three Sisters

translated by Michael Frayn

Characters

Andrey Prozorov
Natasha, *his fiancée, later his wife*
Olga, *his sister*
Masha *his sister*
Irina, *his sister*
Kulygin (*Fyodor*), *a teacher in the local high school, and* **Masha***'s husband*
Lieutenant-colonel Vershinin, *the battery commander*
Lieutenant the Baron Tusenbach
Junior Captain Solyony
Dr Chebutykin, *the medical officer*
Second-lieutenant Fedotik
Second-lieutentant Rode
Ferapont, *an elderly watchman from the local Executive Board*
Anfisa, *the family's nanny, now eighty*

Act One

The interior of the Prozorovs' house. The drawing-room, with a colonnade beyond which the main reception room can be seen. It is noon, and the day is bright and cheerful. The table in the big room beyond is being laid for lunch. **Olga**, *who is wearing the dark blue dress laid down for a teacher in a girls' high school, stands correcting exercise-books the whole time – walks up and down correcting them.* **Masha**, *in a black dress, her hat in her lap, sits reading a book.* **Irina**, *in white, stands lost in her own thoughts.*

Olga It's exactly a year since Father died. A year ago today – May the fifth – it was on your name-day, Irina. It was very cold, we had snow. I thought I should never survive it, and there you were lying in a dead faint. But now here's a year gone by, and we can think about it again quite calmly. You're back in white, your face is shining . . .

The clock strikes twelve.

The clock kept striking then, too.

Pause.

I remember the band playing as they carried Father's body on the bier, I remember them firing the volley over the grave. He was a general, he had a brigade, but not many people came. Though it was raining at the time. Sleeting – sleeting hard.

Irina Why keep harking back?

Baron Tusenbach, **Chebutykin**, *and* **Solyony** *appear on the other side of the colonnade, around the table in the main room.*

Olga It's warm today. We can have the windows wide. The birch trees aren't out yet, though. Father got his brigade and left Moscow with us eleven years ago, and I well remember what Moscow was like at this time of year, at the beginning of May. Everything would be in blossom already, everything would be warm, everything would be awash with sunshine. Eleven years have gone by, but I remember it all as if it were yesterday. Oh God, I woke up this morning, I saw the light flooding in, I saw the spring, and I felt such a great surge of joy, such a passionate longing for home.

Chebutykin   Stuff and nonsense, sir!

Tusenbach   Utter rubbish, of course.

Masha, *lost in thought over her book, quietly whistles a tune.*

Olga   Don't whistle, Masha. How could you?

Pause.

I'm at school each day, then I give lessons for the rest of the afternoon, and I end up with a perpetual headache, I end up thinking the kind of thoughts I'd have if I were an old woman already. And in fact these last four years since I've been teaching I have felt as if day by day, drop by drop, my youth and strength were going out of me. And the only thing that grows, the only thing that gets stronger, is one single dream . . .

Irina   To go to Moscow. To sell up the house, to finish with everything here, and off to Moscow . . .

Olga   Yes! To Moscow, as soon as ever we can!

Chebutykin *and* **Tusenbach** *laugh.*

Irina   Our brother will most likely be a professor. All the same, he won't want to live here. The only one who's stuck here is poor Masha.

Olga   Masha will come to Moscow for the whole summer, every year.

Masha *quietly whistles a tune.*

Irina   God willing, it'll all work itself out (*Looking out of window.*) Beautiful weather. I don't know why my heart is so full of light! This morning I remembered I was the name-day girl, and I felt a sudden rush of joy. I remembered when I was little, and Mama was still alive. And I can't tell you what thoughts I felt stirring, what wonderful thoughts!

Olga   Today you're all shining, you look lovelier than ever. Masha's lovely, too. That brother of ours would be a good-looking man, only he's put on a lot of weight – it doesn't suit him. I've aged, though, I've got terribly thin, I suppose from all my irritation with the girls at school. But today I'm free, I'm home, my headache's gone, and I feel I've got younger overnight. I'm twenty-eight, that's all . . . Everything is for the best, everything is from God, but I can't help feeling it would be better if I were married and stayed at home all day.

Pause.

I should have loved my husband.

Tusenbach (*to* **Solyony**)   What nonsense you do talk! I'm sick of listening to you. (*Coming into the drawing-room.*) I forgot to say. You'll be getting a visit today from our new battery commander, Vershinin (*Sits down at the upright piano.*)

Olga   Good. I shall be delighted.

Irina   Is he old?

Tusenbach   Not particularly. Forty, forty-five, at most. (*Quietly strums on the piano.*) Splendid fellow, by all accounts. Certainly no fool. Talks a lot, that's the only thing.

Irina   Is he an interesting man?

Tusenbach   He's all right, apart from having a wife and mother-in-law and two little girls. Been married before, too. He makes his calls, and everywhere he goes he tells everyone he's got a wife and two little girls. He'll be telling you next. His wife's a bit touched. Long plait like a schoolgirl – all high-flown talk and philosophising. And she makes frequent attempts at suicide, evidently to spite her husband. I'd have left a woman like that long ago, but he puts up with it, and all he does is complain.

Solyony (*coming out of the main room into the drawing-room with* **Chebutykin**)   With one hand I can lift only fifty pounds, whereas with two I can lift 180 – 200 even. From which I conclude that two men are not twice as strong as one, but three times as strong, or even more . . .

Chebutykin (*reading a newspaper as he walks*)   For falling hair . . . dissolve quarter of an ounce of mothballs in half

a bottle of spirit . . . apply daily . . . (*Writes it down in a notebook.*)
Must make a note of that! (*To* **Solyony**:) So there we are, you
put the cork in the bottle, with a glass tube running through it . . .
Then you take a pinch of common or garden alum . . .

Irina   Ivan Romanich! Dear Ivan Romanich!

Chebutykin   My little girl! What is it, my precious?

Irina   Tell me, why am I so happy today? As if I were sailing,
with the wide blue sky above me, and great white birds soaring in
the wind. Why is it? Why?

Chebutykin (*kissing both her hands, tenderly*)   My own white bird . . .

Irina   I woke up this morning, I got up, I washed – and
suddenly I felt everything in this world was clear to me – I felt
I knew how life had to be lived. Dear Ivan Romanich, I can
see it all. A human being has to labour, whoever he happens
to be, he has to toil in the sweat of his face; that's the only way
he can find the sense and purpose of his life, his happiness, his
delight. How fine to be a working man who rises at first light
and breaks stones on the road, or a shepherd, or a teacher, or
an engine driver on the railway . . . Lord, never mind being
human even – better to be an ox, better to be a simple horse,
just so long as you work – anything rather than a young lady
who rises at noon, then drinks her coffee in bed, then takes two
hours to dress . . . that's terrible! In hot weather sometimes you
long to drink the way I began longing to work. And if I don't
start getting up early and working, then shut your heart against
me, Ivan Romanich.

Chebutykin (*tenderly*)   I'll shut it, I'll shut it tight.

Olga   Father trained us to rise at seven. Now Irina wakes at
seven and lies there till nine o'clock at least, just thinking. She
looks so serious, though! (*Laughs.*)

Irina   You're used to seeing me as a child, so then you find it
odd when I look serious. I'm twenty!

Tusenbach   A longing to work – oh, heavens, how well I
know that feeling! I've never done a stroke of work in my life.
I was born in Petersburg, that cold and idle city, and none of

my family had ever known what it was to work, they'd never
known care. When I used to come home from cadet school a
servant would pull my boots off for me, while I played the fool.
My mother regarded me with an indulgent eye, though, and she
was astonished when other people took a different view. I was
protected from work. But I only just managed it by the skin of my
teeth! Because the time has come when the piled thunderclouds
are advancing upon us all. A great healthy storm is brewing, and
it's going to blow our society clean of idleness and indifference,
clean of prejudice against work and rotting boredom. I'm going
to work, but then in twenty years time, in thirty years time,
everyone will be working. Every single one of us!

Chebutykin   I shan't be working.

Tusenbach   You don't count.

Solyony   In twenty years time you won't be alive, thank God.
A couple of years from now and you'll have had a stroke, or I
shall have lost my temper and put a bullet through your lovely
face (*Takes a bottle of scent out of his pocket and sprinkles his chest and
arms.*)

Chebutykin (*laughs*)   But I really never have done anything at
all. From the time I left university I haven't lifted a finger. Not a
solitary book have I read even, nothing but newspapers . . . (*Takes
another newspaper out of his pocket.*) You see . . . ? I know from reading
newspapers who Dobrolyubov was, let's say, I know he was a
famous critic, but what the devil he wrote – heaven knows, not the
slightest idea . . .

The sound of knocking from the floor below.

Ah . . . They want me downstairs, I've got a visitor. Back in a
moment . . . Wait here . . . (*Goes out hurriedly, combing his beard.*)

Irina   He's up to something.

Tusenbach   Yes. He's got his special face on. He's obviously
going to come back in a moment with a present for you.

Irina   Oh, for heaven's sake!

Olga   Yes, it's awful. He's always doing stupid things.

Masha   On a far sea shore an oak tree grows,
And from it hangs a golden chain;
A talking cat forever goes
Around that chain and round again.

She gets up and hums quietly.

Olga   You're not very cheerful today, Masha.

Masha, *still humming, puts on her hat.*

Where are you off to?

Masha   Home.

Irina   What a funny way to behave . . .

Tusenbach   Walking out on your sister's party!

Masha   What does it matter? I'll come this evening. Goodbye,
my sweet . . . (*Kisses* **Irina**.) Best wishes, once again – health and
happiness . . . In the old days, when Father was alive, we'd have
thirty or forty officers coming every time it was someone's name-
day, and there was a lot of noise. Whereas today we've scarcely got
two people to rub together, and it's as silent as the tomb . . . I'm
off . . . I'm down in the dumps today – don't take any notice of
me (*Laughing through her tears.*) We'll have a little talk later. Goodbye
for now, my dear – I'll walk myself somewhere.

Irina (*displeased*)   What an odd creature you are . . .

Olga (*with tears in her eyes*)   I understand you, Masha.

Solyony   If a man philosophises, then what comes out is
philosophy, though it may be full o' sophistry. But if a woman
philosophises, or let's say two women, then it's bound to be not so
much philosophy as full o' gossipy.

Masha   What do you mean by that, you horribly frightening
man?

Solyony   Never mind. The peasant had no time to gasp. Before
he felt the bear's hard clasp. As the poet says.

Pause.

Masha (*to* **Olga**, *angrily*)   Don't howl!

Enter **Anfisa** *and* **Ferapont** *with a cake.*

Anfisa   In here, my dear. Come on, you've got clean feet. (*To* **Irina**:) From the Council, from Protopopov . . . It's a cake.

Irina   Thank you. Will you say thank you to him? (*Takes the cake.*)

Ferapont   What?

Irina (*louder*)   Say thank you to him!

Olga   Nanny, give him a piece of cake. Off you go, then, Ferapont – they'll give you some cake outside.

Ferapont   What?

Anfisa   Come on, my dear. Off we go . . . (*Goes out with* **Ferapont**.)

Masha   I don't like that Protopopov man. There's something about him that reminds me of a bear. He shouldn't have been invited.

Irina   I didn't invite him.

Masha   That's all right, then.

Enter **Chebutykin**, *followed by a* **Soldier** *carrying a silver samovar. There is a murmur of surprise and displeasure.*

Olga (*hides her face in her hands*)   A silver samovar! This is awful! Does he think it's a wedding anniversary? (*Goes out to the table in the main room.*)

Irina   Ivan Romanich, my sweet, what are you doing?

Tusenbach (*laughs*)   I told you!

Masha   Ivan Romanich, you're simply shameless!

Chebutykin   My dears, my loves, you're all I have, you're all that's most precious to me in the world. I'm nearly sixty – I'm an old man, a lonely, useless old man . . . There's no good in me at all except this love I have for you. If it weren't for you I should have departed this world a long time ago . . . (*To* **Irina**:) My dear, my little girl, I've known you since the day you were born . . . I used to carry you in my arms . . . I loved your poor dead mother . . .

Irina   But why such expensive presents?

Chebutykin (*on the verge of tears, angrily*) Expensive presents . . .
Get along with you! (*To the* **Orderly**:) Take the samovar in there . . .
(*Mockingly.*) Expensive presents . . .

The **Orderly** *takes the samovar into the main room.*

Anfisa (*crossing the drawing-room*) Some strange colonel, my
dears! He's taken his coat off, my pets – he's on his way up. Now,
Irinushka, you be nice and polite to him . . . (*Going out.*) It's past
lunchtime already, too . . . Oh my lord . . .

Tusenbach Vershinin, presumably.

Enter **Vershinin**.

Lieutenant-Colonel Vershinin!

Vershinin (*to* **Masha** *and* **Irina**) Allow me to introduce
myself – Vershinin. So very glad to be with you at last. But how
you've changed! Dear me!

Irina Do sit down. This is a great pleasure for us.

Vershinin (*gaily*) I'm so glad! I'm so glad! But there are three
of you, aren't there – three sisters? I remember there being
three girls. Your faces I don't recall, but the fact that your father,
Colonel Prozorov, had three little girls – that I recall perfectly –
indeed I saw it for myself. How time flies! Ah me, how time flies!

Tusenbach The colonel is from Moscow.

Irina From Moscow? You're from Moscow?

Vershinin I am indeed. Your late father was a battery
commander there; I was in the same brigade (*To* **Masha**:) Now
your face I believe I do just remember.

Masha I don't remember you, though!

Irina Olya! Olya! (*Calls into the main room.*) Olya, come here!

Olga *comes out of the main room into the drawing-room.*

Colonel Vershinin turns out to be from Moscow.

Vershinin So you're Olga, you're the eldest . . . You're Maria . . .
And you're Irina, you're the youngest . . .

Olga You're from Moscow?

Vershinin I am. I was at university in Moscow and I began my service career in Moscow. I served there for a long time, until finally I was given a battery here, and transferred, as you see. I don't really remember you – all I remember is that you were three sisters. Your father has stayed in my memory very clearly. I sit here and close my eyes and I see him as if he were standing in front of me. I used to come to your house in Moscow . . .

Olga I thought I remembered them all, and now suddenly . . .

Irina You're from Moscow . . . It's like a bolt from the blue!

Olga We're moving there, you see.

Irina We think we shall actually be there by the autumn. It's our home town – we were born there . . . In Old Basmannaya Street . . .

She and **Olga** *both laugh with delight.*

Masha Out of the blue we've met someone from home (*Animatedly.*) Now it's come back to me! You remember, Olya, we used to talk about 'the lovelorn major'. You were a lieutenant then and you were in love with somebody, and why it was I don't know, but everyone used to tease you by calling you the major . . .

Vershinin (*laughs*) That's me. The lovelorn major – that's right . . .

Masha You only had a moustache in those days . . . Oh, how you've aged! (*Through her tears.*) How you've aged!

Vershinin Yes, when they used to call me the lovelorn major I was young still, and they were right – I was in love. That's not the case now.

Olga But you still don't have a single grey hair. You've aged, yes, but you're not old yet.

Vershinin I shall be forty-three next birthday, nonetheless. Have you been away from Moscow for long?

Irina Eleven years. What are you doing, Masha, you're crying, you funny thing . . . (*Through her tears.*) I'm going to cry, too . . .

Masha   I'm all right. So which street did you live in?

Vershinin   Old Basmannaya.

Olga   So did we . . .

Vershinin   At one time I lived in Nemetzkaya Street. I used to walk from there to the Krasny Barracks. There's a rather depressing bridge on the way – you can hear the noise of the water underneath it. If you're on your own it strikes a chill into your heart.

Pause.

But here you have such a broad and brimming river! A magnificent river!

Olga   Yes, only there's the cold here. The cold and the mosquitoes . . .

Vershinin   Oh, come now! This is a good healthy Russian climate. The forest, the river . . . it's birch country here, too. The good old humble birch – I love it above all trees. It's a fine place to live. The only odd thing is that the railway station is thirteen miles out of town . . . And nobody knows why.

Solyony   I know why.

Everyone looks at him.

Because if the station were near then it wouldn't be far, and if it's far then naturally it can't be near.

An awkward silence.

Tusenbach   Something of a humorist, the captain.

Olga   Now I've placed you, too. I remember you.

Vershinin   I knew your mother.

Chebutykin   A good woman she was, God rest her soul.

Irina   Mama's buried in Moscow.

Olga   In the Novo-Devichi . . .

Masha   Can you imagine, I'm already beginning to forget her face. It will be the same with us – we shan't be remembered, either. We shall be forgotten.

Vershinin   Yes. We shall be forgotten. Such is indeed our fate – there's nothing we can do about it. What we find serious, significant, highly important – the time will come when it's all forgotten, or when it all seems quite unimportant after all.

Pause.

And this is interesting: we can't possibly know now what's eventually going to be considered elevated and important, and what people are going to think pathetic and ridiculous. The discoveries made by Copernicus – or Columbus, let's say – didn't they seem uncalled-for and absurd at first? While some empty nonsense written by a crank looked like the truth? And it may be that our present way of life, with which we feel so much at home, will in time seem odd, uncomfortable, foolish, not as clean as it should be – perhaps even wicked.

Tusenbach   Who knows? Perhaps, on the other hand, our way of life will be thought elevated and remembered with respect. There's no torture now, no executions or invasions; and yet, at the same time, there's so much suffering.

Solyony (*in a little voice*)   Cheep, cheep, cheep . . . If there's one thing the baron loves it's a nice bit of philosophising.

Tusenbach   Will you please leave me alone . . . ? (*Sits elsewhere.*) It's becoming tedious.

Solyony (*in his little voice*)   Cheep, cheep, cheep . . .

Tusenbach (to **Vershinin**)   The suffering to be observed nowadays – and there is so much of it – does nevertheless testify to a certain moral elevation that society has achieved . . .

Vershinin   Yes, yes, of course . . .

Chebutykin   You said just now, baron, that our way of life may one day be thought elevated. But people are still as low as ever . . . (*Stands up.*) Look how low I am. You have to tell me my way of life is elevated just to console me, obviously.

A violin is played, off.

Masha   That's Andrey playing – our brother.

Irina   He's the scholar of the family. He's probably going to be a professor. Papa was a soldier, but his son plumped for an academic career.

Masha   At Papa's wish.

Olga   We've been teasing him today. It appears that he is a tiny bit in love.

Irina   With a certain young lady who lives hereabouts. She'll be coming today, most probably.

Masha   Oh, but the way she dresses! It's not just dowdy, it's not just unfashionable – it's downright pitiful. Some outlandish skirt in a shade of bright yellow, with an appalling little fringe – and a red blouse. And those wishy-washy white cheeks of hers! Andrey isn't in love – that I won't concede – he has some taste, after all. He's just teasing us, just playing the fool. I heard yesterday she's to marry Protopopov, the chairman of the local Executive Council. Very suitable . . . (*Through the side door.*) Andrey! Come here a minute, dear!

Enter **Andrey**.

Olga   This is my brother Andrey.

Vershinin   Vershinin.

Andrey   Prozorov (*Wipes his face, which is covered in perspiration.*) You're our new battery commander?

Olga   Can you imagine, the colonel comes from Moscow.

Andrey   Really? Well, the best of luck to you, because now my sisters will never give you any peace.

Vershinin   I've already managed to weary them.

Irina   Look at the picture-frame that Andrey gave me today! (*Shows the frame.*) He made it himself.

Vershinin (*looking at the frame and not knowing what to say*)   Indeed . . . a thing of . . .

Irina   And that frame there – the one over the piano – he made that as well.

Andrey *flaps his hand and moves away.*

Olga   He's not only the scholar of the family – he also plays the violin and he makes all kinds of little woodwork things. Well, he's the complete all-rounder. Andrey, don't go away! He's got this trick of disappearing all the time. Come back!

Masha *and* **Irina** *take him by the arms and laughingly bring him back.*

Masha   Come on, come on!

Andrey   Leave me alone, will you, please?

Masha   You are absurd! They used to call the colonel here the lovelorn major, and he wasn't the slightest bit cross about it.

Vershinin   Not at all!

Masha   And I'm going to call you the lovelorn fiddler.

Irina   Or else the lovelorn professor!

Olga   He's in love! Our dear Andrey is in love!

Irina *(clapping)*   Bravo, bravo! Encore! Our dear little Andrey is in love!

Chebutykin *(goes up behind* **Andrey** *and seizes him with both arms around his waist).*
For love and love alone
was man put in his earthly home!

(Roars with laughter, still holding the newspaper.)

Andrey   That will do now, that will do . . . *(Wipes his face.)*
I didn't sleep all night, and now I feel a bit the worse for wear. I was reading until four o'clock, then I went to bed, but it was quite fruitless. My thoughts kept going round, and it gets light early here – the sun simply comes stealing into the bedroom. There's a book I want to translate from the English during the course of the summer, while I'm still here.

Vershinin   You read English?

Andrey   Yes. Poor Father – he piled education on to us. It's ridiculous, but I have to confess that after he died I began to put on weight. A year and I'm out to here. It's as if my body had shaken off some load. Thanks to Father my sisters and I know French, German, and English. Irina knows Italian as well. But what it cost us!

Masha Knowing three languages in this town is a pointless embellishment. It's not even an embellishment – it's some kind of useless appendage like a sixth finger. We know much more than we need to.

Vershinin Listen to them! (*Laughs.*) You know much more than you need to, do you? I think the town so dull and dreary that it has no place for someone of intelligence and education truly doesn't exist – couldn't exist. All right, let us concede that among the hundred thousand inhabitants of this town – of this, certainly, rude and backward town – there are no more than three people like you. Obviously you're not going to prevail over the sea of darkness around you. In your own lifetime you'll gradually be forced to give ground to that crowd of a hundred thousand – you'll be swallowed up in it; life will choke you. All the same, you won't disappear, you won't be without influence. After you will come maybe six people of your sort, then twelve, and so on, until in the end people like you are in the majority. In two or three hundred years life on earth will be astonishingly, unimaginably beautiful. This is the life that man must have, and if it eludes him in the meantime then he must have a premonition of it, he must wait and dream and make himself ready for it, and this means he must understand more and know more than his father and grandfather did (*Laughs.*) And you're complaining that you know much more than you need to.

Masha (*takes off her hat*) I'll stay for lunch.

Irina (*with a sigh*) Really, we should have been taking a note of all that . . .

Andrey *is missing. He has gone out unnoticed.*

Tusenbach Many years from now, you tell us, life on earth will be astonishingly beautiful. True. But to have a hand in that life now, albeit a remote hand, we must prepare ourselves for it, we must work . . .

Vershinin (*gets up*) Yes. But what a lot of flowers you've got! (*Looking round.*) And magnificent quarters. I envy you! I've spent all my life knocking about in lodgings with two chairs and a sofa, and a stove that always smokes. Flowers like these are the very thing my life has lacked . . . (*Rubs his hands.*) Ah, well, there we are!

Tusenbach Yes, but we have to work. You're probably thinking, that's what touches a German heart. But I'm Russian, I promise you. I can't even speak German. My father's Russian Orthodox . . .

Pause.

Vershinin (*walks about the stage*) I often think, supposing we could start our life afresh – and this time with our eyes open? Supposing the first life, the one we've already lived, was a kind of rough draft, and the second one was the fair copy! Then what we'd all mostly try to do, I think, would be not to repeat ourselves. Or at any rate we'd create new surroundings for ourselves, we'd set up quarters like these with flowers, with a sea of light . . . I have a wife and two little girls, on top of which my wife is a sick woman, and so it goes on, and anyway, if I were starting life over again I shouldn't get married . . . Not for any money!

Enter **Kulygin** *in a uniform tailcoat.*

Kulygin (*goes up to* **Irina**) My dear sister-in-law, may I offer you all suitable compliments on this happy day? And my most sincere and heartfelt best wishes for your good health, and for everything else a girl of your age might properly be wished. And may I make you a present of this little book? (*Gives it to her.*) The history of our school over the last fifty years, written by me. It's just a little thing I wrote because I had nothing better to do, but read it anyway. Good day, ladies and gentlemen! (*To* **Vershinin**:) Kulygin – teacher in the local high school, Seventh grade of the civil service – a lieutenant-colonel of the civilian world! (*To* **Irina**:) In that little book you'll find a list of all those who passed through our school in the last fifty years. *Feci quod potui, faciant meliora potentes.* I have done what I could; let those who can do better. (*Kisses* **Masha**.)

Irina You gave me some sort of book like this at Easter surely?

Kulygin (*laughs*)   No! Did I? In that case give it back, or better still give it to the colonel here. Take it, colonel. Read it some time when you're bored.

Vershinin   Thank you. (*On the point of leaving.*) I'm so very pleased to have made your acquaintance . . .

Olga   You're not going? No, no, no!

Irina   You'll stay and have lunch with us. Please.

Olga   Do stay!

Vershinin (*bows*)   I seem to have chanced upon a name-day. Forgive me – I had no idea – I didn't offer you my compliments . . . (*Goes out with* **Olga** *into the main room.*)

Kulygin   Today, ladies and gentlemen, is the Sabbath day, the day of rest, and rest we will, rejoice we will, each according to his age and station. The carpets need to be taken up for the summer and put away till winter . . . With insect-powder or mothballs . . . The Romans were healthy because they knew how to work – and they knew how to rest as well. They had *mens sana in corpore sano*. Their mind and body were uniform in their development. Our headmaster says that the most important thing in any life is its attainment to the uniform . . . (*Takes* **Masha** *by the waist, laughing.*) Masha loves me. My wife loves me. The curtains as well as the carpets . . . I'm in merry mood today – I'm in excellent spirits. Masha, we're due at the headmaster's at four o'clock. A little outing is being got up for the teaching staff and their families.

Masha   I'm not going.

Kulygin (*pained*)   My dear Masha, why ever not?

Masha   We'll talk about it later . . . (*Angrily.*) All right, I'll go, only please leave me alone . . . (*Moves away.*)

Kulygin   After which we shall be spending the evening at the headmaster's. In spite of his ill health, that man makes a supreme effort to be sociable. A wonderful person. A splendid man. After the staff meeting yesterday he said to me: 'I'm tired, you know! I'm tired!'

(*Looks at the clock on the wall, then at his watch.*)

Your clock is seven minutes fast. 'Yes,' he says, 'I'm tired.'

The violin plays, off.

Olga   Ladies and gentlemen, this way, please. Lunch is served. We're having a pie!

Kulygin   Ah, my dear Olga! My dear, dear Olga! Yesterday I worked from first thing in the morning until eleven at night, went tired to bed, and am today a happy man (*Goes out to the table in the main room.*) My dear Olga . . .

Chebutykin (*puts the newspaper in his pocket and combs his beard.*)   Pie? Splendid!

Masha (*to* **Chebutykin**, *sternly*)   Just watch you don't drink anything today. Do you hear? It's bad for you to drink.

Chebutykin   Oh, pish and tush! That's all past history. It's two years since I last went on the spree (*Impatiently.*) Goodness, woman, what does it matter?

Masha   Don't you dare start drinking, all the same. Don't you dare, now (*Angrily, but so that her husband shall not hear.*) Damnation, another whole evening of boredom at the headmaster's!

Tusenbach   I shouldn't go, if I were you . . . Very simple answer.

Chebutykin   Don't go, my precious.

Masha   'Don't go,' that's right . . . This damned life, this intolerable life . . . (*Goes into the main room.*)

Chebutykin (*follows her*)   Now, now, now!

Solyony (*going through into the main room*)   Cheep, cheep, cheep . . .

Tusenbach   Stop it, will you? That's enough!

Solyony   Cheep, cheep, cheep . . .

Kulygin (*cheerfully*)   Your health, Colonel! A teacher's what I am, and very much at ease in this house is how I feel. Masha's husband . . . And a dear kind woman she is . . .

Vershinin   I'm going to drink a toast in this dark vodka . . . (*Drinks.*) Your health! (*To* **Olga**:) I feel so much at home here . . . !

Only **Irina** *and* **Tusenbach** *are left in the drawing-room.*

Irina   Masha's out of sorts today. She got married at eighteen, when she thought he was the cleverest man in the world. That's not how it seems now. The kindest, yes, but not the cleverest.

Olga (*impatiently*)   Andrey, will you come!

Andrey (*off*)   Coming. (*Enters and goes to the table.*)

Tusenbach   What are you thinking about?

Irina   Nothing. I don't like that Solyony of yours. He frightens me. He just talks nonsense . . .

Tusenbach   He's a queer fish. I feel sorry for him and irritated by him at the same time. Mostly sorry, though. I think he's shy . . . When we're alone together he's usually very intelligent and friendly, whereas in company he's rude, he's forever picking quarrels. Let me just be near you for a little. What are you thinking about?

Pause.

You're twenty years old – I'm not yet thirty. So many years left in front of us – a long, long corridor of days, full of my love for you . . .

Irina   Please don't talk to me about love.

Tusenbach (*not listening*)   I thirst most desperately to live and strive and labour, and this thirst in my heart has merged into my love for you, Irina. And you're beautiful – it's as if you were taunting me – and life seems beautiful in that same way. What are you thinking about?

Irina   You say that life is beautiful. But supposing it only seems to be? For the three of us, for me and my sisters, life hasn't been beautiful up to now – it's choked us like choking weeds . . . Now the tears have started. Can't have that . . . (*Quickly wipes her face and smiles.*) Work, that's what we must do – work. That's why we feel so gloomy, why we see life in such dark colours – it's because we don't know what it is to work. We were born of people who despised it . . .

Enter **Natasha**. *She is wearing a pink dress with a green belt.*

Natasha   They're sitting down to lunch already . . . I'm late . . . (*Glances in the mirror in passing and sets herself to rights.*) I think my hair's all right, isn't it . . . ? (*Seeing* **Irina**.) Irina, dear – best wishes! (*Kisses her firmly and at length.*) You've got a lot of people here – honestly, I'm ashamed to be seen . . . Hello, baron!

Olga (*coming into the drawing-room*)   And here's Natasha. How are you, my dear?

They exchange kisses.

Natasha   I'm just saying best wishes to Irina. You've got such a lot of company – I feel terribly embarrassed . . .

Olga   Oh, come now – it's just family and friends (*Lowering her voice, startled.*) You're wearing a green belt! My dear, it's wrong!

Natasha   Green means something bad, does it?

Olga   No, it just doesn't go . . . And it looks peculiar, somehow . . .

Natasha (*plaintively*)   Does it? It's not really green, though, you see, it's more sort of neutral (*Follows* **Olga** *into the main room.*)

In the main room people are sitting down to lunch. The drawing-room is deserted.

Kulygin   Irina, here's to a handsome husband. High time you were getting married.

Chebutykin   Natasha, here's to a little someone for you, too.

Kulygin   Natasha already has a little someone.

Masha (*taps her plate with a fork*)   A toast! A short life and a merry one, God help us!

Kulygin   Beta minus for conduct.

Vershinin   Delicious liqueur. What's it made with?

Solyony   Black beetles.

Irina (*plaintively*)   Ugh! How disgusting . . . !

Olga   For supper we're having roast turkey and apple pie. Isn't it wonderful – I've got the whole day at home. I'm home all evening . . . Do come this evening, everyone . . .

Vershinin   May I come, too?

Irina   Please.

Natasha   They're very informal here.

Chebutykin   For love and love alone
Was man put in his earthly home. (*Laughs.*)

Andrey (*angrily*)   Will you stop it, all of you? Aren't you tired of it?

Enter **Fedotik** *and* **Rode** *with a large basket of flowers.*

Fedotik   They've gone in to lunch already, though.

Rode (*loudly, with a guttural accent*)   Gone in to lunch? Oh, yes, so they have . . .

Fedotik   Hold on a moment! (*Takes a photograph.*) One! Just half a moment more . . . (*Takes another photograph.*) Two! Now we're all set!

They take the basket and go into the main room, where they are given a noisy reception.

Rode (*loudly, to* **Irina**)   The best of wishes to you, all the very best! Enchanting weather today, simply magnificent. I've been out walking all morning with some of the boys from the school. I take them for gymnastics. If I have my way, the entire high school will be for the high jump!

Fedotik (*to* **Irina**)   You can move, it's all right! (*Taking a photograph.*) You're looking very pretty today (*Takes a top out of his pocket.*) Oh, and I've got a top for you . . . It makes the most amazing sound . . .

Irina   Oh, how lovely!

Masha   On a far seashore an oak tree grows,
And from it hangs a golden chain . . .
And from it hangs a golden chain . . . (*Pathetically.*) What am I saying that for? I've had those lines on my brain all day . . .

Kulygin   Thirteen at table!

Rode (*loudly*)   No one here, surely, is superstitious?

Laughter.

Kulygin   Thirteen at table means that we have those amongst us who are in love. Not you by any chance, doctor . . . ?

Laughter.

Chebutykin   I'm an old reprobate, but why Natasha here should be blushing I can't understand for the life of me.

Loud laughter. **Natasha** *runs out of the main room into the drawing-room,* **Andrey** *follows her.*

Andrey   Come on, now, don't take any notice of them! Wait . . . stop a moment, I beg you . . .

Natasha   I'm ashamed of myself . . . I don't know what's wrong with me, but they were making me a laughingstock. Leaving the table like that was very ill-mannered, but I can't cope with it . . . I simply can't . . . (*Buries her face in her hands.*)

Andrey   My dear, I beg you, I implore you – don't upset yourself. They're only joking, I assure you – they mean it kindly. My dear, my sweet, they're all kind, good-hearted people who love me and who love you. Come over here by the window – they can't see us here . . . (*Looks round.*)

Natasha   I'm so unused to being in company . . . !

Andrey   Oh, you're so young, you're so miraculously and beautifully young! My dear, my sweet, don't upset yourself so . . . ! Trust me, just trust me . . . I feel so wonderful – my heart is full of love, full of joy . . . They can't see us! They can't, they can't! *Why* I first began to love you – *when* I first began to love you – it's all a mystery to me. My dear, my sweet, my pure in heart, be my wife! I love you, love you . . . as I've never loved before . . .

They kiss.

Enter **Two Officers**. *Seeing the couple kissing, they stop in amazement.*

Curtain.

Act Two

The same

Eight o'clock in the evening. An accordion can just be heard, off, playing in the street outside. Darkness. Enter **Natasha** *in a housecoat, carrying a candle. She goes across and stops outside the door leading to* **Andrey's** *room.*

Natasha   Andryusha? What are you doing in there? Reading, are you? It's all right, I was just wondering . . . (*Goes across and opens another door, looks inside, and closes it again.*) Make sure there isn't a candle burning . . .

Andrey (*enters with a book in his hand*)   What do you want, Natasha?

Natasha   Just making sure there are no candles alight . . . It's Shrovetide – the servants are all excited. You've got to keep a sharp lookout to stop anything happening. Twelve o'clock last night I'm on my way through the dining-room and what do I see? – there's a candle burning. Who lit it? – I still haven't got to the bottom of that. (*Puts her candle down.*) What time is it?

Andrey (*glancing at the clock*)   Quarter past eight.

Natasha   Olga and Irina aren't back yet, either. They're still slaving, poor pets. Olga at her staff meeting, Irina at her telegraph office . . . (*Sighs.*) I was saying to your sister only this morning. 'Irina,' I said, 'you must look after yourself, my pet.' But she won't listen. Quarter past eight, did you say? I'm worried about Bobik. I think he's not at all well, the poor little sweet. Why is he so cold? Yesterday he had a temperature, and today he's like ice . . . I'm so worried!

Andrey   It's all right, Natasha. The child's perfectly well.

Natasha   He'd better go on to invalid food, all the same. I'm worried about him. And at ten o'clock tonight, so I'm told, we're going to have the mummers here. I know it's Shrovetide, but I'd sooner they didn't come, Andryusha.

Andrey   Well, I don't know. They were invited, of course.

Natasha   He woke up this morning, my little baby boy, and he looked at me, and all of a sudden he smiled. He knew it was me! 'Hello, Bobik!' I said. 'Hello, love!' And he laughed. They understand, you see – they understand perfectly well. So, anyway, I'll tell them not to let the mummers in.

Andrey (*irresolutely*)   It's really up to my sisters. They're in charge of the house.

Natasha   They're in charge, too. I'll tell them. They're so kind . . . (*Moves to go.*) I've ordered sour milk for supper. The doctor says you're to eat nothing but sour milk, otherwise you'll never lose weight. (*Stops.*) Bobik's so cold. I'm worried it may be too cold for him in his room. We must put him in another room, at any rate until the weather's warmer. Irina's room, for example – that would be perfect for a baby. It's dry, it gets the sun all day. You'll have to tell her – she can share with Olga for the time being . . . It won't matter – she's not home during the day, she's only here at night . . .

Pause.

Andrey, my pet, why aren't you saying anything?

Andrey   Just thinking. Anyway, there's nothing to say . . .

Natasha   No . . . Something I meant to tell you . . . Oh, yes, Ferapont – he's come round from the Council, he wants to see you.

Andrey (*yawns*)   Send him in.

Natasha *goes.* **Andrey**, *bending close to the candle that she has forgotten, reads his book. Enter* **Ferapont**. *He is wearing an old tattered overcoat, with the collar up and his ears muffled.*

Hello, my old friend. What do you want?

Ferapont   The Chairman's sent a book and a paper of some sort. Here you are . . . (*Hands over a book and a packet.*)

Andrey   Thank you. Right. Why are you so late? It's gone eight now, you know.

Ferapont   What?

Andrey (*louder*)   I said, you're late. It's past eight o'clock.

Ferapont   That's right. It was still light when I got here, but they wouldn't let me in. The master's busy, they said. So, all right, he's busy – I'm not in a hurry to get anywhere. (*Thinking that* **Andrey** *is asking him something.*) What?

Andrey   Nothing. (*Examining the book.*) Friday tomorrow, no one at the office. No matter – I'll go in all the same . . . do some work. Boring at home . . .

Pause.

Oh, my dear old friend, how strangely things do change, how life mocks us! Just out of boredom today, just out of idleness, I picked up this book – my old university lectures, and I had to laugh . . . Dear God, I'm secretary to the local Executive Council – a body that Protopopov is *chairman* of. I'm the secretary, and the most I can hope for is to become a member of it. Me – a member of a local Executive Council! Me – a man who dreams every night that he's a professor of Moscow University, a distinguished scholar, the pride of Russia!

Ferapont   No idea . . . I don't hear too well . . .

Andrey   If you could hear properly I don't suppose I'd be talking to you. I've got to talk to someone, but my wife doesn't understand me, and I'm afraid of my sisters, I don't know why – I'm afraid they'll jeer at me, I'm afraid they'll shame me . . . I don't drink, I've no fondness for taverns, but oh, my friend, what I'd give to be in Moscow now, sitting in Testov's in Theatre Square, or the Grand Hotel in Resurrection.

Ferapont   In Moscow – so one of the contractors was saying at the Council the other day – there were these merchants eating pancakes. One of them ate forty pancakes, and apparently he dropped dead. Either forty or fifty. I don't remember.

Andrey   You can sit in some enormous restaurant in Moscow – you don't know a soul – not a soul knows you – and yet you don't feel a stranger. While here you know everyone, and everyone knows you, and you're a stranger all the same, a total stranger . . . A lonely stranger.

Ferapont   What?

Pause.

And this contractor was saying – may have been a lie, of course – he was saying how they were going to stretch a rope, apparently, right the way across Moscow.

Andrey   What for?

Ferapont   No idea. This contractor was saying.

Andrey   Nonsense. (*Reads his book.*) Have you ever been to Moscow?

Ferapont (*after a pause*)   Never. It wasn't God's will.

Pause.

Am I to go?

Andrey   You may. Take care of yourself.

Ferapont *goes.*

Take care, now. (*Reading.*) You can come back tomorrow and collect these papers . . . Off you go, then . . .

Pause.

He's gone.

Doorbell.

What a business it all is . . . (*Stretches and goes off into his room with no great haste.*)

The **Nurse** *sings, off, as she rocks the baby. Enter* **Masha** *and* **Vershinin**. *While they talk the* **Maid** *is lighting the lamp and the candles.*

Masha   I don't know.

Pause.

I don't know. Being used to something accounts for a lot, of course. For example, it took us a long time after Father died to get used to having no orderlies all of a sudden. But leaving familiarity aside, I think what I'm saying is no more than simple truth. It may not be so in other places, but in our town the most worthwhile people – the most honourable, the most educated – are the military.

Vershinin   I'm thirsty. I shouldn't mind some tea.

Masha (*glancing at the clock*)   They'll be bringing it in a moment. I was married off at eighteen, and I was afraid of my husband because he was a teacher and I was only just out of school. I thought then that he was terribly learned and clever and important. That's no longer the case, though, I regret to say.

Vershinin   Quite . . . indeed . . .

Masha   I'm not talking about my husband – I've got used to him – but among the civilians there are so many people who are vulgar and rude and uneducated. I'm upset by vulgarity – it offends me. I feel pain when I see that someone is lacking in refinement, lacking in gentleness and manners. When I find myself among my husband's teaching colleagues I do quite simply feel pain.

Vershinin   Indeed . . . But so far as I can see it doesn't matter whether they're military or civilians – they're equally uninteresting, in this town at least. It doesn't matter at all! Talk to your local intellectual – be he soldier or be he civilian – and he's fed up with his wife, he's fed up with his home, he's fed up with his estate, he's fed up with his horses . . . What characterises the Russian is above all the loftiness of his thinking, but, tell me, why are his aspirations in life so low? Why?

Masha   Why indeed?

Vershinin   Why is he fed up with his children, why is he fed up with his wife? And then again why are his wife and children fed up with him?

Masha   You're a little out of sorts today.

Vershinin   Possibly. I haven't eaten this evening – I've had nothing to eat all day. My daughter's not very well, and when my girls are ill I'm seized with alarm, I'm racked by guilt for their having such a mother. You should have seen her today! What a squalid creature she is! We started squabbling at seven o'clock in the morning, and at nine I walked out and slammed the door.

Pause.

I never talk about it normally. It's curious – you're the only one I ever complain to (*Kisses her hand.*) Don't be angry with me. You're the only one. I've no one apart from you, no one at all . . .

Pause.

Masha   What a noise the stove's making. The wind was moaning in the chimney just before Father died. That same sound exactly.

Vershinin   Are you superstitious?

Masha   Yes.

Vershinin   Strange (*Kisses her hand.*) You magnificent, magical woman. Magnificent, magical! It's dark in here, but I can see the shining of your eyes.

Masha (*sits on another chair*)   There's more light here . . .

Vershinin   I'm in love, I'm in love, I'm in love . . . In love with your eyes, with the way you move. I dream about it . . . Magnificent, magical woman!

Masha (*laughing quietly*)   When you talk to me like that, I don't know why, but I just find myself laughing, even though it frightens me. Please don't do it again . . . (*Her voice drops.*) Or rather do – what does it matter . . . ? (*Covers her face with her hands.*) What does it matter? There's someone coming, talk about something else . . .

Enter **Irina** *and* **Tusenbach** *through the main room.*

Tusenbach   My surname is triple-barrelled. The Baron Tusenbach-Krone-Altschauer. But I'm Russian and I'm Orthodox, just like you. I have little of the German left in me – only the patience and obstinacy with which I weary you. I escort you home every evening.

Irina   I'm so tired!

Tusenbach   Every day I'm going to come to the telegraph office, and every day I'm going to escort you home. I'll go on

doing it for ten years, for twenty years, until you dismiss me . . .
(*Joyfully, at the sight of* **Masha** *and* **Vershinin**.) Oh, hello, it's you!

Irina   Here I am, home at last (*To* **Masha**:) Some woman
came in just now sending a telegram to her brother in Saratov,
to tell him her son had died today, and she absolutely could not
remember the address. So she sent it without one, just to Saratov.
She was standing there in tears. And suddenly, for no reason at all,
I turned on her. 'Oh,' I said, 'I've no time for all this.' It was such
a stupid thing to happen. Is it today the mummers are coming?

Masha   Yes.

Irina (*sits down in an armchair*)   Rest. Tired.

Tusenbach (*with a smile*)   When you come home from work you
look such a young little, unhappy little thing . . .

Pause.

Irina   Tired. No, I don't like my work, I don't like it at all.

Masha   You've lost weight . . . (*Whistles a tune.*) You've got
younger-looking, and your face has become boyish.

Tusenbach   That's because of the way she does her hair.

Irina   I shall have to look for another job – this one's not for me.
What I so longed for, what I dreamed of, are the very things it
doesn't have. It's work with no poetry in it, mindless labour . . .

Knocking on the floor.

The doctor's knocking (*To* **Tusenbach**:) Be a dear and knock
back . . . I really can't. . . So tired . . .

Tusenbach *knocks on the floor.*

He'll be here in a moment. We ought to be formulating some
plan of action. The doctor and that brother of ours were playing
cards in the Mess yesterday, and they lost again. I gather Andrey
lost two hundred rubles.

Masha (*indifferently*)   Spilt milk.

Irina   A fortnight ago he lost, in December he lost. If only he'd
hurry up and lose the lot maybe we'd get out of this town. Dear

Lord, I dream of Moscow every night – I'm like a woman pos-
sessed (*Laughs.*) We're moving there in June, and before we get to
June we've got to get through . . . February, March, April,
May . . . nearly half a year!

Masha   Just so long as Natasha doesn't somehow find out about
him losing the money.

Irina   Natasha? I don't think it matters much to her.

Chebutykin, *who has only just got out of bed – he has been taking a rest
after dinner – comes into the ballroom and combs his beard, then sits down at
the table and takes a newspaper out of his pocket.*

Masha   Here he is . . . Has he paid his rent?

Irina (*laughs*)   No. Not a kopek for the last eight months. It's
gone out of his head, evidently.

Masha (*laughs*)   Sitting there so full of himself!

They all laugh. Pause.

Irina (*to* **Vershinin**)   Why are you so quiet?

Vershinin   I don't know. I'm longing for some tea. Half my life
for a glass of tea! I haven't eaten all day . . .

Chebutykin   Irina!

Irina   What do you want?

Chebutykin   Come here, would you? *Venezici.*

Irina *goes and sits at the table.*

I can't do it without you.

Irina *lays out the cards for patience.*

Vershinin   Well, then. If we're not going to get any tea, let us
at least refresh ourselves with a little philosophising.

Tusenbach   By all means. What about?

Vershinin   What about? Let us think for a moment about . . .
well, for example, about life as it will be after we are gone, two or
three hundred years from now.

Tusenbach   Well, I suppose that after we are gone, people will
fly about in air balloons, and the cut of a jacket will be different,
and maybe they'll discover a sixth sense and develop it. But life
will remain the same – difficult, full of hidden mysteries, and
happy. And a thousand years from now man will still be sighing,
'Oh, life is hard.' And yet at the same time he'll be just as afraid
of death as he is now, he'll be just as reluctant to die.

Vershinin (*after a moment's thought*)   How can I put it? It seems to
me that everything in this world must gradually change – is
changing already, in front of our eyes. Two hundred years hence,
three hundred years – a thousand, if you like – it's not a question
of how long – but eventually a new and happy life will dawn. No
part in this life shall *we* have, of course, but we are living for it
now – working for it – yes, and suffering for it. We are creating
it – and this alone is the purpose of our existence. This, if you
like, is our happiness.

Masha *laughs quietly.*

Tusenbach   What's got into you?

Masha   I don't know. All day today I've done nothing but laugh.

Vershinin   I went to the same cadet school as you – I didn't go
on to military academy. I read a lot, but I don't know how to
choose my books, and I may be reading quite the wrong things.
But for all that, the longer I live the more I want to know.
I'm going grey, I'm nearly all old man already, but I know so
little – oh, how little I know! All the same, the most important
thing – the most real thing – that I think I do know, and know for
sure. And how I should love to demonstrate to you that there is no
happiness for us – must be none, will be none . . . We have simply
to work and work, and happiness . . . that will be the lot of our
remote descendants.

Pause.

Not me? Then at least my descendants, and their descendants
after them.

Fedotik and **Rode** *appear in the main room. They sit down and hum
quietly, accompanying themselves on the guitar.*

Tusenbach   According to you we can't even dream of happiness. But what if I am in fact happy?

Vershinin   You're not.

Tusenbach (*throws up his hands, claps them together, and laughs*)   We plainly don't understand one another. Let me see, now, how can I convince you?

Masha *laughs quietly*.

(*Raising his finger to her.*) You laugh away! (*To* **Vershinin**:) It's not just two or three hundred years – a million years from now, even, life will still be just the same as it's always been. It doesn't change; it remains constant; it follows its own laws – laws which have nothing to do with you, or which at any rate you'll never discover. The birds that fly south in the autumn – the cranes, for example – on and on they fly, and whatever lofty or petty thoughts they have fermenting inside their heads, on they will continue to fly. On and forever on, whatever philosophers they may have among them. Let them philosophise away to their heart's content, just so long as they go on flying.

Masha   All the same, there is some point?

Tusenbach   Some point . . . Look, it's snowing. Where's the point in that?

Pause.

Masha   It seems to me that a man must have faith, or be seeking it, otherwise his life is empty, quite empty . . . To live and not to know why the cranes fly, why children are born, why the stars are in the sky . . . Either you know why you're alive or it's all nonsense, it's all dust in the wind.

Pause.

Vershinin   All the same, it's sad one's youth has gone . . .

Masha   Gogol's right: 'Living in this world, my friends, is dull work!'

Tusenbach   And I say: arguing with you, my friends, is uphill work! So boo to you.

Chebutykin (*reading the paper*)   Balzac was married in Berdichev.

Irina *hums quietly.*

I might put that down in my little book (*Makes a note.*) Balzac was married in Berdichev (*Reads his newspaper.*)

Irina (*lays out patience. Absently*)   Balzac was married in Berdichev.

Tusenbach   The die is cast. (*To* **Masha**:) You know, do you, that I've resigned my commission?

Masha   So I heard. And no good do I see in that. I've no great love for civilians.

Tusenbach   No matter . . . (*Stands up.*) I'm not a handsome man – what sort of figure do I cut as a soldier? Not that it matters . . . I'm going to work. For one day in my life at any rate I'm going to work so that I go home in the evening, fall into bed exhausted, and go straight to sleep (*Moves away into the main room.*) Working people must sleep so soundly!

Fedotik (*to* **Irina**)   I went into that shop on Moscow Street today and bought you some coloured pencils. Also this penknife . . .

Irina   You've got used to treating me as a child, but I'm grown up now, you realise . . . (*Takes the pencils and the penknife. Joyfully.*) Oh, they're lovely!

Fedotik   And I bought a pocket-knife for myself . . . Take a look at this . . . one blade, two blades, three blades, this is for picking your ears, these are scissors, this is for cleaning your nails . . .

Rode (*loudly*)   Doctor, how old are you?

Chebutykin   Me? Thirty-two.

Laughter.

Fedotik   Now I'm going to show you a different patience. (*Lays out the cards.*)

The samovar is brought in. **Anfisa** *hovers around it.* **Natasha** *enters shortly afterwards and also busies herself about the table. Enter* **Solyony***. He makes his greetings to the company and sits down at the table.*

Vershinin   What a wind, though!

Masha   Yes, I'm sick of the winter. I can't even remember now what summer's like.

Irina (*playing patience*)   It's going to come out, I see. We shall get to Moscow.

Fedotik   On the contrary, it's not going to come out. The eight was on the two of spades, look (*Laughs.*) So you won't get to Moscow.

Chebutykin (*reads the newspaper*)   Manchuria. Smallpox rages.

Anfisa (*crossing to* **Masha**)   Masha, have your tea, dear. (*To* **Vershinin**:) Here you are, colonel . . . I'm sorry, dear, I've forgotten your name . . .

Masha   Bring it here, Nanny. I'm not going over there.

Irina   Nanny!

Anfisa   Coming!

Natasha (*to* **Solyony**)   They understand, you know, babies, they understand perfectly. 'Hello, Bobik!' I said. 'Hello, love!' And he gave me a kind of special look. You think that's just a mother talking, don't you, but no, not at all, I can assure you! He's a most unusual baby.

Solyony   If that baby were mine, I'd fry him in a frying-pan and eat him. (*Takes his glass of tea into the drawing-room and sits down in the corner.*)

Natasha (*covering her face with her hands*)   So coarse! So lacking in breeding!

Masha   Happy the man who never notices whether it's summer or winter. If I were in Moscow, I think I should be indifferent to the weather . . .

Vershinin   The other day I was reading the diary that some French cabinet minister had kept while he was in prison. He'd been convicted for his part in the Panama Affair. With what delight, with what ecstasy, does he write about the birds he can see through his cell window – birds he'd never noticed before, in his days as a minister. Now that he's at liberty again, of course, he notices the birds no more than he did in the past. Nor will you notice Moscow once you're living in it. Happiness is not for us and never can be. All we can do is long for it.

Tusenbach (*picks up a basket from the table*)   Where are the sweets?

Irina   Solyony's eaten them.

Tusenbach   The whole lot?

Anfisa (*serving tea*)   Letter for you, dear.

Vershinin   For me? (*Takes the letter.*) From my daughter. (*Reads it.*) Yes, of course . . . (*To* **Masha***:*) If you'll excuse me I'll just slip quietly away. I won't have any tea (*Stands up, agitated.*) It's the same old story . . .

Masha   What? Or is it a secret?

Vershinin (*quietly*)   My wife has tried to poison herself again. I must go. I'll get away without anyone noticing. It's all very unpleasant. (*Kisses* **Masha***'s hand.*) My dear, my good and wonderful woman . . . I'll slip quietly out through here . . . (*He goes.*)

Anfisa   Where's he off to, then? I've just poured his tea . . . The naughty man.

Masha (*losing her temper*)   Get away from me! Hanging around all the time – there's no rest from you . . . (*Takes her cup of tea to the table.*) Silly old woman, I'm sick of you!

Anfisa   What are you in such a huff about? My sweet!

Andrey (*off*)   Anfisa!

Anfisa (*mimics him*)   'Anfisa!' He just sits in there . . . (*She goes.*)

Masha (*at the table in the main room, angrily*)   Let me sit down, will you? (*Muddles the cards on the table.*) Taking up all the room with cards. Drink your tea!

Irina   Masha, you're in a temper.

Masha   Well, if I'm in a temper don't talk to me. Don't touch me!

Chebutykin (*laughing*)   Don't touch her, don't touch . . .

Masha   You're sixty, but you might as well be six, the way you're always babbling on about God knows what.

Natasha (*sighs*)   My dear Masha, why do you use expressions like that in polite conversation? In good society, with your looks – I'll be quite frank, now – you could be simply enchanting, if it weren't for the language you use. *Je vous prie pardonnez-moi, Marie, mais vous avez des manieres un peu grossierès.*

Tusenbach (*suppressing his laughter*)   May I . . . ? May I . . . ? I think there's some brandy there . . .

Natasha   *Il parait, que man Bobik déjà ne dort pas,* he's woken up. My poor poppet's not very well today. I must go and look at him, do forgive me . . . (*She goes.*)

Irina   Where's the colonel gone?

Masha   Home. Some extraordinary business with his wife again.

Tusenbach (*goes over to* **Solyony**, *holding the brandy decanter*)   You're always sitting on your own thinking about something, I can't imagine what. Come on, let's make it up. Let's have a glass of brandy.

They drink.

I shall probably have to play the piano all night. A lot of rubbish, most likely . . . Well, who cares?

Solyony   What do you mean, make it up? I haven't quarrelled with you.

Tusenbach   You always give me the feeling that something has happened between us. You are an odd fish, I must say.

Solyony (*declaims*)   I may be odd – but who's not odd,
Save fools alike as peas in pod? . . .
Aleko, be not angry!

Tusenbach   Aleko? What, in Pushkin? I don't see what he's got to do with it . . .

Pause.

Solyony   When I'm alone with someone it's all right, I'm like anybody else. But in company I'm morose, I'm awkward, and, I don't know, I talk a lot of rubbish. All the same, I'm more honest, I'm more high-minded than a great many people. And I can prove it.

Tusenbach   I often get angry with you because you keep picking on me in public. I can't help liking you, though, I don't know why. Anyway, who cares? – I'm going to get drunk tonight. Your health.

Solyony   And yours.

They drink.

I've never had anything against you, baron. But I have something of Lermontov's character. (*Quietly.*) I even look rather like him . . . Or so people tell me . . . (*Takes a perfume flask out of his pocket and pours some on to his hands.*)

Tusenbach   I'm resigning my commission. *Basta!* For five years I've been thinking about it, and now at last I've made up my mind. I'm going to work.

Solyony (*declaims*)   Aleko, be not angry . . . Forget, forget your longings and your dreams . . .

As they talk, **Andrey** *enters quietly with his book and sits by the candle.*

Tusenbach   I'm going to work . . .

Chebutykin (*coming into the drawing-room with* **Irina**)   And they entertained us in real Caucasian style – onion soup, followed by a *chekhartmá* of roast meat.

Solyony   *Cheremshá* isn't meat. It's ramson – it's a plant like our onion.

Chebutykin   No, my dear boy. *Chekhartmá* isn't an onion – it's a roast dish made from mutton.

Solyony   I tell you *cheremshá* is onion.

Chebutykin   And I tell you *chekhartmá* is mutton.

Solyony   And I tell you *cheremshá* is onion.

Chebutykin   I'm not going to argue with you. You've never been to the Caucasus and you've never eaten *chekhartmá*.

Solyony I've never eaten it because I can't stand it. It smells like garlic.

Andrey (*beseechingly*)   That will do, now, gentlemen! I beg of you!

Tusenbach When are the mummers coming?

Irina Towards nine, they promised, so any time now.

Tusenbach *begins to hum the music of a folk-song, 'Akh vy, seni'. He puts his arm round* **Andrey** *and leads him in the dance that traditionally accompanies the song. First* **Andrey** *and then* **Chebutykin** *take up both song and dance. Laughter.*

Tusenbach (*kisses* **Andrey**)   Come on, Andryusha, let's drink together, and to hell with it! I'm going to call you Andryusha – you call me Nikolasha – and we'll drink together. And I'm coming with you, Andryusha, I'm coming to Moscow, I'm going to university.

Solyony Which one? There are two universities in Moscow.

Andrey There's one university in Moscow.

Solyony I tell you there are two.

Andrey There can be three, for all I care. The more the merrier.

Solyony There are two universities in Moscow!

Murmuring and hushing.

There are two universities in Moscow – the old one and the new one. But if you don't care to listen, if you're going to be irritated by what I say, then I can perfectly well not speak. In fact I can go and sit in another room . . . (*Goes out through one of the doors.*)

Tusenbach Bravo, bravo! (*Laughs.*) Ladies and gentlemen, let the festivities commence – I'm going to sit down at the piano! He's a funny fellow, that Solyony . . . (*Sits down at the piano and plays a waltz.*)

Masha (*waltzes by herself*)   The baron's drunk, the baron's drunk, the baron's drunk again!

Enter **Natasha**.

Natasha (*to* **Chebutykin**)   Doctor! (*Says something to him, then quietly goes out again.*)

Chebutykin *touches* **Tusenbach** *on the shoulder and whispers something to him.*

Irina   What's happening?

Chebutykin   Time we were going. I'll say goodbye.

Tusenbach   Good night. We must be going.

Irina   I'm sorry, but what about the mummers?

Andrey (*embarrassed*)   There won't be any mummers. The thing is, my dear, that Natasha says Bobik isn't entirely well, and therefore . . . Anyway, I don't know, it doesn't matter to me either way.

Irina (*shrugging*)   Bobik's not well!

Masha   Oh, God help us! If we're being thrown out we'll have to go (*To* **Irina**:) It's not Bobik that's sick – it's her . . . In there! (*She taps her forehead.*) Little shopkeeper!

Andrey *goes out through the righthand door into his own room,* **Chebutykin** *follows him. People make their farewells in the main room.*

Fedotik   What a shame! I was counting on spending the evening, but if the baby's ill then of course . . . I'll bring him some toys tomorrow.

Rode (*loudly*)   I had a good long sleep after dinner specially – I thought I should be dancing all night. It's only nine o'clock, you know.

Masha   Let's go out into the street and talk for a moment. We'll decide what to do.

People can be heard saying goodbye, and there is the sound of **Tusenbach**'s *cheerful laugh. Everyone goes out.* **Anfisa** *and the* **Maid** *clear the table and put out the lights. The* **Nurse** *can be heard singing. Enter* **Andrey** *quietly, in overcoat and hat, with* **Chebutykin**.

Chebutykin   Marrying – that's something I never got around to, because my life has gone by like a flash of lightning. Also because I was madly in love with your mother, who had a husband already.

Andrey   Never marry. Never – it's a bore.

Chebutykin   That may be, but think of loneliness. Philosophise away till you're black in the face, but loneliness is a terrible thing, dear boy . . . Though when you come down to it, what does it matter?

Andrey   Let's be off, then.

Chebutykin   What's the hurry? We've plenty of time.

Andrey   I'm afraid my wife might stop me.

Chebutykin   Ah!

Andrey   This time I'm not going to play. I'll just sit there for a bit. I don't feel too good . . . What should I do about shortness of breath?

Chebutykin   Why ask me? I don't remember, dear boy. No idea.

Andrey   Let's go through the kitchen.

The doorbell rings, then it rings again. There is the sound of voices and laughter. **Andrey** *and* **Chebutykin** *go.*

Irina (*enters*)   What's going on out there?

Anfisa (*in a whisper*)   It's the mummers!

The doorbell rings.

Irina   Nanny, tell them there's no one at home. Say we're sorry.

Anfisa *goes.* **Irina** *walks about the room, agitated and lost in thought. Enter* **Solyony**.

Solyony (*bewildered*)   No one here . . . Where are they all?

Irina   Gone home.

Solyony   Odd. You're all on your own in here?

Irina   All on my own.

Pause.

Goodbye.

Solyony   I lost my self-control just now, I forgot my manners. But you're not like all the rest of them. You're above them, you're pure, you can see the truth . . . You're the only one who can understand me. I'm in love – deeply and boundlessly in love . . .

Irina   Goodbye. Do go.

Solyony   I can't live without you. (*Following her.*) Oh, my heart's delight! (*On the verge of tears.*) Oh, happiness! Sumptuous, magical, amazing eyes, the like of which I have never seen in any other woman . . .

Irina (*coldly*)   Stop! Please!

Solyony   This is the first time I have ever spoken my love for you, and I feel as if I were out of this world, as if I were on some other planet. (*Rubs his forehead.*) Anyway, what does it matter? Feelings obviously can't be forced . . . But happy rivals I will not have . . . I won't . . . I swear to you by all the saints, I'll kill any rival . . . You magical woman!

Natasha *comes through, holding a candle.*

Natasha (*looks first into one room, then into another, and goes past the door leading to her husband's room.*)   Andrey's in there. He can go on reading. (*To* **Solyony***:*) Forgive me, I didn't know you were here, I'm not dressed for visitors . . .

Solyony   That matters very little to me. Goodbye. (*He goes.*)

Natasha   My poor dear girl, but you're tired! (*Kisses* **Irina***.*) You should have been in bed hours ago.

Irina   Is Bobik asleep?

Natasha   He's asleep, but he's very restless. Oh, by the way, my dear, there's something I've been meaning to say to you, only you've been out all the time, or else I've been busy . . . I think it's too cold and damp for Bobik with the nursery where it is. Now your room would be such a lovely one for a baby. My dear, will you move in with Olga for the time being?

Irina (*not understanding*)   Move where?

A troika with bells can be heard approaching the house.

Natasha   You'll be in the same room as Olga, just for the time being, and Bobik will have your room. He's such a love! I said to

him today, 'Bobik, you're mine! All mine!' And he looked at me
with those funny little eyes of his.

Doorbell.

It must be Olga. She's terribly late.

The **Maid** *goes up to* **Natasha** *and whispers in her ear.*

Natasha   Protopopov? What a fool that man is! Protopopov's
here – he's inviting me to go for a troika ride with him (*Laughs.*)
What strange creatures these men are . . .

Doorbell.

Somebody else arriving. I could go for a quick ten or fifteen
minutes perhaps . . . (*To the* **Maid**:) Say I'll be down directly.

Doorbell.

The doorbell . . . That must be Olga . . . (*She goes.*)

The **Maid** *runs out.* **Irina** *sits wrapped in thought. Enter* **Kulygin** *and*
Olga, *followed by* **Vershinin**.

Kulygin   Well, bless my soul! I was told they were having
company tonight.

Vershinin   Odd. I only left half an hour ago, and they were
waiting for the mummers . . .

Irina   Everyone's gone.

Kulygin   Has Masha gone, too? Where's she gone? And
why is Protopopov waiting downstairs in a troika? Who is he
waiting for?

Irina   Don't ask me any questions . . . I'm too tired . . .

Kulygin   Oh, Miss High and Mighty . . .

Olga   The staff meeting has only just finished. I'm exhausted.
Our headmistress is off sick, so at the moment I'm deputising for
her. My head, my head's aching, oh, my head . . . (*Sits.*) Andrey
lost two hundred rubles at cards yesterday . . . The whole town's
talking about it . . .

Kulygin   Yes, the meeting tired me, too. (*Sits.*)

Vershinin   My wife took it into her head to give me a fright just now. She very nearly poisoned herself. Anyway, it's all sorted itself out, and I can breathe again . . . So, we have to go? Well, then, may I wish you all the best? (*To* **Kulygin**:) Come on, let's you and I go on somewhere! I can't stay at home, I absolutely cannot . . . Come on!

Kulygin   No, I'm too tired. (*Stands up.*) Tired, tired. My wife's gone home, has she?

Irina   She must have.

Kulygin (*kisses* **Irina**'s *hand*) Goodbye, then. Tomorrow and the day after we can rest all day. Good night! (*Goes.*) I'd love some tea. I was counting on spending the evening in pleasant company and – oh, *fallacem hominum spem!* – the illusory hopes of men! Exclamation taking the accusative . . .

Vershinin   I'll go on my own, then. (*He goes with* **Kulygin**, *whistling.*)

Olga   My head aches, my poor head . . . Andrey lost at cards . . . The whole town's talking . . . I'm going to bed. (*Goes.*) Tomorrow I'm free . . . Oh, heavens, how sweet that is! Free tomorrow, free the day after . . . My head aches, oh, my poor head . . . (*She goes.*)

Irina (*alone*)   They've all gone. No one here.

An accordion plays in the street; the **Nurse** *sings a song.*

Natasha (*crosses the main room in fur coat and cap, with the* **Maid** *following her*)   I'll be back in half-an-hour. I'm just going to have a bit of an outing. (*She goes.*)

Irina (*left alone, falls into melancholy*)   Moscow! Moscow! To Moscow!

Curtain.

Act Three

Olga's room – now also **Irina**'s. Beds left and right, surrounded by screens. It is past two o'clock in the morning. Offstage the alarm is being sounded for a fire which began much earlier. The household has plainly still not got to bed. **Masha** is lying on a couch, dressed as usual in black. Enter **Olga** and **Anfisa**.

Anfisa   They're sitting in the hall downstairs now . . . I said to them, 'Come upstairs,' I said, 'and then we can do something.' They just kept crying. 'It's Papa,' they said, 'we don't know where he is. Oh, please God he hasn't been burnt to death!' That's what they've got into their heads! There's some outside, too – and they've no clothes to their backs, neither.

Olga (takes clothes out of the wardrobe)   Here, take this grey dress . . . And this one . . . The jacket as well . . . And take this skirt, Nanny . . . Lord in heaven, what a thing to happen! The whole of Kirsanov Lane has burnt down, apparently . . . Take this . . . And this . . . (Tosses clothes into **Anfisa**'s arms.) The Vershinins had a terrible fright, poor things . . . Their house very nearly got caught. They can stay the night here . . . We can't let them go home . . . And poor Fedotik! Everything he possessed – he's nothing left in the world . . .

Anfisa   Olya, love, you'll have to call Ferapont or I'll never carry it all . . .

Olga (rings)   We can ring but we shan't get anyone . . . (Through the doorway.) Could you come here, please, anyone who's there!

Through the open door can be seen a window red from the glow of the fire. The sound of a fire brigade going past the house.

What a nightmare! I'm so sick of it!

Enter **Ferapont**.

Here, take these downstairs . . . The Kolotilin girls are waiting down in the hall . . . give the things to them. And give them this . . .

Ferapont   Right. In 1812 it was Moscow that was on fire. God bless us, weren't the French surprised!

Olga   Off you go, then.

Ferapont   Right. (*He goes.*)

Olga   Nanny, dear, let them have it all. We don't need any of
it – let them have the lot, Nanny, love . . . I'm so tired – I can
hardly stand . . . We can't let the Vershinins go home . . . The
girls can sleep in the drawing-room, and the colonel downstairs
with the baron . . . Fedotik can go in with the baron, too, or else
upstairs in the big living-room . . . The doctor's drunk, horribly
drunk – you'd think he'd picked tonight on purpose – we can't put
anyone in with him. And Vershinin's wife in the drawing-room
with the girls.

Anfisa (*exhausted*)   Olyushka, my dear, don't turn me out! Please
don't!

Olga   Nanny, you're talking nonsense. No one's turning you out.

Anfisa (*lays her head on* **Olga**'s *breast*)   Oh, my own one, oh, my
precious, I toil away, I do my work . . . But I'll get too feeble, and
then they're all going to say: Out you go! But where will I go?
Where can I go? Eighty years old. Eighty-one . . .

Olga   Just you sit down for a moment, Nanny, love . . . You poor
dear, you're worn out . . . (*Sits her down.*) Have a rest, my love.
You've lost all your colour!

Enter **Natasha**.

Natasha   They're saying they'll have to quickly set up a charity
for the people who lost their homes in the fire. I think that's an
excellent idea. We must always help the poor – it's the duty of the
rich. Bobik and Sofochka are fast asleep, for all the world as if
nothing had happened. We've got so many people in the house –
wherever you go it's full. There's influenza in town at the moment –
I'm worried the children might catch it.

Olga (*not listening to her*)   You can't see the fire from this room. It's
quite peaceful in here . . .

Natasha   Isn't it . . . I must be an absolute sight (*In front of the
mirror.*) People keep telling me I've put on weight . . . and it's
not true! Not the slightest bit! Masha's asleep, though – she's

exhausted, the poor love . . . (*To* **Anfisa**, *coldly:*) How dare you sit down in my presence! Get up! Get out!

Anfisa *goes. Pause.*

Why you keep that old woman on I can't understand!

Olga (*taken aback*)   I'm sorry, but *I* don't quite understand . . .

Natasha   She's no use here. She's a peasant – she ought to be living in her village . . . It's just pampering them! I like a little order in the house! There shouldn't be people in the house we don't need (*Looks at* **Olga**'*s face.*) My poor love, you're tired! Our headmistress is tired! When my Sofochka gets bigger and goes to school, though, I'm going to be so frightened of you.

Olga   I'm not going to be headmistress.

Natasha   You'll be the one they choose, Olechka. It's been decided.

Olga   I shall decline. I can't do it . . . I haven't the strength. (*Drinks water.*) You were so rude to Nanny just then . . . I'm sorry, but I can't bear it . . . I thought I was going to faint . . .

Natasha (*alarmed*)   I'm sorry, Olya, I'm sorry . . . I didn't mean to upset you.

Masha *gets up, takes her cushion, and goes out angrily.*

Olga   You do see, my dear . . . We had a peculiar upbringing, perhaps, but I can't bear that sort of thing. It depresses me to see anyone treated like that, it makes me ill . . . I just feel like giving up!

Natasha   I'm sorry, I'm sorry . . . (*Kisses her.*)

Olga   The slightest rudeness, a harshly spoken word, and it upsets me . . .

Natasha   I often say more than I should, it's quite true, but, my dear, you must agree, she could live in her village.

Olga   She's been with us for thirty years.

Natasha   But she can't work now, can she! Either I don't understand what you're saying, or you won't understand what I'm saying . . . She's incapable of work, she does nothing but sleep or just sit there.

Olga   Let her just sit there.

Natasha (*in surprise*)   What do you mean, let her just sit there? She's a servant, isn't she? (*Through her tears.*) I don't understand you, Olya. I have a nanny and a wet-nurse, we have a maid and a cook . . . What do we need that old woman for? What do we want with her?

The alarm is sounded offstage.

Olga   I've aged ten years in this one night.

Natasha   We've got to come to an understanding, Olga. School for you – home for me. You have your teaching – I have the household to run. And if I say something about the servants then I know what I'm talking about, I know – what – I – am – talking about . . . And I want that thieving old hag out of the house by tomorrow . . . (*Stamps her foot.*) That old witch . . . ! How dare people cross me so! How dare they! (*Controlling herself.*) Because really, if you don't move downstairs we shall be forever quarrelling. It's frightful.

Enter **Kulygin**.

Kulygin   Where's Masha? We ought to be getting home. Apparently the fire's dying down. (*Stretches.*) It's only the one block gone, but there was the wind, of course, and for a start it looked as if the whole town was on fire. (*Sits.*) I'm exhausted. Olechka, my dear . . . I often think if it weren't for Masha I should marry you. You're a sweet kind woman . . . I'm worn out. (*Cocks his ear.*)

Olga   What?

Kulygin   You'd think he'd done it tonight on purpose. The doctor – he's gone on the spree, he's quite horribly drunk. You'd think he'd absolutely picked the night! (*Stands up.*) He's coming up here, I think . . . Can you hear? Yes, he is . . . (*Laughs.*) Honestly, what a rascal . . . I'm going to hide . . . (*Goes to the wardrobe and stands in the corner.*) What a villain.

Olga   He hasn't been drinking for two years, and now suddenly he's up and drunk himself silly . . . (*Goes with* **Natasha** *away to the back of the room.*)

Enter **Chebutykin**. *With perfectly steady gait, as if sober, he crosses the room, stops, looks round, then goes over to the washstand and begins to wash his hands.*

Chebutykin (*morosely*)   To hell with the lot of them . . . Lot the rot . . . They think I'm a doctor, they think I know how to treat all the ailments under the sun, but I know absolutely nothing – forgotten anything I ever knew – don't remember a thing – absolutely nothing.

Olga *and* **Natasha** *go without his noticing.*

Well, to hell with them. Wednesday last I treated a woman in town and she died, and it was my fault she died. Yes . . . Twenty-five years back I knew a thing or two, but now I can't remember anything. Not a thing. Maybe I'm not even human – I just put on this appearance of having arms and legs and head. Maybe I don't exist at all – I just think I'm walking and eating and sleeping (*Weeps.*) Oh, if only I could be non-existent! (*Stops weeping. Morosely.*) Well, I don't know . . . Day before yesterday there was this conversation in the Mess. 'Shakespeare!' they go. 'Voltaire . . .' I haven't read a line of any of them – I just put a look on my face as if I had. And the others did the same. But the meanness of it! The shabbiness! And that woman came into my mind, the one I finished off on Wednesday . . . then everything else came back as well, and I felt as if my whole soul was warped and soiled and ugly . . . And off I went and started drinking . . .

Enter **Irina**, **Vershinin**, *and* **Tusenbach**. **Tusenbach** *is wearing new and stylish civilian clothes.*

Irina   Let's sit down here for a moment. No one's going to come in here.

Vershinin   If it hadn't been for the military the whole town would have gone up in flames. Sterling work! (*Rubs his hands with pleasure.*) Sterling lads and sterling work!

Kulygin (*going across to him*)   What time is it?

Tusenbach   Gone three already. It's getting light.

Irina   Everyone's just sitting around in the big living-room. No one's going. That precious Solyony of yours is sitting there, too . . . (*To* **Chebutykin**:) You should be getting to bed, doctor.

Chebutykin   Quite all right . . . I thank you . . . (*Combs his beard.*)

Kulygin (*laughs*)   He's got himself a little spifflicated, has our good doctor! (*Claps him on the shoulder.*) Sterling work! *In vino veritas*, as the ancients would have it.

Tusenbach   People keep asking me to get up a concert in aid of the victims.

Irina   Yes, but who'd be in it?

Tusenbach   It could be managed, if that's what people want. Masha, for instance, is a wonderful pianist.

Kulygin   Wonderful!

Irina   She's forgotten it all. She hasn't played for three years now . . . or is it four?

Tusenbach   Absolutely no one in this town knows anything about music, not a soul, but I do, and I give you my word that Masha is a magnificent pianist – a gifted one, almost.

Kulygin   Quite right, baron. I love Masha very much. She's a splendid woman.

Tusenbach   But imagine being able to play so marvellously, and knowing at the same time that nobody, absolutely nobody, could appreciate it!

Kulygin (*sighs*)   Quite . . . But would it be entirely suitable for her to take part in a concert?

Pause.

I don't know, you see. It might be perfectly all right. Our headmaster is a charming man, I must in all honesty say. Most charming, highly intelligent – but he does have very definite views . . . It's nothing to do with him, of course, but all the same, I could have a word with him if you like . . .

Chebutykin *picks up a china clock and examines it.*

Vershinin   I got absolutely filthy at the fire. I can't imagine what I look like.

Pause.

I heard just in passing yesterday that they're thinking of some rather remote posting for our brigade. Some say the Kingdom of Poland, some reckon Siberia.

Tusenbach   I heard the same thing. Well, the town will be deserted.

Irina   We'll be leaving, too!

Chebutykin (*drops the clock, which breaks*).   Smithereens!

Pause. Everyone is upset and embarrassed.

Kulygin (*picking up the pieces*)   Fancy breaking such a valuable object. Oh, doctor, doctor! Gamma minus for conduct!

Irina   That was poor Mama's clock.

Chebutykin   Maybe it was . . . So, all right, it was Mama's. Maybe I didn't break it, and it only seems I did. Maybe we only seem to exist, and in fact we aren't here at all. I don't know anything; there isn't anything anyone knows (*Reaching the door.*) What are you staring at? Natasha's having a little love-affair with Protopopov, and you don't see it . . . You just sit here and see nothing, and all the time Natasha's having a little affair with Protopopov . . . (*He goes, humming to himself.*)

Vershinin   So . . . (*Laughs.*) How odd all this is, when you come to think about it!

Pause.

When the fire started I ran home as fast as I could, and the first thing I see is there's our house, safe and sound and not in any danger. But there on the doorstep are my two little girls – they've got nothing on but their shifts – there's no sign of their mother – people rushing to and fro – horses galloping – dogs running – and on the girls' faces alarm, terror, entreaty – I don't know what; and at the sight of those faces my heart contracted within me. God in heaven, I thought, what more will these children have to endure in life's long course? I snatched them up and I ran and I kept thinking this same thought: what more will they have to endure in this world!

The sound of the alarm. Pause.

I got here, and here's their mother, shouting and raging.

Enter **Masha** *with her cushion. She sits down on the couch.*

And as my little girls stood on the doorstep in their shifts, and the street was red from the flames, and the noise was terrifying, I found myself thinking that it must have been rather like this many years ago when some enemy made a surprise raid, and looted and burnt . . . Still, when you really come down to it, there's an enormous difference between now and then. And when a little more time has passed, two or three hundred years, say, they'll look back on the life we lead now in just the same way, with just the same mixture of horror and scorn. Everything about the present time will seem awkward and clumsy and terribly uncomfortable and outlandish. Oh, but what a life it's going to be, surely, what a life! (*Laughs.*) Forgive me, I've started to philosophise again. May I continue, though? I've a terrible longing to philosophise – I'm in just the mood for it.

Pause.

It's as if the whole world were still asleep. That's why I say: what a life it's going to be! All you can do is imagine it . . . Here we are now with only three people like you in town; but in succeeding generations there will be more, and more, and ever more, until the day dawns when everything has come round to your way of thinking, and everyone has come round to your way of life; and then you in your turn will be relegated to the past, and there will arise people who are better than you . . . (*Laughs.*) I'm in a rather peculiar mood today. Oh God, but I want to live! (*Begins to hum Prince Gremin's aria from 'Eugene Onegin', Act III, Scene 1 – 'To love must young and old surrender'.*)

Masha   Trum-tum-tum . . .

Vershinin   Tum-tum . . .

Masha   Tra-ra-ra?

Vershinin   Tra-ta-ta (*Laughs.*)

Enter **Fedotik**.

Fedotik (*dances*)   I've lost the lot! Gone up in smoke! I'm cleaned right out!

Laughter.

Irina   How can you joke about it? Everything went?

Fedotik (*laughs*)   The lot. I'm cleaned out. Nothing left. My guitar went, my photographic stuff, all my letters . . . I'd got a little notebook to give you – that went, too.

Enter **Solyony**.

Irina   No, please, go away. No one's allowed in here.

Solyony   Why is the baron, if I'm not?

Vershinin   We must all go, in fact. How is the fire?

Solyony   Dying down, apparently. No, but I do find it positively odd – why the baron and not me? (*Takes out his flask of scent and sprinkles himself.*)

Vershinin   Trum-tum-tum?

Masha   Trum-tum.

Vershinin (*laughs. To* **Solyony**)   Come on, we'll go down to the living-room.

Solyony   All right, then, I shan't forget this. What does the poem say?
We could spell out the moral of this piece –
But let us not provoke the geese.

(*Looking at* **Tusenbach**.) Cheep, cheep, cheep . . . (*He goes with* **Vershinin** *and* **Fedotik**.)

Irina   That wretched Solyony has fumigated the room . . . (*wonderingly.*) The baron's asleep! Baron! Baron!

Tusenbach (*waking up*)   I'm tired, though . . . A brick-works . . . I'm not rambling – I am in fact shortly going to move away from here and start a job at a brickworks . . . I've already had talks about it (*To* **Irina**, *tenderly:*) You're so pale, so lovely, so fascinating . . . Your pale skin seems to brighten the dark air like light . . . You're sad, you're discontented with life . . . Oh, come away with me, come away and we can work together . . . !

Masha   Out you go, now.

Tusenbach (*laughing*)   Oh, you're here, are you? I can't see (*Kisses* **Irina**'s *hand.*) Goodbye, then, I'll be going . . . I look at you now and I remember how once upon a time, long, long ago, on your name-day, you were all bright and cheerful, and you talked about the joys of work . . . And what a happy life I caught a glimpse of then! Where has it gone? (*Kisses her hand.*) You've tears in your eyes. Go to bed, it's getting light already . . . another day's beginning . . . If only I might devote my life to you!

Masha   Out you go! Really . . .

Tusenbach   I'm going . . . (*He goes.*)

Masha (*lying down*)   Fyodor? Are you asleep?

Kulygin   Um?

Masha   You should be getting home.

Kulygin   My dear Masha, my dear sweet Masha . . .

Irina   She's exhausted. You should let her have a rest, Fedya.

Kulygin   I'm going, I'm going . . . My lovely, splendid wife . . . I love you, my one and only . . .

Masha (*angrily*)   *Amo, amas, amat, amamus, amatis, amant.*

Kulygin (*laughs*)   No, truly, she's an amazing woman. I've been married to you for seven years, and it seems like yesterday. On my word of honour. No, truly, you're an amazing woman. I'm content, content, content!

Masha   I'm bored, bored, bored . . . (*Sits up.*) And one thing I can't get out of my head . . . It's absolutely outrageous. It keeps nagging at me – I can't go on not mentioning it. I mean about Andrey . . . He's mortgaged this house to the bank, and his wife's got her hands on all the money. But in fact the house doesn't belong just to him – it belongs to all four of us! He must know that, if he's got a spark of decency in him.

Kulygin   Masha, what do you want him to do? Poor Andrey owes money right, left, and centre, heaven help him.

Masha   All the same, it's an outrageous way to behave (*Lies down.*)

Kulygin   You and I aren't poor. I work – I go off to school each day, then I give private lessons . . . A straightforward man, that's me. A plain, straightforward man . . . *Omnia mea mecum porto,* as they say – all I have I carry with me.

Masha   I'm not in need of anything. I'm just outraged by the unfairness of it.

Pause.

Go on, then, Fyodor!

Kulygin (*kisses her*)   You're tired. Have a little rest for half-an-hour, and I'll sit up and wait for you at home. Off to sleep . . . (*Moves.*) I'm content, content, content. (*He goes.*)

Irina   How much lesser a man has our Andrey become, in fact, living with that woman. How the spark has gone out of him, how he's aged! Once upon a time he was working for a university chair; yesterday he was boasting about getting a seat at last on the local Executive Council. He's got a seat, and Protopopov's the head of it . . . The whole town's talking, the whole town's laughing – he's the only one who doesn't know and can't see . . . Now everyone goes running to the fire while he sits in his room and doesn't bat an eyelid. All he does is play his violin. (*Irritably.*) Oh, it's horrible, horrible, horrible! (*Weeps.*) I just can't bear any more . . . ! I can't, I can't . . . !

Enter **Olga**. *She tidies around her bedside table.*

(*Sobs loudly.*) Throw me away, throw me away, I can't go on . . . !

Olga   What is it? What's the matter? My love!

Irina (*sobbing*)   Where's it all gone? Where is it? Oh, heavens, heavens! I've forgotten it all, I've forgotten it . . . It's all mixed up inside my head . . . I can't remember the Italian for window, or ceiling . . . I'm forgetting it all, day by day forgetting it, and life's going away, and it will never come back, never, and we shall never get to Moscow . . . I see that now – we're not going . . .

Olga   My love, my love . . .

Irina (*controlling herself*)   Oh, I'm so unhappy . . . I can't work, I won't work. I've had enough! First I was in the telegraph office – now I work for the town council, and I loathe and despise everything they give me to do . . . I'll be twenty-four next birthday, I've been working forever, and my brain's dried up, I've grown thin, I've grown old, I've grown ugly, and nothing out of it, nothing, no kind of satisfaction, and time's flying, and I keep feeling as if I'm getting further away from the life that's real and beautiful, further and further away, into some kind of bottomless pit. I'm in despair, and how I'm still alive, how I haven't killed myself before now, I really don't know . . .

Olga   Don't cry, my little girl, don't cry . . . It hurts me to see you.

Irina   I'm not crying, I'm not . . . Enough of that . . . There, now I've stopped crying. Enough . . . Enough!

Olga   My love, I'm talking to you now as your sister, as your friend. If you'll take my advice you'll marry the baron!

Irina *weeps quietly.*

After all, you respect him, you have great regard for him . . . He's not handsome, it's true, but he's a decent, worthwhile man . . . And anyway, women don't marry for love – they do it because it's their duty. That's what I think, at any rate, and I should marry without love. Anyone who proposed to me – I'd marry him, so long as he was someone worthwhile. Even if he was an old man I'd marry him . . .

Irina   I kept waiting for us to be in Moscow. That's where I was going to meet the real one. I dreamt about him, I was in love with him . . . But it's turned out to be nonsense, just so much nonsense . . .

Olga (*embraces her sister*)   My love, my lovely sister, I do understand. When the baron left the service and came here in an ordinary suit I thought he was so plain that I actually started to cry . . . 'Why are you crying?' he asked. What could I say? But if it were God's will for him to marry you, then I should be very happy. Because that's another matter, another matter entirely.

Natasha, *carrying a candle, crosses from the righthand door to the left in silence.*

Masha (*sits*)   She's roaming about as if she were the one who'd started the fire.

Olga   You are a silly, Masha. Shall I tell you who's the biggest silly in our family? – It's you. I'm sorry.

Pause.

Masha   Dear sisters, I want to make confession. I think I shall die if I don't say it. I'm going to make my confession to you, then never to another soul . . . I'm going to say it, this very minute (*Quietly.*) It's my secret, but you both must know it . . . I can't not say it . . .

Pause.

I'm in love, I'm in love . . . I'm in love with that man . . . The one you saw just now . . . Oh, what's the use? – I'm in love with Vershinin . . .

Olga (*goes to her own corner behind the screens*)   Stop that. I can't hear, in any case.

Masha   But what can I do? (*Clutches her head.*) First of all I thought, What a strange man! Then I felt sorry for him . . . then I began to be in love with him . . . I began to be in love with his voice, and with the things he said, and with his misfortunes, and with his two little girls . . .

Olga (*behind the screen*)   I can't hear. Whatever nonsense you're talking, I can't hear.

Masha   Oh, Olya, you're the one who's the silly. I'm in love – all right, so that's my fate. So that's my lot in life . . . He loves me, too . . . It's terrifying. Isn't it? Is it wrong? (*Takes* **Irina** *by the hand, and draws her nearer.*) Oh, my sweet . . . Somehow we shall live our lives, whatever happens to us . . . You read some novel and you think, that's all old stuff, everyone knows all that. But as soon as you fall in love yourself you realise that no one knows anything, and that we each have to solve our own lives . . . My loves, my sisters . . . I've confessed to you. Now I shall be silent . . . Now I shall be like the madman in that story of Gogol's . . . silence . . . silence . . .

Enter **Andrey**, *followed by* **Ferapont**.

Andrey (*angrily*)   What do you want? I don't understand.

Ferapont (*in the doorway, unhurriedly*)   If I've said it once I've said it a dozen times.

Andrey   First of all you can address me as 'sir'! I do have a rank, you know, I do happen to be a member of the Council.

Ferapont   Sir, it's the firemen, sir, they're asking please may they take their carts down to the river through the garden. Otherwise they have to keep going round – it's backbreaking.

Andrey   Very well. Tell them, very well.

Ferapont *goes*.

I'm sick of them. Where's Olga?

Olga *comes out from behind the screen*.

You're the person I'm looking for. Give me the key to the cupboard, will you – I've lost mine. You know that little key you've got.

Olga *silently gives him the key*. **Irina** *goes to her own corner behind the screen*.

Pause.

What an enormous fire, though! It's begun to die down now. Damn it, he made me so cross, that man Ferapont. That was a stupid thing I said to him . . . Making him call me sir.

Pause.

Why don't you say something, then, Olya?

Pause.

It's time you stopped all this nonsense. It's time you stopped pouting about like that for no earthly reason. You're here, Masha. Irina's here. All right, then, let's have it out in the open, once and for all. What have you three got against me? What is it?

Olga   Stop it now, Andryusha. We'll talk about it tomorrow (*Becoming upset.*) What a torment this night has been!

Andrey (*very embarrassed*)   Don't get upset. I'm simply asking you, perfectly calmly: what is it you've got against me? Just tell, me straight out.

Vershinin (*off*)   Trum-tum-tum!

Masha (*stands up. Loudly*)   Tra-ta-ta! (*To* **Olga**:) Good night, Olga, God bless you (*Goes behind the screen and kisses* **Irina**.) Sleep well . . . Good night, Andrey. Do go away, now, they're exhausted . . . you can have it all out tomorrow . . . (*She goes.*)

Olga   That's right, Andryusha – let's postpone it till tomorrow . . . (*Goes to her corner behind the screen.*) Time for bed.

Andrey   I'll just say what I have to say and then I'll go Forthwith . . . In the first place you've got something against Natasha, my wife – and this I've been aware of from the very day we got married. Natasha is a fine person – honest, straightforward, and upright – that's my opinion. I love and respect my wife – I respect her, you understand? – and I insist that others respect her, too. I say it again – she is an honest and upright person, and all your little marks of displeasure – forgive me, but you're simply behaving like spoilt children.

Pause.

Secondly, you seem to be angry that I'm not a professor, that I'm not a scientist. But I serve in local government, I am a member of the local Council, and this service I consider just as sacred, just as elevated, as any service I could render to science. I am a member of the local Council and proud of it, if you wish to know . . .

Pause.

Thirdly . . . I have something else to say . . . I mortgaged the house without asking your consent . . . To this I plead guilty, and

indeed I ask you to forgive me . . . I was driven to it by my debts
. . . thirty-five thousand . . . I don't play cards now – I gave it up
long since – but the main thing I can say in my own justification
is that you're girls, and you get an annuity, whereas I had no . . .
well, no income . . .

Pause.

Kulygin (*in the doorway*)   Masha's not in here? (*Alarmed.*) Where is
she, then? That's odd . . . (*He goes.*)

Andrey   They're not listening. Natasha is an outstanding
woman, someone of great integrity (*Walks about in silence, then stops.*)
When I got married I thought we were going to be happy . . . all
going to be happy . . . But my God . . . (*Weeps.*) My dear sisters, my
own dear sisters, don't believe me, don't trust me . . . (*He goes.*)

Kulygin (*in the doorway, alarmed*)   Where's Masha? She isn't in
here, is she? Surprising thing (*He goes.*)

The sound of the alarm; an empty stage.

Irina (*behind the screens*)   Olya! Who's that banging on the floor?

Olga   That's the doctor. He's drunk.

Irina   No peace tonight.

Pause.

Olya! (*Looks out from behind the screen.*) Have you heard? They're
taking the brigade away from us, they're posting them somewhere
far away.

Olga   It's only rumours.

Irina   We shall be left all on our own if they go . . . Olya!

Olga   What?

Irina   Dear Olya, I do have a lot of respect for the baron, I do
have a great regard for him, he's a fine man, and I'll marry him,
all right – only we must go to Moscow! We must – I implore you!
There's nowhere like Moscow in the whole wide world! We must
go, Olya! We must!

Curtain.

Act Four

The old garden of the Prozorovs' house. A long avenue of fir-trees, at the end of which can be seen the river. On the further bank of the river is the forest. Right – the verandah of the house, with a table on which there are bottles and glasses; people have evidently just been drinking champagne. Noon. From time to time people go through the garden on their way from the road to the river; half a dozen soldiers go by in quick time. **Chebutykin**, *in a genial mood which never abandons him throughout the act, is sitting in an armchair in the garden, waiting to be summoned. He is wearing a peaked military cap and carrying a stick.* **Kulygin** – *wearing a decoration round his neck and no moustache* – **Irina**, *and* **Tusenbach** *are standing on the verandah seeing off* **Fedotik** *and* **Rode**, *who are coming down the steps. Both officers are in marching order.*

Tusenbach (*embraces* **Fedotik**)   You're a good man. We've got on so well together. (*Embraces* **Rode**.) One more for you, then . . . Goodbye, old friend.

Irina   We'll see each other again.

Fedotik   No, we shan't. We never will.

Kulygin   Who knows? (*Wipes his eyes and smiles.*) Now here I am starting to cry.

Irina   We'll meet again one day.

Fedotik   What – in ten, fifteen years time? We'll scarcely recognise each other by then. We'll greet each other like strangers. (*Takes a photograph.*) Keep still . . . One last one.

Rode (*embraces* **Tusenbach**)   We'll never see each other again . . . (*Kisses* **Irina***'s hand.*) Thank you for everything, thank you!

Fedotik (*with irritation*)   Stand still, will you!

Tusenbach   God willing, we'll meet again. Write to us, though. Be sure to write.

Rode (*looks round the garden*)   Goodbye, trees! (*Calls.*) Hup-hup!

Pause.

Rode   Goodbye, echo!

Kulygin   Who knows, you may get married over there in Poland . . . A little Polish wife to put her arms round you and whisper soft words in Polish! (*Laughs.*)

Fedotik (*glancing at his watch*)   We've less than an hour in hand. Solyony's the only one from our battery who's travelling on the barge – the rest of us will be marching. Three batteries are leaving today in battalion order, and another three tomorrow – then peace and quiet will descend upon the town.

Tusenbach   Also frightful boredom.

Rode (*to* **Kulygin**)   And your wife is where?

Kulygin   Masha? In the garden.

Fedotik   We must say goodbye to her.

Rode   Goodbye, then! We must go, or I shall start crying . . . (*Quickly embraces* **Tusenbach** *and* **Kulygin**, *and kisses* **Irina**'s *hand.*) We've had a wonderful life here . . .

Fedotik (*to* **Kulygin**)   Something for you to remember me by . . . A notebook with its own little pencil . . . We'll go down to the river through here . . .

They depart, both gazing about them.

Rode (*calls*)   Hup-hup!

Kulygin (*calls*)   Goodbye!

Fedotik *and* **Rode** *meet* **Masha** *away upstage and make their farewells. She goes off with them.*

Irina   They've gone . . . (*Sits down on the bottom step of the verandah.*)

Chebutykin   They forgot to say goodbye to me.

Irina   Did you remember to say goodbye to them?

Chebutykin   No, I forgot, too, somehow. Anyway, I shall be seeing them again shortly – I'm off tomorrow. Yes . . . One more day left, that's all. A year from now and I'll be getting my discharge. Then I'll come back here again and live out my time with you . . . Only one year left before my pension, one short year . . . (*Puts his newspaper in his pocket and takes out another one.*) I'm going to come and stay with you and be a completely reformed character . . . I'm going to become such a quiet little – I don't know – proper little, decorous little fellow . . .

Irina   You ought to reform, though, my dear. You really ought to, one way or another.

Chebutykin   I know. I'm aware of that. (*Sings quietly.*)
                    Ta-ra-ra boom-de-ay,
                    Ta-ra-ra boom-de-ay . . .

Kulygin   Incorrigible, the doctor! Quite incorrigible!

Chebutykin   Yes, I should have come to you for lessons. Made you my reform-master.

Irina   Fyodor has shaved off his moustache. I can't bear to look!

Kulygin   Why ever not?

Chebutykin   I'd tell you what you look like now, but it's beyond my powers of description.

Kulygin   Come, come. This is the done thing, this is the *modus vivendi*. Our headmaster is clean-shaven, and I shaved, too, as soon as I became an inspector. No one likes it, but I don't care. I'm content. With or without a moustache, I'm equally content (*Sits.*)

At the end of the garden **Andrey** *wheels the baby, asleep, in its perambulator.*

Irina   Doctor, dear, I'm terribly worried. You were there yesterday, weren't you, outside the theatre? Tell me what happened.

Chebutykin   What happened? Nothing. Lot of nonsense. (*Reads his newspaper.*) What does it matter?

Kulygin   The story I heard is that Solyony and the baron met yesterday in the street outside the theatre. . .

Tusenbach   Do stop it! Really! (*Flaps his hand and goes off into the house.*)

Kulygin   Anyway, that's where it was . . . Solyony began to pick on the baron, and the baron lost patience and made some slighting remark . . .

Chebutykin   I don't know. It's all nonsense.

Kulygin   The tale is told of a Latin teacher in a seminary who wrote 'Tripe!' on a pupil's essay. 'Please, sir,' said the boy, 'does that mean it's good or bad, *tri-pe*?' He thought it was Latin, you see! (*Laughs.*) You can't help laughing. Apparently Solyony's in love with Irina, and he's conceived a great hatred for the baron . . . It's quite understandable. Irina's a very nice girl. She's like Masha, in fact – the same dreamy type. Only you have a more gentle nature, Irina. Though of course Masha has a very nice nature, too. I love her – Masha.

Voices (*off, at the end of the garden*)   Hulloo! Hup-hup!

Irina (*shudders*)   I don't know, I'm jumping at the slightest thing today.

Pause.

I've got everything ready – I'm sending my things off after dinner. The baron and I are getting married tomorrow, and it's tomorrow we're leaving for the brickworks. Then the very next day I shall be working in the school there, and a new life will be starting. Somehow God will give me strength! When I was taking the examination to be a teacher I actually cried for joy.

Pause.

The cart will be coming for our things very shortly . . .

Kulygin   That's all very fine, but it's a little head-in-the-clouds, somehow. Just a lot of ideas, not quite down to earth. You have my sincerest good wishes, though.

Chebutykin (*emotionally*)   My sweet and lovely girl, my precious . . . Up and away you've gone – there's no catching you. I've dropped behind, like a bird heading south that's got too old to fly. Fly on, my loves, fly on, and God go with you!

Pause.

Mistake, you know, shaving your moustache off.

Kulygin   Don't keep on about it! (*Sighs.*) So the troops will be off today, and everything will go back to the way it was. They can say what they like – Masha is a fine upstanding woman. I love her very much, and I bless my lot in life . . . Odd how much one person's lot in life can differ from another's . . . In the excise department here there works one Kozyrev. He was at school with me, but he got himself thrown out of the fifth form because he simply could not grasp *ut* followed by a consecutive clause. Now he lives in terrible poverty – he's a sick man into the bargain – and whenever I run into him I say, 'Hello, consecutive *ut*!' 'Yes,' he says, 'exactly, it's all consecutive.' And he coughs . . . Whereas I've been lucky all my life, I'm a happy man, I even have the Order of St Stanislaus, second class, and now I'm teaching others that famous consecutive *ut* in my turn. I'm a man of some intelligence, of course – more so than many – but that's not the secret of happiness . . .

The sound of 'The Maiden's Prayer' being played on the piano inside the house.

Irina   The Maiden's Prayer. And tomorrow evening I shan't be hearing it – I shan't be coming face to face with Protopopov . . .

Pause.

He's sitting there in the drawing-room. He's even come today . . .

Kulygin   Hasn't our headmistress arrived yet?

Irina   Not yet. She has been sent for. If only you knew how hard it's been for me, living here alone without Olya . . . She's resident at the school, and she's the headmistress, so she's busy all day, while I'm on my own, I'm bored, I've nothing to do, and I hate the room I live in . . . So I simply decided – if I'm not destined to live in Moscow, then so be it. That's my lot in life. There's nothing to be done about it . . . Everything is in the hands of God, that's the truth of the matter. The baron proposed to me . . . So – I thought about it for a while, and I made up my mind to it. He's a good, kind man – in fact it's surprising how good and kind he is . . . And suddenly it was as if my heart had grown wings. My spirits rose, and I was seized again by the desire to work, to work . . . But then yesterday something happened, some mysterious thing came looming over me . . .

Chebutykin   *Tri-pe.* As the boy said. Nonsense.

Natasha (*out of the window*)   It's our headmistress!

Kulygin   Our headmistress has arrived. Come on, then.

He goes with **Irina** *into the house.*

Chebutykin (*reads the paper, singing quietly*).

>Ta-ra-ra boom-de-ay,
>Ta-ra-ra boom-de-ay . . .

Masha *approaches; at the end of the garden* **Andrey** *wheels the perambulator.*

Masha   So he's just quietly sitting here, is he? Just having a little sit.

Chebutykin   What if I am?

Masha (*sits*)   Nothing . . .

Pause.

You were in love with my mother?

Chebutykin   Very much.

Masha   And she with you?

Chebutykin (*after a pause*)   That I don't remember.

Masha   Is my one here? We had a cook once who called her policeman that – my one. Is he here, my one?

Chebutykin   Not yet.

Masha   When you snatch happiness in fits and starts and bits and pieces the way I have, and then lose it again the way I am, you find yourself getting gradually coarser and more foul-tempered . . . (*Indicates her breast.*) It boils up inside me here . . . (*Looking at her brother* **Andrey**, *who is wheeling the perambulator.*) Look at Andrey, our lovely brother . . . All our hopes have foundered. Thousands of people raised the great bell up, much toil and money were expended, then suddenly it fell and shattered. Suddenly, just like that, for no good reason. And so did Andrey . . .

Andrey   When are they going to quieten down a bit in the house? Such a row.

Chebutykin   Won't be long. (*Looks at his watch.*) I've got an old-fashioned striking watch . . . (*Winds the watch, and it strikes.*) The first, second, and fifth batteries are leaving on the dot of one . . .

Pause.

And me tomorrow.

Andrey   Forever?

Chebutykin   Don't know. Might come back in a year's time. Though heaven knows . . . What does it matter?

The sound of a harp and fiddle being played somewhere in the distance.

Andrey   The town's going to be deserted. It's like a candle being snuffed out.

Pause.

Something happened yesterday outside the theatre. Everyone's talking about it, but I don't know what it was.

Chebutykin   Nothing. A lot of nonsense. Solyony began picking on the baron, the baron flared up and insulted him, and the end of it was that Solyony felt obliged to challenge him to a duel (*Looks at his watch.*) About time for it now, I think . . . Half-past twelve, in those woods you can see on the other side of the river . . . Bang bang. (*Laughs.*) Solyony thinks he's Lermontov – he even writes verse. Well, a joke's a joke, but this will be his third duel.

Masha   Will be whose third duel?

Chebutykin   Solyony's.

Masha   What about the baron?

Chebutykin   What about the baron?

Pause.

Masha Everything's going round and round inside my head.
I say they ought to be stopped, though. He could wound the
baron – or kill him, even.

Chebutykin The baron's a nice chap, but one baron more or
less – what does it matter? Let them go ahead. It doesn't matter!

A Voice (*calling, from beyond the garden*) Hulloo! Hup-hup!

Chebutykin They're waiting. That's Skvortzov shouting. One
of the seconds. He's sitting in the boat.

Pause.

Andrey If you want my opinion, taking part in a duel is quite
straightforwardly immoral. So is attending one, even as a doctor.

Chebutykin It only seems so . . . We're not here, there's
nothing in the world, we don't exist, we only seem to exist . . .
Anyway, what does it matter?

Masha That's right, talk, talk, talk, the whole day long . . .
(*Makes a move to go.*) It's bad enough living in a climate like this –
because it will be snowing before we know where we are – but to
have to listen to these conversations into the bargain . . . (*Stopping.*)
I'm not going into the house – I can't go in there . . . You'll tell
me when Vershinin arrives . . . (*Goes along the avenue.*) The birds are
flying south already . . . (*Looks up.*) Swans or geese . . . My loves,
my happy loves . . . (*She goes.*)

Andrey Our house is going to be deserted. The officers will
have gone, you'll have gone, my sister will have got married, and I
shall be left alone in the place.

Chebutykin What about your wife?

Enter **Ferapont** *with some papers.*

Andrey A wife's a wife. She's honest, she's decent, she's – yes –
good-hearted. But at the same time there's something in her
that reduces her to the level of a little blind furry animal. She's
certainly not a human being. I'm telling you all this because
you're a friend, the only person I can open my heart to. I love
Natasha, it's true, but sometimes she seems to me amazingly

squalid, and then I don't know where I am – I can't understand why I love her so, or at any rate did love her . . .

Chebutykin (*stands up*)   My friend, I'm leaving tomorrow – we may never see each other again. So here is my advice to you. Put on your cap, pick up your stick, and walk out of here . . . Walk out and keep walking, without so much as a backward glance. And the further you go the better.

Solyony *crosses the end of the garden with two other officers. Seeing* **Chebutykin**, *he turns towards him, while the other officers continue on their way.*

Solyony   It's time, doctor! Half-past twelve already. (*Greets* **Andrey**.)

Chebutykin   Coming. I'm sick of the lot of you (*To* **Andrey**:) Andryusha, if anyone wants me, tell them I'll be back directly . . . (*Sighs.*) Oh-oh-oh!

Andrey *goes.*

Solyony   The peasant had no time to gasp
Before he felt the bear's hard clasp.

(*They move off together.*) What's all that groaning for, Grandpapa?

Chebutykin   Mind your own business.

Solyony   Fit and well, are we?

Chebutykin (*angrily*)   Fit as a flea.

Solyony   There's no need for Grandpapa to get excited. I shan't overdo it. I shall just wing him like a woodcock. (*Takes out his scent and sprinkles it over his hands.*) I've used up a whole flaskful today, and still they smell. They smell like a corpse.

Pause.

Well, there we are . . . You remember Lermontov's poem?

'Rebelliously he seeks the storm,
As if in storms there promised peace . . .'

Chebutykin   That's right.

The peasant had no time to gasp.
Before he felt the bear's hard clasp. (*He goes with* **Solyony**.)

Voices (*calling, off*)   Hup-hup!

Enter **Andrey** *and* **Ferapont**.

Ferapont   Will you sign the papers . . .

Andrey (*irritably*)   Get away from me! Get away! I beg of you!
(*He goes with the perambulator.*)

Ferapont   That's what papers are for, you know, to be signed
(*Goes away upstage.*)

Enter **Irina** *and* **Tusenbach** *in a straw hat.* **Kulygin** *crosses the stage.*

Kulygin (*calling*)   Hulloo, Masha, hulloo!

Tusenbach   There, by the look of it, goes the only man in
town who's glad the troops are leaving.

Irina   That's understandable.

Pause.

Our town's going to be deserted now.

Tusenbach (*glancing at his watch*)   My love, I shall be back
directly.

Irina   Where are you going?

Tusenbach   I've got to go into town. I've got to . . . see some of
my friends off.

Irina   You're not telling the truth . . . Nikolai, why are you so
preoccupied today?

Pause.

What happened yesterday outside the theatre?

Tusenbach (*makes an impatient movement*)   In an hour I shall be
back, and with you again (*Kisses her hands.*) My precious . . .
(*Gazes into her face.*) Five years have gone by now since I first loved
you, and still I can't get used to it, still you seem to grow more
beautiful. Your hair . . . your eyes . . . Tomorrow I'm going to

take you away, we're going to work, we're going to be rich, all my
dreams will come true. You're going to be happy. Only one thing
wrong with it all – just one. You don't love me!

Irina   That's not within my control. I'll be your wife, I'll be your
loyal and submissive wife, but there's no love there, and there's
nothing I can do about that (*Weeps.*) Not once in my life have I
ever been in love! Oh, I've dreamt so much about love – dreamt
about it for so long now, night and day. But my heart is like some
priceless grand piano that's been locked up, and the key to it lost.

Pause.

You look anxious.

Tusenbach   I didn't sleep all night. There's nothing terrible in
my life, nothing I should be afraid of. It's just this lost key that tor-
ments me and gives me sleepless nights . . . Say something to me.

Pause.

Say something . . .

Irina   What? Say what? What is there to say?

Tusenbach   Anything.

Irina   Stop, stop!

Pause.

Tusenbach   Ridiculous how such silly little things can sometimes
take on a sudden importance in your life, for no reason you can
put your finger on. You laugh at them just as you always did, you
think how absurd they are, and yet you go along with it all and
feel you haven't the strength to stop. Oh, let's not talk about it! I
feel cheerful. I look at these fir-trees, at these maples and birches,
and it's as if I'm seeing them for the first time in my life. And
everything's looking at me – with curiosity – waiting. Such lovely
trees, and really, such a lovely life there ought to be around them!

Voices (*off*)   Hulloo! Hup-hup!

Tusenbach   I must go, it's past time . . . Here's a tree that's
withered up, yet still it sways in the wind with the others. It will

be like that with me, I think, if I should die. I shall still have a
hand in life one way or another. Goodbye, my love . . . (*Kisses her
hands.*) Those papers you gave me are on the table in my room,
underneath the calendar.

Irina   I'll come with you.

Tusenbach (*in alarm*)   No, no! (*Quickly goes, then stops in the avenue.*)
Irina!

Irina   What?

Tusenbach (*not knowing what to say*)   I didn't have any coffee this
morning. Will you tell them to make me some . . . (*Quickly goes off.*)

Irina *stands lost in her own thoughts, then goes away upstage and sits on the
swing. Enter* **Andrey** *with the perambulator,* **Ferapont** *appears.*

Ferapont   Look, they're not my papers, you know – they're
official. It wasn't me that thought them up.

Andrey   Oh, where is it, where has it gone, that past of mine,
when I was young and clever and light of heart, when I thought
and reasoned elegantly, when present and future were both alight
with hope? Why, when we have still scarcely begun to live, do we
become dull and grey and uninteresting and idle and indifferent
and useless and unhappy . . . ? Our town has been here for
two hundred years, it's got a hundred thousand inhabitants,
and not one of them who hasn't been exactly like all the others –
not one, past or present, who's been ready to die for a cause – not
one scholar, not one artist, nobody even faintly remarkable, who
might have aroused envy, or some passionate desire to emulate
him . . . They've just eaten, and drunk, and slept, and then died . . .
The next lot have been born, and they in their turn have eaten,
drunk, slept, and then, to avoid being stupified by boredom,
they've introduced a little variety into their lives by vile scandal-
mongering and vodka and cards and quibbling lawsuits; and the
wives have deceived their husbands, while the husbands have
turned a blind eye; and irresistibly this sordid influence
has crushed the children, and the divine spark within them
has guttered out, and they have become the same miserable,
indistinguishable corpses as their mothers and fathers . . . (*To*
Ferapont, *angrily.*) What do you want?

Ferapont What? Oh, sign the papers.

Andrey I'm sick of the sight of you.

Ferapont (*handing him the papers*) The doorman at the revenue office was telling me just now . . . In Petersburg last winter by all accounts, he said, they had two hundred degrees of frost.

Andrey The present is loathsome, but then when I think about the future – well, that's another story. It all becomes so easy and spacious; and in the distance there's a gleam of light – I can see freedom, I can see me and my children being freed from idleness, from roast goose and cabbage, from little naps after dinner, from ignoble sponging off others . . .

Ferapont Two thousand people froze to death, by all accounts. Everyone was terrified, he said. Either in Petersburg or in Moscow – I can't remember.

Andrey (*seized by tender feeling*) My dear sisters, my wonderful sisters! (*On the verge of tears.*) Masha, my sister . . .

Natasha (*at the window*) Who's that talking so loudly out here? Is it you, Andryusha? You'll wake Sofochka. *Il ne faut pas faire du bruit, la Sophie est dormée déjà. Vous êtes un ours.* (*Getting angry.*) If you want to talk, give the perambulator to someone else. Ferapont, take the perambulator from the master.

Ferapont Take the perambulator, right. (*Takes it.*)

Andrey (*embarrassed*) I'm talking quietly.

Natasha (*inside the window, petting her baby boy*) Bobik! Isn't Bobik a rascal now! Isn't Bobik a naughty boy!

Andrey (*glancing at the papers*) All right, I'll look through them and sign whatever's necessary, and you can take them back to the Council . . .

Andrey *goes into the house, reading the papers,* **Ferapont** *pushes the perambulator down to the end of the garden.*

Natasha (*inside the window*) What's mama called, then, Bobik? There's a good boy! Who's that, then? That's Auntie Olya. Say, 'Hello, Auntie Olya!'

Enter two wandering musicians, a man and a girl, playing fiddle and harp, **Vershinin**, **Olga**, *and* **Anfisa** *come out of the house and listen to them for a moment in silence.* **Irina** *approaches.*

Olga   Our garden is like a public highway – people come walking through, they come riding through. Nanny, give these people something . . .

Anfisa (*gives the musicians something*)   Off you go, then, my dears, and God go with you.

The musicians bow and go off.

Poor wretches. It's not a full stomach makes them play (*To* **Irina**:) Hello, Irisha! (*Kisses her.*) Eh, child, but I'm having the time of my life! At the school, my precious, in the official Government living quarters, along with Olyushka. Appointed to me by the Lord in the fullness of my years. Sinner that I am, in all my born days I've never lived so . . . Great big apartment it is, and me with a room and a bed all to myself. And everything official from the Government. I wake up in the night – and oh my Lord, oh Mother of God, there's not a happier soul in all the world!

Vershinin (*glances at his watch. To* **Olga**)   We shall be leaving directly. It's time for me to go.

Pause.

I should like to wish you all the best . . . Where's Masha?

Irina   She's somewhere in the garden. I'll go and look for her.

Vershinin   If you'd be so kind. I am pressed for time.

Anfisa   I'll go and look as well (*Calls.*) Mashenka, hulloo! (*Goes off with* **Irina** *to the end of the garden.*) Hulloo-oo! Hulloo-oo!

Vershinin   All things come to an end sooner or later. Now it's our turn to part. (*Looks at his watch.*) The town has been giving us something in the style of a luncheon. We drank champagne, the mayor made a speech. I sat there eating and listening, but in spirit I was here, with all of you . . . (*Looks round the garden.*) I've grown accustomed to you all.

Olga   Shall we ever see each other again?

Vershinin   Probably not.

Pause.

My wife and the two girls will stay on here for a couple of months. Please, if anything should happen, if anything should be needed . . .

Olga   Yes, yes, of course. Rest assured.

Pause.

By tomorrow there won't be a soldier left in town. It will all have become nothing but a memory. And for us, of course, a new life will be commencing.

Pause.

Nothing works out as we would have it. I didn't want to be headmistress, but headmistress I've nonetheless become. So there's no question of my living in Moscow . . .

Vershinin   Anyway . . . Thank you for everything . . . Forgive me for anything I may have done wrong . . . I've talked a great deal – a very great deal, I'm afraid. Forgive me for that, too, and remember me kindly.

Olga (*wipes her eyes*)   Where has Masha got to?

Vershinin   What else can I say to wish you farewell? What is there to philosophise about . . . ? (*Laughs.*) Life is hard. To many of us it appears blank and hopeless, but we have to concede nonetheless that it is becoming steadily easier and brighter. And by all appearances the time is not far off when it will be quite cloudless. (*Looks at his watch.*) Time for me to be going, it really is! In days gone by the human race kept itself busy with wars. It filled out its life with campaigns and raids and conquests. But all that now has become a thing of the past, leaving behind a vast empty space which we for the time being lack the means to fill. But mankind seeks, and will of course find. Ah, speed the day!

Pause.

I tell you, if human industry could be complemented by education, and education by industry. (*Looks at his watch.*) Time for me to go, though . . .

Olga   Here she comes.

Enter **Masha**.

Vershinin   I've come to say goodbye . . .

Olga *goes off a little to one side so as not to hinder their farewells.*

Masha (*looking into his face*) Goodbye . . . my love . . .

A prolonged kiss.

Olga   Come on, now . . .

Masha *sobs bitterly.*

Vershinin   Write to me . . . my love, yes . . . Don't forget! Let me go . . . It's time . . . (*To* **Olga**:) Take her, please, it really is . . . time . . . I'm late already . . . (*Shaken, he kisses* **Olga***'s hands, then once again embraces* **Masha***, and quickly goes off.*)

Olga   Come on, Masha! Stop it, now, my precious . . .

Enter **Kulygin**.

Kulygin (*in embarrassment*)   Never mind, let her cry, let her cry . . . My dear Masha, my good, kind Masha . . . You're my wife, and I'm happy no matter what . . . I'm not complaining, I'm not reproaching you . . . Olga can be my witness to that . . . We'll go back to the same old way of life we had before, and not a word will I breathe, not a hint . . .

Masha   (*restraining her sobs*)   On a far sea shore an oak tree grows,
And from it bangs a golden chain . . .
And from it hangs a golden chain . . .
I'm going out of my mind . . .
On a far sea shore . . . an oak tree grows . . .

Olga   Calm down, now, Masha . . . Calm down . . . Give her some water.

Masha   I've stopped crying.

Kulygin   She's stopped crying . . . She's good, she's kind . . .

The sound of a shot, dull and distant.

Masha   On a far sea shore an oak tree grows,
     And from it hangs a golden chain . . .
     A golden cat forever goes . . . A talking cat . . .
I'm getting mixed up . . . (*Drinks water.*) A failed life . . . Nothing left now that I want . . . I shall calm down in a moment . . . Not that it matters . . . What is all this about a far sea shore? Why have I got this phrase in my head? My thoughts are getting all mixed up.

Enter **Irina**.

Olga   Calm down, Masha. There's a good girl . . . Let's go inside, shall we?

Masha (*angrily*)   I'm not going in there. (*Sobs, but then immediately stops.*) I've stopped going into that house – I'm not going in now . . .

Irina   Let's all sit down together for a moment, even if we don't say anything. I am leaving tomorrow, after all . . .

Pause.

Kulygin   Look what I took away from some little chap in the third form yesterday . . . (*Puts on a beard complete with moustache.*) I look like the German master . . . (*Laughs.*) Don't I? You have to laugh at some of these boys.

Masha   You do look like that German.

Olga (*laughs*)   Yes, you do.

Masha *weeps*.

Irina   Come on, Masha.

Kulygin   Very like him . . .

Enter **Natasha**.

Natasha (*to the maid*)   What is it? Protopopov will sit with Sofochka for a bit, and Andrey can push Bobik. What a business children are . . . (*To* **Irina**:) Irina, you're leaving tomorrow – it's such a shame. Stay a few more days, anyway, why don't you. (*Sees* **Kulygin** *and cries out.*)

Kulygin *laughs and takes off the beard.*

Honestly! You gave me a fright! (*To* **Irina**:) I've got used to having
you around. Don't think I'm going to find it easy to part with you.
I shall have Andrey and that violin of his moved into your
room – he can scrape away in there to his heart's content! And
then in his old room we'll put Sofochka. She really is an amazing
child! Such a poppet! Today she looked at me with eyes like this,
and – 'Mama!'

Kulygin   An admirable child, it must be said.

Natasha   So tomorrow I shall be all on my own here. (*Sighs.*)
The first thing I'm going to do is to have that avenue of fir-trees
cut down, and then this maple here . . . It looks such a sight in the
evening . . . (*To* **Irina**:) My love, that belt doesn't suit you at all . . .
Terrible taste . . . You need something a little brighter. And all
round here I'm going to have flowers planted – flowers and more
flowers – and we shall have the scent . . . (*Sharply.*) Why is there
a fork lying about on the seat out here? (*Goes into the house. To the*
Maid:) Why is there a fork lying about on the seat out here, I want
to know! (*Shouts.*) Be quiet!

Kulygin   She's off!

A band, off, plays a march. They all listen.

Olga   They're leaving.

Enter **Chebutykin**.

Masha   Our men . . . our ones. So – fare them well! (*To her*
husband.) We must go home . . . Where are my hat and shawl?

Kulygin   I put them inside . . . I'll go and fetch them. (*Goes into*
the house.)

Olga   That's right, we can all go home now. It's time to be
moving.

Chebutykin   Olga Sergeyevna!

Olga   What?

Pause.

What?

Chebutykin   Nothing . . . I don't know how to say it to you . . . (*Whispers in her ear.*)

Olga (*frightened*)   It's not possible!

Chebutykin   I know . . . It's a nasty business . . . I've had enough, I don't want to say any more . . . (*With irritation.*) Anyway, what does it matter?

Masha   What's happened?

Olga (*puts her arms round* **Irina**)   A terrible day this is . . . My dear, I don't know how to say it to you . . .

Irina   What? Tell me quickly, somebody – what is it? For the love of God! (*Weeps.*)

Chebutykin   There's been a duel. The baron was killed . . .

Irina (*weeps quietly*)   I knew it, I knew it . . .

Chebutykin (*sits on a garden seat upstage*)   I've had enough . . . (*Takes a newspaper out of his pocket.*) Let them have their little cry . . . (*Sings quietly.*)

> Ta-ra-ra boom-de-ay,
> Ta-ra-ra boom-de-ay . . .
> Doesn't matter, does it?

The three sisters stand huddled against each other.

Masha   Oh, but listen to the band! They're leaving us. One has left us altogether – left us forever. We shall remain behind, on our own, to start our life again. We have to live . . . We have to live . . .

Irina (*puts her head on* **Olga**'s *breast*)   A time will come when people will understand what it was all for, what the purpose was of all this suffering, and what was hidden from us will be hidden no more. In the meantime, though, we have to live . . . we have to work, that's all, we have to work! Tomorrow I shall go on my way alone. I shall take up my teaching post, and devote my life to those who may have some use for it. It's autumn now. Soon winter will come and bring the first falls of snow, and I shall be working, I shall be working . . .

Olga (*embraces both her sisters*)   The band plays so bravely – you feel you want to live! Merciful God! Time will pass, and we shall depart forever. We shall be forgotten – our faces, our voices, even how many of us there were. But our sufferings will turn to joy for those who live after us. Peace and happiness will dwell on earth, and people living now will be blessed and spoken well of. Dear sisters, our life is not ended yet. We shall live! And the band plays so bravely, so joyfully – another moment, you feel, and we shall know why we live and why we suffer . . . If only we could know, if only we could know!

The music grows quieter and quieter. **Kulygin**, *smiling cheerfully, brings* **Masha**'s *hat and shawl.* **Andrey** *pushes the perambulator with* **Bobik** *sitting in it.*

Chebutykin (*sings quietly*)   Ta-ra . . . ra . . . boom-de-ay . . . Ta-ra-ra boom-de-ay . . . (*Reads his newspaper.*)

Anyway, it doesn't matter. It doesn't matter.

Olga   If only we could know, if only we could know!

Curtain.

JOHN GALSWORTHY

Strife

A Drama in Three Acts

Characters

John Anthony
Edgar Anthony
Frederic Wilder
William Scantlebury
Oliver Wanklin
Henry Tench
Francis Underwood
Simon Harness
David Roberts
James Green
John Bulgin
Henry Thomas
George Rous
Jago
Evans
Frost
Enid Underwood
Annie Roberts
Madge Thomas
Mrs Rous
Mrs Bulgin
Mrs Yeo

The action takes place on February 7th between the hours of noon and six in the afternoon, close to the Trenartha Tin Plate Works, on the borders of England and Wales, where a strike has been in progress throughout the winter.

Act One

It is noon. In the **Underwoods'** *dining-room a bright fire is burning. On one side of the fireplace are double doors leading to the drawing-room, on the other side a door leading to the hall. In the centre of the room a long dining-table without a cloth is set out as a board table. At the head of it, in the Chairman's seat, sits* **John Anthony**, *an old man, big, clean shaven, and high-coloured, with thick white hair, and thick dark eyebrows. His movements are rather slow and feeble, but his eyes are very much alive. There is a glass of water by his side. On his right sits his son* **Edgar**, *an earnest-looking man of thirty, reading a newspaper. Next him* **Wanklin**, *a man with jutting eyebrows, and silver-streaked light hair, is bending over transfer papers.* **Tench**, *the secretary, a short and rather humble, nervous man, with side whiskers, stands helping him. On* **Wanklin's** *right sits* **Underwood**, *the Manager, a quiet man, with a long, stiff jaw, and steady eyes. Back to the fire is* **Scantlebury**, *a very large, pale, sleepy man, with grey hair, rather bald. Between him and the Chairman are two empty chairs.*

Wilder (*who is lean, cadaverous, and complaining, with drooping grey moustaches, stands before the fire*)   I say, this fire's the devil! Can I have a screen, Tench?

Scantlebury   A screen, ah!

Tench   Certainly, Mr Wilder. (*He looks at* **Underwood**.) That is – perhaps the Manager – perhaps Mr Underwood –

Scantlebury   These fireplaces of yours, Underwood –

Underwood (*roused from studying some papers*)   A screen? Rather! I'm sorry. (*He goes to the door with a little smile.*)
We're not accustomed to complaints of too much fire down here just now.

He speaks as though he holds a pipe between his teeth, slowly, ironically.

Wilder (*in an injured mice*)   You mean the men. H'm!
Underwood *goes out.*

Scantlebury   Poor devils!

Wilder   It's their own, fault, Scantlebury.

Edgar (*holding out his paper*)   There's great distress amongst them, according to the *Trenartha News*.

Wilder   Oh, that rag! Give it to Wanklin. Suit his Radical views. They call us monsters, I suppose. The editor of that rubbish ought to be shot.

Edgar (*reading*)   'If the Board of worthy gentlemen who control the Trenartha Tin Plate Works from their armchairs in London, would condescend to come and see for themselves the conditions prevailing amongst their workpeople during this strike – '

Wilder   Well, we *have* come.

Edgar (*continuing*)   'We cannot believe that even their leg-of-mutton hearts would remain untouched.'

Wanklin *takes the paper from him.*

Wilder   Ruffian! I remember that fellow when he hadn't a penny to his name; little snivel of a chap that's made his way by blackguarding everybody who takes a different view to himself.

Anthony *says something that is not heard.*

Wilder   What does your father say?

Edgar   He says 'The kettle and the pot'.

Wilder   H'm!

He sits down next to **Scantlebury**.

Scantlebury (*blowing out his cheeks*)   I shall boil if I don't get that screen.

Underwood *and* **Enid** *enter with a screen, which they place before the fire.* **Enid** *is tall; she has a small, decided face, and is twenty-eight years old.*

Enid   Put it closer, Frank. Will that do, Mr Wilder? It's the highest we've got.

Wilder   Thanks, capitally.

Scantlebury (*turning, with a sigh of pleasure*)   Ah! Merci, madame!

Enid   Is there anything else you want, father? (**Anthony** *shakes his head.*) Edgar – anything?

Edgar   You might give me a 'J' nib, old girl.

Enid   There are some down there by Mr Scantlebury.

Scantlebury (*handing a little box of nibs*)   Ah! your brother uses 'J's'. What does the Manager use? (*With expansive politeness.*) What does your husband use, Mrs Underwood?

Underwood   A quill!

Scantlebury   The homely product of the goose. (*He holds out quills.*)

Underwood (*dryly*)   Thanks, if you can spare me one. (*He takes a quill.*) What about lunch, Enid?

Enid (*stopping at the double doors and looking back*)   We're going to have lunch here, in the drawing-room, so you needn't hurry with your meeting.

Wanklin *and* **Wilder** *bow, and she goes out.*

Scantlebury (*rousing himself, suddenly*)   Ah! Lunch! That hotel – Dreadful! Did you try the whitebait last night? Fried fat!

Wilder   Past twelve! Aren't you going to read the minutes, Tench?

Tench (*looking for the Chairman's assent, reads in a rapid and monotonous voice*)   'At a Board Meeting held the 31st of January at the Company's Offices, 512 Cannon Street, E.C. Present – Mr Anthony in the chair, Messrs F. H. Wilder, William Scantlebury, Oliver Wanklin, and Edgar Anthony. Read letters from the Manager dated January 20th, 23rd, 25th, 28th, relative to the strike at the Company's Works. Read letters to the Manager of January 21st, 24th, 26th, 29th. Read letter from Mr Simon Harness, of the Central Union, asking for an interview with the Board. Read letter from the Men's Committee, signed David Roberts, James Green, John Bulgin, Henry Thomas, George Rous, desiring conference with the Board; and it was resolved that a special Board Meeting be called for February 7th at the house of the Manager, for the purpose of discussing the situation with Mr Simon Harness and the Men's Committee on the spot. Passed twelve transfers, signed and sealed nine certificates and one balance certificate.'

He pushes the book over to the Chairman.

Anthony (*with a heavy sigh*)   If it's your pleasure, sign the same.

He signs, moving the pen with difficulty.

Wanklin   What's the Union's game, Tench? They haven't made up their split with the men. What does Harness want this interview for?

Tench   Hoping we shall come to a compromise, I think, sir; he's having a meeting with the men this afternoon.

Wilder   Harness! Ah! He's one of those cold-blooded, cool-headed chaps. I distrust them. I don't know that we didn't make a mistake to come down. What time'll the men be here?

Underwood   Any time now.

Wilder   Well, if we're not ready, they'll have to wait – won't do 'em any harm to cool their heels a bit.

Scantlebury (*slowly*)   Poor devils! It's snowing. *What* weather!

Underwood (*with meaning slowness*)   This house'll be the warmest place they've been in this winter.

Wilder   Well, I hope we're going to settle this business in time for me to catch the 6.30. I've got to take my wife to Spain tomorrow. (*Chattily.*) My old father had a strike at his works in '69; just such a February as this. They wanted to shoot him.

Wanklin   What! In the close season?

Wilder   By George, there was no close season for employers then! He used to go down to his office with a pistol in his pocket.

Scantlebury (*faintly alarmed*)   Not seriously?

Wilder (*with finality*)   Ended in his shootin' one of 'em in the legs.

Scantlebury (*unavoidably feeling his thigh*)   No? God bless me!

Anthony (*lifting the agenda paper*)   To consider the policy of the Board in relation to the strike.

There is a silence.

Wilder   It's this infernal three-cornered duel – the Union, the men, and ourselves.

Wanklin   We needn't consider the Union.

Wilder   It's my experience that you've always got to consider the Union, confound them! If the Union were going to withdraw their support from the men, as they've done, why did they ever allow them to strike at all?

Edgar   We've had that over a dozen times.

Wilder   Well, I've never understood it! It's beyond me. They talk of the engineers' and furnacemen's demands being excessive – so they are – but that's not enough to make the Union withdraw their support. What's behind it?

Underwood   Fear of strikes at Harper's and Tinewell's.

Wilder (*with triumph*)   Afraid of other strikes – now, that's a reason! Why couldn't we have been told that before?

Underwood   You were.

Tench   You were absent from the Board that day, sir.

Scantlebury   The men must have seen they had no chance when the Union gave them up. It's madness.

Underwood   It's Roberts!

Wilder   Just our luck, the men finding a fanatical firebrand like Roberts for leader.

A pause.

Wanklin (*looking at* **Anthony**)   Well?

Wilder (*breaking in fussily*)   It's a regular mess. I don't like the position we're in; I don't like it; I've said for a long time. (*Looking at* **Wanklin**.) When Wanklin and I came down here before Christmas it looked as if the men must collapse. You thought so too, Underwood.

Underwood   Yes.

Wilder   Well, they haven't! Here we are, going from bad to worse – losing our customers – shares going down!

Scantlebury (*shaking his head*)   M'm! M'm!

Wanklin   What loss have we made by this strike, Tench?

Tench   Over fifty thousand, sir!

Scantlebury (*pained*)   You don't say!

Wilder   We shall never get it back.

Tench   No, sir.

Wilder   Who'd have supposed the men were going to stick out like this – nobody suggested that. (*Looking angrily at* **Tench**.)

Scantlebury (*shaking his head*)   I've never liked a fight – never shall.

Anthony   No surrender!

All look at him.

Wilder   Who wants to surrender? (**Anthony** *looks at him.*) I – I want to act reasonably. When the men sent Roberts up to the Board in December – then was the time. We ought to have humoured him; instead of that, the Chairman – (*Dropping his eyes before* **Anthony**'s.) – er – we snapped his head off. We could have got them in then by a little tact.

Anthony   No compromise!

Wilder   There we are! This strike's been going on now since October, and as far as I can see it may last another six months. Pretty mess we shall be in by then. The only comfort is, the men'll be in a worse!

Edgar (*to* **Underwood**)   What sort of state are they really in, Frank?

Underwood (*without expression*)   Damnable!

Wilder   Well, who on earth would have thought they'd have held on like this without support!

Underwood   Those who know them.

Wilder   I defy anyone to know them! And what about tin? Price going up daily. When we do get started we shall have to work off our contracts at the top of the market.

Wanklin   What do you say to that, Chairman?

Anthony   Can't be helped!

Wilder   Shan't pay a dividend till goodness knows when!

Scantlebury (*with emphasis*)   We ought to think of the shareholders. (*Turning heavily.*) Chairman, I say we ought to think of the shareholders.

Anthony *mutters.*

Scantlebury   What's that?

Tench   The Chairman says he *is* thinking of you, sir.

Scantlebury (*sinking back into torpor*)   Cynic!

Wilder   It's past a joke. *I* don't want to go without a dividend for years if the Chairman does. We can't go on playing ducks and drakes with the Company's prosperity.

Edgar (*rather ashamedly*)   I think we ought to consider the men.

All but **Anthony** *fidget in their seats.*

Scantlebury (*with a sigh*)   We mustn't think of our private feelings, young man. That'll never do.

Edgar (*ironically*)   I'm not thinking of our feelings. I'm thinking of the men's.

Wilder   As to that – we're men of business.

Wanklin   That is the little trouble.

Edgar   There's no necessity for pushing things so far in the face of all this suffering – it's – it's cruel.

No one speaks, as though **Edgar** *had uncovered something whose existence no man prizing his self-respect could afford to recognize.*

Wanklin (*with an ironical smile*)   I'm afraid we mustn't base our policy on luxuries like sentiment.

Edgar   I detest this state of things.

Anthony   We didn't seek the quarrel.

Edgar   I know that, sir, but surely we've gone far enough.

Anthony   No.

All look at one another.

Wanklin   Luxuries apart, Chairman, we must look out what we're doing.

Anthony   Give way to the men once and there'll be no end to it.

Wanklin   I quite agree, but – (**Anthony** *shakes his head.*) You make it a question of bedrock principle? (**Anthony** *nods.*) Luxuries again, Chairman! The shares are below par.

Wilder   Yes, and they'll drop to a half when we pass the next dividend.

Scantlebury (*with alarm*)   Come, come! Not so bad as that.

Wilder (*grimly*)   You'll see! (*Craning forward to catch* **Anthony**'s *speech.*) I didn't catch –

Tench (*hesitating*)   The Chairman says, sir, 'Fais que – que – devra –'

Edgar (*sharply*)   My father says: 'Do what we ought – and let things rip.'

Wilder   Tcha!

Scantlebury (*throwing up his hands*)   The Chairman's a Stoic – I always said the Chairman was a Stoic.

Wilder   Much good that'll do us.

Wanklin (*suavely*)   Seriously, Chairman, are you going to let the ship sink under you, for the sake of – a principle?

Anthony   She won't sink.

Scantlebury (*with alarm*)   Not while I'm on the Board I hope.

Anthony (*with a twinkle*)   Better rat, Scantlebury.

Scantlebury   What a man!

Anthony   I've always fought them; I've never been beaten yet.

Wanklin   We're with you in theory, Chairman. But we're not all made of cast-iron.

Anthony   We've only to hold on.

Wilder (*rising and going to the fire*)   And go to the devil as fast as we can!

Anthony   Better go to the devil than give in!

Wilder (*fretfully*)   That may suit you, sir, but it doesn't suit me, or anyone else I should think.

Anthony *looks him in the face – a silence.*

Edgar   I don't see how we can get over it that to go on like this means starvation to the men's wives and families.

Wilder *turns abruptly to the fire, and* **Scantlebury** *puts out a hand to push the idea away.*

Wanklin   I'm afraid again that sounds a little sentimental.

Edgar   Men of business are excused from decency, you think?

Wilder   Nobody's more sorry for the men than I am, but if they (*Lashing himself.*) choose to be such a pig-headed lot, it's nothing to do with us; we've quite enough on *our* hands to think of ourselves and the shareholders.

Edgar (*irritably*)   It won't kill the shareholders to miss a dividend or two; I don't see that *that's* reason enough for knuckling under.

Scantlebury (*with grave discomfort*)   You talk very lightly of your dividends, young man; I don't know where we are.

Wilder   There's only one sound way of looking at it. We can't go on ruining *ourselves* with this strike.

Anthony   No caving in!

Scantlebury (*with a gesture of despair*)   Look at him! **Anthony** *is leaning back in his chair. They do look at him.*

Wilder (*returning to his seat*)   Well, all I can say is, if that's the Chairman's view, I don't know what we've come down here for.

Anthony   To tell the men that we've got nothing for them – (*Grimly.*) They won't believe it till they hear it spoken in plain English.

Wilder   H'm! Shouldn't be a bit surprised if that brute Roberts hadn't got us down here with the very same idea. I hate a man with a grievance.

Edgar (*resentfully*)   We didn't pay him enough for his discovery. I always said that at the time.

Wilder   We paid him five hundred and a bonus of two hundred three years later. If that's not enough! What does he want for goodness sake?

Tench (*complainingly*)   Company made a hundred thousand out of his brains, and paid him seven hundred – that's the way he goes on, sir.

Wilder   The man's a rank agitator! Look here, I hate the Unions. But now we've got Harness here let's get him to settle the whole thing.

Anthony   No!

Again they look at him.

Underwood   Roberts won't let the men assent to that.

Scantlebury   Fanatic! Fanatic!

Wilder (*looking at* **Anthony**)   And not the only one!

Frost *enters from the hall.*

Frost (*to* **Anthony**)   Mr Harness from the Union, waiting, sir. The men are here too, sir.

Anthony *nods.* **Underwood** *goes to the door, returning with* **Harness**, *a pale, clean-shaven man with hollow cheeks, quick eyes and lantern jaw –* **Frost** *has retired.*

Underwood (*pointing to* **Tench**'s *chair*)   Sit there next the Chairman, Harness, won't you?

At **Harness**'s *appearance, the Board have drawn together, as it were, and turned a little to him, like cattle at a dog.*

Harness (*with a sharp look round, and a bow*)   Thanks! (*He sits – his accent is slightly nasal.*) Well, gentlemen, we're going to do business at last, I hope.

Wilder   Depends on what you *call* business, Harness. Why don't you make the men come in?

Harness (*sardonically*)   The men are far more in the right than you are. The question with us is whether we shan't begin to support them again.

He ignores them all, except **Anthony**, *to whom he turns in speaking*.

Anthony   Support them if you like; we'll put in free labour and have done with it.

Harness   That won't do, Mr Anthony. You can't get free labour, and you know it.

Anthony   We shall see that.

Harness   I'm quite frank with you. We were forced to withhold our support from your men because some of their demands are in excess of current rates. I expect to make them withdraw those demands today: if they do, take it straight from me, gentlemen, we shall back them again at once. Now, I want to see something fixed up before I go back tonight. Can't we have done with this old-fashioned tug-of-war business? What good's it doing you? Why don't you recognize once for all that these people are men like yourselves, and want what's good for them just as you want what's good for you – (*Bitterly*.) Your motor-cars, and champagne, and eight-course dinners.

Anthony   If the men will come in, we'll do something for them.

Harness (*ironically*)   Is that your opinion too, sir – and yours – and yours? (*The Directors do not answer*.) Well, all I can say is: It's a kind of high and mighty aristocratic tone I thought we'd grown out of – seems I was mistaken.

Anthony   It's the tone the men use. Remains to be seen which can hold out longest – they without us, or we without them.

Harness   As business men, I wonder you're not ashamed of this waste of force, gentlemen. You know what it'll all end in.

Anthony   What?

Harness   Compromise – it always does.

Scantlebury Can't you persuade the men that their interests are the same as ours?

Harness (*turning ironically*) I could persuade them of that, sir, if they were.

Wilder Come, Harness, you're a clever man, you don't believe all the Socialistic claptrap that's talked nowadays. There's no real difference between their interests and ours.

Harness There's just one very simple little question I'd like to put to you. Will you pay your men one penny more than they force you to pay them?

Wilder *is silent.*

Wanklin (*chiming in*) I humbly thought that not to pay more than was necessary was the A B C of commerce.

Harness (*with irony*) Yes, that seems to be the A B C of commerce, sir; and the A B C of commerce is between your interests and the men's.

Scantlebury (*whispering*) We ought to arrange something.

Harness (*dryly*) Am I to understand then, gentlemen, that your Board is going to make no concessions?

Wanklin and **Wilder** *bend forward as if to speak, but stop.*

Anthony (*nodding*) None.

Wanklin and **Wilder** *again bend forward, and* **Scantlebury** *gives an unexpected grunt.*

Harness You were about to say something, I believe?

But **Scantlebury** *says nothing.*

Edgar (*looking up suddenly*) We're sorry for the state of the men.

Harness (*icily*) The men have no use for your pity, sir. What they want is justice.

Anthony Then let *them* be just.

Harness For that word 'just' read 'humble', Mr Anthony. Why should they be humble? Barring the accident of money, aren't they as good men as you?

Anthony   Cant!

Harness   Well, I've been five years in America. It colours a man's notions.

Scantlebury (*suddenly, as though avenging his uncompleted grunt*)   Let's have the men in and hear what they've got to say!

Anthony *nods, and* **Underwood** *goes out by the single door.*

Harness (*dryly*)   As I'm to have an interview with them this afternoon, gentlemen, I'll ask you to postpone your final decision till that's over.

Again **Anthony** *nods, and taking up his glass drinks.* **Underwood** *comes in again, followed by* **Roberts**, **Green**, **Bulgin**, **Thomas**, **Rous**. *They file in, hat in hand, and stand silent in a row.* **Roberts** *is lean, of middle height, with a slight stoop. He has a little ratgnawn, brown-grey beard, moustaches, high cheekbones, hollow cheeks, small fiery eyes. He wears an old and grease-stained, blue serge suit, and carries an old bowler hat. He stands nearest the Chairman.* **Green**, *next to him, has a clean, worn face, with a small grey-goatee beard and drooping moustaches, iron spectacles, and mild, straightforward eyes. He wears an overcoat, green with age, and a linen collar. Next to him is* **Bulgin**, *a tall, strong man, with a dark moustache, and fighting jaw, wearing a red muffler, who keeps changing his cap from one hand to the other. Next to him is* **Thomas**, *an old man with a grey moustache, full beard, and weatherbeaten, bony face, whose overcoat discloses a lean, plucked-looking neck. On his right,* **Rous**, *the youngest of the five, looks like a soldier; he has a glitter in his eyes.*

Underwood (*pointing*)   There are some chairs there against the wall, Roberts; won't you draw them up and sit down?

Roberts   Thank you, Mr Underwood; we'll stand – in the presence of the Board. (*He speaks in a biting and staccato voice, rolling his r's, pronouncing his a's like an Italian a, and his consonants short and crisp.*) How are you, Mr Harness? Didn't expect t' have the pleasure of seeing you till this afternoon.

Harness (*steadily*)   We shall meet again then, Roberts.

Roberts   Glad to hear that; we shall have some news for you to take to your people.

Anthony   What do the men want?

Roberts (*acidly*)   Beg pardon, I don't quite catch the Chairman's remark.

Tench (*from behind the Chairman's chair*)   The Chairman wishes to know what the men have to say.

Roberts   It's what the Board has to say we've come to hear. It's for the Board to speak first.

Anthony   The Board has nothing to say.

Roberts (*looking along the line of men*)   In that case we're wasting the Directors' time. We'll be taking our feet off this pretty carpet.

He turns, the men move slowly, as though hypnotically influenced.

Wanklin (*suavely*)   Come, Roberts, you didn't give us this long cold journey for the pleasure of saying that.

Thomas (*a pure Welshman*)   No, sir, an', what I say iss –

Roberts (*bitingly*)   Go on, Henry Thomas, go on. You're better able to speak to die – Directors than me.

Thomas *is silent.*

Tench   The Chairman means, Roberts, that it was the men who asked for the conference, the Board wish to hear what they have to say.

Roberts   Gad! If I was to begin to tell ye all they have to say, I wouldn't be finished today. And there'd be some that'd wish they'd never left their London palaces.

Harness   What's your proposition, man? Be reasonable.

Roberts   You want reason, Mr Harness? Take a look round this afternoon before the meeting. (*He looks at the men; no sound escapes them.*) You'll see some very pretty scenery.

Harness   All right, my friend; you won't put me off.

Roberts (*to the men*)   We shan't put Mr Harness off. Have some champagne with your lunch, Mr Harness; you'll want it, sir.

Harness   Come, get to business, man!

Thomas   What we're asking, look you, is just simple justice.

Roberts (*venomously*)   Justice from London? What are you talking about, Henry Thomas? Have you gone silly? (**Thomas** *is silent.*) We know very well what we are – discontented dogs – never satisfied. What did the Chairman tell me up in London? That I didn't know what I was talking about. I was a foolish, uneducated man, that knew nothing of the wants of the men I spoke for.

Edgar   Do please keep to the point.

Anthony (*holding up his hand*)   There can only be one master, Roberts.

Roberts   Then, be Gad, it'll be us.

There is a silence; **Anthony** *and* **Roberts** *stare at one another.*

Underwood   If you've nothing to say to the Directors, Roberts, perhaps you'll let Green or Thomas speak for the men.

Green *and* **Thomas** *look anxiously at* **Roberts**, *at each other, and the other men.*

Green (*an Englishman*)   If I'd been listened to, gentlemen –

Thomas   What I'fe got to say iss what we'fe all got to say –

Roberts   Speak for yourself, Henry Thomas.

Scantlebury (*with a gesture of deep spiritual discomfort*)   Let the poor men call their souls their own!

Roberts   Aye, they shall keep their souls, for it's not much body that you've left them, Mr (*With biting emphasis, as though the word were an offence.*) Scantlebury! (*To the men.*) Well, will you speak, or shall I speak for you?

Rous (*suddenly*)   Speak out, Roberts, or leave it to others.

Roberts (*ironically*)   Thank you, George Rous. (*Addressing himself to* **Anthony**.) The Chairman and Board of Directors have honoured us by leaving London and coming all this way to hear what we've got to say; it would not be polite to keep them any longer waiting.

Wilder   Well, thank God for that!

Roberts   Ye will not dare to thank Him when I have done, Mr Wilder, for all your piety. May be your God up in London has no time to listen to the working man. I'm told He is a wealthy God; but if He listens to what I tell Him, He will know more than ever He learned in Kensington.

Harness   Come, Roberts, you have your own God. Respect the God of other men.

Roberts   That's right, sir. We have another God down here; I doubt He is rather different to Mr Wilder's. Ask Henry Thomas; he will tell you whether his God and Mr Wilder's are the same.

Thomas *lifts his hand, and cranes his head as though to prophesy.*

Wanklin   For goodness' sake, let's keep to the point, Roberts.

Roberts   I rather think it is the point, Mr Wanklin. If you can get the God of Capital to walk through the streets of Labour, and pay attention to what he sees, you're a brighter man than I take you for, for all that you're a Radical.

Anthony   Attend to me, Roberts! (**Roberts** *is silent.*) You are here to speak for the men, as I am here to speak for the Board. (*He looks slowly round.*)

Wilder, **Wanklin**, *and* **Scantlebury** *make movements of uneasiness, and* **Edgar** *gazes at the floor. A faint smile comes on* **Harness'** *face.*

Anthony   Now then, what is it?

Roberts   Right, sir!

Throughout all that follows, he and **Anthony** *look fixedly upon each other. Men and Directors show in their various ways suppressed uneasiness, as though listening to words that they themselves would not have spoken.*

Roberts   The men can't afford to travel up to London; and they don't trust you to believe what they say in black and white. They know what the post is (*He darts a look at* **Underwood** *and* **Tench**.), and what Directors' meetings are: 'Refer to the Manager – let the Manager advise us on the men's condition. Can we squeeze them a little more?'

Underwood (*in a low voice*)   Don't hit below the belt, Roberts!

Roberts   Is it below the belt, Mr Underwood? The men know.
When I came up to London, I told you the position straight.
An' what came of it? I was told I didn't know what I was talkin'
about. I can't afford to travel up to London to be told that
again.

Anthony   What have you to say for the men?

Roberts   I have this to say – and first as to their condition. Ye
shall 'ave no need to go and ask your Manager. Ye can't squeeze
them any more. Every man of us is well-nigh starving. (*A surprised
murmur rises from the men.* **Roberts** *looks round.*) Ye wonder why I tell
ye that? Every man of us is going short. We can't be no worse off
than we've been these weeks past. Ye needn't think that by waiting
ye'll drive us to come in. We'll die first, the whole lot of us. The
men have sent for ye to know, once and for all, whether ye are
going to grant them their demands. I see the sheet of paper in
the Secretary's hand. (**Tench** *moves nervously.*) That's it, I think,
Mr Tench. It's not very large.

Tench (*nodding*)   Yes.

Roberts   There's not one sentence of writing on that paper
that we can do without.

A movement amongst the men. **Roberts** *turns on them sharply.*

Roberts   Isn't that so?

The men assent reluctantly. **Anthony** *takes from* **Tench** *the paper and
peruses it.*

Roberts   Not one single sentence. All those demands are fair.
We have not asked anything that we are not entitled to ask. What
I said up in London, I say again now: there is not anything on
that piece of paper that a just man should not ask, and a just man
give.

A pause.

Anthony   There is not one single demand on this paper that we
will grant.

In the stir that follows on these words, **Roberts** *watches the Directors and*
Anthony *the men.* **Wilder** *gets up abruptly and goes over to the fire.*

Roberts   D'ye mean that?

Anthony   I do.

Wilder *at the fire makes an emphatic movement of disgust.*

Roberts (*noting it, with dry intensity*)   Ye best know whether the condition of the Company is any better than the condition of the men. (*Scanning the Directors' faces.*) Ye best know whether ye can afford your tyranny – but this I tell ye: If ye think the men will give way the least part of an inch, ye're making the worst mistake ye ever made. (*He fixes his eyes on* **Scantlebury**.) Ye think because the Union is not supporting us – more shame to it! – that we'll be coming on our knees to you one fine morning. Ye think because the men have got their wives an' families to think of – that it's just a question of a week or two –

Anthony   It would be better if you did not speculate so much on what we think.

Roberts   Aye! It's not much profit to us! I will say this for you, Mr Anthony – ye know your own mind! (*Staring at* **Anthony**.) I can reckon on ye!

Anthony (*ironically*)   I am obliged to you!

Roberts   And I know mine. I tell ye this. The men will send their wives and families where the country will have to keep them; an' they will starve sooner than give way. I advise ye, Mr Anthony, to prepare yourself for the worst that can happen to your Company. We are not so ignorant as you, might suppose. We know the way the cat is jumping. Your position is not all that it might be – not exactly!

Anthony   Be good enough to allow, us to judge of our position for ourselves. Go back, and reconsider your own.

Roberts (*stepping forward*)   Mr Anthony, you are not a young man now; from the time that I remember anything ye have been an enemy to every man that has come into your works. I don't say that ye're a mean man, or a cruel man, but ye've grudged them the say of any word in their own fate. Ye've fought them down four times. I've heard ye say ye love a fight – mark my words – ye're fighting the last fight ye'll ever fight –

Tench *touches* **Roberts'** *sleeve.*

Underwood   Roberts! Roberts!

Roberts   Roberts! Roberts! I mustn't speak my mind to the Chairman, but the Chairman may speak his mind to me!

Wilder   What are things coming to?

Anthony (*with a grim smile at* **Wilder**)   Go on, Roberts; say what you like.

Roberts (*after a pause*)   I have no more to say.

Anthony   The meeting stands adjourned to five o'clock.

Wanklin (*in a low voice to* **Underwood**)   We shall never settle anything like this.

Roberts (*bitingly*)   We thank the Chairman and Board of Directors for their gracious hearing.

He moves towards the door; the men cluster together stupefied; then **Rous***, throwing up his head, passes* **Roberts** *and goes out. The others follow.*

Roberts (*with his hand on the door – maliciously*)   Good day, gentlemen!

He goes out.

Harness (*ironically*)   I congratulate you on the conciliatory spirit that's been displayed. With your permission, gentlemen, I'll be with you again at half-past five. Good morning!

He bows slightly, rests his eyes on **Anthony***, who returns his stare unmoved, and, followed by* **Underwood***, goes out. There is a moment of uneasy silence.* **Underwood** *reappears in the doorway.*

Wilder (*with emphatic disgust*)   Well!

The double doors are opened.

Enid (*standing in the doorway*)   Lunch is ready.

Edgar*, getting up abruptly, walks out past his sister.*

Wilder   Coming to lunch, Scantlebury?

Scantlebury (*rising heavily*)   I suppose so, I suppose so. It's the only thing we can do.

They go out through the double doors.

Wanklin (*in a low voice*)   Do you really mean to fight to a finish, Chairman?

Anthony *nods.*

Wanklin   Take care! The essence of things is to know when to stop.

Anthony *does not answer.*

Wanklin (*very gravely*)   This way disaster lies. The ancient Trojans were fools to your father, Mrs Underwood.

He goes out through the double doors.

Enid   I want to speak to father, Frank.

Underwood *follows* **Wanklin** *out.* **Tench**, *passing round the table, is restoring order to the scattered pens and papers.*

Enid   Aren't you coming, dad?

Anthony *shakes his head.* **Enid** *looks meaningly at* **Tench**.

Enid   Won't you go and have some lunch, Mr Tench.

Tench (*with papers in his hand*) Thank you, ma'am, thank you!

He goes slowly, looking back.

Enid (*shutting the doors*)   I *do* hope it's settled, father!

Anthony   No!

Enid (*very disappointed*)   Oh! Haven't you done anything?

Anthony *shakes his head.*

Enid   Frank says they all want to come to a compromise, really, except that man Roberts.

Anthony   *I* don't.

Enid   It's such a horrid position for us. If you were the wife of the Manager, and lived down here, and saw it all. You can't realize, dad!

Anthony   Indeed?

Enid We see *all* the distress. You remember my maid Annie, who married Roberts? (**Anthony** *nods.*) It's so wretched, her heart's weak; since the strike began, she hasn't even been getting proper food. I know it for a fact, father.

Anthony Give her what she wants, poor woman!

Enid Roberts won't let her take anything from *us*.

Anthony (*staring before him*) I can't be answerable for the men's obstinacy.

Enid They're all suffering. Father! Do stop it, for my sake!

Anthony (*with a keen look at her*). You don't understand, my dear.

Enid If I were on the Board, I'd do something.

Anthony What would you do?

Enid It's because you can't bear to give way. It's so –

Anthony Well?

Enid So unnecessary.

Anthony What do *you* know about necessity? Read your novels, play your music, talk your talk, but don't try and tell *me* what's at the bottom of a struggle like this.

Enid I live down here; and see it.

Anthony What d'you imagine stands between you and your class and these men that you're so sorry for?

Enid (*coldly*) I don't know what you mean, father.

Anthony In a few years you and your children would be down in the condition they're in, but for those who have the eyes to see things as they are and the backbone to stand up for themselves.

Enid You don't know the state the men are in.

Anthony I know it well enough.

Enid You don't, father; if you did, you wouldn't –

Anthony It's you who don't know the simple facts of the position. What sort of mercy do you suppose you'd get if no one stood between you and the continual demands of labour? This sort of mercy – (*He puts his hand up to his throat and squeezes it.*) First would go your sentiments, my dear; then your culture, and your comforts would be going all the time!

Enid I don't believe in barriers between classes.

Anthony You – don't – believe – in – barriers – between the classes?

Enid (*coldly*) And I don't know what that has to do with this question.

Anthony It will take a generation or two for you to understand.

Enid It's only you and Roberts, father, and you know it!

Anthony *thrusts out his lower lip.*

Enid It'll ruin the Company.

Anthony Allow me to judge of that.

Enid (*resentfully*) I won't stand by and let poor Annie Roberts suffer like this! And think of the children, father! I warn you.

Anthony (*with a grim smile*). What do you propose to do?

Enid That's my affair.

Anthony *only looks at her.*

Enid (*in a changed voice, stroking his sleeve*) Father, you *know* you oughtn't to have this strain on you – you know what Dr Fisher said!

Anthony No old man can afford to listen to old women.

Enid But you *have* done enough, even if it really is such a matter of principle with you.

Anthony You think so?

Enid Don't, dad! (*Her face works.*) You – you might think of *us!*

Anthony I am.

Enid It'll break you down.

Anthony (*slowly*) My dear, I am not going to funk; you may rely on that.

Re-enter **Tench** *with papers; he glances at them, then plucking up courage.*

Tench   Beg pardon, madam, I think I'd rather see these papers were disposed of before I get my lunch.

Enid, *after an impatient glance at him, looks at her father, turns suddenly, and goes into the drawing-room.*

Tench (*holding the papers and a pen to* **Anthony**, *very nervously*)   Would you sign these for me, please sir?

Anthony *takes the pen and signs.*

Tench (*standing with a sheet of blotting-paper behind* **Edgar***'s chair, begins speaking nervously*)   I owe my position to you, sir.

Anthony   Well?

Tench   I'm obliged to see everything that's going on, sir; I – I depend upon the Company entirely. If anything were to happen to it, it'd be disastrous for me. (**Anthony** *nods.*) And, of course, my wife's just had another; and so it makes me doubly anxious just now. And the rates are really terrible down our way.

Anthony (*with grim amusement*)   Not more terrible than they are up mine.

Tench   No, sir? (*Very nervously.*) I know the Company means a great deal to you, sir.

Anthony   It does; I founded it.

Tench   Yes, sir. If the strike goes on it'll be very serious. I think the Directors are beginning to realize that, sir.

Anthony (*ironically*)   Indeed?

Tench   I know you hold very strong views, sir, and it's always your habit to look things in the face; but I don't think the Directors – like it, sir, now they – they see it.

Anthony (*grimly*)   Nor you, it seems.

Tench (*with the ghost of a smile*)   No, sir; of course I've got my children, and my wife's delicate; in my position I *have* to think of these things, (**Anthony** *nods.*) It wasn't *that* I was going to say, sir, if you'll excuse me (*Hesitates.*) –

Anthony   Out with it, then!

Tench   I know – from my own father, sir, that when you get on in life you do feel things dreadfully –

Anthony (*almost paternally*)   Come, out with it, Tench!

Tench   I don't *like* to say it, sir.

Anthony (*stonily*)   You must.

Tench (*after a pause, desperately bolting it out*)   I think the Directors are going to throw you over, sir.

Anthony (*sits in silence*)   Ring the bell!

Tench *nervously rings the bell and stands by the fire.*

Tench   Excuse me saying such a thing. I was *only* thinking of you, sir.

Frost *enters from the hall, he comes to the foot of the table, and looks at* **Anthony**; **Tench** *covers his nervousness by arranging papers.*

Anthony   Bring me a whisky and soda.

Frost   Anything to eat, sir?

Anthony *shakes his head –* **Frost** *goes to the sideboard, and prepares the drink.*

Tench (*in a low voice, almost supplicating*)   If you *could* see your way, sir, it would be a great relief to my mind, it would indeed. (*He looks up at* **Anthony**, *who has not moved.*) It does make me so very anxious. I haven't slept properly for weeks, sir, and that's a fact.

Anthony *looks in his face, then slowly shakes his head.*

Tench (*disheartened*)   No, sir?

He goes on arranging papers. **Frost** *places the whisky and soda on a salver and puts it down by* **Anthony**'s *right hand. He stands away, looking gravely at* **Anthony**.

Frost   *Nothing* I can get you, sir? (**Anthony** *shakes his head.*) You're aware, sir, of what the doctor said, sir?

Anthony   I am.

A pause. **Frost** *suddenly moves closer to him, and speaks in a low voice.*

Frost   This strike, sir; puttin' all this strain on you. Excuse me, sir, is it – is it worth it, sir?

Anthony *mutters some words that are inaudible.*

Frost   Very good, sir!

He turns and goes out into the hall – **Tench** *makes two attempts to speak; but meeting his Chairman's gaze he drops his eyes, and turning dismally, he too goes out.* **Anthony** *is left alone. He grips the glass, tilts it, and drinks deeply; then sets it down with a deep and rumbling sigh, and leans back in his chair.*

The curtain falls.

Act Two

Scene One

It is half-past three. In the kitchen of **Roberts'** *cottage a meagre little fire is burning. The room is clean and tidy, very barely furnished, with a brick floor and white-washed walls, much stained with smoke. There is a kettle on the fire. A door opposite the fireplace opens inwards from a snowy street. On the wooden table are a cup and saucer, a teapot, knife, and plate of bread and cheese. Close to the fireplace in an old armchair, wrapped in a rug, sits* **Mrs Roberts,** *a thin and dark-haired woman about thirty-five, with patient eyes. Her hair is not done up, but tied back with a piece of ribbon. By the fire, too, is* **Mrs Yeo,** *a red-haired, broad-faced person. Sitting near the table is* **Mrs Rous,** *an old lady, ashen-white, with silver hair; by the door, standing, as if about to go, is* **Mrs Bulgin,** *a little pale, pinched-up woman. In a chair, with her elbows resting on the table, and her face resting in her hands sits* **Madge Thomas,** *a good-looking girl, of twenty-two, with high cheekbones, deep-set eyes, and dark, untidy hair. She is listening to the talk but she neither speaks nor moves.*

Mrs Yeo   So he give me a sixpence, and that's the first bit o' money *I* seen this week. There an't much 'eat to this fire. Come and warm yerself, Mrs Rous, you're lookin' as white as the snow, you are.

Mrs Rous (*shivering – placidly*)   Ah! but the winter my old man was took was the proper winter. Seventy-nine that was, when none of you was hardly born – not Madge Thomas, nor Sue Bulgin. (*Looking at them in turn.*) Annie Roberts, 'ow old were you, dear?

Mrs Roberts   Seven, Mrs Rous.

Mrs Rous   Seven – well ther'! A tiny little thing!

Mrs Yeo (*aggressively*)   Well, I was ten myself, *I* remembers it.

Mrs Rous (*placidly*)   The Company hadn't been started three years. Father was workin' on the acid that's 'ow he got 'is pisoned leg. I kep' sayin' to 'im 'Father, you've got a pisoned leg.' 'Well,' 'e said, 'Mother, pison or no pison, I can't afford to go a-layin' up.'

An' two days after he was on 'is back, and never got up again. It was Providence! There wasn't none o' these Compension Acts then.

Mrs Yeo   Ye hadn't no strike that winter! (*With grim humour.*) This winter's 'ard enough for me. Mrs Roberts, you don't want no 'arder winter, do you? Wouldn't seem natural to 'ave a dinner, would it, Mrs Bulgin?

Mrs Bulgin   We've had bread and tea last four days.

Mrs Yeo   You got that Friday's laundry job?

Mrs Bulgin (*dispiritedly*)   They said they'd give it me, but when I went last Friday, they were full up. I got to go again next week.

Mrs Yeo   Ah! There's too many after that. I send Yeo out on the ice to put on the gentry's skates an' pick up what 'e can. Stops 'im from broodin' about the 'ouse.

Mrs Bulgin (*in a desolate, matter-of-fact voice*)   Leavin' out the men – it's bad enough with the children. I keep 'em in bed, they don't get so hungry when they're not running about; but they're that restless in bed they worry your life out.

Mrs Yeo   You're lucky they're all so small. It's the goin' to school that makes 'em 'ungry. Don't Bulgin give you *any*thin'?

Mrs Bulgin (*shakes her head, then, as though by after-thought*)   Would if he could, I s'pose.

Mrs Yeo (*sardonically*)   What! 'Aven't 'e got no shares in the Company?

Mrs Rous (*rising with tremendous cheerfulness*)   Well, goodbye, Annie Roberts, I'm going along home.

Mrs Roberts   Stay an' have a cup of tea, Mrs Rous?

Mrs Rous (*with the faintest smile*)   Roberts'll want 'is tea when he comes in. I'll just go an' get to bed; it's warmer there than anywhere.

She moves very shakily towards the door.

Mrs Yeo (*rising and giving her an arm*)   Come on, mother, take my arm; we're all goin' the same way.

Mrs Rous (*taking the arm*)   Thank you, my dearies!

They go out, followed by **Mrs Bulgin**.

Madge (*moving for the first time*)   There, Annie, you see that! I told George Rous, 'Don't think to have my company till you've made an end of all this trouble. You ought to be ashamed,' I said, 'with your own mother looking like a ghost, and not a stick to put on the fire. So long as you're able to fill your pipes, you'll let us starve.' 'I'll take my oath, Madge,' he said, 'I've not had smoke nor drink these three weeks!' 'Well, then, why do you go on with it?' 'I can't go back on Roberts!' . . . That's it! Roberts, always Roberts! They'd all drop it but for him. When *he* talks it's the devil that comes into them. (*A silence.* **Mrs Roberts** *makes a movement of pain.*) Ah! *You* don't want him beaten! He's your man. With everybody like their own shadows! (*She makes a gesture towards* **Mrs Roberts**.) If Rous wants me he must give up Roberts. If *he* gave him up – they all would. They're only waiting for a lead. Father's against him – they're all against him in their hearts.

Mrs Roberts   You won't beat Roberts! (*They look silently at each other.*)

Madge   Won't I? The cowards – when their own mothers and their own children don't know where to turn.

Mrs Roberts   Madge!

Madge (*looking searchingly at* **Mrs Roberts**)   I wonder he can look *you* in the face. (*She squats before the fire, with her hands out to the flame.*) Harness is here again. They'll have to make up their minds today.

Mrs Roberts (*in a soft, slow voice, with a slight West-country burr*)   Roberts will never give up the furnacemen and engineers. 'Twouldn't be right.

Madge   You can't deceive me. It's just his pride.

A tapping at the door is heard, the women turn as **Enid** *enters. She wears a round fur cap, and a jacket of squirrel's fur. She closes the door behind her.*

Enid   Can I come in, Annie?

Mrs Roberts (*flinching*)   Miss Enid! Give Mrs Underwood a chair, Madge.

Madge *gives* **Enid** *the chair she has been sitting on.*

Enid   Thank you! Are you any better?

Mrs Roberts   Yes, m'm; thank you, m'm.

Enid (*looking at the sullen* **Madge** *as though requesting her departure*)   Why did you send back the jelly? I call that really wicked of you!

Mrs Roberts   Thank you, m'm, I'd no need for it.

Enid   Of course! It was Roberts' doing, wasn't it? How can he let all this suffering go on amongst you?

Madge (*suddenly*)   What suffering?

Enid (*surprised*)   I beg your pardon?

Madge   Who said there was suffering?

Mrs Roberts   Madge!

Madge (*throwing her shawl over her head*)   Please to let us keep ourselves to ourselves. We don't want you coming here and spying on us.

Enid (*confronting her, but without rising*)   I didn't speak to you.

Madge (*in a low, fierce voice*)   Keep your kind feelings to yourself. You think you can come amongst us, but you're mistaken. Go back and tell the Manager that.

Enid (*stonily*)   This is not your house.

Madge (*turning to the door*)   No, it is not my house; keep clear of my house, Mrs Underwood.

She goes out. **Enid** *taps her fingers on the table.*

Mrs Roberts   Please to forgive Madge Thomas, m'm; she's a bit upset today.

A pause.

Enid (*looking at her*)   Oh, I think they're so *stupid,* all of them.

Mrs Roberts (*with a faint smile*)   Yes, m'm.

Enid   Is Roberts out?

Mrs Roberts   Yes, m'm.

Enid   It is *his doing,* that they don't come to an agreement. Now isn't it, Annie?

Mrs Roberts   (*softly, with her eyes on* **Enid**, *and moving the fingers of one hand continually on her breast*)   They do say that your father, m'm –

Enid   My father's getting an old man, and you know what old men are.

Mrs Roberts   I am sorry, m'm.

Enid   (*more softly*)   I don't expect *you* to feel sorry, Annie. I know it's his fault as well as Roberts'.

Mrs Roberts   I'm sorry for anyone that gets old, m'm; it's dreadful to get old, and Mr Anthony was such a fine old man I always used to think.

Enid   (*impulsively*)   He always liked you, don't you remember? Look here, Annie, what can I do? I do so want to know. You don't get what you ought to have. (*Going to the fire, she takes the kettle off, and looks for coals.*) And you're so naughty sending back the soup and things!

Mrs Roberts   (*with a faint smile*)   Yes, m'm?

Enid   (*resentfully*)   Why, you haven't even got coals?

Mrs Roberts   If you please, m'm, to put the kettle on again; Roberts won't have long for his tea when he comes in. He's got to meet the men at four.

Enid   (*putting the kettle on*)   That means he'll lash them into a fury again. Can't you stop his going, Annie? (**Mrs Roberts** *smiles ironically.*) Have you tried? (*A silence.*) Does he know how ill you are?

Mrs Roberts   It's only my weak 'eart, m'm.

Enid   You used to be so well when you were with us.

Mrs Roberts   (*stiffening*)   Roberts is always good to me.

Enid   But you ought to have everything you want, and you have nothing!

Mrs Roberts (*appealingly*)   They tell me I don't look like a dyin' woman?

Enid   Of course you don't; if you could only have proper – Will you see my doctor if I send him to you? I'm sure he'd do you good.

Mrs Roberts (*with faint questioning*)   Yes, m'm.

Enid   Madge Thomas oughtn't to come here; she only excites you. As if I didn't know what suffering there is amongst the men! I do feel for them dreadfully, but you know they *have* gone too far.

Mrs Roberts (*continually moving her fingers*)   They say there's no other way to get better wages, m'm.

Enid (*earnestly*)   But, Annie, that's why the Union won't help them. My husband's very sympathetic with the men, but he says they're not underpaid.

Mrs Roberts   No, m'm?

Enid   They never think how the Company could go on if we paid the wages they want.

Mrs Roberts (*with an effort*)   But the dividends having been so big, m'm.

Enid (*taken aback*)   You all seem to think the shareholders are rich men, but they're not – most of them are really no better off than working men. (**Mrs Roberts** *smiles.*) They have to keep up appearances.

Mrs Roberts   Yes, m'm?

Enid   You don't have to pay rates and taxes, and a hundred other things that they do. If the men didn't spend such a lot in drink and betting they'd be quite well off!

Mrs Roberts   They say, workin' so hard, they must have some pleasure.

Enid   But surely not low pleasure like that.

Mrs Roberts (*a little resentfully*)   Roberts never touches a drop; and he's never had a bet in his life.

Enid   Oh! but he's not a com – I mean he's an engineer – a superior man.

Mrs Roberts   Yes, m'm. Roberts says they've no chance of other pleasures.

Enid (*musing*)   Of course, I know it's hard.

Mrs Roberts (*with a spice of malice*)   And they say gentlefolk's just as bad.

Enid (*with a smile*)   I go as far as most people, Annie, but you know, yourself, that's nonsense.

Mrs Roberts (*with painful effort*)   A lot o' the men never go near the Public; but even they don't save but very little, and that goes if there's illness.

Enid   But they've got their clubs, haven't they?

Mrs Roberts   The clubs only give up to eighteen shillin's a week, m'm, and it's not much amongst a family. Roberts says workin' folk have always lived from hand to mouth. Sixpence today is worth more than a shillin' tomorrow, that's what they say.

Enid   But that's the spirit of gambling.

Mrs Roberts (*with a sort of excitement*)   Roberts says a working man's life is all a gamble, from the time 'e's born to the time 'e dies.

Enid *leans forward, interested.* **Mrs Roberts** *goes on with a growing excitement that culminates in the personal feeling of the last words.*

Mrs Roberts   He says, m'm, that when a working man's baby is born, it's a toss-up from breath to breath whether it ever draws another, and so on all 'is life; an' when he comes to be old, it's the workhouse or the grave. He says that without a man is very near, and pinches and stints 'imself and 'is children to save, there can't be neither surplus nor security. That's why he wouldn't have no children (*She sinks back.*), not though I *wanted* them.

Enid   Yes, yes, I know!

Mrs Roberts   No, you don't, m'm. You've got your children, and you'll never need to trouble for them.

Enid (*gently*)   You oughtn't to be talking so much, Annie. (*Then, in spite of herself.*) But Roberts was paid a lot of money, wasn't he, for discovering that process?

Mrs Roberts (*on the defensive*)   All Roberts' savin's have gone. He's always looked forward to this strike. He says he's no right to a farthing when the others are suffering. 'Tisn't so with all o' them! Some don't seem to care no more than that – so long as they get their own.

Enid   I don't see how they can be expected to when they're suffering like this. (*In a changed voice.*) But Roberts ought to think of *you!* It's all terrible! The kettle's boiling. Shall I make the tea? (*She takes the teapot, and seeing tea there, pours water into it.*) Won't you have a cup?

Mrs Roberts   No, thank you, m'm. (*She is listening, as though for footsteps.*) I'd sooner you didn't see Roberts, m'm, he gets so wild.

Enid   Oh! but I must, Annie; I'll be quite calm, I promise.

Mrs Roberts   It's life an' death to him, m'm.

Enid (*very gently*)   I'll get him to talk to me outside, we won't excite you.

Mrs Roberts (*faintly*)   No, m'm.

She gives a violent start. **Roberts** *has come in, unseen.*

Roberts (*removing his hat – with subtle mockery*)   Beg pardon for coming in; you're engaged with a lady, I see.

Enid   Can I speak to you, Mr Roberts?

Roberts   Whom have I the pleasure of addressing, ma'am?

Enid   But surely you know me! I'm Mrs Underwood.

Roberts (*with a bow of malice*)   The daughter of our Chairman.

Enid (*earnestly*)   I've come on purpose to speak to you; will you come outside a minute?

She looks at **Mrs Roberts**.

Roberts (*hanging up his hat*)   I have nothing to say, ma'am.

Enid   But I *must* speak to you, please.

She moves towards the door.

Roberts (*with sudden venom*)   I have not the time to listen!

Mrs Roberts   David!

Enid   Mr Roberts, *please*!

Roberts (*taking off his overcoat*)   I am sorry to disoblige a lady – Mr Anthony's daughter.

Enid (*wavering, then with sudden decision*)   Mr Roberts, I know you've another meeting of the men. (**Roberts** *bows*.) I came to appeal to you. Please, please try to come to some compromise; give way a little, if it's only for your own sakes!

Roberts (*speaking to himself*)   The daughter of Mr Anthony begs me to give way a little, if it's only for our own sakes.

Enid   For everybody's sake; for your wife's sake.

Roberts   For my wife's sake, for everybody's sake – for the sake of Mr Anthony.

Enid   Why are you so bitter against my father? He has never done anything to you.

Roberts   Has he not?

Enid   He can't help his views, any more than you can help yours.

Roberts   I really didn't know that I had a right to views!

Enid   He's an old man, and you –

Seeing his eyes fixed on her, she stops.

Roberts (*without raising his voice*)   If I saw Mr Anthony going to die, and I could save him by lifting my hand, I would not lift the little finger of it.

Enid   You – you –

She stops again, biting her lips.

Roberts   I would not, and that's flat!

Enid (*coldly*)   You don't mean what you say, and you know it!

Roberts   I mean every word of it.

Enid   But why?

Roberts (*with a flash*)   Mr Anthony stands for tyranny! That's why!

Enid   Nonsense!

Mrs Roberts *makes a movement as if to rise, but sinks back in her chair.*

Enid (*with an impetuous movement*)   Annie!

Roberts   Please not to touch my wife!

Enid (*recoiling with a sort of horror*)   I believe – you are mad.

Roberts   The house of a madman then is not the fit place for a lady.

Enid   I'm not afraid of you.

Roberts (*bowing*)   I would not expect the daughter of Mr Anthony to be afraid. Mr Anthony is not a coward like the rest of them.

Enid (*suddenly*)   I suppose you think it brave, then, to go on with this struggle.

Roberts   Does Mr Anthony think it brave to fight against women and children? Mr Anthony is a rich man, I believe; does he think it brave to fight against those who haven't a penny? Does he think it brave to set children crying with hunger, an' women shivering with cold?

Enid (*putting up her hand, as though warding off a blow*)   My father is acting on his principles, and you know it!

Roberts   And so am I!

Enid   You hate us; and you can't bear to be beaten.

Roberts   Neither can Mr Anthony, for all that he may say.

Enid   At any rate you might have pity on your wife.

Mrs Roberts, *who has her hand pressed to her heart, takes it away, and tries to calm her breathing.*

Roberts   Madam, I have no more to say.

He takes up the loaf. There is a knock at the door, and **Underwood** *comes in. He stands looking at them.* **Enid** *turns to him, then seems undecided.*

Underwood   Enid!

Roberts (*ironically*)   Ye were not needing to come for your wife, Mr Underwood. We are not rowdies.

Underwood   I know that, Roberts. I hope Mrs Roberts is better.

Roberts *turns away without answering.*

Underwood   Come, Enid!

Enid   I make one more appeal to you, Mr Roberts, for the sake of your wife.

Roberts (*with polite malice*)   If I might advise ye, ma'am – make it for the sake of your husband and your father.

Enid, *suppressing a retort, goes out.* **Underwood** *opens the door for her and follows.* **Roberts**, *going to the fire, holds out his hands to the dying glow.*

Roberts   How goes it, my girl? Feeling better, are you?

Mrs Roberts *smiles faintly. He brings his overcoat and wraps it round her.*

Roberts (*looking at his watch*)   Ten minutes to four! (*As though inspired.*) I've seen their faces, there's no fight in them, except for that one old robber.

Mrs Roberts   Won't you stop and eat, David? You've 'ad nothing all day!

Roberts (*putting his hand to his throat*)   Can't swallow till those old sharks are out o' the town. (*He walks up and down.*) I shall have a bother with the men – there's no heart in them, the cowards. Blind as bats, they are – can't see a day before their noses.

Mrs Roberts   It's the women, David.

Roberts   Ah! So they say! They can remember the women when their own bellies speak! The women never stops them from the drink; but from a little suffering to themselves in a sacred cause, the women stop them fast enough.

Mrs Roberts   But think o' the children, David.

Roberts   Ah! If they will go breeding themselves for slaves, without a thought o' the future o' them they breed –

Mrs Roberts (*gasping*)   That's enough, David; don't begin to talk of that – I won't – I can't –

Roberts (*staring at her*)   Now, now, my girl!

Mrs Roberts (*breathlessly*)   No, no, David – I won't!

Roberts   There, there! Come, come! That's right. (*Bitterly.*) Not one penny will they put by for a day like this. Not they! Hand to mouth – Gad! – I know them! They've broke my heart. There was no holdin' them at the start, but now the pinch 'as come.

Mrs Roberts   How can you expect it, David? They're not made of iron.

Roberts   Expect it? Wouldn't I expect what I would do meself? Wouldn't I starve an' rot rather than give in? What one man can do, another can.

Mrs Roberts   And the women?

Roberts   This is not women's work.

Mrs Roberts (*with a flash of malice*)   No, the women may die for all you care. That's their work.

Roberts (*averting his eyes*)   Who talks of dying? No one will die till we have beaten these –

He meets her eyes again, and again turns his away. Excitedly.

Roberts   This is what I've been waiting for all these months. To get the old robbers down, and send them home again without a farthin's worth o' change. I've seen their faces, I tell you, in the valley of the shadow of defeat.

He goes to the peg and takes down his hat.

Mrs Roberts (*following with her eyes – softly*)   Take your overcoat, David; it must be bitter cold.

Roberts (*coming up to her – his eyes are furtive*)   No, no! There, there, stay quiet and warm. I won't be long, my girl!

Mrs Roberts (*with soft bitterness*)   You'd better take it. *She lifts the coat. But* **Roberts** *puts it back, and wraps it round her. He tries to meet her eyes, but cannot.* **Mrs Roberts** *stays huddled in the coat, her eyes, that follow him about, are half malicious, half yearning. He looks at his watch again, and turns to go. In the doorway he meets* **Jan Thomas**, *a boy of ten in clothes too big for him, carrying a penny whistle.*

Roberts   Hallo, boy!

He goes, **Jan** *stops within a yard of* **Mrs Roberts**, *and stares at her without a word.*

Mrs Roberts   Well, Jan!

Jan   Father's coming; sister Madge is coming.

He sits at the table, and fidgets with his whistle; he blows three vague notes; then imitates a cuckoo.

There is a tap on the door. Old **Thomas** *comes in.*

Thomas   A very coot tay to you, ma'am. It is petter that you are.

Mrs Roberts   Thank you, Mr Thomas.

Thomas (*nervously*)   Roberts in?

Mrs Roberts   Just gone on to the meeting, Mr Thomas.

Thomas (*with relief, becoming talkative*)   This is fery unfortunate, look you! I came to tell him that we must make terms with London. It is a fery great pity he is gone to the meeting. He will be kicking against the pricks, I am thinking.

Mrs Roberts (*half rising*)   He'll never give in, Mr Thomas.

Thomas   You must not be fretting, that is very pat for you. Look you, there iss hartly any mans for supporting him now, but the engineers and George Rous. (*Solemnly.*) This strike is no longer coing with Chapel, look you! I have listened carefully an' I have

talked with her. (**Jan** *blows*.) Sst! I don't care what th' others say,
I say that *Chapel means us* to be stopping the trouble, that is what
I make of her; and it is my opinion that this is the fery best thing
for all of us. If it wasn't my opinion, I ton't say – but it is my
opinion, look you.

Mrs Roberts (*trying to suppress her excitement*)   I don't know what'll
come to Roberts, if you give in.

Thomas   It iss no disgrace whateffer! All that a mortal man
coult do he hass tone. It iss against Human Nature he hass gone;
fery natural – any man may to that; but Chapel has spoken and
he must not co against *her*.

Jan *imitates the cuckoo*.

Thomas   Ton't make that squeaking! (*Going to the door*.) Here iss
my taughter come to sit with you. A fery goot day, ma'am – no
fretting – rememper!

Madge *comes in and stands at the open door, watching the street*.

Madge   You'll be late, father; they're beginning. (*She catches him
by the sleeve*.) For the love of God, stand up to him, father – this
time!

Thomas (*detaching his sleeve with dignity*)   Leave me to do what's
proper, girl!

He goes out, **Madge**, *in the centre of the open doorway, slowly moves in, as
though before the approach of someone*.

Rous (*appearing in the doorway*)   Madge!

Madge *stands with her back to* **Mrs Roberts**, *staring at him with her
head up and her hands behind her*.

Rous (*who has a fierce distracted look*)   Madge! I'm going to the
meeting.

Madge, *without moving, smiles contemptuously*.

Rous   D'ye hear me?

They speak in quick low voices.

Madge   I hear! Go, and kill your own mother, if you must.

Rous *seizes her by both her arms. She stands rigid, with her head bent back. He releases her, and he too stands motionless.*

Rous   I swore to stand by Roberts. I swore that! Ye want me to go back on what I've sworn.

Madge (*with slow soft mockery*)   You are a pretty lover!

Rous   Madge!

Madge (*smiling*)   I've heard that lovers do what their girls ask them – (**Jan** *sounds the cuckoo's notes.*) – but that's not true, it seems!

Rous   You'd make a blackleg of me!

Madge (*with her eyes half-closed*)   Do it for me!

Rous (*dashing his hand across his brow*)   Damn! I can't!

Madge (*swiftly*)   Do it for me!

Rous (*through his teeth*)   Don't play the wanton with me!

Madge (*with a movement of her hand towards* **Jan** *– quick and low*)   I'd do *that* to get the children bread!

Rous (*in a fierce whisper*)   Madge! Oh, Madge!

Madge (*with soft mockery*)   But *you* can't break your word with me!

Rous (*with a choke*)   Then, Begod, I can!

He turns and rushes off.

Madge *stands with a faint smile on her face, looking after him. She moves to the table.*

Madge   I have done for Roberts!

She sees that **Mrs Roberts** *has sunk back in her chair.*

Madge (*running to her, and feeling her hands*)   You're as cold as a stone! You want a drop of brandy. Jan, run to the 'Lion'; say I sent you for Mrs Roberts.

Mrs Roberts (*with a feeble movement*)   I'll just sit quiet, Madge. Give Jan – his – tea.

Madge (*giving* **Jan** *a slice of bread*)   There, ye little rascal. Hold your piping. (*Going to the fire, she kneels.*) It's going out.

Mrs Roberts (*with a faint smile*)   'Tis all the same!

Jan *begins to blow his whistle.*

Madge   Tsht! Tsht! – you –

Jan *stops.*

Mrs Roberts (*smiling*)   Let 'im play, Madge.

Madge (*on her knees at the fire, listening*)   Waiting an' waiting. I've no patience with it; waiting an' waiting – that's what a woman has to do! Can you hear them at it – I can!

She leans her elbows on the table, and her chin on her hands. Behind her, **Mrs Roberts** *leans forward, with painful and growing excitement, as the sounds of the strikers' meeting come in.*

The curtain falls.

Scene Two

It is past four. In a grey, failing light, an open muddy space is crowded with workmen. Beyond, divided from it by a barbed-wire fence, is the raised towing-path of a canal, on which is moored a barge. In the distance are marshes and snow-covered hills. The 'Works' high wall runs from the canal across the open space, and in the angle of this wall is a rude platform of barrels and boards. On it, **Harness** *is standing.* **Roberts,** *a little apart from the crowd, leans his back against the wall. On the raised towing-path two bargemen lounge and smoke indifferently.*

Harness (*holding out his hand*)   Well, I've spoken to you straight. If I speak till tomorrow I can't say more.

Jago (*a dark, sallow, Spanish-looking man, with a short, thin beard*)   Mister, want to ask you! Can they get blacklegs?

Bulgin (*menacing*)   Let 'em try.

There are savage murmurs from the crowd.

Brown (*a round-faced man*)   Where could they get 'em then?

Evans (*a small restless, harassed man, with a fighting face*)   There's always blacklegs; it's the nature of 'em. There's always men that'll save their own skins.

Another savage murmur. There is a movement, and old **Thomas**, *joining the crowd, takes his stand in front.*

Harness (*holding up his hand*)   They can't get them. But that won't help you. Now men, be reasonable. Your demands would have brought on us the burden of a dozen strikes at a time when we were not prepared for them. The Unions live by Justice, not to one, but all. Any fair man will tell you – you were ill-advised! I don't say you go too far for that which you're entitled to, but you're going too far for the moment; you've dug a pit for yourselves. Are you to stay there, or are you to climb out? Come!

Lewis (*a clean-cut Welshman with a dark moustache*)   You've hit it, mister! Which is it to be?

Another movement in the crowd, and **Rous**, *coming quickly, takes his stand next* **Thomas**.

Harness   Cut your demands to the right pattern, and we'll see you through; refuse, and don't expect me to waste my time coming down here again. I'm not the sort that speaks at random, as you ought to know by this time. If you're the sound men I take you for – no matter who advises you against it – (*He fixes his eyes on* **Roberts**.) you'll make up your minds to come in, and trust to us to get your terms. Which is it to be? Hands together, and victory – or – the starvation you've got now?

A prolonged murmur from the crowd.

Jago (*sullenly*)   Talk about what you know.

Harness (*lifting his voice above the murmur*)   Know? (*With cold passion.*) All that you've been through, my friend, I've been through – I was through it when I was no bigger than (*Pointing to a youth.*) that shaver there; the Unions then weren't what they are now. What's made them strong? It's hands together that's made them strong. I've been through it all, I tell you, the brand's on my soul yet. I know what you've suffered – there's nothing you can tell me that I don't know; but the whole is greater than the part, and you are only the part. Stand by us, and we will stand by you.

Quartering them with his eyes, he waits. The murmuring swells; the men form little groups. **Green**, **Bulgin**, *and* **Lewis** *talk together.*

Lewis   Speaks very sensible, the Union chap.

Green (*quietly*)   Ah! if I'd a been *listened* to, you'd 'ave 'eard sense these two months past.

The bargemen are seen laughing.

Lewis (*pointing*)   Look at those two blanks over the fence there!

Bulgin (*with gloomy violence*)   They'd best stop their cackle, or I'll break their jaws.

Jago (*suddenly*)   You say the furnacemen's paid enough?

Harness   I did not say they were paid enough; I said they were paid as much as the furnacemen in similar works elsewhere.

Evans   That's a lie. (*Hubbub.*) What about Harper's?

Harness (*with cold irony*)   You may look at home for lies, my man. Harper's shifts are longer, the pay works out the same.

Henry Rous (*a dark edition of his brother George*)   Will ye support us in double pay overtime Saturdays?

Harness   Yes, we will.

Jago   What have ye done with our subscriptions?

Harness (*coldly*)   I have told you what we *will* do with them.

Evans   Ah! *will*, it's always will! Ye'd have our mates desert us.

Hubbub.

Bulgin (*shouting*)   Hold your row!

Evans *looks round angrily.*

Harness (*lifting his voice*)   Those who know their right hands from their lefts know that the Unions are neither thieves nor traitors. I've said my say. Figure it out, my lads; when you want me you know where I shall be.

*He jumps down, the crowd gives way, he passes through them, and goes away. A bargeman looks after him, jerking his pipe with a derisive gesture. The men close up in groups, and many looks are cast at **Roberts**, who stands alone against the wall.*

420   Strife

Evans   He wants ye to turn blacklegs, that's what he wants. He wants ye to go back on us. Sooner than turn blackleg – I'd starve, I would.

Bulgin   Who's talkin' o' blacklegs – mind what you're saying, will you?

Blacksmith (*a youth with yellow hair and huge arms*)   What about the women?

Evans   They can stand what we can stand, I suppose, can't they?

Blacksmith   Ye've no wife?

Evans   An' don't want one.

Thomas (*raising his voice*)   Aye! Give us the power to come to terms with London, lads.

Davies (*a dark, slow-fly, gloomy man*)   Go up the platform, if you got anything to say, go up an' say it.

There are cries of 'Thomas!' He is pushed towards the platform; he ascends it with difficulty, and, bares his head, waiting for silence. A hush!

Red-haired Youth (*suddenly*)   Coot old Thomas!

A hoarse laugh; the bargemen exchange remarks; a hush again, and **Thomas** *begins speaking.*

Thomas   We are all in the tepth together, and it iss Nature that has put us there.

Henry Rous   It's London put us there!

Evans   It's the Union.

Thomas   It iss not London; nor it iss not the Union – it iss Nature. It iss no disgrace whateffer to a potty to give in to Nature. For this Nature iss a fery pig thing; it is pigger than what a man is. There iss more years to my hett than to the hett of any one here. It is fery pat, look you, this coing against Nature. It is pat to make other potties suffer, when there is nothing to pe cot py it.

A laugh. **Thomas** *angrily goes on.*

Thomas   What are ye laughing at? It is pat, I say! We are fighting for a principle; there is nopotty that shall say I am not a peliever in principle. Putt when Nature says 'No further,' then it is no coot snapping your fingers in her face.

A laugh from **Roberts**, *and murmurs of approval.*

Thomas   This Nature must be humort. It is a man's pisiness to be pure, honest, just and merciful. That's what Chapel tells you. (*To* **Roberts**, *angrily:*) And, look you, David Roberts, Chapel tells you ye can do that without coing against Nature.

Jago   What about the Union?

Thomas   I ton't trust the Union; they haf treated us like tirt. 'Do what we tell you, said they. I haf peen captain of the furnacemen twenty years, and I say to the Union – (*Excitedly.*) – 'Can you tell me then, as well as I can tell you, what iss the right wages for the work that these men do?' For fife and twenty years I haf paid my moneys to the Union and – (*With great excitement.*) – for nothings! What iss that but roguery, for all that this Mr Harness says!

Murmurs.

Evans   Hear, hear.

Henry Rous   Get on with you! Cut on with it then!

Thomas   Look you, if a man toes not trust me, am I coing to trust him?

Jago   That's right.

Thomas   Let them alone for rogues, and act for ourselves.
Murmurs.

Blacksmith   That's what we been doin', haven't we?

Thomas (*with increased excitement*)   I was brought up to do for meself. I wass brought up to go without a thing, if I hat not moneys to puy it. There iss too much, look you, of doing things with other people's moneys. We haf fought fair, and if we haf peen beaten, it iss no fault of ours. Gif us the power to make terms with London for ourself; if we ton't succeed, I say it iss petter to take our peating like men, than to tie like togs, or hang on to others' coat-tails to make them do our pusiness for us!

Evans (*muttering*)   Who wants to?

Thomas (*craning*)   What's that? If I stand up to a potty, and he knocks me town, I am not to go hollering to other potties to help me; I am to stand up again; and if he knocks me town properly, I am to stay there, isn't that right?

Laughter.

Jago   No Union!

Henry Rous   Union!

Others take up the shout.

Evans   Blacklegs!

Bulgin *and the* **Blacksmith** *shake their fists at* **Evans**.

Thomas (*with a gesture*)   I am an olt man, look you.

A sudden silence, then murmurs again.

Evans   Olt fool, with his 'No Union!'

Bulgin   Them furnace chaps! For twopence I'd smash the faces o' the lot of them.

Green   If I'd 'a been listened to at the first –

Thomas (*wiping his brow*)   I'm comin' now to what I was coing to say –

Davies (*muttering*)   An' time too!

Thomas (*solemnly*)   Chapel says: Ton't carry on this strike! Put an end to it!

Jago   That's a lie! Chapel says go on!

Thomas (*scornfully*)   Inteet! I haf ears to my head.

Red-haired Youth   Ah! long ones!

A laugh.

Jago   Your ears have misbeled you then.

Thomas (*excitedly*)   Ye cannot be right if I am, ye cannot haf it both ways.

Red-haired Youth   Chapel can though!

'The Shaver' laughs; there are murmurs from the crowd.

Thomas (*fixing his eye on 'The Shaver'*)   Ah! ye're coing – the roat to tamnation. An' so I say to all of you. If ye co against Chapel I will not pe with you, nor will any other Got-fearing man.

He steps down from the platform. **Jago** *makes his way towards it. There are cries of 'Don't let 'im go up!'*

Jago   Don't let him go up? That's free speech, that is. (*He goes up.*) I ain't got much to say to you. Look at the matter plain; ye've come the road this far, and now you want to chuck the journey. We've all been in one boat; and now you want to pull in two. We engineers have stood by you; ye're ready now, are ye, to give us the goby? If we'd a-known that before, we'd not a-started out with you so early one bright morning! That's all I've got to say. Old man 'Thomas a'n't got his Bible lesson right. If you give up to London, or to Harness, now, it's givin' us the chuck – to save your skins – you won't get over that, my boys; it's a dirty thing to do.

He gets down; during his little speech, which is ironically spoken, there is a restless discomfort in the crowd. **Rous**, *stepping forward, jumps on the platform. He has an air of fierce distraction. Sullen murmurs of disapproval from the crowd.*

Rous (*speaking with great excitement*)   I'm no blanky orator, mates, but wot I say is drove from me. What I say is yuman nature. Can a man set an' see 'is mother starve? Can 'e now?

Roberts (*starting forward*)   Rous!

Rous (*staring at him fiercely*)   Sim 'Arness said fair! I've changed my mind.

Evans   Ah! Turned your coat you mean!

The crowd manifests a great surprise.

Evans (*apostrophizing* **Rous**)   Hallo! What's turned him round?

Rous (*speaking with intense excitement*)   'E said fair. 'Stand by us,'
'e said, 'and we'll stand by you.' That's where we've been makin'
our mistake this long time past; and who's to blame for't? (*He points
at* **Roberts**.) That man there! 'No,' 'e said, 'fight the robbers,' 'e
said, 'squeeze the breath out o' them!' But it's not the breath out
o' them that's being squeezed; it's the breath out of *us* and *ours*,
and that's the book of truth. I'm no orator, mates, it's the flesh and
blood in me that's speakin', it's the heart o' me. (*With a menacing, yet
half-ashamed movement towards* **Roberts**.) He'll speak to you again,
mark my words, but don't ye listen. (*The crowd groans*.) It's hell fire
that's on that man's tongue. (**Roberts** *is seen laughing*.) Sim 'Arness is
right. What are we without the Union – handful o' parched leaves –
a puff o' smoke. I'm no orator, but I say: Chuck it up! Chuck it up!
Sooner than go on starving the women and the children.

The murmurs of acquiescence almost drown the murmurs of dissent.

Evans   What's turned *you* to blacklegging?

Rous (*with a furious look*)   Sim 'Arness knows what he's talkin'
about. Give us power to come to terms with London; I'm no
orator, but I say – have done wi' this black misery!

*He gives his muffler a twist, jerks his head back and jumps off the platform.
The crowd applauds and surges forward. Amid cries of 'That's enough!' 'Up
Union!' 'Up Harness!'* **Roberts** *quietly ascends the platform. There is a
moment of silence.*

Blacksmith   We don't want to hear you. Shut it!

Henry Rous   Get down!

Amid such cries they surge towards the platform.

Evans (*fiercely*)   Let 'im speak! Roberts! Roberts!

Bulgin (*muttering*)   He'd better look out that I don't crack 'is skull.

Roberts *faces the crowd, probing them with his eyes till they gradually
become silent. He begins speaking. One of the bargemen rises and stands.*

Roberts   You don't want to hear me, then? You'll listen to
Rous and to that old man, but not to me. You'll listen to Sim

Harness of the Union that's treated you *so fair;* maybe you'll
listen to those men from London? Ah! You groan! What for? You
love their feet on your necks, don't you? (*Then as* **Bulgin** *elbows
his way towards the platform, with calm pathos.*) You'd like to break
my jaw, John Bulgin. Let me speak, then do your smashing, if
it gives you pleasure. (**Bulgin** *stands motionless and sullen.*) Am I
a liar, a coward, a traitor? If only I were, ye'd listen to me, I'm
sure. (*The murmurings cease, and there is now dead silence.*) Is there
a man of you here that has less to gain by striking? Is there a
man of you that had more to lose? Is there a man of you that
has given up *eight hundred* pounds since this trouble here began?
Come now, is there? How much has Thomas given up – ten
pounds or five, or what? You listened to him, and what had he
to say? 'None can pretend,' he said, 'that I'm not a believer
in principle – (*With biting irony.*) – but when Nature says: "No
further, 'tes going agenst Nature." ' *I* tell you if a man cannot
say to Nature: 'Budge me from this if ye can!' – (*With a sort of
exaltation.*) – his principles are but his belly. 'Oh, but,' Thomas
says, 'a man can be pure and honest, just and merciful, and
take off his hat to Nature!' *I* tell you Nature's neither pure nor
honest, just nor merciful. You chaps that live over the hill, an'
go home dead beat in the dark on a snowy night – don't ye fight
your way every inch of it? Do ye go lyin' down an' trustin' to the
tender mercies of this merciful Nature? Try it and you'll soon
know with what ye've got to deal. 'Tes only by that – (*He strikes
a blow with his clenched fist.*) – in Nature's face that a man can be
a man. 'Give in,' says Thomas, 'go down on your knees; throw
up your foolish fight, an' perhaps,' he said, 'perhaps your enemy
will chuck you down a crust.'

Jago   Never!

Evans   Curse them!

Thomas   I nefer said that.

Roberts (*bitingly*)   If ye did not say it, man, ye meant it. An'
what did ye say about Chapel? 'Chapel's against it,' ye said. 'She's
against it!' Well, if Chapel and Nature go hand in hand, it's the
first I've ever heard of it. That young man there – (*Pointing to*
Rous) – said I 'ad 'ell fire on my tongue. If I had I would use it

all to scorch and wither this talking of surrender. Surrendering's
the work of cowards and traitors.

Henry Rous (*as* **George Rous** *moves forward*)   Go for him,
George – don't stand his lip!

Roberts (*flinging out his finger*)   Stop there, George Rous, it's no
time this to settle personal matters. (**Rous** *stops*.) But there was
one other spoke to you – Mr Simon Harness. We have not much
to thank Mr Harness and the Union for. They said to us 'Desert
your mates, or we'll desert you.' An' they did desert us.

Evans   They did.

Roberts   Mr Simon Harness is a clever man, but he has come
too late. (*With intense conviction*.) For all that Mr Simon Harness
says, for all that Thomas, Rous, for all that any man present here
can say – *We've won the fight!*

The crowd sags nearer, looking eagerly up. With withering scorn.

Roberts   You've felt the pinch o't in your bellies. You've
forgotten what that fight 'as been; many times I have told you; I
will tell you now this once again. The fight o' the country's body
and blood against a blood-sucker. The fight of those that spend
theirselves with every blow they strike and every breath they draw,
against a thing that fattens on them, and grows and grows by the
law of *merciful* Nature. That thing is Capital! A thing that buys the
sweat o' men's brows, and the tortures o' their brains, at its own
price. *Don't I* know that? Wasn' the work o' *my* brains bought for
seven hundred pounds, and hasn't one hundred thousand pounds
been gained them by that seven hundred without the stirring of
a finger? It is a thing that will take as much and give you as little
as it can. That's *Capital!* A thing that will say – 'I'm very sorry for
you, poor fellows – you have a cruel time of it, I know,' but will not
give one sixpence of its dividends to help you have a better time.
That's Capital! Tell me, for all their talk is there one of them that
will consent to another penny on the Income Tax to help the poor?
That's Capital! A white-faced, stonyhearted monster! Ye have got
it on its knees; are ye to give up at the last minute to save your
miserable bodies pain? When I went this morning to those old men
from London, I looked into their very 'earts. One of them was

sitting there – Mr Scantlebury, a mass of flesh nourished on us: sittin' there for all the world like the shareholders in this Company, that sit not moving tongue nor finger, takin' dividends – a great dumb ox that can only be roused when its food is threatened. I looked into his eyes and I saw *he was afraid* – afraid for himself and his dividends, afraid for his fees, afraid of the very shareholders he stands for; and all but one of them's afraid – like children that get into a wood at night, and start at every rustle of the leaves. I ask you, men – (*He pauses, holding out his hand till there is utter silence.*) – Give me a free hand to tell them: 'Go you back to London. The men have nothing for you!' (*A murmuring.*) Give me that, an' I swear to you, within a week you shall have from London all you want.

Evans, **Jago**, *and* **Others**   A free hand! Give him a free hand! Give him a free hand! Bravo – bravo!

Roberts   'Tis not for this little moment of time we're fighting (*The murmuring dies.*), not for ourselves, our own little bodies, and their wants, 'tis for all those that come after, throughout all time. (*With intense sadness.*) Oh! men – for the love o' them, don't roll up another stone upon their heads, don't help to blacken the sky, an' let the bitter sea in over them. They're welcome to the worst that can happen to me, to the worst that can happen to us all, aren't they – aren't they? If we can shake (*Passionately.*) that white-faced monster with the bloody lips, that has sucked the life out of ourselves, our wives and children, since the world began. (*Dropping the note of passion, but with the utmost weight and intensity.*) If we have not the hearts of men to stand against it breast to breast, and eye to eye, and force it backward till it cry for mercy, it will go on sucking life; and we shall stay for ever what we are (*In almost a whisper.*) less than the very dogs.

An utter stillness, and **Roberts** *stands rocking his body slightly, with his eyes burning the faces of the crowd.*

Evans *and* **Jago** (*suddenly*)   Roberts!

The shout is taken up.

There is a slight movement in the crowd, and **Madge** *passing below the towing-path stops by the platform, looking up at* **Roberts**. *A sudden doubting silence.*

Roberts   'Nature,' says that old man, 'give in to Nature.' *I* tell you, strike your blow in Nature's face – an' let it do its worst!

He catches sight of **Madge**, *his brows contract, he looks away.*

Madge   (*in a low voice – close to the platform*)   Your wife's dying!

Roberts *glares at her as if torn from some pinnacle of exaltation.*

Roberts   (*trying to stammer on*)   I say to you – answer them – answer them –

He is drowned by the murmur in the crowd.

Thomas   (*stepping forward*)   Ton't you hear her, then?

Roberts   What is it?

A dead silence.

Thomas   Your wife, man!

Roberts *hesitates, then with a gesture, he leaps down, and goes away below the towing-path, the men making way for him. The standing bargeman opens and prepares to light a lantern. Daylight is fast failing.*

Madge   He needn't have hurried! Annie Roberts is dead. (*Then in the silence, passionately.*) You pack of blinded hounds! How many more women are you going to let die?

The crowd shrinks hack from her, and breaks up in groups, with a confused, uneasy movement. **Madge** *goes quickly away below the towing-path. There is a hush as they look after her.*

Lewis   There's a spitfire, for ye!

Bulgin   (*growling*)   I'll smash 'er jaw.

Green   If I'd a-been listened to, that poor woman –

Thomas   It's a judgment on him for coing against Chapel. I tolt him how 'twould be!

Evans   All the more reason for sticking by 'im. (*A cheer.*) Are you goin' to desert him now 'e's down? Are you goin' to chuck him over, now 'e's lost 'is wife?

The crowd is murmuring and cheering all at once.

Rous (*stepping in front of platform*)   Lost his wife! Aye! Can't ye see? Look at home, look at your own wives! What's to save them? Ye'll have the same in all your houses before long!

Lewis   Aye, aye!

Henry Rous   Right! George, right!

There are murmurs of assent.

Rous   It's not us that's blind, it's Roberts. How long will ye put up with 'im!

Henry Rous, **Bulgin**, **Davies**   Give 'im the chuck!

The cry is taken up.

Evans (*fiercely*)   Kick a man that's down? Down?

Henry Rous   Stop his jaw there!

Evans *throws up his arm at a threat from* **Bulgin**. *The bargeman, who has lighted the lantern, holds it high above his head.*

Rous (*springing on to the platform*)   What brought him down then, but 'is own black obstinacy? Are ye goin' to follow a man that can't see better than that where he's goin'?

Evans   He's lost 'is wife.

Rous   An' whose fault's that but his own? 'Ave done with 'im, I say, before he's killed your own wives and mothers.

Davies   Down im!

Henry Rous   He's finished!

Brown   We've had enough of 'im!

Blacksmith   Too much!

The crowd takes up these cries, excepting only **Evans**, **Jago**, *and* **Green**, *who is seen to argue mildly with the* **Blacksmith**.

Rous (*above the hubbub*)   We'll make terms with the Union, lads.

Cheers.

Evans (*fiercely*)   Ye blacklegs!

Bulgin (*savagely – squaring up to him*)   Who are ye callin' blacklegs, Rat?

Evans *throws up his fists, parries the blow, and returns it. They fight. The bargemen are seen holding up the lantern and enjoying the sight. Old* **Thomas** *steps forward and holds out his hands.*

Thomas   Shame on your strife!

The **Blacksmith, Brown, Lewis** *and the* **Red-haired Youth** *pull* **Evans** *and* **Bulgin** *apart. The stage is almost dark.*

The curtain falls.

Act Three

It is five o'clock. In the **Underwoods'** *drawing-room, which is
artistically furnished.* **Enid** *is sitting on the sofa working at a baby's
frock.* **Edgar**, *by a little spindle-legged table in the centre of the room, is
fingering a china-box. His eyes are fixed on the double doors that lead into
the dining-room.*

Edgar (*putting down the china-box, and glancing at his watch*)   Just on
five, they're all in there waiting, except Frank. Where's he?

Enid   He's had to go down to Gasgoyne's about a contract. Will
you want him?

Edgar   He can't help us. This is a Directors' job. (*Motioning
towards a single door half hidden by a curtain.*) Father in his room?

Enid   Yes.

Edgar   I wish he'd stay there, Enid.

Enid *looks up at him.*

Edgar   This is a beastly business, old girl?

He takes up the little box again and turns it over and over.

Enid   I went to the Roberts's this afternoon, Ted.

Edgar   That wasn't very wise.

Enid   He's simply killing his wife.

Edgar   We are, you mean.

Enid (*suddenly*)   Roberts *ought* to give way!

Edgar   There's a lot to be said on the men's side.

Enid   I don't feel half so sympathetic with them as I did before
I went. They just set up class feeling against you. Poor Annie
was looking dreadfully bad – fire going out, and nothing fit for
her to eat.

Edgar *walks to and fro.*

Enid But she would stand up for Roberts. When you see all this wretchedness going on and feel you can do nothing, you have to shut your eyes to the whole thing.

Edgar If you can.

Enid When I went I was all on their side, but as soon as I got there I began to feel quite different at once. People talk about sympathy with the working classes, they don't know what it means to try and put it into practice. It seems hopeless.

Edgar Ah! well.

Enid It's dreadful going on with the men in this state. I do hope the Dad will make concessions.

Edgar He won't. (*Gloomily.*) It's a sort of religion with him. Curse it! I know what's coming! He'll be voted down.

Enid They wouldn't dare!

Edgar They will – they're in a funk.

Enid (*indignantly*) He'd never stand it!

Edgar (*with a shrug*) My dear girl, if you're beaten in a vote, you've got to stand it.

Enid Oh! (*She gets up in alarm.*) But would he resign?

Edgar Of course! It goes to the roots of his beliefs.

Enid But he's so *wrapped up in this company*, Ted!

There'd be nothing left for him! It'd be dreadful!

Edgar *shrugs his shoulders.*

Enid Oh, Ted, he's so old now! You mustn't let them!

Edgar (*hiding his feelings in an outburst*) My sympathies in this strike are all on the side of the men.

Enid He's been Chairman for more than thirty years! He made the whole thing! And think of the bad times they've had, it's always been he who pulled them through. Oh, Ted, you must –

Edgar   What is it you want? You said just now you hoped he'd make concessions. Now you want me to back him in not making them. This isn't a game, Enid!

Enid (*hotly*)   It isn't a game to *me* that the Dad's in danger of losing all he cares about in life. If he won't give way, and he's beaten, it'll simply break him down!

Edgar   Didn't you say it was dreadful going on with the men in this state?

Enid   But can't you see, Ted, father'll never get over it! You must stop them somehow. The others are afraid of him. If you back him up –

Edgar (*putting his hand to his head*)   Against my convictions – against yours! The moment it begins to pinch one personally –

Enid   It isn't personal, it's the Dad!

Edgar   Your family or yourself, and over goes the show!

Enid (*resentfully*)   If you don't take it seriously, I do.

Edgar   I am as fond of him as you are; that's nothing to do with it.

Enid   We can't tell about the men; it's all guess-work. But we know the Dad might have a stroke any day. D'you mean to say that he isn't more to you than –

Edgar   Of course he is.

Enid   I don't understand you then.

Edgar   H'm!

Enid   If it were for oneself it would be different, but for your own father! You don't seem to realize.

Edgar   I realize perfectly.

Enid   It's your first duty to save him.

Edgar   I wonder.

Enid (*imploring*)   Oh, Ted! It's the only interest he's got left; it'll be like a death-blow to him!

Edgar (*restraining his emotion*)   I know.

Enid   Promise!

Edgar   I'll do what I can.

He turns to the double doors.

The curtained door is opened, and **Anthony** *appears.*

Edgar *opens the double doors, and passes through.*

Scantlebury's *voice is faintly heard: 'Past five; we shall never get through – have to eat another dinner at that hotel!' The doors are shut.* **Anthony** *walks forward.*

Anthony   You've been seeing Roberts, I hear.

Enid   Yes.

Anthony   Do you know what trying to bridge such a gulf as this is like?

Enid *puts her work on the little table, and faces him.*

Anthony   Filling a sieve with sand!

Enid   Don't!

Anthony   You think with your gloved hands you can cure the trouble of the century.

He passes on.

Enid   Father! (**Anthony** *stops at the double doors.*) I'm only thinking of you!

Anthony (*more softly*)   I can take care of myself, my dear.

Enid   Have you thought what'll happen if you're beaten – (*She points.*) – in there?

Anthony   I don't mean to be.

Enid   Oh! Father, don't give them a chance. You're not well; need you go to the meeting at all?

Anthony (*with a grim smile*)   Cut and run?

Enid   But they'll outvote you!

Anthony (*putting his hand on the doors*)   We shall see!

Enid   I beg you, dad!

Anthony *looks at her softly.*

Enid   Won't you?

Anthony *shakes his head. He opens the door. A buzz of voices comes in.*

Scantlebury   Can one get dinner on that 6.30 train up?

Tench   No, sir, I believe not, sir.

Wilder   Well, I shall speak out; I've had enough of this.

Edgar (*sharply*)   What?

It ceases instantly. **Anthony** *passes through, closing the doors behind him.* **Enid** *springs to them with a gesture of dismay. She puts her hand on the knob, and begins turning it; then goes to the fireplace, and taps her foot on the fender. Suddenly she rings the bell.* **Frost** *comes in by the door that leads into the hall.*

Frost   Yes, m'm?

Enid   When the men come, Frost, please show them in here; the hall's cold.

Frost   I could put them in the pantry, m'm.

Enid   No. I don't want to – to offend them; they're so touchy.

Frost   Yes, m'm. (*Pause.*) Excuse me, Mr Anthony's 'ad nothing to eat all day.

Enid   I know, Frost.

Frost   Nothin' but two whiskies and sodas, m'm.

Enid   Oh! you oughtn't to have let him have those.

Frost (*gravely*)   Mr Anthony is a little difficult, m'm. It's not as if he were a younger man, an' knew what was good for 'im; he will have his own way.

Enid   I suppose we all want that.

Frost   Yes, m'm. (*Quietly*). Excuse me speakin' about the strike. I'm sure if the other gentlemen were to give up to Mr Anthony, and quietly let the men 'ave what they want, afterwards, that'd be the best way. I find that very useful with him at times, m'm.

Enid *shakes her head.*

Frost   If he's crossed, it makes him violent (*With an air of discovery.*)*,* and I've noticed in my own case, when I'm violent I'm always sorry for it afterwards.

Enid (*with a smile*)   Are *you* ever violent, Frost?

Frost   Yes, m'm; oh! sometimes very violent.

Enid   I've never seen you.

Frost (*impersonally*)   No, m'm; that is so.

Enid *fidgets towards the door's back.*

Frost (*with feeling*)   Bein' with Mr Anthony, as you know, m'm, ever since I was fifteen, it worries me to see him crossed like this at his age. I've taken the liberty to speak to Mr Wanklin (*Dropping his voice.*) – seems to be the most sensible of the gentlemen – but 'e said to me: 'That's all very well, Frost, but this strife's a very serious thing,' 'e said. 'Serious for all parties, no doubt,' I said, 'but yumour 'im, sir,' I said, 'yumour 'im. It's like this, if a man comes to a stone wall, 'e doesn't drive 'is 'ead against it, 'e gets over it.' 'Yes,' 'e said, 'you'd better tell your master that.' (**Frost** *looks at his nails.*) That's where it is, m'm. I said to Mr Anthony this morning: 'Is it worth it, sir?' 'Damn it,' he said to me, 'Frost! Mind your own business, or take a month's notice!' Beg pardon, m'm, for using such a word.

Enid (*moving to the double doors, and listening*)   Do you know that man Roberts, Frost?

Frost   Yes, m'm; that's to say, not to speak to. But to *look* at 'im you can tell what *he's* like.

Enid (*stopping*)   Yes?

Frost   He's not one of these 'ere ordinary 'armless Socialists. 'E's violent; got a fire inside 'im. What I call 'personal'. A man may 'ave what opinion 'e likes, so long as 'e's not personal; when 'e's that 'e's *not* safe.

Enid   I think that's what my father feels about Roberts.

Frost   No doubt, m'm, Mr Anthony has a feeling against him.

Enid *glances at him sharply, but finding him in perfect earnest, stands biting her lips, and looking at the double doors.*

Frost   It's a regular right down struggle between the two. I've no patience with this Roberts, from what I 'ear he's just an ordinary workin' man like the rest of 'em. If he did invent a thing he's no worse off than 'undreds of others. My brother invented a new kind o' dumb waiter – nobody gave *him* anything for it, an' there it is, bein' used all over the place.

Enid *moves closer to the double doors.*

Frost   There's a kind o' man that never forgives the world, because 'e wasn't born a gentleman. What I say is – no man that's a gentleman looks down on another man because 'e 'appens to be a class or two above 'im, no more than if 'e 'appens to be a class or two below.

Enid *(with slight impatience)*   Yes, I know, Frost, of course. Will you please go in and ask if they'll have some tea; say I sent you.

Frost   Yes, m'm.

He opens the doors gently and goes in. There is a momentary sound of earnest, rather angry talk.

Wilder   I don't agree with you.

Wanklin   We've had this over a dozen times.

Edgar *(impatiently)*   Well, what's the proposition?

Scantlebury   Yes, what does your father say? Tea? Not for me, not for me!

Wanklin   What I understand the Chairman to say is this –

Frost *re-enters, closing the door behind him.*

Enid *(moving from the door)*   Won't they have any tea, Frost?

She goes to the little table, and remains motionless, looking at the baby's frock.

*A **Parlourmaid** enters from the hall.*

Parlourmaid   A Miss Thomas, m'm.

Enid *(raising her head)*   Thomas? What Miss Thomas – d'you mean a – ?

Parlourmaid Yes, m'm.

Enid (*blankly*) Oh! Where is she?

Parlourmaid In the porch.

Enid I don't want – (*She hesitates.*)

Frost Shall I dispose of her, m'm?

Enid I'll come out. No, show her in here, Ellen.

The **Parlourmaid** *and* **Frost** *go out.* **Enid** *pursing her lips, sits at the little table, taking up the baby's frock. The* **Parlourmaid** *ushers in* **Madge Thomas** *and goes out;* **Madge** *stands by the door.*

Enid Come in. What is it? What have you come for, please?

Madge Brought a message from Mrs Roberts.

Enid A message? Yes.

Madge She asks you to look after her mother.

Enid I don't understand.

Madge (*sullenly*) That's the message.

Enid But – what – why?

Madge Annie Roberts is dead.

There is a silence.

Enid (*horrified*) But it's only a little more than an hour since I saw her.

Madge Of cold and hunger.

Enid (*rising*) Oh! that's not true! the poor thing's heart – What makes you look at me like that? I tried to help her.

Madge (*with suppressed savagery*) I thought you'd like to know.

Enid (*passionately*) It's so unjust! Can't you see that I want to help you all?

Madge I never harmed anyone that hadn't harmed me first.

Enid (*coldly*) What harm have I done you? Why do you speak to me like that?

Madge (*with the bitterest intensity*)   You come out of your comfort to spy on us! A week of hunger, that's what *you* want!

Enid (*standing her ground*)   Don't talk nonsense!

Madge   I saw her die; her hands were blue with the cold.

Enid (*with a movement of grief*)   Oh! why wouldn't she let me help her? It's such senseless pride!

Madge   Pride's better than nothing to keep your body warm.

Enid (*passionately*)   I won't talk to you! How can you tell what I feel? It's not my fault that I was born better off than you.

Madge   We don't want your money.

Enid   You don't understand, and you don't want to; please to go away!

Madge (*balefully*)   You've killed her, for all your soft words, you and your father –

Enid (*with rage and emotion*)   That's wicked! My father is suffering himself through this wretched strike.

Madge (*with sombre triumph*)   Then tell him Mrs Roberts is dead! That'll make him better.

Enid   Go away!

Madge   When a person hurts us we get it back on them.

She makes a sudden and swift movement towards **Enid**, *fixing her eyes on the child's frock lying across the little table.* **Enid** *snatches the frock up, as though it were the child itself. They stand a yard apart, crossing glances.*

Madge (*pointing to the frock with a little smile*)   Ah! You felt *that!* Lucky it's her mother – not her children – you've to look after, isn't it. *She* won't trouble you long!

Enid   Go away!

Madge   I've given you the message.

She turns and goes out into the hall. **Enid**, *motionless till she has gone, sinks down at the table, bending her head over the frock, which she is still clutching to her. The double doors are opened, and* **Anthony** *comes slowly in; he passes his daughter, and lowers himself into an armchair. He is very flushed.*

Enid (*hiding her emotion – anxiously*)   What is it, dad? (**Anthony** *makes a gesture, but does not speak.*) Who was it?

Anthony *does not answer.* **Enid** *going to the double doors meets* **Edgar** *coming in. They speak together in low tones.*

Enid   What is it, Ted?

Edgar   That fellow Wilder! Taken to personalities! He was downright insulting.

Enid   What did he *say?*

Edgar   Said, father was too old and feeble to know what he was doing! The Dad's worth six of him!

Enid   Of course he is.

They look at **Anthony**.

The doors open wider, **Wanklin** *appears with* **Scantlebury**.

Scantlebury (*sotto voce*)   I don't like the look of this!

Wanklin (*going forward*)   Come, Chairman! Wilder sends you his apologies. A man can't do more.

Wilder, *followed by* **Tench**, *comes in, and goes to* **Anthony**.

Wilder (*glumly*)   I withdraw my words, sir. I'm sorry.

Anthony *nods to him.*

Enid   You haven't come to a decision, Mr Wanklin?

Wanklin *shakes his head.*

Wanklin   We're all here, Chairman; what do you say? Shall we get on with the business, or shall we go back to the other room?

Scantlebury   Yes, yes; let's get on. We must settle something.

He turns from a small chair, and settles himself suddenly in the largest chair, with a sigh of comfort.

Wilder *and* **Wanklin** *also sit; and* **Tench**, *drawing up a straight-backed chair close to his Chairman, sits on the edge of it with the minute-book and a stylographic pen.*

Enid (*whispering*)   I want to speak to you a minute, Ted.

They go out through the double doors.

Wanklin   Really, Chairman, it's no use soothing ourselves with a sense of false security. If this strike's not brought to an end before the General Meeting, the shareholders will certainly haul us over the coals.

Scantlebury (*stirring*)   What – what's that?

Wanklin   I know it for a fact.

Anthony   Let them!

Wilder   And get turned out?

Wanklin (*to* **Anthony**)   I don't mind martyrdom for a policy in which I believe, but I object to being burnt for someone else's principles.

Scantlebury   Very reasonable – you must see that, Chairman.

Anthony   We owe it to other employers to stand firm.

Wanklin   There's a limit to that.

Anthony   You were all full of fight at the start.

Scantlebury (*with a sort of groan*)   We thought the men would give in, but they – haven't!

Anthony   They will!

Wilder (*rising and pacing up and down*)   I can't have my reputation as a man of business destroyed for the satisfaction of starving the men out. (*Almost in tears.*) I can't have it! How can we meet the shareholders with things in the state they are?

Scantlebury   Hear, hear – hear, hear!

Wilder (*lashing himself*)   If anyone expects me to say to them I've lost you fifty thousand pounds and sooner than put my pride in my pocket I'll lose you another – (*Glancing at* **Anthony**.) It's – it's unnatural! *I don't want* to go against you, sir –

Wanklin (*persuasively*)   Come, Chairman, we're *not* free agents. We're part of a machine. Our only business is to see the Company earns as much profit as it safely can. If you blame me for want of principle: I say that we're Trustees. Reason tells us we shall never get back in the saving of wages what we shall lose if we continue this struggle – really, Chairman, we *must* bring it to an end, on the best terms we can make.

Anthony No!

There is a pause of general dismay.

Wilder It's a deadlock then. (*Letting his hands drop with a sort of despair.*) Now I shall never get off to Spain!

Wanklin (*retaining a trace of irony*) You hear the consequences of your victory, Chairman?

Wilder (*with a burst of feeling*) My wife's *ill*!

Scantlebury Dear, dear! You don't say so!

Wilder If I don't get her out of this cold, I won't answer for the consequences.

Through the double doors **Edgar** *comes in looking very grave.*

Edgar (*to his father*) Have you heard this, sir? Mrs Roberts is dead!

Everyone stares at him, as if trying to gauge the importance of this news.

Edgar Enid saw her this afternoon, she had no coals, or food, or anything. It's enough!

There is a silence, everyone avoiding the other's eyes, except **Anthony**, *who stares hard at his son.*

Scantlebury You don't suggest that we could have helped the poor thing?

Wilder (*flustered*) The woman was in bad health. Nobody can say there's any responsibility on us. At least – not on me.

Edgar (*hotly*) I say that we *are* responsible.

Anthony War is war!

Edgar Not on women!

Wanklin It not infrequently happens that women are the greatest sufferers.

Edgar   If we knew that, all the more responsibility rests on us.

Anthony   This is no matter for amateurs.

Edgar   Call me what you like, sir. It's sickened me. We had no right to carry things to such a length.

Wilder   I don't like this business a bit – that Radical rag will twist it to their own ends; see if they don't! They'll get up some cock-and-bull story about the poor woman's dying from starvation. I wash my hands of it.

Edgar   You can't. None of us can.

Scantlebury (*striking his fist on the arm of his chair*)   But I protest against this –

Edgar   Protest as you like, Mr Scantlebury, it won't alter facts.

Anthony   That's enough.

Edgar (*facing him angrily*)   No, sir. I tell you exactly what I think. If we pretend the men are not suffering, it's humbug; and if they're suffering, we know enough of human nature to know the women are suffering more, and as to the children – well – it's damnable!

Scantlebury *rises from his chair.*

Edgar   I don't say that we meant to be cruel, I don't say anything of the sort; but I do say it's criminal to shut our eyes to the facts. We employ these men, and we can't get out of it. I don't care so much about the men, but I'd sooner resign my position on the Board than go on starving women in this way.

All except **Anthony** *are now upon their feet,* **Anthony** *sits grasping the arms of his chair and staring at his son.*

Scantlebury   I don't – I don't like the way you're putting it, young, sir.

Wanklin   You're rather overshooting the mark.

Wilder   I should think so indeed!

Edgar (*losing control*)   It's no use blinking things! If *you* want to have the death of women on your hands – *I* don't!

Scantlebury   Now, now, young man!

Wilder   On *our* hands? Not on *mine*, I won't have, it!

Edgar   We are five members of this Board; if we were four against it, why did we let it drift till it came to this? You know perfectly well why — because we hoped we should starve the men out. Well, all we've done is to starve one woman out!

Scantlebury (*almost hysterically*)   I protest, I protest! I'm a humane man — we're all humane men!

Edgar (*scornfully*)   There's nothing wrong with our *humanity*. It's our imaginations, Mr Scandebury.

Wilder   Nonsense! My imagination's as good as yours.

Edgar   If so, it isn't good enough.

Wilder   I foresaw this!

Edgar   Then why didn't you put your foot down!

Wilder   Much good that would have done.

He looks at **Anthony**.

Edgar   If you, and I, and each one of us here who say that our imaginations are so good —

Scantlebury (*flurried*)   I never said so.

Edgar (*paying no attention*)   — had put our feet down, the thing would have been ended long ago, and this poor woman's life wouldn't have been crushed out of her like this. For all we can tell there may be a dozen other starving women.

Scantlebury   For God's sake, sir, don't use that word at a — at a Board meeting; it's — it's monstrous.

Edgar   I *will* use it, Mr Scantlebury.

Scantlebury   Then I shall not listen to you. I shall not listen! It's painful to me.

He covers his ears.

Wanklin   None of us are opposed to a settlement, except your father.

Edgar   I'm certain that if the shareholders knew –

Wanklin   I don't think you'll find their imaginations are any better than ours. Because a woman happens to have a weak heart –

Edgar   A struggle like this finds out the weak spots in everybody. Any child knows that. If it hadn't been for this cut-throat policy, she needn't have died like this; and there wouldn't be all this misery that anyone who isn't a fool can see is going on.

Throughout the foregoing **Anthony** *has eyed his son; he now moves as though to rise, but stops as* **Edgar** *speaks again.*

Edgar   I don't defend the men, or myself, or anybody.

Wanklin   You may have to! A coroner's jury of disinterested sympathizers may say some very nasty things. We mustn't lost sight of our position.

Scantlebury (*without uncovering his ears*)   Coroner's jury! No, no, it's not a case for that?

Edgar   I've had enough of cowardice.

Wanklin   Cowardice is an unpleasant word, Mr Edgar Anthony. It will look very like cowardice if we suddenly concede the men's demands when a thing like this happens; we must be careful!

Wilder   Of course we must. We've no knowledge of this matter, except a rumour. The proper course is to put the whole thing into the hands of Harness to settle for us; that's natural, that's what we *should* have come to anyway.

Scantlebury (*with dignity*)   Exactly! (*Turning to* **Edgar**.) And as to you, young sir, I can't sufficiently express my – my distaste for the way you've treated the whole matter. You ought to withdraw! Talking of starvation, talking of cowardice! Considering what our views are! Except your own father – we're all agreed the only policy is – is one of goodwill – it's most irregular, it's most improper, and all I can say is it's – it's given me pain –

He places his hand on the centre of his scheme.

Edgar (*stubbornly*)   I withdraw nothing.

He is about to say more when **Scantlebury** *once more covers up his ears.*
Tench *suddenly makes a demonstration with the minute-book. A sense of
having been engaged in the unusual comes over all of them, and one by one
they resume their seats.* **Edgar** *alone remains on his feet.*

Wilder (*with an air of trying to wipe something out*)　I pay no attention
to what young Mr Anthony has said. Coroner's jury! The idea's
preposterous. I – I move this amendment to the Chairman's
Motion: That the dispute be placed at once in the hands of
Mr Simon Harness for settlement, on the lines indicated by him
this morning. Anyone second that?

Tench *writes in the book.*

Wanklin　I do.

Wilder　Very well, then; I ask the Chairman to put it to the
Board.

Anthony (*with a great sigh – slowly*)　We have been made the
subject of an attack. (*Looking round at* **Wilder** *and* **Scantlebury**
with ironical contempt.) I take it on *my* shoulders. I am seventy-six
years old. I have been Chairman of this Company since its incep-
tion two-and-thirty years ago. I have seen it pass through good
and evil report. My connection with it began in the year that this
young man was born.

Edgar *bows his head.* **Anthony**, *gripping his chair, goes on.*

Anthony　I have had to do with 'men' for fifty years; I always
stood up to them; I have never been beaten yet. I have fought the
men of this Company four times, and four times I have beaten
them. It has been said that I am not the man I was. (*He looks at*
Wilder.) However that may be, I am man enough to stand to
my guns.

His voice grows stronger. The double doors are opened.

Enid *slips in, followed by* **Underwood**, *who restrains her.*

Anthony　The men have been treated justly, they have – had
fair wages, we have always been ready to listen to complaints. It
has been said that times have changed; if they have, I have not
changed with them. Neither will I. It has been said that masters

and men are equal! Cant! There can only be one master in a house! Where two men meet the better man will rule. It has been said that Capital and Labour have the same interests. Cant! Their interests are as wide asunder as the poles. It has been said that the Board is only part of a machine. Cant! We *are* the machine; its brains and sinews; it is for us to lead and to determine what is to be done, and to do it without fear or favour. Fear of the men! Fear of the shareholders! Fear of our own shadows! Before I am like that, I hope to die!

He pauses, and meeting his son's eyes, goes on.

Anthony   There is only one way of treating 'men' – with *the iron hand*. This half-and-half business, the half-and-half manners of this generation has brought all this upon us. Sentiment and softness, and what this young man, no doubt, would call his social policy. You can't eat cake and have it! This middle-class sentiment, or Socialism, or whatever it may be, is rotten. Masters are masters, men are men! Yield one demand, and they will make it six. They are (*He smiles grimly.*) like Oliver Twist, asking for more. If I were in *their* place I should be the same. But I am not in their place. Mark my words: one fine morning, when you have given way here, and given way there – you will find you have parted with the ground beneath your feet, and are deep in the bog of bankruptcy; and with you, floundering in that bog, will be the very men you have given way to. I have been accused of being a domineering tyrant, thinking only of my pride – I am thinking of the future of this country, threatened with the black waters of confusion, threatened with mob government, threatened with what I cannot see. If by any conduct of mine I help to bring this on us, I shall be ashamed to look my fellows in the face.

Anthony *stares before him, at what he cannot see, and there is perfect stillness.* **Frost** *comes in from the hall, and all but* **Anthony** *look round at him uneasily.*

Frost (*to his master*)   The men are here, sir.

Anthony *makes a gesture of dismissal.*

Frost   Shall I bring them in, sir?

Anthony   Wait!

Frost *goes out,* **Anthony** *turns to face his son.*

Anthony I come to the attack that has been made upon me.

Edgar, *with a gesture of deprecation, remains motionless with his head a little bowed.*

Anthony A woman has died. I am told that her blood is on my hands; I am told that on my hands is the starvation and the suffering of other women and of children.

Edgar I said 'on *our* hands', sir.

Anthony It is the same. (*His voice grows stronger and stronger, his feeling is more and more made manifest.*) I am not aware that if my adversary suffer in a fair fight not sought by me, it is *my* fault. If I fall under *his* feet – as fall I may – I shall not complain. That will be *my* lookout – and this is – his. I cannot separate, as I would, these men from their women and children. A fair fight is a fair fight! Let them learn to think before they pick a quarrel!

Edgar (*in a low voice*) But is it a fair fight, father? Look at them, and look at us! They've only this one weapon!

Anthony (*grimly*) And you're weak-kneed enough to teach them how to use it! It seems the fashion nowadays for men to take their enemy's side. I have not learnt that art. Is it my fault that they quarrelled with their Union too?

Edgar There is such a thing as Mercy.

Anthony And Justice comes before it.

Edgar What seems just to one man, sir, is injustice to another.

Anthony (*with suppressed passion*) You accuse me of injustice – of what amounts to inhumanity – of cruelty –

Edgar *makes a gesture of horror – a general frightened movement.*

Wanklin Come, come, Chairman!

Anthony (*in a grim voice*) These are the words of my own son. They are the words of a generation that I don't understand; the words of a soft breed.

A general murmur. With a violent effort **Anthony** *recovers his control.*

Edgar (*quietly*)   I said it of *myself,* too, father.

A long look is exchanged between them, and **Anthony** *puts out his hand with a gesture as if to sweep the personalities away; then places it against his brow, swaying as though from giddiness. There is a movement towards him. He waves them back.*

Anthony   Before I put this amendment to the Board, I have one more word to say. (*He looks from face to face.*) If it is carried, it means that we shall fail in what we set ourselves to do. It means that we shall fail in the duty that we owe to all Capital. It means that we shall fail in the duty that we owe ourselves. It means that we shall be open to constant attack to which we as constantly shall have to yield. Be under no misapprehension – run this time, and you will never make a stand again! You will have to fly like curs before the whips of your own men. If that is the lot you wish for, yon will vote for this amendment.

He looks again from face to face, finally resting his gaze on **Edgar**; *all sit with their eyes on the ground.* **Anthony** *makes a gesture, and* **Tench** *hands him the book. He reads.*

Anthony   'Moved by Mr Wider, and seconded by Mr Wanklin: "That the men's demands be placed at once in the hands of Mr Simon Harness for settlement on the lines indicated by him this morning." ' (*With sudden vigour.*) Those in favour: Signify the same in the usual way!

For a minute no one moves; then hastily, just as **Anthony** *is about to speak,* **Wilder***'s hand and* **Wanklin***'s are held up, then* **Scantlebury***'s and last* **Edgar***'s, who does not lift his head.*

Anthony   Contrary?

Anthony *lifts his own hand.*

Anthony (*in a clear voice*)   The amendment is carried. I resign my position on this Board.

Enid *gasps, and there is dead silence.* **Anthony** *sits motionless, his head slowly drooping; suddenly he heaves as though the whole of his life had risen up within him.*

Anthony   Fifty years! You have disgraced me, gentlemen. Bring in the men!

He sits motionless, staring before him. The Board draws hurriedly together, and forms a group. **Tench** *in a frightened manner speaks into the hall.* **Underwood** *almost forces* **Enid** *from the room.*

Wilder (*hurriedly*)   What's to be said to them? Why isn't Harness here? Ought we to see the men before he comes? I don't –

Tench   Will you come in, please?

Enter **Thomas**, **Green**, **Bulgin** *and* **Rous**, *who file up in a row past the little table.* **Tench** *sits down and writes. All eyes are fixed on* **Anthony**, *who makes no sign.*

Wanklin (*stepping up to the little table, with nervous cordiality*)   Well, Thomas, how's it to be? What's the result of your meeting?

Rous   Sim Harness has our answer. He'll tell you what it is. We're waiting for him. He'll speak for us.

Wanklin   Is that so, Thomas?

Thomas (*sullenly*)   Yes. Roberts will not be coming, his wife is dead.

Scantlebury   Yes, yes! Poor woman! Yes! Yes!

Frost (*entering from the hall*)   Mr Harness, sir!

As **Harness** *enters he retires.*

Harness *has a piece of paper in his hand, he bows to the Directors, nods towards the men, and takes his stand behind the little table in the very centre of the room.*

Harness   Good evening, gentlemen.

Tench, *with the paper he has been writing, joins him, they speak together in low tones.*

Wilder   We've been waiting for you, Harness. Hope we shall come to some –

Frost (*entering from the hall*)   Roberts.

He goes.

Roberts *comes hastily in, and stands staring at* **Anthony**. *His face is drawn and old.*

Roberts   Mr Anthony, I am afraid I am a little late. I would have been here in time but for something that – has happened. (*To the men:*) Has anything been said?

Thomas   No! But, man, what made ye come?

Roberts   Ye told us this morning, gentlemen, to go away and reconsider our position. We have reconsidered it; we are here to bring you the men's answer. (*To* **Anthony**:) Go ye back to London. We have nothing for you. By no jot or tittle do we abate our demands, nor will we until the whole of those demands are yielded.

Anthony *looks at him but does not speak. There is a movement amongst the men as though they were bewildered.*

Harness   Roberts!

Roberts (*glancing fiercely at him, and back to* **Anthony**)   Is that clear enough for ye? Is it short enough and to the point? Ye made a mistake to think that we would come to heel. Ye may break the body, but ye cannot break the spirit. Get back to London, the men have nothing for ye!

Pausing uneasily he takes a step towards the unmoving **Anthony**.

Edgar   We're all sorry for you, Roberts, but –

Roberts   Keep your sorrow, young man. Let your father speak!

Harness (*with the sheet of paper in his hand, speaking from behind the little table*)   Roberts!

Roberts (*to* **Anthony**, *with passionate intensity*)   Why don't ye answer?

Harness   Roberts!

Roberts (*turning sharply*)   What is it?

Harness (*gravely*)   You're talking without the book; things have travelled past you.

He makes a sign to **Tench**, *who beckons the Directors. They quickly sign his copy of the terms.*

Harness　Look at this, man!

Holding up his sheet of paper.

Harness　'Demands conceded, *with the exception of those relating to the engineers and furnacemen.* Double wages for Saturday's overtime. Night-shifts as they are.' These terms have been agreed. The men go back to work again tomorrow. The strike is at an end.

Roberts (*reading the paper, and turning on the men. They shrink back from him, all but* **Rous**, *who stands his ground. With deadly stillness.*) Ye have gone back on me? I stood by ye to the death; ye waited for *that* to throw me over!

The men answer, all speaking together.

Rous　It's a lie!

Thomas　Ye were past endurance, man.

Green　If ye'd listen to me –

Bulgin (*under his breath*)　Hold your jaw!

Roberts　Ye waited for *that!*

Harness (*taking the Directors' copy of the terms, and handing his own to* **Tench**)　That's enough men. You had better go.

The men shuffle slowly, awkwardly away.

Wilder (*in a low, nervous voice*)　There's nothing to stay for now, I suppose. (*He follows to the door.*) I shall have a try for that train! Coming, Scantlebury?

Scantlebury (*following with* **Wanklin**)　Yes, yes; wait for me.

He stops as **Roberts** *speaks.*

Roberts (*to* **Anthony**)　But *ye* have not signed them terms! They can't make terms without their Chairman! Ye would never sign them terms!

Anthony *looks at him without speaking.*

Roberts　Don't tell me ye have! for the love o' God! (*With passionate appeal.*) I reckoned on ye!

Harness (*holding out the Directors' copy of the terms*)   *The Board* has signed!

Roberts *looks dully at the signatures – dashes the paper from him, and covers up his eyes.*

Scantlebury (*behind his hand to* **Tench**)   Look after the Chairman! He's not well; he's not well – he had no lunch. If there's any fund started for the women and children, put me down for – for twenty pounds.

He goes out into the hall, in cumbrous haste; and **Wanklin**, *who has been staring at* **Roberts** *and* **Anthony** *with twitchings of his face, follows.* **Edgar** *remains seated on the sofa, looking at the ground;* **Tench**, *returning to the bureau, writes in his minute-book.* **Harness** *stands by the little table, gravely watching* **Roberts**.

Roberts   Then you're no longer Chairman of this Company! (*Breaking into half-mad laughter.*) Ah! ha – ah, ha, ha! They've thrown ye over – thrown over their Chairman! Ah – ha – ha! (*With a sudden dreadful calm.*) So – they've done us both down, Mr Anthony?

Enid, *hurrying through the double doors, comes quickly to her father and bends over him.*

Harness (*coming down and laying his hands on* **Roberts**' *sleeve*) For shame, Roberts! Go home quietly, man; go home!

Roberts (*tearing his arm away*)   Home? (*Shrinking together – in a whisper.*) Home!

Enid (*quietly to her father*) Come away, dear! Come to your room!

Anthony *rises with an effort. He turns to* **Roberts**, *who looks at him. They stand several seconds, gazing at each other fixedly;* **Anthony** *lifts his hand, as though to salute, but lets it fall. The expression of* **Roberts**' *face changes from hostility to wonder. They bend their heads in token of respect.* **Anthony** *turns, and slowly walks towards the curtained door. Suddenly he sways as though about to fall, recovers himself and is assisted out by* **Tench** *and* **Edgar**, *who has hurried across the room.* **Roberts** *remains motionless for several seconds, staring intently after* **Anthony**, *then goes out into the hall.*

Tench (*approaching* **Harness**)   It's a great weight off my mind, Mr Harness! But what a painful scene, sir!

He wipes his brow.

Harness, *pale and resolute, regards with a grim half-smile the quavering* **Tench**.

Tench   It's all been so violent! What did he mean by: 'Done us both down?' If he has lost his wife, poor fellow, he oughtn't to have spoken to the Chairman like that!

Harness   A woman dead; and the two best men both broken!

Underwood *enters suddenly.*

Tench (*staring at* **Harness** – *suddenly excited*)   D'you know, sir – these terms, they're the *very same* we drew up together, you and I, and put to both sides before the fight began? All this – all this – and – and what for?

Harness (*in a slow grim voice*)   That's where the fun comes in!

Underwood *without turning from the door makes a gesture of assent.*

The curtain falls.

Play Anthologies available from Methuen Drama

Recent and Forthcoming titles

THE METHUEN DRAMA ANTHOLOGY OF IRISH PLAYS
edited by Patrick Lonergan

(*The Hostage* by Brendan Behan; *Bailegangaire* by Tom Murphy; *The Belle of the Belfast City* by Christina Reid; *The Steward of Christendom* by Sebastian Barry; *The Cripple of Inishmaan* by Martin McDonagh)
ISBN 978 1 408 106785

THE METHUEN DRAMA BOOK OF BLACK BRITISH PLAYS
edited by Lynnette Goddard

(*Welcome Home Jacko* by Mustapha Matura; *Chiaroscuro* by Jackie Kay; *Talking in Tongues* by Winsome Pinnock; *Sing Yer Heart Out For The Lads* by Roy Williams; *Fix Up* by Kwame Kwei-Armah; *Gone Too Far!* by Bola Agbaje)
ISBN 978 1 408 131244

NOT BLACK AND WHITE
(*Category B* by Roy Williams; *Seize the Day* by Kwame Kwei-Armah; *Detaining Justice* by Bola Agbaje)
ISBN 978 1 408 127445

THE METHUEN DRAMA BOOK OF ROYAL COURT PLAYS
edited by Ruth Little

(*Under the Blue Sky* by David Eldridge; *Fallout* by Roy Williams; *Motortown* by Simon Stephens; *My Child* by Mike Bartlett; *Enron* by Lucy Prebble)
ISBN 978 1 408 123935

THE METHUEN DRAMA BOOK OF TWENTY-FIRST CENTURY BRITISH PLAYS
edited by Aleks Sierz

(*Blue/Orange* by Joe Penhall; *Elmina's Kitchen* by Kwame Kwei-Armah; *Realism* by Anthony Neilson; *Gone Too Far!* by Bola Agbaje; *Pornography* by Simon Stephens)
ISBN 978 1 408 123911

PRODUCERS' CHOICE: SIX PLAYS FOR YOUNG PERFORMERS
edited by Paul Roseby

(*Promise* by Megan Barker; *Oedipus/Antigone* by D. J. Britton; *Tory Boyz* by James Graham; *The Butterfly Club* by Sarah May; *Alice's Adventures in Wonderland* by Simon Reade; *Punk Rock* by Simon Stephens)
ISBN 978 1 408 128855

SIX ENSEMBLE PLAYS FOR YOUNG ACTORS
edited by Paul Roseby

(*East End Tales* by Fin Kennedy; *Wan2tlk?* by Kevin Fegan; *Stuff I Buried in a Small Town* by Mike Bartlett; *Sweetpeter* by John Retallack and Usifu Jalloh; *The Playground* by Kay Adshead; *The Odyssey* by Hattie Naylor)
ISBN 978 1 408 106730